The Future of Business Schools

Also by Thomas Durand

Strategic Networks – Learning to Compete (2007) (*editor with Michael Gibbert*)

Bringing Technology and Innovation into the Boardroom (2004) (*editor with Ove Granstrand, Cornelius Herstatt, Arie Nagel, David Probert and Hugo Tschirky*)

Nouvelles perspectives en Management Stratégique (2000) (*editor with Gérard Koenig and Eleonore Mounoud*)

The Future of Business Schools

Scenarios and Strategies for 2020

Written and Edited by

Thomas Durand

and

Stéphanie Dameron

First published in 2008 by
PALGRAVE MACMILLAN
Houndmills, Basingstoke, Hampshire RG21 6XS and
175 Fifth Avenue, New York, N.Y. 10010
Companies and representatives throughout the world

PALGRAVE MACMILLAN is the global academic imprint of the Palgrave Macmillan division of St. Martin's Press, LLC and of Palgrave Macmillan Ltd. Macmillan® is a registered trademark in the United States, United Kingdom and other countries. Palgrave is a registered trademark in the European Union and other countries.

ISBN-13: 978–0–230–51548–2 hardback
ISBN-10: 0–230–51548–7 hardback

This book is printed on paper suitable for recycling and made from fully managed and sustained forest sources. Logging, pulping and manufacturing processes are expected to conform to the environmental regulations of the country of origin.

A catalogue record for this book is available from the British Library.

A catalog record for this book is available from the Library of Congress.

10   9   8   7   6   5   4   3   2   1
17 16 15 14 13 12 11 10 09 08

Printed and bound in Great Britain by
CPI Antony Rowe, Chippenham and Eastbourne

Contents

Part I   A Foresight View

Part II   Current Situation and Trends in Management Education in Various Countries and Regions

List of Tables

List of Illustrations

Figures

Chart

Exhibit

Acknowledgements

This is to thank our colleagues who accepted to write a piece for Part II of this book, about the current context of University education and research in management in their home country or about a region which they know well: JC Spender for the US, Donatella Depperu for Italy, Isabel Gutiérrez and Jaime Ortega for Spain, Kathrin Moslein and Anne Huff for Germany, Joao Neves for Portugal, Niels Noorderhaven and Aswin Van Oijen for the Netherlands, Howard Thomas for the UK, Bengt Stymne for Sweden, as well as Georges Blanc for Latin America, Christian Koenig and Pierre Tapie for Asia, Jean-Paul Larçon and Nassef Hmimda for Central Europe, Lassaâd Mezghani for Middle East and North Africa. Some of them also participated in discussions with us about our scenarios for the future of Business Schools. An additional special word of thanks goes to JC spender who contributed to the "US base line" in the introductory part.

The preparation of the book would also not have been possible without the contributions of members of a working group which met in 2005–2006. We would like to kindly thank Tugrul Atamer, Jean-Claude Cuzzi, Jean-François Germe, Isabelle Huault, Patrick Joffre, Arnaud Langlois Meurinne, Pierre-Xavier Meschi, Christophe Midler, Jean-Pierre Nioche, Catherine Paradeise, Bernard Pras and Pierre Tapie.

We must also thank those who gave some of their time to discuss the future of higher education in management. These conversations were extremely helpful in feeding our thinking.

Finally our thanks go to Peter Houston and Sylvie Zavallone who helped us shape the manuscript.

Notes on Contributors

Georges Blanc is Professor Emeritus at Groupe HEC where he has been teaching Business Strategy and Policy since 1968. His research interests are in organizational structures and management of change in large multinational organizations. He has been visiting professor at the University of California (Berkeley), University of Otago (New Zealand), Foundation Getulio Vargas (Brazil), and Warsaw University of Technology (Poland). He has been active with the Fundaçao Dom Cabral in Brazil since 1976. He was one of the initiators and first Academic Director of the Trium program (with LSE and Stern School at NYU).

Donatella Depperu is Full Professor of Business Administration and Strategy at Università Cattolica del Sacro Cuore. Her research interests include internationalization strategies, international competitiveness of firms, and the strategy process. She has served on the Università Commerciale L. Bocconi. She is Head of Department and is a member of the executive committee of the European Academy of Management.

Isabel Gutiérrez is Professor of Management at Universidad Carlos III de Madrid. She holds a PhD in Business Administration and Licentiate degree in Economics from University of Seville. Her research focuses on organization theory and competitive strategy. Her research interests include competitive and spatial dynamics affecting the outcomes of firms that face radical innovation and environmental discontinuities. She teaches management, organization theory, and organizational design to undergraduates and doctoral students.

Nassef Hmimda is Associate Professor of Strategic Management at Amiens Business School and researcher at Ecole Centrale Paris. He holds a PhD in Strategic Management from Ecole Centrale Paris. His research interests include technology management, market creation, and innovation. Nassef Hmimda also leads research projects in strategic technology management in cooperation with French companies.

Anne Sigismund Huff is Permanent Visiting Professor of Strategy and Innovation at the TUM Business School in Munich, Germany. She is also an Academic Director of CLIC (the Center for Leading Innovation and Cooperation at HHL) Leipzig Graduate School of Management and

Visiting Professor in the Communications Department of the University of Colorado. Before moving to Germany, she was Founding Director of the United Kingdom's Advanced Institute of Management Research (AIM). In 1998–99 she was President of the Academy of Management (AoM) and held associated leadership positions from 1995 to 2001. Her research interests focus on sustained innovation and strategic change.

Christian Koenig holds a PhD in Management from the University of Paris-Dauphine and a Masters degree in Business Economics from Harvard University. He is Associate Professor in the Management department at ESSEC business school, of which he has been Chair. When Director of the Grande Ecole-MBA program from 1998 to 2002, he developed several partnerships and double-degree programs with leading Asian institutions. He created the ESSEC campus and research center in Singapore which he now directs. His recent research work deals with partnership management.

Jean-Paul Larçon is a Professor of Strategy and the Senior Associate Dean of HEC Paris for International Development. He was Visiting Professor at CEIBS (Shanghai), ESADE (Barcelona), NHH (Bergen), St Petersburg State University, and Warsaw University of Technology. He is specialized in international business and strategy in emerging markets.

Lassaâd Mezghani holds a BSc and an MSc in Industrial Engineering (UW-Madison, United States) and a PhD in Strategic Management (Ecole Centrale Paris). Lassaâd Mezghani is Professor of Strategic Management at the University of Sfax, Tunisia. He is a member of the University of Sfax Council. Since 2003, he is an elected member of the Executive Council for the French speaking International Association for Strategic Management (AIMS). He is also a founding member of the Tunisian Management Association. His research interests concern competitive strategy, family business development, and information and communication technology implementation.

Kathrin M. Möslein is Professor of Information Systems – Innovation & Value Creation, University Erlangen-Nuremberg, Germany. Before joining the University Erlangen-Nuremberg, she has served as Associate Director of the United Kingdom's Advanced Institute of Management Research (AIM) and Chair for Strategic Management and Organisation at HHL – Leipzig Graduate School of Management. She is also an Academic Director of CLIC – the Center for Leading Innovation and Cooperation at HHL and Vice President of the European Academy of

Management (EURAM). Her current research and teaching focuses on innovation, cooperation, and leadership systems.

João C. Neves is Professor of Finance Accounting and Real Estate and Director of the Real Estate Management Programme at ISEG School of Economics and Management of the Technical University of Lisbon. He is a member of the Continental European Standard Board of RICS, an institution that accredits academic degrees in real estate. He has been Visiting Professor of Finance and Control at HEC Paris, EM Lyon, and Copenhagen Business School. He was awarded a PhD in Business Administration by Manchester Business School. Before his academic career, he was controller, management consultant, and turnaround manager. He was also trainer and general director of a leading executive training in Portugal.

Niels Noorderhaven is Professor of International Management at Tilburg University. He served as Associate Dean for Education for four years, and during that time developed an interest in international differences in management education. His research interests include the management of collaboration and learning across cultural boundaries.

Jaime Ortega is Associate Professor of Management, Universidad Carlos III de Madrid, Spain. Dr. Ortega has a Licenciate degree in Economics from Universidad Autónoma de Madrid and a PhD in Economics from the Massachusetts Institute of Technology. He is the Director of the Graduate Program in Business and Quantitative Methods and Assistant Director of the MBA program at Carlos III. His research deals with the economics of human resource management practices.

John-Christopher Spender is *Svenska Handelsbanken* Visiting Professor of Knowledge Management, Lund University, Lund, Sweden. Initially trained as a nuclear engineer, Dr. Spender went on to work in computers, consulting, and banking before heading back to graduate school to do a PhD in corporate strategy. He has served on the faculties of City University (London), UCLA, Glasgow University, and Rutgers. He has also served as Dean of the School of Business and Technology at FIT/SUNY before retiring in 2003. He is now researching, writing, and teaching in the field of knowledge management.

Bengt Stymne is Professor Emeritus of Organization Theory at the Stockholm School of Economics. He was Cofounder and Managing Director of SIAR (Scandinavian Institutes of Administrative Research), Managing Director of EFI (Economics Research Institute, Stockholm) and IMIT (Institute for Management of Innovation and Technology, Gothenburg), Cofounder of SSES (Stockholm School of Entrepreneurship), and Director of Research at the FENIX Research and Executive PhD Program (Gothenburg and Stockholm). He has published books and articles on innovation, organization design and strategy, organizational values, industrial democracy, IT and management, and research methodology.

Pierre Tapie has been Dean and President of ESSEC Business School (Paris and Singapore) since September 2001. Previously he was Dean of a graduate school of Engineering and CEO of a venture capital company. Educated at The Ecole Polytechnique (Paris), he has a PhD in Biophysics and an MBA from INSEAD. He teaches Business Ethics. He is a member of Board for numerous academic associations, in France and internationally.

Howard Thomas holds a BSc (London), an MSc (London, an MBA (Chicago), a PhD (Edinburgh), a DSc (Edinburgh). Howard Thomas is Dean of Warwick Business School and Professor of Strategic Management. He is internationally recognized as a leading expert in the field of strategic management, with research interests spanning competitive strategy, risk analysis, strategic change, international management, and strategic decision making.

Aswin Van Oijen is Associate Professor at Tilburg University. He has extensive experience in the administration of management education, for example as Director of the International Business program. He is also representative of the Business group of Tuning, a large project aimed at improving the comparability of higher education across Europe. His research interests include the antecedents, implementation, and performance outcomes of corporate strategy.

Introduction

North America stands as the Mecca for management. It took less than a century for American Management to establish itself as a leader in both practice and academia. As a result, Business and Business Education throughout the world are strongly influenced and, to a large extent, dominated by the US.

Will this remain so? Could it be that some of the various criticisms periodically formulated from within the US academic community itself and most often targeted at the MBA, the most visible symbol of American management education, would turn out to undermine an otherwise quite successful model? Could the model also be affected by some of the rare but incredibly damaging scandals of the beginning of the twenty-first century (unethical behavior, inappropriate governance, top management and board greediness, leading to focus all attention on financial profit whatever the social or environmental costs, such as child labor or improper disposal of hazardous wastes, etc.)?

In this context, will other regions of the world continue to choose to follow the US model? Could some regions be waking up to challenge the current dominant model? Could the dominant model be challenged through other means, e.g. technological innovation via e-learning? Could some alternate models emerge?

We conducted a Foresight exercise to bring some light on these issues. We did this by adopting a European viewpoint looking at both the US and EU models but we also discussed other regions of the world. We believe that most of our findings may be useful beyond North America and Europe, as they can be extrapolated and adapted to other regional contexts, at least to some extent.

All in all, we came to the conclusion that while the US is dominating the scene of management education worldwide, other players, including

Europe, may be waking up, not necessarily in a catching up paradigm, but possibly on a differentiation mode, thus offering the world alternate ways of thinking and educating for business practice. The game is not over yet, but we argue that this is a relevant scenario, i.e. a potential context for which the stakeholders in the world of Management Education may want to prepare. (Along the way, as Europeans, we go one step further. Turning specifically to Europe we argue that some key players there need to recognize the importance of the issue of proper management education and react accordingly. We thus send a call to key European players in the system: the Commission of the European Union, governments in member states, regional governments and Industry). "The *future is not to be discovered. The future is primarily to be invented*" (Gaston Berger). *"A Foresight exercise aims at thinking about a variety of possible futures (the 'futurible') as a way to bring light on what we intend to do today*" (Michel Godet).

*   *   *

History is filled with stories of empires which were built through military conquest, maintained through economic domination and then in-printed or rooted via the cultural influence of the leading power, until the softening of the whole empire made it a tempting prey for external attacks or implosive internal pressures. The old Egypt, the Greeks and then the Romans in the Mediterranean sea, the Arab domination from Spain to Pakistan and Indonesia, the Spanish and Portuguese colonies from the Americas to the Philippines or Macao, or more recently, the Victorian British empire give us examples of a sequential model of domination: first the soldier for the territory, then the merchant and businessman for the economy, and the teacher and the priest for the mind and the soul of the people.

This may appear as an overly simplified and rather deterministic view of historical cycles. Yet, this may bring some light on the current domination of the US on management education.

The nineteenth century saw the rise of the US as a giant-to-be. In his "De la démocratie en Amérique" (1832) Alexis de Tocqueville clearly identified the potential of the fascinating country emerging at that time in North America. He recognized the immense reservoir of open space on the land, the political promise of the democracy prevailing in the young nation, the pragmatism of the American people, the blending power of free initiative as a way to reach for money and status – away from the old European tradition of aristocracy through birth, etc. He described a promising nation, a power-to-be.

The twentieth century saw the fall of the British and French empires and the full establishment of the US as a super-power. The two world wars brought the GI around the globe as the sword against anti-democratic rulers. From then on, apart from a trail of US military bases left along the way, businessmen progressively substituted for the GIs in most countries, with some painful exceptions such as Korea or Vietnam as the cold war was in fact being hotly fought on the territories of third parties. At the same time, American universities soon become the place where the elite throughout the world would send their children for a good education. And Hollywood also followed, disseminating images of the American way of life and its cultural heritage around the globe. The implosion of the former USSR and the fall of the Berlin wall finalized the establishment of the US as the one and only superpower offering its model to the world for the 21st century.

It may be too early to tell whether the 9/11 attack and the subsequent Afghanistan – Iraq move will be remembered as the sign of the beginning of some form of a (relative) decline – the withdrawal from Vietnam in 1975 being thus essentially an early signal. In any case, it may be argued that America will stay on as a key power throughout the century, as our modern times may be witnessing the emergence of a multi-polar world with several blocks of power bound to co-exist as co-opetitive entities.

Some may oppose the above analysis arguing that the American way of running business became dominant not because of wars but primarily thanks to the excellence of the model of management and the competitiveness of the American-based multinational corporation. This would just be another interpretation of the same historical data, which would open an interesting debate. We could argue that the Japanese or German modes of management have been rather successful, while significantly differing from what is being taught in US business schools. But we will not go in that direction here.

What we suggest retaining from our brief historical interpretation is two-fold:

Firstly, the long-lasting effect of a dominating power stems from the resilience of the cultural footprint which is brought in the wake of the military and economic domination. This effect may last many decades after the decline of the military and economic power. In a way, the sequence of domination in our simplified model of historical cycles mirrors the path of a comet. The comet itself may be relatively short, but the tail is gigantic. In our analogy, the comet stands for the military conquest while the tail would represent the cultural footprint. The Roman Empire is still present throughout the world in many ways (language, calendar, law and institutions, religion, etc.). The prestige of

Ox-bridge or Sorbonne remains decades after the fall of the empires, to a certain extent irrespective of the strength of the economies of the UK or France. The same may apply to Humboldt in Berlin – despite several decades behind the wall. In that sense, one may expect the US domination on culture, if not on economy, and in any case on management education, to last much longer than the GI presence outside the US.

Secondly, if the world of geopolitics is leaning towards a multi-polar arrangement, one may legitimately ask whether this could have an influence on the variety of models for management and management education which may co-exist in such a new international setting. Things may not change immediately but one may wonder whether the days of the one-model-for-all in management may not soon be behind us.

And if this line of reasoning is worth pursuing, it soon appears that among the emerging blocks in the world which is currently shaping up in front of us in this beginning of the 21st century, and more specifically when it comes to management education, Europe is a typical candidate to be a challenger to the US model of business schools.

Other candidates may be thought of, Japan being one of them. (We did not give a close enough look at the Japanese system of management education but this would most certainly be an interesting exercise). Apart from Japan, Asia is in great demand for western management training, especially China and India. (China may actually end up building a specific managerial model in the long run, but for the time being it seems that Chinese authorities are doing their best to learn from the outside, primarily from the US and Europe).

Australia and New Zealand are in a situation similar to Europe, facing the US model, but they are geographically part of the Pacific Rim and are thus interested in connecting further with Japan, the emergent economies of China and India and the rest of Asia. Canada may also be seen in a similar cultural situation but its geographic proximity to the US, the very close links existing between the two economies and the high level of mobility of students and managers across the border create a very peculiar situation. As a result, Canada is both very integrated into the North American model of management and, in a way, still searching for its own differentiated path.

Russia is in an intermediate position, having opened up to the West but eager to limit the influence on the way it will run business. Management education in Russia is thus an open but sensitive question.

Latin America is under strong Northern influence and may be interested in getting access to an alternate way to train their elite in business, thus leaning towards Europe as a second source, at least in part. The Middle East is also trying to train managers for its developing businesses beyond oil, thus turning to America but also Europe. And Africa is trailing, with many difficulties.

All in all, beyond the US itself, Europe is the most obvious candidate which could possibly influence the future of management education in a way which would somehow differ from the dominant current US model. We thus felt that it would make sense to use European lenses to study the future of management education in general.

Yet, some would argue that Europe is currently trying to catch up through direct imitation, importing the US business school model and thus the rules of the game – and its shortcomings. In that sense, Europe would be increasingly aligned on the US model, thus simply running behind.

However, some others would suggest that Europe may be on the verge of choosing to play a slightly different game, at least to a certain extent, leveraging some of its historical and cultural specificities to depart from the dominant mainstream US model of business schools, in a differentiation strategy. But this is yet to be seen.

Our book is precisely a contribution to discuss this possible bifurcation in management education.

It should be stressed that our aim is not to try to oppose Europe to the US. This would be both irrelevant and fruitless. Our intent is to use the case of Europe as a way to discuss whether the future of business schools worldwide may or may not remain aligned to the US dominant model of today. We thus first look at the US model as the baseline and we then look at the future of business schools through the lenses of Europe.

It should also be noted that some may argue that there is more than a single model of management in America. We agree that there are variants as the US managerial stage is a complex and lively community where many views and practices confront and interact. As a result, management style and methods in America do vary across sectors, from mature to emerging industries, from the large multinational to the Hi-tech start-up, from the Iron Belt to the Silicon Valley. Yet, in a broader context, we wish to stress that all these tend to belong to the same management paradigm, what we refer to as the American managerial way. This may sound as a sweeping generalization, but this macro view will help us discuss the future of management education and research adopting a worldwide perspective.

*   *   *

The research behind this book all started when we were invited to write a Foresight report for the French Foundation for Management Education (Fnege) on the future of Business schools in France and Europe. At that point we invited colleagues to join in a working group to contribute through a series of monthly half-day discussions for about 6 months. We used a Foresight technique known as "Mactor" (Godet, 2005). We also interviewed a panel of insiders from the international academic community (mostly business school Deans and business professors) and practitioners from Industry. Most interviewees came from Europe and North America. We also reviewed the available literature dealing with the topic. This initial Foresight exercise led to five scenarios for European business schools. These scenarios, together with the report, were then extensively discussed in a series of seminars with various audiences. The Foresight report raised a lot of interest and led us to consider extending the analysis.

We thus subsequently decided to broaden our perspective, calling upon European colleagues to establish an informed descriptive base of the current situation and trends in their respective countries or about regions they would know well. We also asked them to revisit the Foresight scenarios with us. We are thus deeply indebted to these colleagues who contributed to the making of the book. Yet, apart from the edited chapters of Part II, the usual disclaimers apply as we, the authors, are fully and solely responsible for the ideas presented and discussed here.

This book is the result of the above process. It is about the future of business schools. It looks at the world of business education in 2020, adopting a broad perspective. This is a Foresight exercise. The book first describes the present situation as it is in various countries, starting obviously from the US as the baseline and then discussing the case of Europe, in the diversity of European countries. We actually use the case of Europe as a "system of systems of management education" typically confronted with the US dominant model of business schools. This serves as a case material to conduct the Foresight analysis: searching for the main families of players in the system, identifying challenges facing the families of players from within the system as well as exogenous pressures exerted onto the system from the outside. In turn, this leads to

Given the lack of overall statistics for worldwide management education, we have made some gross evaluations to generate orders of magnitude. We believe that some 200 000 management faculties teach about 4 to 5 million students every year in about 7600 management programs around the globe, for a business of about 10 to 12 billion US $. Although these figures are gross estimates, they provide some indication of the scale of the activity conducted in business schools. But the real importance of management education should be looked at through the influence of business schools on the overall economy. To a large extent, this is why we wrote this book.

building scenarios for the future of business schools. On that basis, the book draws strategic implications for the main players in management education in the main regions of the world. We discuss strategies for North America, Europe, the Brics (Brazil, Russia, India, China and South Africa) and RoW (rest of the World).

We feel that a European system of management education may be currently emerging. We also feel that this emerging European management education raises interest in the rest of the world and may soon challenge the US dominant model. Clearly, Harvard will remain Harvard and the power of American management research will remain for many years ahead. Yet, we feel that something may be happening in the world of business schools and this may be coming from Europe.

The design of the book follows the line of reasoning which we just developed in this introduction.

We start with the US baseline: we invite JC Spender to present his vision of where North American business schools currently stand and where they are heading. We use this as our baseline.

We develop our Foresight view as Part I. The first chapter presents a systematic transversal analysis of the European situation in its diversity, thus introducing the families of players within a typical system of management education (Chap 1). We then introduce the challenges facing the players from within the system (Chap 2). We also introduce the exogenous pressures exerted onto the system from the outside (Chap 3). On that basis, we go for the presentation of our Foresight output in the form of 5 scenarios for the future of business schools (Chap 4). We then draw the strategic implications of the scenarios for stakeholders in management education in various regions of the world (Chap 5). Finally, as Europeans, we go one step further to send a call to key European players, asking them to better support management education and research in the EU (Chap 6).

The background descriptions of the current situations in various geographical zones and specific countries are presented in Part II. In other words, Part II provides the detailed background material which made it possible to discuss the future of business education both in context and in perspective.

The US Base Line: Revisiting the American Dominant Model

The US model of management education has a clear leadership worldwide. Not only is the US the Mecca of management through the practice of business in the American Corporation, it is also the Mecca of Business Schools. The business of business education is doing well in America.

Yet, this model is periodically challenged by intense internal debates about the relevance of what is being taught, the way it is being taught and what the alumni do with that knowledge once they work as managers or executives in companies.

Despite these debates – a rather healthy practice which America is proud of, and legitimately so – the rest of the world tends to refer to the US model with a variety of feelings: attraction, envy, willingness to compete with, criticism, etc.

We asked JC Spender to give us his view of the American dominant model of Management Education.

(We are fully aware that the US university system of business education is made up of a complex variety of components. The wording "US model" as if it were single and fully homogenous is thus inappropriate. Yet, we use it here for the sake of simplicity. We also mean to mention explicitly the absence of Canada in our analysis. We simply could not cover all countries of the world, not even all OECD countries. We briefly touched upon the specific situation of Canada in the introduction of the book).

The Business School in America:
A Century Goes By

J.C. Spender

Background

The Harvard Business School (HBS) was founded in 1907.[1] It was not the first US university business school; those of the universities of Louisiana and Wisconsin were founded in 1851 and 1852 respectively.[2] Nor were business schools "invented" in the US, as some believe; there were several in Europe even before American independence.[3] Nor was HBS the first of the top US schools, Wharton being founded in 1881.[4] But HBS is arguably the best known and has become the model for many other schools in the US and around the world.[5]

So one hundred years on from the founding we might look at it and at the other top US schools and ask about their circumstances and condition.[6] HBS received a serious shock in the Harvard President's report in 1978.[7] Bok chided the school for being overly quantitative, paying insufficient attention to globalization and business ethics, and ill-equipping young people who were often destined for high office. He noted that although HBS's students were mostly headed into the private sector, in the US's mixed economy career success necessarily led to social responsibilities beyond their firm. 30 years later, not much seems to have changed. When Yale's Business School Dean stepped down in 2005 he repeated similar concerns about US graduate business education, arguing the top schools needed radical change.[8] He reflected on events like 9/11 and Enron, and the BSchools' abandoned vision of spearheading a world-wide movement towards globalization and privatization while governments learned to leave the management of their increasingly complex and globally integrated economies to a new generation of BSchool educated senior managers. This, it seemed, was how Europe and America should best prepare for the economic invasion from China and India, the addition of 2 billion producing and consuming people to the developed world's economy. But the private sector's scandals and organizational failures revealed in the law courts, and by Hurricane Katrina and other failures in the public sector, reminded us that business's senior managers are no more trustworthy or capable than those in government, and that mendacity, corruption and utter incompetence are as widespread as ever. So new questions are being asked about the schools, such as NorthWestern which Skilling attended, and elsewhere where his fellows in failure were trained.[9] Overall, as Gartner noted, senior managers seem to be refocusing more narrowly on their own businesses and personal opportunities as their pay differentials over their average worker widen ever further.

At the same time long-term rumbles of concern that US BSchool students are not being taught adequately or correctly continue. HBS's house journal, the Harvard Business Review (HBR), now one of the most influential of American management journals, followed up critical pieces by Livingston,[10] Hayes and Abernathy,[11] Linder and Smith,[12] and Lataif,[13] with a fresh attack from Bennis and O'Toole,[14] suggesting business schools had "lost their way." As with Mintzberg's critique,[15] the complaints are mostly about course content, that students are taught too much theory, much of it irrelevant and overly quantitative, and providing too little exposure to the "soft" people aspects of organizations, leadership, and business ethics. These complaints and breast-beatings are visible well beyond HBR, indeed they are widespread across US journals and campuses.[16] They were recognized and legitimated as topics of concern within the US Academy of Management as several Academy Presidents used their inaugural speeches to provoke the membership to think anew.[17] Similar concerns have surfaced in the UK, with calls to broaden the business schools' relationships to the "real world" and to embrace publics and objectives beyond maximizing shareholder value.[18] In fact these complaints about BSchools and what and how they teach have been part of management education in Europe for at least two centuries.[19] Ghoshal touched an old wound, suggesting business schools may actually be damaging the nations and economies in which they thrive, especially if they infuse their students with inappropriate ethical and moral standards,[20] and prompted at flurry of discussion.[21]

The Profession responds

What action has there been beyond this continual breast-beating? American in origin, the AACSB International is now the world's leading and most highly regarded business school accrediting agency. It estab-lished a Management Education Task Force in part to address these on-going complaints, and in 2002 issued a report "Management Education at Risk."[22] Its conclusions were far from radical, dealing with but three topics: doctoral education, curriculum changes, and the relationship between degree programs and executive education. The first noted a crisis in PhD program enrollment, threatening the supply of future fac-ulty, though this may have had the unanticipated and beneficial effect of increasing the number of women professors and faculty born and trained overseas. The second is a perennial topic for energetic Deans and reluctant faculty committees as they struggle to leave their mark on their schools. To help them move this agenda forward the AACSB com-mittee suggested a new task force of business and academic leaders to "identify core management skills that span traditional functional areas of expertise and prepare managers for global adaptability" leading us to wonder what the last century of business school research had produced if not such basic knowledge. The third topic drew attention to the paradox facing our industry for, in spite of the many complaints and passionate critiques, there appears to be continuing rising demand for both its credentialed and un-credentialed products. In fact the business of business education is remarkably healthy. Demand continues to ex-pand, though lately US MBA program enrollments have hesitated and the rate of return on the student's investment in the degree seems to have declined.[23] Notwithstanding such clouds, wealthy sponsors con-tinue to appear and take their opportunities to fund and name ever fancier new business schools.

And our industry is not just about MBAs and post-graduate education. The continuing appeal and success of undergraduate programs is re-markable, and the income is of great importance to the host university. Doctoral programs are typically loss leaders so the real money is at the undergraduate and executive levels. US educational legislation generally demands undergraduates take 50 percent of their credits outside their major, so the business enrollment is of huge political and economic importance for the liberal arts and science faculties who supply the sup-porting credits. 20 years ago Miles reminded us business degrees make up the largest single element of many universities' output,[24] and now the MBA programs have expanded to make up 25% of total US Masters degrees.[25] Likewise Mowday hurrahs the expansion of the Academy of Management and its journals over the last 40 years.[26] Teaching in these undergraduate, graduate and executive programs the Academy members now number around 17,000 and hail from 98 countries.

The sheer volume of students, classes, instructors, and publications rises steadily. Fernandes, the AACSB's current President and CEO, reminds members the MBA is the "most popular, most flexible, and most successful degree in the world."[27] Many US BSchools have globalized, offering programs in such exotic locations as Singapore, Beijing, Shanghai, Rome, Dubai, and elsewhere; though some US schools opened overseas campuses with mixed success. BSchools are also home to rising numbers of academics who do not regard the Academy of Management as their professional institution; e.g. economists, lawyers, psychologists, business ethicists, accountants, computer scientists, economic and business historians, and others. Overall it is clear the business of business education has never been better. On top of that the MBAs' and undergraduates' salaries and career opportunities continue to improve, especially as business bachelors are seen as cheap MBAs and the MBA has become the entry-credential of choice in many industries, and increasingly in the public sector as it seeks to emulate the private sector's efficiencies.

Pondering the complaints

So, given our industry's successes what are these complaints really about? Do we need to take notice? Why do we not simply celebrate our industry's progress? To take one issue, on what basis should we worry about the ethical standards evident in business practice today? Who are we to call these shots? As political theorists we can fret that we have no adequate theory of capitalist society and its ethical dimensions, but why would we think ourselves responsible for business practice? There are bad apples in every barrel and senior managements' objectives are surely not ours to determine; we merely help prepare intellectual tools and should be celebrating the quality of the training we provide and the strength of the research on which it is based. Are we to go beyond education and try to control what business people do? This kind of discussion raises questions for all manner of educators, especially in a democratic society which ultimately expects individuals to be accountable and responsible for their own actions.[28] Should schools go beyond generating an awareness of the ethical and aesthetic issues around organizational management and get into fostering or even proselytizing particular positions, such as a blind commitment to free market principles? Even more immediately, how can the critics accuse business schools of being irrelevant, and in the same breath berate them for having students like Skilling? Are engineering schools to hold such students who become weapons designers responsible for the uses to which their inventions are put? Our educational processes may influence students negatively – there are suggestions that teaching economics makes students more self-interested and greedy[29] – and maybe BSchool students survive the experience of being educated and go on to lead the nation only because they are already the best.[30]

We should not lose sight of the fact that there is always a drumbeat of complaint within every academic discipline as traditionalists mourn the passing of the old, first-learned, and familiar, while young Turks rail at the slowness of change. Complaining is part of the academics' critical attitude, and within business education the complaints are not notably different from those within public policy,[31] economics,[32] accounting,[33] engineering,[34] information systems,[35] to say nothing of the centuries of vigorous and sometimes vicious debate about the right path within disciplines like history, sociology, and psychology. But the business schools' critics are particularly troubled because, ironically, our discipline lacks the clear and strong connections between theory and practice that are evident in disciplines such as accounting, law, engineering, and medicine. This raises deeper questions about whether business schools really are professional schools, like those of accounting, law and engineering, and even whether business should be properly considered a profession.[36]

A profession is often defined as a community of practitioners trained into an established body of knowledge whose access to that community is policed through credentialing entry processes generally overseen and sometimes directly controlled by an institutionalized professional body – such as the American Bar Association or the American Society of Civil Engineers.[37] The profession's body of knowledge can be research- or theory-based, as for engineering, or practice-based, as for lawyers and accountants. The institutions policing this body of knowledge control the relationships between the researchers and the innovative practitioners, thereby prescribing what is professionally relevant and acceptable; though there are additional governmentally established rules, regulations, and informal standards of behavior often put in place with the assistance of the professional institutions. In collaboration with government, these institutions may exclude people from the profession if they are under-qualified, or are guilty of criminal or un-ethical conduct. Thus doctors, engineers, and others display their professional and academic credentials in their offices from necessity as well as with pride.

Business is not a profession according to these criteria.[38] Entry is free to anyone able to register a company; bankruptcy is no impediment and even the legal prohibition debarring convicted felons from serving on the boards of public companies can be gotten around, as in Martha Stewart's case. In the end anyone in any kind of business can be described as a valid member of the business community. Qualifications and professional standards are all but irrelevant. At the same time it is clear business schools are not typically staffed by people with deep knowledge of business or management, nor is the research they do of immediate relevance to those in business – as it might be in medical or engineering schools. Nor are US universities generally managed by the BSchool's professoriate. But it is also clear the MBA certification process acts as a powerful selection mechanism for certain types of industrial activity, such as consulting and financial services. Indeed this selection and credentialing function, even when applied informally during the process of seeking a recruitment interview, seems to be growing and extending into other industries. But what appears paradoxical may appear so simply because we have mis-framed the issues. Behind the complaints and our satisfactions lie assumptions about what business schools are and do. Their success tells us they are definitely serving the interests of some people and institutions, their students and those in the corporate world included. Where complaints arise they spring from the different interests and expectations held by quite different communities who have different ideas about what the schools are or should be doing.[39] We can see the complaints fall into different categories: (a) the course content is inappropriate, (b) the research is not of the quality or relevance appropriate to professional standing, (c) the profession of management is not institutionalized and thus the schools cannot be professional schools, and (d) business schools have lost sight of their function, and even which community they serve. The first category is exemplified in Mintzberg's work. The second is behind the hand-wringing of the Academy presidents and the "theory police."[40] Little has been said in the US about the third, but in the UK the Chartered Management Institute, with over 70,000 members, is making a serious attempt to create a cadre of professionally qualified and recognized managers. However some industries traditionally regard MBAs as trained into dys-functionality and vastly over inflated egos.

So perhaps the most troubling category is the fourth, that the US business schools have "lost their way" and are not only failing to provide the nation and the managerial community with the necessary skills but may actually be doing tangible damage to the economy or to the students. The core concern is less that they have become a hot-bed of anti-social or anti-capitalist ideology, leveraging the academics' traditional Democratic and left-leaning tendencies into a student revolt. Rather the concern is that competition between the schools as businesses themselves, far from improving the breed, is leading to "goal displacement" as they focus on their Business Week and US News & World Report ranking at the expense of their deeper mission.[41] While the business of business education is healthier than ever, it has clearly become more competitive, along with much university activity in the US.[42] The peculiar lack of relevance characteristic of BSchools' body of knowledge means the educational products are not significantly differentiated by course content. From this point of view Podunk U.'s MBA, or that of an on-line for-profit, is little different from those from Stanford or Chicago Business Schools, or any other BSchool. The degree's principal differentiator is the school's reputation, even though the basis for a school's reputation is extremely difficult to establish.[43] Branding and other forms of reputation management become hugely important in the struggle to attract the best students. Funding the university's sports teams may have more impact than hiring a Nobel economist. If the students coming into the school are the best available, they are likely to remain so when the recruiters come to call at the end of their programs. A virtuous cycle is established for the schools with the best reputations, while a vicious cycle confronts those trying to climb the ladder. 18 of the schools ranked within the top 20 in Business Week's original listing in 1986 have never been off the list. Only 35 schools have ever been ranked as in the top 30,[44] so Podunk U.'s chances of getting on the list are virtually zero, even though hundreds of schools hire new Deans and build new buildings with the declared objective of getting into the top 30. The AACSB convened another committee to report on this rankings dilemma.[45] They concluded the media needed to be educated into the real issues shaping schools' qualities (i.e. to ignore Business Week and the US News and World Report rankings), that the media should come to the AACSB for the real data, that AACSB accreditation was the most relevant quality measure, and that more research into rankings and their effects was required. Some research has been done, reinforcing the divergence between research quality and school ranking,[46] so mostly increasing our confusion.

Conclusions and methodological issues

Can we draw any tentative conclusions about the state of the US business schools? As Wensley suggests, it may make sense to applaud their obviously successful short-term accommodation to the economic and institutional pressures, while expressing concern about the longer term issues.[47] The counter argument is that during the history of business education, at least since the 1960s and the post-Foundation Report transformation,[48] we have seen an on-going series of short-term adjustments, and that these will continue satisfactorily as the BSchools respond competitively to the latest concerns, such as the renewed post-Enron focus on business ethics and personal morality, and the rising post-US-globalization concerns with ecology, sustainability, and alternative cultures.[49] In this case there is little more to be said, beyond looking at the historical record and, perhaps, teasing out the relevant mechanisms of institutional change. How effective are the AACSB's initiatives, for instance? Will it be necessary to recruit new faculty with new skills? Will the competitive nature of the BSchool process need modification to ensure students compete less with each other? Should BSchools be rated rather than ranked? These seem to be worthwhile questions and moves, but there may be something more fundamental going on here. That business is not a profession, in spite of the rhetoric to the contrary, tells us something important about the educational and research processes involved. The key insight may be that business is about entrepreneurship and permanent innovation while professionalization is about ensuring an established body of knowledge is applied in ways overseen by institutions. Business normally makes room for the novel product, leaving its evaluation to market forces and *caveat emptor*, while the engineering and medical professions, for instance, are intent on protecting the public from the under-qualified and novel ideas that have not yet been subjected to expert appraisal. The whole point of the professional institutions is to deny open access to market forces, especially under conditions of poor knowledge and the tendency to run after new fads,[50] and business continually seeks to break out of such institutional structures.[51]

The deeper implications go beyond researching narrowly into entrepreneurial firms and SMEs, for large firms and not-for-profits can be entrepreneurial, as can public sector bureaucracies; so the real underlying issues are methodological.[52] The BSchool response to the Foundation Reports was to prioritize rational theorizing and positivistic methods over the then-prevailing historical and discursive methods of enquiry and education. The Carnegie Mellon work conducted in the 1960s under Dean Bach was especially influential in developing techniques of rational decision analysis and establishing these as the fashionable metaphor for good management.[53] But there has been little corresponding advance or uptake of entrepreneurship theory to re-balance this preferment of rational and quantitative analysis. Those who criticize the BSchools' curriculum content as overly rational or quantitive seldom suggest alternatives, beyond vaguely suggesting greater attention to the social and psychological "soft" topics. Yet in practice these too are equally likely to be fitted into rationalist and positivistic straightjackets.

This struggle is familiar to all social scientists, yet is curiously ignored in the BSchools which are evidently reluctant to admit they are in the social science discipline. Among economists, for instance, the work of Knight and Schumpeter focused on the response to uncertainty and broke out of the framework of naïve rationality. In contrast Kirzner, and a number of current authors such as Casson and Shane, see entrepreneurship as the process of discovering the opportunities existing in imperfect market-places.[54] Knight, Schumpeter, and the Austrian economists took a different view and saw entrepreneurship as the activity of creating something new, not the discovery of what already existed.[55] This methodological switch raises quite different questions. While the entrepreneurial process approach can be reduced to rational theorizing,[56] it is not easy to see how entrepreneurial creativity can be similarly reduced to positivistic theorizing. Nor can we imagine how to teach it. Even creativity researchers are puzzled about creativity.[57] There may be lessons to be learned from, for instance, Schools of Art and Music, educational enterprises that seek a better balance between the rational and the creative aspects of our lives.[58] Along the same lines Bennis and O'Toole argued that MBA programs would benefit from paying more attention to "fast-breaking news" and Shakespeare[59] (Business Week On-Line, 5/25/2005).

But the real lessons are epistemological and philosophical – and very difficult. In the business schools we are struggling with the overhang of two centuries of commitment to rationality as the appropriate methodology for investigating social and economic questions. These underplay, and even ignore, human agency, the fact that we create a world as well as live within it.[60] Ironically, agency theory, as taught by business school economists, is about the use of incentives that appeal to the agent's rationality and thereby align the agent's creativity with that of the principal.[61] The agent's creativity is otherwise neglected and theorized out of the analysis, while the principal's is ignored under that surprising assumption that they can set whatever goals they choose. The challenge with this almost blind commitment to rationality and positivistic method in the pursuit of uncritically accepted goals is not that it is wrong; the sciences, natural, psychological, and social, have been hugely productive and are of huge importance to our understanding of business, economics, psychology, and so forth. It is that if we really do the academic spadework to see what underpins all our knowledge of business and management we find rationality itself is no more than a dialectical companion to the human imagination. Some would argue it is a prisoner of class interests, others of an overly functional orientation, yet others that rationality is culturally and historically shaped. In the same way, entrepreneurial creativity is not a mode of managerial operation all to itself. It too is a dialectical companion to managing bureaucratic organizations and engaging in rational market behavior. The problem is that our discipline's uncritical attitude towards rationality does much to sustain the urban myth that rationality alone can be sufficient for dealing with the managers' responsibilities and consequently for distancing BSchools from practicing managers. Inasmuch as students adopt such hyper-rationality as a managerial ideology they are visibly harmed by the business school process. For the most part, of course, they are too street-wise, of the "real world", and too ethically informed, to believe all they are told. The downside of the state of the US business school is that they are exclusivity-seeking temples to a purely rational approach to social and economic affairs, as Bok argued over a generation ago. The upside is that most business school students are smart enough to take what they hear with a large pinch of salt as they focus on the short-term issues of getting credentialed and advancing their careers.

Part I

A Foresight View

Current situation, dynamics, scenarios and strategic implications

Our intent is to use the case of Europe as a case study to discuss the future of business schools in general. It is also to use our European lenses to discuss whether European business schools will remain aligned to the US dominant model of today, e.g. in a "catching up" mode, or whether they may find other possible routes.

Now that we have had a critical review of the US model (as our baseline), we start the Foresight discussion by looking at the variety of management education across Europe (Chap 1). This will help better understand the system for which we conduct a Foresight. This will also help identify the families of players being part of a typical system of management education and thus the contour of the system. On that basis, we shall then look at the challenges facing the players from within (Chap 2) and the external pressures exerted on the system from the outside (Chap 3). In turn this discussion will lead to the presentation of the results of our Foresight exercise in the form of 5 scenarios (Chap 4). Strategic implications of the scenarios for business schools and other key stakeholders in major regions of the world will then be drawn (Chap 5). Finally, as Europeans, we send a specific call to EU leaders asking them to contribute to strengthen the emerging European system of management education and research (Chap 6). (See Table 1.1).

The discussion of the variety of management education across Europe is based on a series of contributions which are presented in details in Part II.

1

Management Education as a System: A Case Study on Europe

The aim of this chapter is to study and compare management education in Europe. We base our analysis on the country studies presented in part II: France, Italy, Germany, Netherlands, Portugal, Spain, Sweden and the U.K, plus a brief review of Central Europe.

Europe has a long tradition in business studies. The first business school was created in Lisbon, Portugal, in 1759, followed by the ESCP (Ecole Supérieure de Commerce de Paris) in Paris, France, in 1819. Public universities began to launch business administration programs only in the mid-twentieth century. The number of students in business studies then grew dramatically in all European countries. For instance, in Spain the number of Faculties of Economics and Business doubled between the mid 70s and the mid 80s. Nowadays, one of the European students' preferred subjects is Business Studies, accounting for 22 percent of all postgraduate students in the U.K, 16 percent of all higher education students in France, 10 percent of the graduate students in Sweden.[1] In some cases, this development of business studies was a response to the one-sided reliance upon, and the perceived lack of practical orientation of the discipline of economics (e.g. in the Netherlands and France).

Despite this enduring tradition and the social visibility of business studies within European countries, European management education today lags behind the American model for business schools. This is partly ironic, given that the US system was modeled on the German higher education system of the 19th century. European spending on higher education represents only 1.1 percent of gross domestic product, compared with 2.7 percent in the US. The A-ranked academic journals in business studies are American; US rankings specify the criteria by which the business schools are evaluated worldwide, and all international rankings demonstrate the ascendancy of American business schools.

Indeed, the US model in management education seems never to have been more dominant. In this context, and in an increasingly globalized world, we asked ourselves whether a European model for management education already exists or might be emerging.

National specificities – clustering

Throughout Europe, higher education systems are mainly public with state-owned universities. Each national system emerged over time as the result of a specific historical context with specific public policies. Part II of the book presents typical details for some of the countries. It is thus hard to look at "European management education" as if it were homogenous. As a result, the job market for business professors remains essentially national; student mobility is still low despite EU effort to foster cross border exchange programs, and the specificity of each national higher education structure is still high. Nevertheless, we suggest clustering management education in Europe around three models: the Latin, the German and the Anglo-saxon models.

We discuss the commonalities and major differences of the national systems of management education in the first section. Section two then presents the result of our clustering exercise.

An excessive compartmentalization

For the moment, the European system of Higher Education still shows certain defining features: the compartmentalization of national job markets, low student mobility, and distinct national institutional settings for higher education.

The job market for faculty is still compartmentalized

European professors often hold jobs for life and are usually civil servants. With the exception of the UK and the Netherlands, professors have to pass a national exam or achieve some sort of accreditation to secure tenure. The price a professor has to pay for mobility is to give up job security. Furthermore, regulations and/or practices within most EU member states make it difficult to hire non-nationals who are not already embedded in the national system. As a result, a pan-European job market is difficult to implement. (See Table 1.1).

This compartmentalization contributes to noticeable wage differences across Europe. Germany, Netherlands and the U.K. offer the most attractive salaries for management professors. However, while a young professor has to be mentored to enter into the German system, along

Table 1.1 Salaries and tenure policies in European countries and the U.S.

	France	Italy	Portugal	Spain	Germany	Netherlands	Sweden	UK	U.S.
Approximate Salaries (net monthly remuneration, before income tax) in universities	Lecturer and Senior Lecturer: €2000 to €4250 Professor: up to €5800	Lecturer: €1750 to €3250 Professor: up to €4300	Lecturer and Senior Lecturer: from €3500 to €4650 Full Professor: up to €5900	Senior Lecturer: from €2300 to €4200 Professor: up to €5100	From €2900 up to €7500; New salary system since 2006	From €2700 to €8000 universities have leeway to pay bonuses for exceptional achievements	Lecturer: from €2700 up to €5250 Professor: from €3500 up to €6750	Lecturer (€3000–4000) Senior Lecturer (€5000–5600) Professor (€6800–€11100) £1 ~ €1.5	From €5000€ to €23500€ (€1 ~ $1.3)
Tenure/How to get professorship in universities	National habilitation for permanent position in Lectureship + national competitive exam to get professorship (aggrégation)	National public examination (Associate professor) and another national public examination to become Professor	National public examination to become full Professor	National habilitation for permanent position (senior lecturer and professor)	Habilitation thesis	The universities have the authority to recruit and appoint full professors; there is no national exam or evaluation.	Recruitment process is managed by a standing recruitment committee with a panel of experts	Tenure at the level of the university	Tenure at the level of the university
Number of professors in business studies	Around 2000 professors and lecturers (1400 in public universities)	Around 1400		2032 (2003)	1826 (2004)		109 professors, 4 associate professors, 360 lecturers, 316 assistant professors		

the lines of the "medieval guild," the U.K. and the Netherlands have a more open market in which the universities have the authority to recruit and appoint professors. As a result, we believe that we perceive a "weak signal": a growing tendency for young and promising new PhDs to begin their career in the U.K. Broadly speaking, the current situation markedly reduces the attractiveness of the European job market compared to the United States. There, wage and employment policies are entirely at the discretion of each university. The development of a significant and efficient EU job market for management faculty will require a profound change of the wage and employment policies in most European countries.

The Socrates/Erasmus program aims at promoting the mobility of students, teachers and administrative staff within the EU (and other participating European countries). Even Erasmus has not significantly improved faculty mobility. Since its launch by the European Commission (EC) in 1987, only 12,000 professors, across all disciplines, have benefited from the program according to Eurostat. In a 2005 survey, the EC has even noted a trend towards reduced teaching staff mobility.[2] Broadly speaking, current support for professor mobility is considered insufficient to meet the challenge of delivering management education with truly European scope to non-mobile students. Finally, it should be stressed that mobility conditions for a professor are too precarious and incentives too limited to turn such exchanges into a viable program for faculty.

Student mobility is still low

The students' demand for mobility is steadily increasing: the Erasmus program sent 145,000 students to other European member states in 2005, compared to barely 3,000 students at its launch. Moreover, business students outnumber other disciplines in this respect: in 2005, they represented more than 30 percent of the French Erasmus students (EC). German, French and Spanish students are the most mobile and these countries are also the most popular destinations for Erasmus students. European students consider learning a foreign language, and notably English, both a great opportunity and a challenge. This may help explain the low number of English students that study in other European countries, compared to the attractiveness of the UK (which nonetheless competes with the US) for foreign students. It is worth noting that in each country, it is the responsibility of the higher institutions themselves to attract and recruit foreign applicants, while there is no particular incentive to encourage them to do so. Despite this, more and more

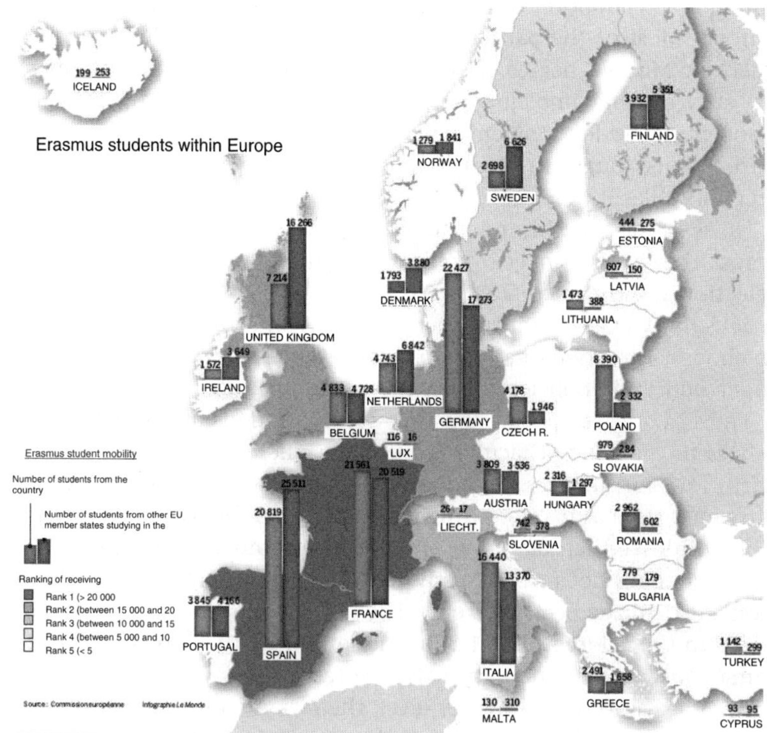

Figure 1.1. Where do Erasmus students study?
Source: Le Monde, 15 November 2006, EU Commission.

universities across Europe are offering courses in English in order to attract foreign students. See Figure 1.1 for Erasmus-related mobility.

However, among the 16 million students in European higher education, only 2 percent spent at least one year studying in another European country between 1998 and 2002, and today, the Erasmus program deals with less than 1 percent of the total European student population per year.

National degrees remain very specific despite the Bologna process

The Bologna process offered a significant impetus towards the creation of a truly European system of higher education. The Bologna agreements, signed in 1998 and 1999, launched a concrete process to harmonize the university diplomas throughout the Union. It has already largely facilitated the development of a more meaningful system through the adoption of the same two-step university degrees across Europe. Most of the participating countries have already created the Bachelor/Master's degree clarification, Germany being the only member state to delay implementation until 2010 (Table 1.2). An EC study also reports the development of specific curricula targeted to "European" participants, taught in English and designed for national and foreign students alike.

However, despite this move to harmonize higher education offerings across the EU, two major problems remain to be addressed: student selection and the doctorate degree.

Selectivity at entry into higher education and the student's freedom to choose a program or a university vary widely across the EU, according to education policies in each country (Table 1.2).

The PhD degree is the "missing piece" of the Bologna process. It relates to the issue of faculty recruitment and tenure, which remains within the jurisdiction of each member state. This will become particularly important as many retiring professors from the babyboom generation will leave their faculty position in the coming years. Moreover, a doctorate does not mean exactly the same thing across Europe (duration, curricula, expectation, etc.). The PhD titles have not been harmonized in the EU (see Table 1.2) in the sense that they do not open the same doors in the same ways. (Also see Table 1.3).

Even at Bachelor and Master level, the lack of curricula harmonization increases the difficulty of evaluating the relative quality of the various degrees awarded across Europe. As a matter of fact, some institutions prefer to develop bilateral agreements instead of entering the European credit transfer system. This may be an indication that the issue of quality recognition is not yet properly addressed. This also contributes to limiting student mobility. As the EC report concludes, European countries would like to achieve improved international recognition, as they seem to have realized "that their degrees are not automatically recognized at their real level."

Some universities in a few countries have begun setting up joint, integrated or double degree programs. This means that two institutions accept to award a combined degree when a student follows a combined curriculum. A "European diploma" however is yet to be seen. This does not seem to prevent some institutions to use the wording "European degree" to sell their programs. This leads to some form of confusion regarding the academic curricula made available in Europe, and makes it hard for European students, not to mention the non-Europeans, to understand what a "European" diploma track might be.

Table 1.2 Structure of higher education in business studies in Europe (and US) in 2007

	Entrance in university	+2	+3	+4	+5	+6	+8 (or more)
Germany	Hochschulneife	Zwischeprüfung (undergraduate degree)		Magister (graduate degree)		Zweltestaaptsrüfung	Doctorate
Italy	Maturita+selection or not, depending on each university		Laurea triennale	Master universitario di primo livello	Laurea magistralis		Dottorato di ricerca
Netherlands	The final year of primary school (age of 11–12) on the advice of the school and a national test, only one type of secondary school grants direct access to university bachelor programs		Bachelor		Master		PhD
France – University	Baccalauréat	Licence		Master 1	Master 2		Doctorat
France – business schools		Entrance exam after 2 years of preparation			"Grande Ecole" program Specialized Mastère		
Portugal	National examen + Access to university		Licenciatura		Master		Doctoral
Spain	Bachiller+National entry examination (selectividad)		Diplomas degree in BA	Undergraduate degree (Licenciate)	Master degree (Master of science-professional)	Master degree (Master of science-academic)	Doctorate
Sweden		College exam	Bachelor	Master/Business Economist	Advanced Master		Licenciate (5+2); PhD (5+4)
UK	University Selection with conditional offers		Bachelor (BA or BS)	Master	Master		PhD
USA	College selection			Bachelor	Master	Master/MBA	PhD

Table 1.3 Governance of higher education in business studies in Europe in 2006

	France	Italy	Portugal	Spain	Germany	Netherlands	Sweden	UK
Private/public	The market is segmented between public universities and semi-public business schools which offer Masters' degrees.	The market is segmented, development of professional education	Market share of undergraduate management studies is 20% private; at the Master level it's 10%. the Università Cattolica del Sacro Cuore has the largest offer of MBAs	Public (majority) Private Catholic, private schools specialized in professional education and MBA	Public system covers far more than 90% of the graduate. 10% of the universities and 20% of the universities of applied science are privately held.	Only public	Mainly public	Public; Private schools more specialized in professional education and MBA
Who delivers doctorate degree	Mostly public universities: 232 PhD in management in 2005	Public universities	Public universities	Public: about 50 in 2003	Public universities: 463 in 2004	Public universities	Mainly public, about 10 per year	Public universities: 244 in 2001–2002
Governance	Funding from State depends on the number of students. A university strategic plan is negotiated every four years	Funding from the State varies with research and teaching performance; universities are responsible for their P&L and balance sheet				Funding from the State is related to the results of research and teaching activities	Funding from the State depends on the number of students	

Three clusters of business schools in Europe

Higher education in Europe is mainly public. In most European countries, public universities "control" the Bachelor's degree and have a monopoly on the doctorate degree. Private sector institutions are more specialized in executive education and MBAs. (See Table 1.3).

Except for the noteworthy domination of public governance on higher education, the situation in each country tends to be specific. Nonetheless, broadly speaking, we suggest grouping European business schools into three models. (See Table 1.4).

The Latin model

This model includes the Portuguese, Spanish, French and Italian management education systems. (Each national system has its own distinctive features that do not strictly fit in, but we feel that there are enough commonalities to justify grouping these countries together).

The Latin model has an old tradition in business education, which was first established by the private sector, and in which religious institutions played a major role. The first business schools were created in the mid-18th century in Portugal and during the 19th century in France and Spain. The Paris Catholic Institute set up the ESSEC business school in France in 1907; the Jesuits played a major role in the creation of the most famous business schools in Spain, and the catholic universities are central players in management education in Portugal and Italy.

Although public education in business studies developed during the second part of the 20th century, business education remains split between the public and private systems. Public universities offer undergraduate and doctoral degrees while private or semi-private business schools play a central role in delivering Master's degrees and executive/ professional education. Furthermore, while the public system dominates in volume, private or semi-private business schools are more selective and more prestigious at Master's level: for example, Bocconi in Italy; IESE, Esade or Instituto de Empresa in Spain, and the Università Cattolica del Sacro Cuore in Portugal or HEC, ESSEC, ESCP-EAP, EM Lyon or Edhec in France. Within the public system of the "Latin" cluster, tuition and fees are very low – of the order of €800 per year, on average – and are regulated by the State, unlike private or semi-private business schools which may charge students and their families about 10 times that amount for undergraduates and more for Masters. (See Table 1.5).

Within the "Latin" public system, recruitment to academic positions and career evolution (for example, to a full professorship) are regulated by a national evaluation committee, and/or a specific national examination.

In most countries of the cluster, this led to a system characterized by a closed job market and low mobility. As a result, wages tend to be lower in this cluster than in the other two clusters. Incentives for research are limited and salary increases are modest throughout one's career. For example, as described in the chapter on Spain, the "best full professors in terms of research output would multiply their salary by only 2.2 over a lifetime career and, by the end of their career, the research bonus would represent only 14 percent of total remuneration." For faculty in the public sector in these countries, executive training and consultancy are, in financial terms, more attractive than research.

The German model

This model includes the German and Swedish management education systems, even if Swedish business schools in fact fall between the German and Latin models. The German model has its own roots, and is quite distinct from the rest of Europe. Its influence at the end of the 19th century was significant, when the German higher education system inspired the organization of American universities.

Like the Latin model, the German model has grown out of an old tradition in business education. The first business schools (departments of economics and business at universities) were created at the end of the 19th century in Germany and at the beginning of the 20th century in Sweden. Although the distinction between private and public management education also exists in this cluster, it is the public system that is the dominant player in terms of quantity and prestige. Public higher education is traditionally free, and university revenues essentially come from State funding.

The universities are renowned, and an academic career is still considered prestigious. Socialization and mentorship are the drivers of knowledge creation, and the career path for professors follows a "medieval guild" model. As a result, there is no formal career path and no national evaluation. Universities are organized around chairs run by professors, who have broad freedom in teaching and research, helped by assistants and "Habilitands." Doctoral candidates are fully employed as research and teaching staff at a chair. The "habilitation," or qualification process, to secure professorships is a challenging step. A candidate has to be mentored to pass it and obtain a full-chaired professorship. In this model, the PhD is the most prestigious diploma and the most reliable foundation for a career in management practice, despite the competition from the MBA diploma. The job market in the "German" model is thus characterized by professors who are deeply embedded in the community, which limits the possibilities for outsiders to enter the system. The established tradition of academic education and the prestige granted to professorships result in relatively higher wages than those prevailing in the Latin model.

The Anglo-Saxon model

English and Dutch business schools, and certain specific institutions like INSEAD or IMD, can be included under the Anglo-Saxon model. Within Europe, this cluster may be regarded as the most recent as it has been directly influenced by the US model. For example, London Business School (LBS) and Manchester Business School (MBS) were founded in the mid-60s and were the first business schools in the UK. In the Netherlands, business programs were started in the 30s, and were further developed after World War II. The main aim was the development of practical tools and close links exist between the academic and business communities in the countries of the cluster.

In this model, the business schools are, by and large, public and university-based. However, they have their own governance. Private schools do exist but are often less prestigious: they focus on continued education and play a minor role in the overall management education system.

Business school revenues come not only from State funding, but also from private funding and tuition and fees. For example, as noted in the chapter on the UK, "large donations from major British companies provided approximately £57 million in today's terms" thus permitting the creation of the first UK business school. Cambridge University has a £1.2 billion endowment fund (€1.8 billion), financed principally through alumni donations; the State's contribution represents only 30 percent of its revenue.[3]

Tuition and fees are regulated by the State, and although fees are higher in this cluster than in the rest of Europe, they are still low compared to the US. In the UK, tuition fees vary according to the degree, and there is a significant difference between undergraduate and graduate degrees. A 2004 reform raised the tuition fees in the UK to £3000 (€4500) for a Bachelor's degree, while those for a Master's degree are between £8000 and £20000 (€12000 and €30000). Financial aid for disadvantaged students is offered by the State.

Within this model, academic positions are open to competition, with a tenure-track system. In most universities of the Netherlands, a full professor is appointed by the university board, upon recommendation of an evaluation committee (at faculty level), with the support and involvement of the Dean. The tenure-track system was first adopted in

Table 1.4   Three clusters to describe higher education in management in the EU

	Latin model	German model	Anglo-Saxon model
Leading players	private/semi-public	public	public
Endowment funds	no	no	yes
Tuition fees (average)	Very low compared to the cost of the student (about 10%) Except "private" BSchools	Free of charge €1,000 since 2005	€4,500 (BA) up to €30,000
Career path	Regulated, national competitive exam	Mentored, accreditation process called "habilitation"	open competition tenure-track system
Wages (approximate average)	€2,000–€6,000	€3,000–€7,500	€3,000–€11,000

£1 ~ €1.5.

the Netherlands in the mid-1990s at the business school of Tilburg University. It is broadly established in the UK. The teaching load depends on past research performance, and faculty members on tenure track have guaranteed research time.

The spur to the foundation of a European management education system

Business schools across Europe are confronted with the same issues

Regardless of the cluster they belong to, business schools have to grapple with the same difficulties.

Inadequate funding and under-investment explain the financial shortfall experienced by universities. Funding sources and regulated fees do not cover the full economic cost of offering a high quality educational experience. Some universities have run into serious financial trouble, for example in Germany, in France, and even in the UK where institutions have greater control over financial matters. The unattractiveness of academic careers in most European countries, particularly in those of the Latin model, jeopardizes the ability of business schools to retain the best talents. Some are attracted by better wages and work conditions in the US. European public universities receive the vast majority of their funding from governments, and cannot charge students for tuition as much as American schools do. Politically, the US model of private payments is difficult to imitate in Europe, where free higher education is an emotional issue as it is seen as a symbol of fairness and equality. When the UK, in 2003, allowed universities to charge £3,000 (€4,500) a year, the measure faced such fierce opposition that an exemption for poor students was introduced. In Germany, a 2005 regulation made it possible for universities to start charging tuition – but only €1,000 a year: previously, it had been free.[4]

Recruiting top faculty in business studies is a strategic concern: demand for management education is growing at the same time as most western countries are experiencing, and will continue to experience, a wave of retirement. In the UK, for example, the current students/faculty ratio in management is 26:1, compared to the average higher education sector ratio of 13:1 across disciplines. Yet, there were only 244 newly awarded PhD in Business and Management in 2001–2002. At the same time, more than 4,000 faculty members were already over fifty years old. Most of them are set to retire over the next decade, a trend similar to that in the US (see the UK chapter). Hiring competition between the universities promises to be a merciless struggle and the United States will be one of the most serious competitors for Europe on that matter. Should a European job market emerge, the issue of wage policy will certainly come at the top of the agendas for deans, university presidents and their Ministries of Education.

Attracting the best students is another challenge posed by worldwide competition. Even given the appeal of management education, demographic shifts are reducing the number of potential students. For example, as we see in the UK chapter, MBA applicants are declining in number and quality, and the USA is experiencing a similar phenomenon. Secondly, as competition moves beyond national borders, European business schools struggle to attract not only the best students from home but also the best foreign students. Some European business schools are addressing this challenge: for example, several French business schools are developing "International Master's" degrees, 12-month programs taught in English.

Internationalization makes it possible to offer students the opportunity to study abroad and contributes to enrich campus life via intercultural interactions. Yet this poses the question of assessing the

Table 1.5 Comparison of tuition and fees in Europe and in the U.S.

	France	Italy	Portugal	Spain	Germany	Netherlands	Sweden	UK	U.S.
Fees per annum	Public universities €150 (Bachelor) €190 (Master) €290 (doctorate) free, depending on financial means; Private business schools: up to €8,000 (up to Master level included)	Public: €250 to €2300 – €800. on average, (Depending on the income of the student family) Private: €2,000 to €10,000 (Bocconi, Università Cattolica del Sacro Cuore)	From €487 to €902	Public university: €800 Private university: from €3,500 to €6,500 p	Free; New reform to charge €1,000	Depending on the income of the family student: €1,200 on average	Free	Tuitions fees reform in 2004, brought into play in 2006 €4,500. max (BA) from €12,000 to €30,000 (Master) €32500£ (MBA)	
Average estimated cost per student in public university	€8,800 in universities €10,500 n business schools	€7,500 12% are covered by students fees in public universities, 50% to 90% in private Business Schools		€3,200 to €4,000	€8,500			€9,000	€16,000

£1 ~ €1.5/$1 ~ €1.3.

quality of students recruited internationally. Experience shows that the quality of international students may vary significantly. It is not easy to compare curricula and merits in very specific contexts, in different languages, where selection processes are embedded in historical and socio-cultural specificities. It appears that many European institutions are still at the beginning of a learning process when it comes to assessing the quality of students coming from zones of the world new to their recruiting teams. As a result, the variance in the quality of the international students may be too great to ensure academic consistency at entry level. Wrong decisions on such matters may end up being very detrimental to the institution's reputation. European Business Schools are clearly working on this.

International visibility is then, increasingly, a necessity if the business schools are to be successful in attracting the best of both international students and professors. The business schools' interest in attracting the international elite is fueled by the growing demand from companies for executives who are fluent in foreign languages, and who are prepared to work with multilingual and multicultural teams.

This evolution is contributing to the increasing influence of the international accreditation bodies, particularly the American AACSB (Association to Advance Collegiate Schools of Business, created in 1916), the British AMBA (Association of MBAs, founded in 1967), and the European Foundation for Management Development (offering EQUIS since 1997). These accreditation bodies receive a growing number of requests for audits. (Business schools pay for the process of accreditation). The institutions that are officially accredited are asked to accept common rules for research, and quality of teaching and administration. Notably, accreditation increases the pressure on faculty to publish in top international journals.

The international rankings provided by non European universities (e.g. the Shanghai ranking) or the press (e.g. the Financial Times and Wall Street Journal) are also significantly influencing the organization of the management education system in Europe. The first Financial Times's ranking of European business schools in 2006, for example, will most certainly have consequences for both the strategies of these institutions and the organization of an evolving European system of management education (Appendix 1.1).

The extensive influence of such external players, often American, on European management education is resulting in a situation where European stakeholders have lost control of some of the important rules of the game. Europe is thus not fully in a position to drive the direction and speed of evolution of its system of management education.

As the influence of these international organizations for quality assessment and accreditation increases, European universities tend to seek even more international accreditations. As a result, national accreditation bodies may lose their significance. This trend reinforces the threat of new entrants into the management education market, and that of imported education. National regulators are no longer in a position to stop the development of international private education. In a liberal economy, privately owned international business schools do not seek, and probably do not need, to be integrated in the existing national educational framework (EC reports). For example, a private American graduate institution has established the International School of Management (ISM) in Paris, offering MBA, IeMBA, DBA, and PhD programs in partnership with three other campuses (St. John's University in New York, Temple University Japan in Tokyo, the School of Management at Fudan University in Shanghai), without seeking any French accreditation.

Weaker links with business is another distinctive feature of many universities in Europe, compared to the United States. Historically, education in Europe was the domain of the government and/or the religious authorities. Universities were created before the industrial age and, unlike the American universities, were not designed to train students to grapple with the real economic and practical challenges faced by companies. As a result, firms are less involved in management education in Europe than in the US. This is why private or semi-private business schools were created in European countries of the Latin cluster, outside traditional universities. Thus this does not mean that European Firms are not monitoring or supporting business schools' activities at all, especially the first league institutions. It simply means that there is still a wider gap in the EU compared to the US between Industry and the academic world of management.

The premise of a European model

Three elements are laying the potential foundations of a European management education system: the growing links between European institutions, the development of European academic associations and the European Commission priority to promote a knowledge economy.

Management education institutions are developing strategies to connect with each other, and to create a European area for management education. Business schools are developing strategic partnerships with their European counterparts to develop programs that permit students to study in various member states. For example, Aston Business School (UK) EM Lyon (France) and Ludwig Maximilian Universität (Germany) established a "European Master in Management" in 2002. The program is dedicated to applicants with a Bachelor's degree from all over the world. It is a general management course, offering a specialization in the second year. In the first year, students are all on the same campus (EM Lyon) where they take core management courses: they are supervised by a team of three professors representing each institution, and the teaching takes into account the perspectives of the three countries involved. Students then specialize during the second year: marketing with Aston Business School; organisation, change and strategy with Ludwig Maximilian Universität, or corporate finance with EM Lyon. Students receive a triple degree (Aston+EM Lyon+LMU). These "International Master's" programs are taught in English. The tuition fees of this program are €10,000 for European students, and €15,000 for non-Europeans.

Some other business schools and universities are experimenting with broader multi-lateralist strategies. For example, the Community of European Management Schools (CEMS) was founded in 1988. CEMS is an alliance that incorporates 4 non-European academic institutions along with 17 European business schools and universities, each country being represented by a single institution. CEMS collaborates with 50 multinational firms, and one of its leading programs, the Pan-European Master's in International Management (MIM), has now 3,700 alumni worldwide.

In many countries (e.g. the Netherlands, Sweden, Germany), universities are setting up a new generation of internationally oriented, primarily postgraduate, programs that are taught in English. These are either specifically for foreign students or for a mixed group of local and international participants. These programs illustrate a growing awareness of the need for Europe to offer unique programs globally, drawing from joint curricula from participating institutions based in various countries. Some countries are establishing support centers to promote such programs in target countries (e.g. Netherlands, Germany; the UK has already established such centers around the world).

Finally, the old line of division between public and private academic institutions is blurring in Europe as these institutions are basically following the same strategies (e.g., Italy, Germany, France). First, they have moved from their traditional national diplomas to the Bachelor's and Master's structure, as required by the Bologna process. The private system increasingly awards degrees that qualify as PhD, or at least claims the right to do so. At the same time, the growing need for new sources of revenue is encouraging public universities to develop MBA and executive education programs. Second, both public and private institutions try to attract research professors who can compete internationally. These talents are rare and increasingly expensive. Furthermore, the institutions aim at attracting the best students and executives. Hence the quality of campus infrastructure and education facilities becomes of the utmost importance. As a result, all institutions – public and private – search for more money. Typically, they try to develop new sources of income by creating foundations and professorships financed by alumni and firms. This situation has also led to a general trend towards rising tuition fees, even in the public system. In all European countries (see part II), there are ongoing discussions about the raising of fees and/or the option for universities to set up their own fee levels.

Academic Societies and Associations created at the European level are playing a major role in the development of a European area for management studies. The European Institute for Advanced Studies in Management (EIASM) broke new ground in this domain. Founded in 1971 with five years of private funding from the Ford Foundation, the institute has striven to create an identity for European management research in its relations with both the other well-established scientific disciplines and the business world (http://www.eiasm.org/index1.html). Its mission is to contribute "to the awareness that rather than having to depend solely on American models of management development, higher educational institutions in Europe can now refer to their own bodies of knowledge." One may ask the question whether this is happening or not; yet the mission statement is very clear. In the 1970s, this was done with an in-residence faculty. In the mid-1980s, this gave way to a looser structure and a wider network of affiliated faculty members. Nowadays, EIASM can best be described as "the node of a set of networks bringing together management scholars from throughout Europe – as well as between Europe and other parts of the World. EIASM claims a worldwide network with 40,000 researchers involved in management research or teaching" (http://www.eiasm.org/index1.html). Notably, its actions have contributed to the development of several dynamic groups of management scientists in Europe: the European Academy of Management (EURAM), the European Accounting Association (EAA), the European Association for Research in Industrial Economics (EARIE), the European Finance Association (EFA), the European International Business Academy (EIBA), the European Marketing Academy (EMAC), and the European Operations Management Association (EurOMA).

Furthermore, through these scientific associations, EIASM supports the development of European reviews such as European Management Review or International Journal of Research in Marketing. EIASM also sponsors education and development of European management scholars through the EDEN program, launched in June 1988. The network also organizes doctoral tutorials: from its inception through to December 2005, it brought together 2,010 PhD students and 238 professors.

Other academic societies, like the European Group for Organizational Studies (EGOS), also play a significant role. Although they do not explicitly aim to promote a European identity within management studies and research, they contribute to developing specific standards for research. For example, Organization Studies is a scientific journal created by EGOS that sustains research-action and qualitative methodologies, a far cry from the standards of deductive and quantitative research that prevail in many of the mainstream leading US academic journals.

Similarly, the European Foundation for Management Development ("EFMD"), which was created more than 30 years ago, has established the European Quality Improvement Systems (EQUIS). This is a system of assessment and accreditation for higher education institutions in management and business administration. So far, 97 schools have been accredited from 29 different countries (*http://www.efmd.org*). EQUIS pays special attention, for example, to criteria covering the quality of the training provided at the business school.

As European management education is primarily public, delivered through state-owned universities (even the French business schools are partly owned by the Chambers of Commerce and Industries which are public bodies), the creation of a European area for management education will need a strong *political will*. Currently, reforms (Spain, Italy, Germany, UK) are undertaken to deal with some of the major issues discussed in the first section of this chapter: for example, the decline in public subsidies for public universities and increased fees (Portugal, Italy, Germany, UK); the development of assessment agencies to evaluate and determine career paths for professors (UK); the development of administrative autonomy for universities (Portugal, Italy); universities' freedom to manage academic, administrative, and financial affairs, as well as the creation of agencies to fund research (France).

The European Commission is a major player in this game. The Bologna process was a first step – useful but not sufficient. Based on EC recommendations, a number of initiatives have been launched: for example, the Tune project is a collective action financed by the EC to define common curricula in business studies across the EU; or the

European Association for Quality Assurance in Higher Education (ENQA), was founded in 2000 to disseminate information, experiences and good practices in the field of quality assurance (QA) in higher education. The targets of ENQA are European QA agencies, public authorities and higher education institutions. However, several key issues remain on the agenda of the EU Commission: the creation of a European job market for academics (a "Bologna for Faculty"), a clarification around the PhD and the access to faculty positions, the sensitive issue of student selection at university entrance and obviously the issue of resources to make it possible for European business schools to compete internationally.

Conclusion

Europe has a strong academic base. Yet, in the field of management, Europe is clearly running behind North America. In fact, several systems of management education and research co-exist in Europe. Some form of convergence may be taking place due to a combination of factors: the Bologna process, the expectations from other countries looking for a second source of management knowledge apart from the US, the competitive pressures from leading US BSchools, the slow emergence of a thin layer of a European job market for faculty, a permanent hunt for more funding, etc.

The EU may be in the process of building a European system of management education and research but this is a rather slow and bumpy process. In any case, the role played by the European Commission will be pivotal to any future development in the teaching and research of management studies within Europe.

Along the way, as we have been discussing the current situation of business schools in Europe, we in fact reviewed most of the key players active in management education and research. Broadly speaking, we identify ten actors or families of actors who play a significant role in a typical system of management education: business schools, universities, faculty, students, alumni, business executives, firms, new entrants, state authorities (including the EU Commission in the case of Europe) and quality assessment bodies. Although these families of players may not be fully homogenous (e.g. large multinationals corporations may not have the same objectives and needs as SMEs when it comes to management education), we will use these to build the analysis leading to our foresight scenarios.

We now turn to the challenges faced by the 10 families of players within the system of business schools.

Appendix 1.1   The 2006 Financial Times ranking of the 25 best European business schools

Business school	Country	Rank 2006	Full time global MBA 2006	Executive MBA 2006	European Masters in Mangmt. 2006 +	Open progs. – Exec. Education 2006	Custom progs. – Exec. Education 2006
HEC Paris	France	1	7	2	1	7	2
London Business School	U.K.	2	1	1	–	5	3
IMD	Switzerland	3	5	6	–	4	1
Instituto de Empresa	Spain	4	3	3	–	2	17
Iese Business School	Spain	5	4	7	–	1	5
ESCP-EAP	France/U.K./ Germany/Spain/ Italy	6	26	12	3	15	17
RSM Erasmus University	Netherlands	7	9	9	13	–	9
University of Bradford/ TiasNimbas	U.K./ Netherlands/ Germany	8	19	14	20	–	#
Cranfield School of Management	U.K.	8	14	15	–	6	3
Insead	France/Singapore	10	2	–	–	2	6
Esade Business School	Spain	11	10	–	11	10	12
Stockholm School of Economics	Sweden/Russia/ Latvia	12	–	13	8	16	11
EM Lyon	France	13	–	24	5	18	14

Continued

Appendix 1.1   Continued

Business school	Country	Rank 2006	Full time global MBA 2006	Executive MBA 2006	European Masters in Mangmt. 2006 +	Open progs. – Exec. Education 2006	Custom progs. – Exec. Education 2006
Vlerick Leuven Gent	Belgium	14	–	20	12	9	16
Essec Business School	France/Singapore	14	–	10	6	11	10
Ashridge	U.K.	16	18	19	-	13	7
Warwick Business School	U.K.	17	17	4	-	–	20
University of Durham Business School	U.K.	18	25	24	19	–	–
City University: Cass	U.K.	19	15	5	-	–	–
University College Dublin: Smurfit	Ireland	20	24	17	30	–	–
Imperial College London: Tanaka	U.K.	21	15	7	-	–	–
Lancaster University Management School	U.K.	22	11	–	26	–	21
London School of Economics and Political Science	U.K.	23	–	2	8	–	–
University of Oxford: Saïd	U.K.	24	6	–	–	–	8
Helsinki School of Economics	Finland	24	30*	26	24	18	–
Edhec Business School	France	24	28*	–	7	–	19

Source Financial Times: http://rankings.ft.com/rankings/ebsw

Appendix 1.2 Additional data on management education in EU member states

	France	Italy	Portugal	Spain	Germany	Netherlands	Sweden	UK
Number of students in BSchools	16% of all higher education students		8% of undergraduate students	261 633 (2003)	162 608 (2004)		10% of the graduate students	14% of all higher education students; 22% of all postgraduates
Agency of Evaluation of a BS; Funding of research	Commission nationale des universités (peer evaluation) Commission Helfer (Master accreditation) ANR (research) funds selected research projects		CNAVES (National Evaluation Council) in 1998, but no link with the funding	CNEAI (1989) research evaluation of tenured professors every six years ANECA (2002) certify the quality of graduate and undergraduate programs ANEP (1986) evaluation of research grant		Public accreditation system (education) NVAO (Dutch-Flemish Accreditation Organisation) accredits higher education programs on the basis of external evaluation Bsik (research) funds thematic researches a necessary condition is that private sector also funds at least 33 percent of the cost.	National Agency for Education	RAE (research) peer-based assessment, QAA (teaching)

Continued

Appendix 1.2 Continued

	France	Italy	Portugal	Spain	Germany	Netherlands	Sweden	UK
Selection in higher education based on record or test	University: At the master's level, between the first and the second year at the university			Yes			At the Master's level, with certain restrictions	Yes
Date of the first creation of a Business School	1819: ESCP 1881: HEC 1907: ESSEC (Institut Catholique de Paris)		1759	1897	1898	Business Economics programs originated from the 1930s	1909 (SSE)	1960's

44

2
Nine Challenges for Business Schools

We have described the main characteristics of the system of higher education in management across Europe. We identified ten families of players typically constituting such a system.

We now identify nine issues or challenges for the system from within. For the sake of clarity, we present these challenges in three blocks, relating to "what" (contents), "who" (parties), and "how" (teaching and research methods in management).

Exogenous forces, affecting the system from the outside, will be addressed in Chapter 3.

Again, note that Europe serves here as a case study. We believe that most of the challenges identified below for the case of Europe may in fact apply or be adapted to other regions of the world.

What: management knowledge produced and taught at business schools

The current BSchool system is challenged by a first set of fundamental questions: to what extent is the knowledge produced by management research solid, general and relevant? And to what extent is the knowledge taught in business schools useful, applicable and relevant? In other words, are business schools producing and teaching well-established knowledge which fits managerial needs in a variety of contexts and situations? To what extent is management knowledge context-specific? This actually leads to an even more important underlying question: what will be the core pieces of knowledge, skills and capabilities to be taught in business schools by 2020 and beyond?

Management: best practices and/or scientific knowledge?

> **Is management a science?** Or is it more of a set of documented best-practices? Can theories be built about business? Can a scientific approach to business studies bring more insight into, and enrich, practice?

Although the question of the scientific legitimacy of management research may be of little concern for companies, students and executives in continuous education, it may be very much a concern for those involved in management research. The issue relates to the nature of the knowledge produced about management, whether it is **"scientific,"** or **"reasoned practices."** Although there is no clear-cut answer to this question of the scientific status of management, we feel that the matter seems to be less sensitive in North America. The current status on this in America may be assessed as follows: management would be considered more or less as a science for a large part of the academic community in business schools; it would be more of a set of reasonably well-documented practices for managers and practitioners in firms. We believe that the question is far from being settled in Europe – and possibly elsewhere. We argue that one possible explanation for this could be the influence of the more established social sciences such as sociology or psychology, and even more so economics, as all of these may not fully recognize business studies as a scientific domain of its own. These "disciplines" would see management as just another field where to conduct their own empirical research to feed into their own theorizing. They would look upon the sort of *"bricolage"* conducted by self-proclaimed management scholars, sometimes even denying any real scientific merit to management research. One may even argue that the "overly quantified, positivist" bias of the current mainstream management research may be essentially an attempt to respond to these critics.

The question of the "scientificity" of management would thus relate to its autonomy, i.e. its capacity to generate its own body of theories from the observation and analysis of what is going on within and around companies and organizations. As a matter of fact, a significant part of the so-called management theories are essentially imports from other fields (economics, sociology, psychology, etc.).

This situation may evolve in time as we should keep in mind the three following aspects:

Management is still a young field, which probably needs more time to establish itself in the way economics or sociology did. One should probably expect that many more years – in fact decades – are needed before the field may be considered as fully established.

As discussed already, the field has so far drawn to a large extent on knowledge from other disciplines: sociology, psychology, economy, history, etc. It is very likely that management will keep calling upon these disciplines in the future. Needless to say, these conceptual imports are both useful and healthy. Yet, the real sign of management gaining a scientific status will be when management theories start being called upon by other disciplines. This is yet to be seen but management research is working hard in this direction.

As a social science (or a social-science-to-be), business studies face the unavoidable ontological and epistemological difficulty of dealing with human activities in organizations, while aiming at building "valid" (or at least useful) theories with some claims for a degree of generality. Management is thus under the dual scrutiny of, on the one hand, the positivists adopting the hard line of hard science, including most of the close colleagues from Economics, and, on the other hand, the constructivists in social sciences and humanities. This is a rather difficult posture. There is no reason why this should not remain so in the coming years. However, this dialectic tension may turn out to be productive. This is a key point we want to make in this book.

Given the richness of the European tradition in humanities and social sciences – a real asset in fact, if not one of the best cards in the hand of European management research – we expect the dual question of the scientificity and autonomy of the field of management to take some time before it is settled in Europe. It is not clear whether this matter will be resolved or not in Europe by 2020. However, it might be that Europe will successfully leverage its strong tradition in humanities to contribute to management research in a substantially differentiated way. Indeed, beyond using Europe as a case study, we argue that something may be happening in Europe regarding management education and research. We develop this point at length in Chapters 5 and 6.

One of the main tasks of business schools is to train managers: do business schools really have the capacities to educate the managers of tomorrow?

Is it realistic to enrol young undergraduate students in business studies? Is it a relevant way to help them structure their thinking and build analytical skills? Should we prefer to educate first in more fundamental disciplines and then train in management? Is the functional split of business schools in departmental silos relevant or should the training in management be more transverse, across sub-domains?

Mathematics, hard sciences, law, economics or philosophy are known to contribute to pave the way for further studies. But is it the case for Business Studies as well? Some serious doubts are already expressed in various countries. Is this mostly due to the lack of scientific legitimacy of the field, as previously discussed, with a possible hope that this status will evolve, or is it a specificity of an applied field, bound to remain applied, to be unfit or at least not fully fit for structured (and structuring) undergraduate studies?

In addition, the usual functional split of business schools in departmental silos (HR, marketing, finance, strategy, etc.) is questionable as most managerial issues are in fact more transverse (seen from a practical viewpoint). The extensive use of case studies in teaching does not properly solve the matter, although it contributes to present managerial issues in trans-functional contexts. At the same time, the attempts to generate some theories in management require some form of segmentation, which so far has been primarily functional. Yet, more thematic views (law, psychology, organizational behavior, etc.) are also considered.

As far as the production of management research is concerned, business schools face some degree of perplexity coming from the practitioners' side. If optimization methods in logistics or new simulation techniques in finance or sophisticated analytical tools in psychology applied to marketing may raise significant interest in companies, a large part of management research appears abstract, theoretical, inapplicable, not understandable, if not uninteresting by most managers. This relates to the nature of the dominant model of management research, what we call the Mainstream, where relevance of the themes and results tends to be traded away for rigor in the process of conducting the research. In other words the knowledge produced and thus taught in

Business Schools may be statistically validated but runs the risk of being of limited relevance for practitioners. This sounds disturbing. This is also a paradox as participants in Executive Education demand professors who conduct research but have no real idea of what the norms in management research in fact are. Should they really know, they would most probably reformulate their demands. This may also be why academic gurus most often built their reputation on books, not on academic papers in A journals.

Towards the emergence of a European form of management, with a European system of management education?

> **Is there, will there be such a thing as a European way to manage?**
> Is European diversity, within and beyond the European Union, a source of specificity which will drive the contents of curricula in European Business Schools? Is this desirable?

Should one try to claim that a European form of management exists, relative to the North American dominant way to run business, one would argue that this European management is more transverse, somehow more integrated and systemic. Also, one would argue that it pays more attention to intercultural issues, ethical concerns, sustainable development and corporate social responsibility, etc. This does not mean that North America ignores such matters. It simply means that Europe seems even keener to deal with these issues.

In addition, cross-cultural issues in managing across borders turns out to be a challenge which European companies face very early on. The cultural diversity within the EU remains high, not to speak of the issue of languages, thus imposing some form of managerial adaptation to companies which aim at developing across the EU. This is much less so for their North American counterparts operating in a more homogeneous legal, regulatory and cultural context.

Whether Europe has or has not something different to offer in management is far from being a minor point. Indeed several emerging countries, e.g. those symbolized by the BRICS (Brazil, Russia, China, India, and South Africa), are looking for alternatives to the dominant managerial model coming from the US. A European specificity in management may thus turn out to be a way to gain market share for European Business Schools in the worldwide competition in higher education in management.

The emergence of some form of harmonization in European university education, with common levels of degrees and diploma, and a shared system of credits to encourage student mobility throughout the EU proved to be a strong driver for change and triggered a move towards the re-establishment of Europe as a place where to study, in a specific organizational and multi-cultural context. In management education, a discipline traditionally dominated by North American business schools, this leads to raising the question of the existence of a body of knowledge and practices which would be Europe-specific. In turn, this opens a debate about the relevance of and interest in offering such contents for teaching in European business schools.

Some of the players in the system may tend to oppose this view: most of North American leading business schools, US-based (or US-influenced) accreditation bodies, US-based (or US-influenced) academic journals, or even some of the students and participants in executive education programs who view America as the Mecca of Business would probably prefer to advocate that Europe bridge the gap in management by keeping on imitating the American way. They would claim that geography should have no impact on management studies.

However, other players may call for a different posture in both management teaching and research, advocating a more differentiated approach, more fitted for the evolution and specificities of the EU as a cultural entity, with specific issues and specific ways of handling problems within and around organizations.

In turn, this raises the question of the ability of business schools and universities to grasp and capture the specificities of the socio-economic model of the EU, to conceptualize the corresponding managerial model, if it exists, and to train students for it.

Who: players from within the educational system

All of those players who are involved in providing higher education in management are in a search for new resources. This search tends to both revive and blur the traditional distinctions made between public and private spheres of education. As an illustration, some professors in publicly funded business schools already use their bargaining power to enter directly into the market when their institution does not sufficiently support them in their projects. From this point of view, the system is confronted with at least three challenges:

the strengthening of the market logic,
the question of the autonomy of universities and business schools,

the branding issue, i.e. who owns and symbolizes the most important brand: the university, the business school, the department, the research team, the professor-guru?

Towards more market in academia (in business studies)? Towards an increasingly commercial approach?

Is the public logic, prevailing in most European academic institutions, likely to gradually disappear into a market logic? Is the commercial reasoning compatible with the culture of European higher education? Are market forces likely to weaken the position of universities and other established educational institutions in management?

The problem of limited access to human and financial resources is crucial for Business Schools. This goes much farther than the traditional lack of resources in universities.

There are strong inflationary pressures in management to recruit the best teachers as a way to reach international standards.

We already witness in Europe the emergence of an international job market for university professors in management. This is fuelled by the launch of international programs at schools where the in-house faculty is not necessarily fit for such courses. This is also fuelled by the recruitment policy of first league business schools which deliberately ignore the national bureaucratic constraints to fish for talents outside the usual national pool, etc.

Some of the Corporate Universities openly search for the best professors and their team. They try to contract directly with them to cover their specific in-house needs, without having to pay the university and Business School overheads. This is a form of cherry-picking which the universities tend to fight by requesting their faculty to ask for permission before accepting any outside teaching engagement. Some academics sometimes negotiate some degree of freedom, choose to work part time, go on leave of absence or even resign from their university in order to respond to such market attraction.

This creates tensions as professors tend to build market value by combining academic publications with more visible and readable outputs such as books and conferences, targeted at audiences of practitioners. Business schools expect the academic publications to reinforce their academic reputation, but at the same time need good performers in the MBA and Executive Education programs. Those professors who are capable of doing both are then pressured by external offers, and tend to negotiate with their dean for a better package (lighter teaching load, more research money, less administrative responsibilities, etc.). At the end of the day, this is costly for business schools.

In addition, as a way to promote their image, some business schools run communication campaigns. As the cost of advertising is high, with uncertain return, this requires even more financial resources.

In a market where so many public and private players put out such a large diversity of offerings to compete for revenues, it is logical that students, especially in MBA programs, and executives in exec education tend to become more demanding. Although Europe has a tradition of free education (or at least with extremely low fees, even at university level), there is a clear tendency for students, and obviously even more so for executives, to behave as customers demanding a quality service, evaluating programs, professors and sessions, making sure that they receive the value they expect for the time and money they invest in.

The current system of financing for higher management education in Europe is clearly insufficient, when compared to North America. Interestingly enough, in a country known for its aversion to public subsidies and government intervention, the American tradition of donations by companies or by alumni to their universities, leads to significant endowments, especially in the most prestigious schools. This basically does not exist in Europe, known for a rather different social model, or when it does, it is not to the same extent.

All in all, demands from companies, expectations from participants increasingly behaving as customers, competitive pressures from new entrants are typical forces which call for evolutions in the system to compensate for insufficient resource allocation.

Should a more market oriented approach win in the future, it would severely affect the institutions (universities and business schools), the dominant logic of academia known to serve public interest, the way faculty and students operate and interact, etc.

Towards more institutional autonomy for universities and business schools?

Several European countries still have a university system centrally controlled by a national Ministry: is this sustainable in the years to come? **Will European universities and business schools eventually be in a position to take care of themselves, with an autonomous governance?**

European business schools have to cope with the regulatory context in which they operate. This is usually, although with some exceptions, the context of the national university system they belong to. They simultaneously try to control:

their sources of financing and in particular to freely diversify these sources
the selection and admission of students
the selection and promotion (including the compensation scheme) of their faculty
their strategy of external growth and partnership

As business schools contribute to fulfil a public need, namely higher education, they tend to be funded, at least in part, by governments. As a result they tend to be heavily controlled, if not managed by national bureaucracies. This has direct and concrete implications for business schools which have to follow the rules imposed on the university system. Typically three constraints are known to limit manoeuvrability:

rules to select students (e.g., admission of students on a geographical basis);
ceiling on the fees and tuitions allowed (as low as a few hundred euros) which illustrates the idea prevailing in many European countries that university education, at least for undergraduate levels, should be free;
national recruitment of faculty, or at least heavy central control on eligibility (despite EU regulations tearing down legal barriers to mobility, the process of recruitment in several countries *de facto* prevents most non nationals to run for the positions).
In addition, as universities are pressured by a variety of forces, they tend to look for resources where some slack is generated. In several

countries, it appears that business schools are being "taxed" to transfer part of their specific external incomes to contribute to funding the university as a whole. For business schools, this does not go in the direction of autonomy.

The result is a loss of strategic, if not operational, autonomy for the business schools and the deans. In the worldwide competition for reputation, attraction of the best students, attraction of the best professors and researchers, business schools in Europe are still struggling for more autonomy.

Interestingly enough, although numerically marginal in several countries, student unions have proved influential enough to scare politicians away from any attempt to give more autonomy to public universities. Student unions oppose any such reform as they fear it would lead to some form of ranking among universities, thus leading to second and third tier diploma. One may object that it is *de facto* already the case, as some universities and business schools are clearly more recognized than others. One may also object that explicit competition would stimulate the university system. Yet, many European politicians seem to be extremely cautious regarding universities. When they are part of the university system, European business schools are thus locked in that game.

All in all, public authorities are pulled between two arguments:

centralization allowing for more control and supposedly a better optimization of resources, at least in theory, with national validation of diplomas;

decentralization and autonomy, making it possible for local governance to be more efficient than a complex centralized system – but with the explicit or implicit recognition that not all universities are equal.

Towards internal battles around branding?

> Could it be that too many programs in the same business school dilute the overall brand name instead of reinforcing it? Could brands attached to specific degrees and programs gain autonomy and thus weaken the mother brand ? Could some individuals or teams build their own brand name, thus playing down the name of their home institution?

Many factors affect brand names: word of mouth, aggressive communication campaigns, visibility of publications, rankings, influence of alumni, etc. All these contribute to build, maintain and reinforce brand names over the years.

As an example, rankings distinguish business schools where quality teaching programs and research activities are sheltered. Some rankings lay stress on MBA programs, others on salaries of graduates, others on publications, while others adopt a broader perspective. Yet, the result is always to affect the reputation of the business schools and thus their brand name.

Who bears and owns the brand then becomes a key issue.

Some programs, departments, groups of professors or more often guru-professors tend to build their own name and thus, sometimes indirectly and unintentionally, their own brand. This is quite normal and natural as universities expect their faculty to build their scientific reputation. Yet, in business schools, an academic reputation soon becomes saleable on the market place as it may mean commercial value, either for executive training, seminar in executive committees or even consulting. Business schools – like medical schools – tend to permit a fast connection between theory and practice, knowledge production and knowledge use, at least for those with the capability of operating in both worlds.

The result is somewhat paradoxical: as business schools expect their faculty to build their reputation – through their publications, their teaching, their programs, etc-, the resulting "local" brand names built along the way tend to both complement and challenge the overall brand name of the mother institution.

One may view this as a positive self reinforcing mechanism. Others may sense a risk of tension and potential discord.

When the reputation of a faculty member transforms into a negotiation lever with the dean, then things may become difficult. A time may come when freedom is no longer granted but taken, when external activities are no longer complementary but conflicting, when the local brand name no longer supports but blurs the overall name of the school. At times, parallel affiliations and overlapping engagements may become too much. Some schools attempt to pre-empt such problems by limiting the outside engage-ments of their faculty but this is not easy nor totally desirable. Indeed, academia requires openness and cross fertilization. In addition, business schools can clearly benefit from having their faculty interact with a vari-ety of situations, including real life problems with practitioners. Such activities may actually be a healthy sign of relevance, adding legitimacy to the scientific recognition of the participating faculty.

In any case, it is often difficult to draw a clear line between a single consulting assignment, a piece of work with an executive committee in a company, a seminar in an organization and a full training program com-peting with the Executive Education Department at the business school.

Similarly, accepting a round of conferences to promote a new book may not be so different from a set of seminars, which may also be in fact close to contributing to a corporate university program.

As often happens, social pressure, good faith and informal control work better than bureaucratic rules. And this is enough to solve most difficulties.

Yet, there are cases when professors start hiring "franchised" teachers to disseminate their own material. Then, where is the limit? Where exactly does the stance of a trusted professor, loyal to his or her school, end? Where do we start to see an autonomous producer of knowledge selling via a variety of distribution channels beyond the mother institution?

Conversely, the blunt but explicit comment *"Oh, it's just a teaching place"* tells us a lot about how pure teaching schools may be looked upon as simple distribution channels of management knowledge produced elsewhere.

This leads us to the theme of e-learning. New technologies, offering remote teaching possibilities, combined with the issue of branding may lead to a potential unbundling of the value chain (or value network) in management education.

How: process and method of teaching management

The manner in which business schools will deliver their education can be another strain on the system. Information technologies permit training solutions which can for the most part be freed from the confines of the classroom through remote training. How will institutions utilise such new solutions in order to better serve their clientele?

The corresponding challenges deal with:

the relative attention paid to the various activities in the portfolio of business schools (undergrad, MBA, exec education, research) and the need to deliver quality teaching;
a potential reconfiguration of the value chain (or more appropriately the value network), and
life-long training needs for managers.

Back to teaching?

Periodically in recent years, concerns have been expressed about not enough **attention being paid to teaching** while too much emphasis was put on research. Could business schools strike a better balance? Is there a need to help young faculty first focus on **research and publications** while accompanying them progressively towards **excellence in the classroom**, including when facing seasoned executives?

Education and research are the two legs of a university. These two roles are complementary and permit synergies. Yet the two activities are not always easy to combine as they compete for the same resources.

The pressure for international rankings and the competition from their North American counterparts led most European business schools to stress research and publications as their top priorities. Yet, students and executives in the classroom are clients, demanding to be treated as such. Quality teaching requires time, attention and dedication. This cannot be done in passing, in between two research projects.

This structurally creates a tension on faculty members having to face two sets of time-consuming tasks. As a result, we already see the emergence of a fundamental split, with some faculty operating as "researcher professors" dedicated to their research and aiming at publishing in the best journals, while some other faculty operate primarily as "teaching professors" with the ability to capture the attention of a variety of audiences, combining theoretical inputs, concrete examples and practical implications in their teaching.

> *"Well, as I understand it, your faculty professors teach and conduct research. This is fine. But how do they touch base with reality? They probably do some consulting as well. Don't they?"* Source: interview (a practitioner).

Ideally, one could hope that most management faculty would be able to excel in both research and teaching. Some actually do. They are the pride of the profession. Yet, many others are keen (and/or better fit) to dedicate their talent primarily to one of the two sets of academic activities.

More generally, a business school dean faces several issues relating to the "back to teaching?" challenge:

What balance to strike between producing management knowledge and teaching? (How the portfolio of activities is balanced has direct implications on the financial resources accessible, the visibility and reputation of the school, the profile of new recruits, and the quality of the teaching).

What balance between the production of public goods and the sales of privatized offerings? The point here is not to oppose activities which are complementary, at least in part. The idea is to recognize that there are choices to be made in the allocation of resources, as academic activities compete for the time of the key resource of the business schools, namely their faculty.

In turn, this leads to a questioning around the dynamics over time of a balanced portfolio (research and teaching; undergraduate, MBA and executive education; money-contributing vs money-consuming activities; demand driven vs mainstream theory research projects; etc.). Such dynamic choices are obviously path dependent and clearly affect how the faculty is recruited, motivated, evaluated and compensated. These challenges are at the heart of the strategic dilemmas facing business schools.

Towards a reconfiguration of the value network?

> What impact on teaching methods should one expect from **ICT**? What combination of remote vs classroom teaching should we anticipate? How will management knowledge be made accessible in the future? What should we expect from e-learning? Should one anticipate a redistribution of the roles between knowledge producers, knowledge packagers in multimedia format, facilitators of the learning process using the packaged knowledge?

The burst of the internet bubble may have dissipated some of the early dreams about a radical transformation of university teaching due to **Information and Communication Technologies**. It remains that ICT keep challenging the traditional way of conveying knowledge through classroom teaching. This clearly applies to management education. Among other things, ICT may in fact stress the issue of decoupling the academic role of creating new knowledge from that of disseminating the knowledge.

> *"We are not far away from being in a position to teach without being physically with the students. We are actually getting very close to that point. This will be a dramatic change. Think of the number of business schools we have less than 200 miles around this university. I am not sure that we will need all them anymore. We might actually merge or reshuffle the roles."* Source: interview
>
> *"In executive education, I do not believe for a second that these "high flyers" will still be ready to pay what we charge them today for our seminars if all that we have to offer them is to face their computer screen. This cannot be serious."* Source: interview

In addition, management teaching seems to evolve increasingly towards some form of "individual learning experience." This appears in the form of projects in small groups, follow-up questions to the teacher after the class, during office hours or via the internet. This is even more so in Executive education where the teacher is no longer mainly a facilitator whose task is to animate a group of experienced managers, have them share their experience as they search for the hidden key in a complex case study, bring in some useful concepts and models, and finally help them access what may be seen as the golden clue. Instead, the teacher increasingly becomes a sort of personal coach, helping participants individually through a reflexive process to revisit their behaviour, cognitive representations, fears and beliefs, etc. As a result, a significant part of the role of the teacher is now performed outside the classroom. This evolution has tremendous implications for the profiles needed for this role and for the organization adjusting to this new learning scheme:

> *"Once we had set up the Internet platform where the participants to our Exec Program could interact with us and among themselves, we had to re-organize quite fundamentally the way we work."*
>
> *"In this emerging new setting, our faculty not only had to deal with all the preparation of the sessions (pre-readings, submitting questions to raise participants' interest and trigger their thinking, etc.) but teachers also had to embark on heavy follow-up after the sessions. As this turned out to be too much for them, we had to hire a new breed of "advanced teaching assistants", capable of doing most of this follow-up work. This is quite new for us."* Source: interviews

Some business schools hesitate to respond to the requirements of such an organization, as these are time-consuming and necessitate new profiles. However, one may observe that some of the new entrants in the market, e.g. consulting firms, carefully position themselves to fulfil that sort of need as a way of differentiating from the incumbents.

Another implication of ICTs is worth mentioning. It turns out that the packaging of knowledge in a multimedia format is a rather capital intensive process requiring more resources than most business schools have so far been used to invest. This is truly an additional aspect of the challenge represented by ICT and e-learning, especially when many schools struggle with financial constraints.

When and how to address managers' learning needs?

When should a student interested in management join a management program? Is a management curriculum relevant at undergraduate level? How many years of practice are relevant before enrolling in an MBA? Would it be feasible to review managers' knowledge and ability periodically as for a driving license? What format for life-long learning in management?

The role of continuous education throughout a professional career is both reinforcing and evolving. The pace of renewal, the need to adapt to a changing world, the continuous flow of new ideas and new practices in management make it difficult to stick with the usual split: learning in the early years of life, purely practicing afterwards. Some form of refreshing is needed along the way. This may be done through a variety of settings but the point remains that pure empirical learning through the "university of life" may be a limited answer to post graduation training needs in management.

> *"Maybe we should deliver **diploma with vanishing ink!**"* Source: interview
>
> *"I do not understand how we let some of these people be appointed top manager of a company, in charge of billions of dollars and thousands of jobs, with no clear **professional certification.** I think that managers should be certified like medical doctors or lawyers (with the bar exam). And I think this certificate should be re-validated periodically."* Source: interview

In a typical European way of addressing such issues, some of the European countries have passed bills to impose legal training obligations. Companies are asked to spend a certain amount of money every year on training their staff. And the result is known: most of the continued education money goes for rather young professionals of a higher level in the hierarchy of the organization. Among other things, this thus contributes to generating a market for continuous education in management.

Similarly, several countries are trying to imitate the German tradition of internships and apprenticeships, which is seen as one of the reasons behind a relatively better integration process of young workers on the German job market. As internships and apprenticeships tend to develop quite rapidly in Europe, the idea of combining phases of work and phases of study in time becomes more natural.

At the same time, while the cost of education in Europe is often paid by governments, a variety of programs at Master level is now being offered for a significant fee. This leads some of the students to enrol on a part time basis in order to be able to cover the cost of their study. This is somewhat new in most European countries. As a result again, it is becoming more natural to combine work and study either in parallel or in short sequences.

Along these lines, business schools are tempted to pursue this trend a bit further by trying to build loyalty, creating a long-lasting customer relation through the professional careers of the managers. This is not easy. The point remains, however, that answering the life-long learning needs stands as another challenge for business schools.

Table 2.1 below summarizes the nine main challenges which we identified for business schools in the years to come. These are internal to the dynamics of the "management education system."

Table 2.1   Main challenges for business schools

What: management knowledge produced and taught at business schools		
1		Management: best practices and/or scientific knowledge?
2		Do business schools really have the capacities to educate the managers of tomorrow?
3		Towards the emergence of a European form of management, with a European system of management education?
Who: players from within the research and educational system		
4		Towards more market in academia (for business studies)?
5		Towards more institutional autonomy for universities and BSchools
6		Towards internal battles around branding?
How: process and methods to management teaching		
7		Back to teaching? Towards more attention paid to teaching?
8		Towards a reconfiguration of the value network?
9		When and how to provide life long learning?

We now turn to review the context in which the "system" operates and thus the exogenous pressures exerted onto the system from the outside.

3
Exogenous Pressures Exerted on the System

We are discussing the future of the system of management education. The system includes a variety of players which were introduced in the descriptions of Chapter 1. In Chapter 2, we have subsequently discussed the challenges faced by business schools as they have a pivotal role among the players in the system. These challenges, listed in Table 2.1 above were mostly internal to the system.

We now turn to the effect of the external environment on the system. More specifically, we are going to discuss here the "exogenous" pressures exerted on management education. Indeed this system of management education does not operate in a vacuum. It interacts with the world economy and society at large. On the one hand, the system feeds these macro social and economic dynamics at work but more importantly, on the other hand, it is influenced by the context in which it operates. In other words, after having discussed the drivers inside the system, we need to identify the external forces affecting its evolution.

We identify seven such external trends or exogenous pressures which will contribute to shaping the scenarios for business schools 2020 (presented in Chapter 4).

The construction of the European Union is a major process affecting the future of Europe and its role in the world. Among other things, the emergence of the EU leads to a strong political thrust towards a common overall policy in favour of education and research. The Lisbon strategy is high on the agenda. Innovation became a priority. Europe is known to have excellent basic research, with a missing link when it comes to connecting this research potential to the world of application in Industry.

Education. The Bologna agreement signed in 1999 launched a concrete process to harmonize the university diplomas throughout the Union. Extending what was the Erasmus programme, this fostered the mobility of students and collaborations between universities. After a bumpy implementation, the process is advancing well and proves to be quite beneficial. Along the way, this led to reshuffling the programs of many universities in Europe, thus reopening margins of manoeuvre for change.

In turn this contributes to paving the way for the so-called European Research Area.

Research. The Lisbon agenda aims at reaching the target of 3% of GDP for R&D by 2010.[1] Research became a clear priority with the EU Research and Technological Development (RTD) framework programs. This funding is essential as the R&D expenditure gap widens with respect to Japan and the US (FT, Oct 30, 2006). The RTD framework programs also contribute to foster cooperation across the EU, especially between public research and private companies.

The EU may help transform our universities

«French universities do not have international visibility, except may be Sorbonne and Sciences po. This is a problem we share with most other European countries, with the exception of the UK. (...) I believe that the European Union can be of great help to reform our universities. Harmonizing the university degrees in Europe already contributed to generate change in the system. (...) The University-Industry relationships are not developed enough. We need centers of competence bringing together universities across Europe. (...) We also need to give more autonomy to the governance of universities. Finally, we need to improve the way we attract and take care of foreign students».

Interview Michel Herbillon, député, French parliament.
Les Echos, 15 novembre 2004, p. 4

Role of regions in Europe. Finally, the emergence of the European Union together with the role played by the EU Commission has the effect of strengthening the political power of regions within the members' States. The weight of regions in Europe may turn out to be extremely important in reshaping the university system in the EU in the years to come.

The liberal thrust clearly dominates the evolution of the world economies. This is a much debated topic that goes far beyond the future of management education, although it is a fact that business schools contribute to feed that trend.

There is obviously a variety of ways to accommodate the liberal ideology according to political and socio-historical contexts. In the European tradition where concerns for social protection and solidarity in society through public transfers remain high, policies tend to smooth the short-term effects of the primarily liberal thrust stemming from the ideology prevailing in the economic and political thinking behind the EU construction.

This means that the irruption of market dynamics in academia may face internal opposition in universities, but the overall climate may be leading to it, at least to a certain extent.

Aging is a third major trend affecting most European Countries as well as most other developed countries. Living longer should mean working longer, thus generating new needs for continued education beyond 50 and even beyond 60. This is a paradox, as we know that in several countries most funding for continuous education goes to the younger, most qualified staff (managers in this context).

In addition, many managers actually start a new professional life after retiring from their managerial positions. Some offer to share their experience through teaching; others register as consultants; others even consider writing a PhD thesis. This trend is far from being a marginal topic for business schools! Yet, there are not so many business schools having targeted this particular group at this stage.

The rise of the Brics (Brazil, Russia, India, China and South Africa), especially **China and India**, represents the fourth driver affecting the external environment of the system we study here.

The case of China is striking. China has had economic growth of around 10 percent per year for the last 15 years, with R&D expenditure ranking third behind the US and Japan. Between 1998 and 2001, the central government of China increased the budget for universities from 6,7 to 13,6b$. The number of students in Chinese universities will have doubled from 2000 to 2015, up to 40 million. For reasons having to do with family planning regulations in China, this increase will take place between 2004 and 2008, with growth rates of 30 percent annually. (This may explain why foreign universities have rushed to China in recent years). With the so-called project 211, started in 1995, the Chinese government aimed at boosting around 100 elite universities in the country.

India is in a similar dynamic. "Between 2000 and 2015, the student population in India will increase from 11 to 41 million." Although India has had a history of established management institutes (the six Indian Management Institutes, plus literally hundreds of MBAs), the growth potential for management studies is enormous.

The Chinese and Indian markets became major targets where considerable investments are being made by most multinational companies. Quite logically, several business schools have targeted China and India to recruit students, develop ad hoc programs, invest locally in partnership with Chinese or Indian universities, etc.

The rise of the Knowledge economy is another important trend affecting the world economy – and management education.

This is a much debated topic as some argue that human activities have always been based on some clever use of some form of knowledge. Yet, it is broadly recognized that the world economy is currently organized around a group of economic powers, namely the OECD countries, chief among which is the triad composed of North America, the EU and Japan, each building its competitive advantage on advanced technology, innovation, design and added value services. While many other countries are clearly in a race to catch up, these more advanced zones leverage knowledge derived from science as well as organizational and managerial capabilities to stay ahead in the global race. University education and research are at the heart of their strategy.

The fast growing followers place their bets on specific added value steps such as manufacturing for China, or software development for India. This is used as a way to learn, imitate and bridge the gap. These countries heavily invest in education, and send their best talents to study abroad, especially in engineering and management. The aim for them is to generate elites capable of managing the development of their economies. At the same time, these countries try to develop their own university systems. This creates both a clear opportunity and a challenge for western business schools.

A better governance is largely consolidating in most countries.

This affects the corporate governance, as scandals at the beginning of the 21st century raised much turmoil in various countries. Several topics are on the agenda: ethical concerns about top management behavior in large and not so large companies, sustainable development and the effect of human activities on global warming, the corporate social responsibility *vis a vis* the work force not only in the home country but in developing countries as well, etc.

This theme has been regularly addressed at the Davos World Economic Forum, with many sessions on the issue of corporate governance and corporate social responsibility, e.g. "Corporate Governance: from scandals to sustainability" or "How responsible is responsible enough?"

In this context The Sarbanes Oxley regulation in the US, often referred to as "Sox," actually affects multinational companies doing business in the US, especially those listed on the New York stock exchange.

Corporate Legitimacy discussed at the World Economic Forum in Davos
What is the role of corporations?
(...) The shareholder is one among other stakeholders. Rakesh Khurana from Harvard Business School makes the point: « *Companies do not just exist to return profit to the investor. They have to combine financial and social objectives*». Otherwise they may lose their legitimacy as Arthur Andersen, a well etablished firm from long ago, disappeared in a few weeks after the Enron scandal.

Source: Les Echos, Jan 28, 2005

The issue of better governance also affects emerging countries which are put under pressure to accept the rules of the game: a stable legal system, enforcement of intellectual property rights (patents, brands, etc.), fair treatment of non-national companies in public tenders, active anti-corruption policies, etc. As they try to join the world community of business, countries such as China, India, Russia or Brazil are clearly moving in that direction.

The dominance of English as the language of business worldwide is now well established. English became the *lingua franca* of modern management. It is very likely that this will last for a long time, far beyond the 2020 time horizon of our foresight exercise here.

This has tremendous implications for management education and business schools, even in countries with a strong identity and culture based on a different language. Among many others, Germany, Spain and Latin America, France, China, Russia, and even Japan face the same challenge. Some other countries like the UK, Canada, Ireland, Australia, and to some extent India have a de facto competitive advantage on this matter. Other countries like Scandinavia have already largely adopted English as almost a second language and are well prepared to face the challenge.

Most top-ranked journals are in English. Management researchers eager to publish must build a refined and subtle command of English and/or rely on English-speaking editing services to submit drafts of their papers. As an example, when most PhD theses are written in the mother tongue, this literally means drafting a text twice. This is time consuming, costly and not fully adequate, as part of the finesse of the initial thinking may be lost along the way. Classroom teaching may in part or in total be done in English, but again non native speakers tend to somehow degrade the quality of what is taught and thus learned.

These seven exogenous trends are pressures put on the system of management education. These do not originate from within the system itself, but we argue that they will undoubtedly contribute to shaping the social and economic context of the evolution of business schools in the future.

7 Exogenous Pressures on the System

- European Construction (Europe and Regions)
- The liberal thrust
- Aging
- The rising of the BRICS: Brazil, Russia, India, China and South Africa
- The Knowledge Economy
- Issues of Governance
- English as the language of business

In a way, the EU Lisbon strategy recapitulates these external forces. The Lisbon strategy bets on education and research as a way to construct a dynamic Knowledge Economy in a liberal EU with improved governance, open to international business with the rest of the world.

Again, most of these external forces identified for the case of Europe, may apply (or may be adapted) to the situation of other Regions of the world.

So far we have identified and discussed 10 families of players participating in the system of management education. We have identified 9 challenges facing the players in the system, especially the business schools. These challenges are issues internal to the system. Obviously, as in any system, families of players can group in coalitions to face some of the challenges while opposing on others. We have then just identified and discussed seven major exogenous pressures exerted on the management education system by external forces or trends in the world economy and society.

These are the ingredients to our Foresight cooking. On that basis we built five scenarios in an attempt to grasp the potential futures of business schools around 2020.

The five scenarios are presented in the next chapter.

4
Five Foresight Scenarios for Business Schools 2020

Figure 4.1 represents schematically what we have described so far of the management education system. The system (shown as the dotted ellipse) is composed of 10 families of players (shown as the bubbles on the diagram), each with its own margins of manoeuvre and strategic intents (shown as arrows from one bubble towards the others); 9 challenges "drive" the system from within (the dotted arrows) while 7 exogenous forces affect the social and economic environment of management education (the external arrows).

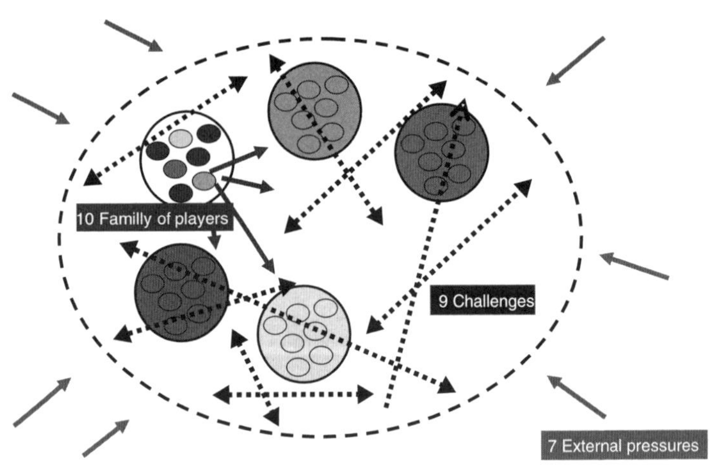

Figure 4.1 The system: players, challenges, pressures

All of the above is mostly descriptive (chapter 1 – see also detailed presentations in part II) and analytical (Chapters 2–3). We now want to get a picture of how the system could evolve in the future. We suggest that a set of scenarios may provide such a Foresight picture.

The five scenarios which we built to attempt to grasp the "futurible" of management education are:

1. Drifting away
2. European Management stands up
3. Unbundling: Business Schools as vendors (distribution channels)
4. M&A's
5. Reactive adaptation

Each scenario is described using a set of **key variables** which appeared in the previous analysis of the system. The key variables used are: the sources and structures of funding, career attractiveness for faculty, networks of alliances or mergers, institutional or market dominance, new entrants, management as a science?, role of e-learning.

About Foresight Scenarios

We follow Pierre Wack who argued that "when carefully looking at the data, for long enough periods of time, new visions may emerge." Pierre Wack was head of strategic planning at Shell. These "new visions" are no longer simple descriptions of the system as it is with its current trends. Instead, these "visions" or scenarios are intentionally integrated, articulated stories which recombine previously available pieces of knowledge in a way which gives more meaning. These scenarios are stories that add value for the strategist. Scenarios may be viewed as strategic representations, "re-presenting" the knowledge, i.e. presenting it differently, thus helping the strategist at work.

In this sense, Foresight is a way of integrating available pieces of knowledge about a complex system into useful representations about potential futures. Scenarios are coherent, self-sustained and meaningful stories describing possible future states of the system. Scenarios are strategic representations built from accessible knowledge, through a Foresight exercise which this book discusses. As strategic representations, the scenarios mediate the complexity of the knowledge base, the uncertainty of future outcomes and the work of the strategist.

The aim of the scenarios is to provide an insight into the variety of possible futures (the "futurible"). The objective is not to forecast what the most probable future will be. Instead, the overall objective is to shed light on a plurality of visions, from the most to the least desirable and from the least probable to the most probable, as a way to revisit the strategic issues of today.

Scenarios are useful constructs as they help stimulate creative responses from players participating in the system.

Each scenario is also illustrated using a current **example** which forebodes what the system would look like, should that scenario unfold.

A synoptic view of the scenarios is then presented first as Table 4.1 and then as a mapping on Figure 4.2.

Scenario I: "Drifting away"

In this scenario, North American dominance in management and management education remains unchallenged. Funding in most European universities remains low, including for business schools. Career attractiveness for faculty is thus low as well. Demographics make it even worse as faculty positions opening (due to "baby boomer" retiring professors and increasing student enrolment) are difficult to fill with enough talents from the younger generation. The quality of teaching suffers; PhD programs have to search for students essentially from developing countries and leading schools have to recruit their new faculty from outside Europe.

The gap between a handful of leading European business schools competing in the international arena and the rest of the schools widens. Players in the European "first league" manage to secure some additional funding and increasingly move towards a market dominant approach while the others are stuck in a predominantly institutional public stance. There are a few exceptions in the public context, serving as examples to justify the status quo under the misleading pretext that "it is quite possible to launch innovative strategic projects even with a centralized public governance and national Ministries of Education." Funding remains stable, mostly public, with some limited additional contributions from continued education and master programs.

Ad hoc networks of alliances appear in some instances but these are exceptions. Some of the leading European business schools develop and intensify specific collaborations internationally and forge ahead into some form of closed club integration.

In this context, the research output from academia diverges even more from managerial needs and expectations. The world of practice is intrigued but skeptical in the face of the academic production of knowledge. E-learning develops slowly as an add-on to classroom teaching. Videos and multimedia case studies complement the usual textbooks and standard cases. Yet, the value chain of management education is not affected much.

As most European business schools and universities are not in a position to occupy the market field, corporate universities and consulting firms address market needs quite successfully. The best MBA candidates and top executives continue to cross the Atlantic Ocean to access the sources of management in the American Mecca of business, ready to pay the corresponding fees.

The driver (or rather the brake) of this scenario is the lack of financial resources and the corollary limitations on human resources available, thus affecting the capacity of European universities and business schools to adapt and compete properly. This greyish "drifting away" scenario may be exemplified by the Shanghai ranking or the financial difficulties encountered by some visible European universities (e.g. in Berlin) and their incapacity to help their young faculty conduct research (e.g. by limiting the high teaching load imposed by too high a ratio of students per faculty).

Scenario II: "European management stands up"

In this scenario, Europe is on the move. EU member countries choose to invest heavily in higher education as a way to compete more successfully in the world economy. European management claims some form of specificity, thus feeding into business schools' curricula. Governments across the EU as well as the European Commission allocate additional resources for university research and education, especially in management. Firms agree to follow the same path and invest in Foundations created by universities.

The institutional public thinking remains strong but some autonomy is given to universities. This directly affects business schools. As a result, business schools can select their students, and charge significantly higher tuitions and fees – while offering scholarships both for those who cannot afford to pay and for the best students whom they want to attract. In addition, business schools are free to hire the faculty they want at market conditions.

In this context, academic careers become attractive. Young European talents enrol in PhD programs. This leads to revitalizing the profession, while the job market for management faculty becomes increasingly European with a flow across the Atlantic Ocean. Most business schools recruit their faculty as well as their students throughout Europe and beyond. Cooperation and alliances spread among business schools across Europe as a way to gain visibility and critical mass.

In this scenario, American business schools have difficulty in entering Europe, corporate universities are careful not to appear as direct competitors of universities which they respect and support, as they need their expertise. Significant investments are made in e-learning, without too greatly affecting the structure of the value chain or value network.

A European specificity of management research steadily emerges, gaining international recognition. A special strength in clinical studies is being developed in Europe. This research calls upon humanities and social sciences. At the same time, however, some other researchers conduct quantitative studies as a way to publish in the leading best ranked quantitative American journals. Among these European academics that chose to compete in the US led arena, some are quite successful, thus showing that European management research can do it. Altogether, the gap is being bridged, at least in part. On the one hand, some European researchers play it "mainstream" successfully. On the other hand, European research builds its own specificity through clinical studies which, among other things, contributes to reconciling management research and practitioners.

The prime driver of this scenario is the awareness among European politicians and Industry of the importance of management education. Another element is the wider recognition of the relevance of clinical research, leveraging humanities and social sciences, both on the academic front and on the practitioners' side. As a result, firms tend to invest more heavily in European business schools through "foundations."

The significant improvements of European business schools in rankings over the years is an indication of what European management could do if it decided to stand up and play it their way.

The ability of European MBAs to deal with business across a variety of cultural contexts adds significant value, William Parrot, AACSB.

Source: FT

Scenario III: "Unbundling: business schools as vendors"

In this scenario, the development of e-learning triggers a significant transformation of the value network in management education. ICTs now make it possible to distribute the same teaching content simultaneously in a variety of locations without losing the strength of the messages. This in turn affects the way courses are taught, the nature of business faculty work and the structure of higher education in management.

In this context, some academics decide to surf the wave of e-learning by focusing on becoming "**knowledge producers**." They design highly visible teaching contents which they market via a variety of institutions which operate as franchisees or vendors. When needed, these "knowledge producers" accept to appear in some of the premium programs via visio-conferencing, thus minimizing travel time and costs. They invest the time they saved into publications, partly academic to build legitimacy, and partly applied to target executives and managers. They thus build up their positioning as gurus and, as such, generate significant additional income along the way. As some other academics try to imitate the successful gurus, they find out that this is a complex game where only the best talents succeed. Market logic clearly prevails.

A second group of faculty chooses to focus on classroom teaching and coaching in executive education. They operate as distributors of knowledge which they did not really help to create. Consultants enter this activity as well. This leads to significant career segmentation.

This also leads to some form of unbundling. As guru professors emerge, they establish their own brand name if not their own "knowledge producing factory," in the same way as TV show producers did. They sell their specialized contents to business schools and corporate universities which, in this scenario, become predominantly distribution channels. If their home university attempts to limit this sort of *de facto* positioning, they threaten to move to another place, and some go as far as leaving the *alma mater* and start operating on a fully independent private basis.

While the classroom teachers tend to stay in the business schools and develop strong ties to their institution, other faculty members choose to mimic the gurus and try to develop and package their own concepts. They offer their packages to vendors (other business schools, corporate universities, companies via in-house training or quasi-consulting assignments, etc.), hoping to gain autonomy and/or generate revenues with minimal time spent in the classroom.

In this scenario, some of the faculty members try to leverage ICT, and market mechanisms to solve some of the problems which their institution faces, while improving their own situation. Business schools are the losers of this scenario.

As some professors openly operate in a market mode, the blurring of academic borders allows non-academics (practitioners as well as consultants) to enter both businesses of content creation and classroom animation. "Best practices" are dressed up as conceptual inputs if not theories. In-house company seminars offered by consultants or managers call upon the latest teaching package bought from a guru. Many opportunistic new entrants try to benefit from this unbundling process.

Market thinking is dominant. Funding stems from a variety of sources, as services are paid for at market price with fees and tuitions charged according to the perceived quality of the service delivered. The institutional academic logic of universities is considerably weakened. Business schools slowly become selling channels with a vending brand name to distribute knowledge created elsewhere.

E-learning is a key driver of this unbundling process where some of the most influential faculty members partly escape from the control of the university which employs them. There are several examples which forebode this scenario: the Open University in the UK which awards several thousand MBA degrees every year with distant learning and a network of franchisees, Ron Meyer's and Bob de Witt's Strategy Academy in the Netherlands, or the Theseus Institute which spun off from being an in-house MBA of the Orange group in the early 90s before being bought by Edhec in France.

Theseus, the former France Telecom – Orange MBA

Theseus was initially founded by France Telecom in 1989 in Sophia-Antipolis. The institute offered an MBA specializing in the management of information technologies. At that point, representatives from other large companies and academic institutions were sitting on the board of Theseus.

When France Telecom decided to withdraw from the institute, a group of Theseus professors decided to go for an MBO. (France Telecom subsequently created the France Telecom Group University, now Orange University – a typical corporate university).

As a result, Theseus became a privately owned, independent entity and operated as such for several years, at the periphery of the formal academic world. In 2004, Edhec, a fully private business school, acquired the Theseus MBA to merge it with its own full time MBA. The new program now focuses on the management of technology.

Yet, the team owning Theseus had organized the ownership through two entities: the MBA for teaching activities (which they sold to Edhec), and a second entity for all other activities (which they kept operating on their own). They were thus teaching via Edhec while independently conducting their other activities alongside. In other words they were considering the Edhec MBA as a vending channel. At some point, tensions were too high and the setting was dismantled as the team disbanded.

Source: interviews

Scenario IV: "M&As"

This scenario is made of joint-ventures, alliances, acquisitions or mergers. Three main drivers are at work, pressing business schools to go for M&As: becoming international, gaining visibility through size, building economies of scale.

In this scenario, business schools find out that there are three dominant, rather distinct ways to go:

an integrated network of international campuses,
a closed club of partners sharing part of their activities and strategy while remaining independent,
a local cluster within a city or a district, relying upon geographic proximity and collecting funding from local public authorities.

The integrated network of international campuses serves several purposes. It aims at fostering student mobility through flexible curricula, offering the opportunity to study on different campuses while remaining within the design of the same program within the same institution. It also aims at consolidating preferred linkages to multinational companies eager to recruit well trained graduates in various countries or continents, while fishing in a diversified pool of talents.

The closed club of independent partners is a scheme designed for smaller (in size) business schools desperately searching for more visibility through collective size. Most of the leading European business schools such as INSEAD in Fontainebleau, IMD in Lausanne, SSE in Stockholm, IESE or ESADE in Barcelona, HEC or ESSEC in Paris tend to have a rather limited size. Obviously, beyond absolute size, a key factor is the amount of resource available per student or per faculty. Yet, in this scenario, the visibility of a larger network of business schools contributes to reinforcing the overall visibility of its members.

The regional cluster is the third form of M&As forming this scenario. New institutions emerge from a combination of local universities and private or public business schools, under the auspices of the local Chamber of Commerce, the regional government, and with the support of local companies. These re-combinations, which can take the form of full mergers, gather similar or complementary institutions (e.g., several business schools together or business schools plus an engineering school plus a design/art institution, etc.). The settings of such local aggregates face many difficulties, including historical oppositions and jealousies, thus requiring a strong drive from a dedicated leader, the support of local politicians and the prospect of additional funding from local stakeholders.

Altogether, these moves contribute to reshaping the competitive arena in which business schools operate. In this scenario, e-learning helps consolidate the links among distant partners as well as distant sites within the same institution.

The job market for business faculty is affected by these institutional changes. As newly formed groups of partners and increasingly visible entities are better at collecting additional funding from various sources, more resources are made available for the best teaching and research talents, offering attractive careers in the most visible settings. Some institutions are deeply embedded locally; others pursue a multi-regional strategy, while some others reinforce a global scope. Commercial logic is at work but business schools continue to tap public sources of funding both locally and from the national government and the EU Commission.

In this scenario, the M&As reinforce the typical European tradition, whereby public funding is combined with, and reinforced by, some additional private sources, in a semi-commercial way. Most M&As are *de facto* or even explicitly supported by public bodies (local and regional governments, Chambers of Commerce, Ministries of Education). In this context, purely private institutions (foreign business schools, consultants, corporate universities, etc.) find it hard to enter the market. Incumbents having restructured through a set of mergers, acquisitions and alliances are well positioned to consolidate barriers to entry on the market. As a way to control the business, they insist that the knowledge that is produced and taught on their premises is scientific. They defend and leverage the academic dimension of management

---

The "global MBA"

The Wharton-Insead alliance signed in March 2001 makes it possible for students and executives to have access to four campuses: Philadelphia, San Francisco, Fontainebleau and Singapore. This is a typical example of geographic complementarity through an alliance.

The same rationale applies to the International Master's in Management (IMM), offered by Purdue, Tias Business School in the Netherlands, ESCP-EAP in Paris and Budapest University. IMM includes six modules, of two weeks each, on the premises of each of the partners. The program leads to a dual MBA degree, both European and American. *The "global MBA" formula makes it possible to recruit globally in all countries says* Patrick Gougeon, dean for MBA at ESCP-EAP. *Relation with students may not be as strong as for a full time program but we do provide significant distant interaction with participants and ad hoc individual follow up.*

The development of the "global MBA" concept illustrates the idea of international networks of alliances among business schools worldwide. As Gabriel Hawanini, former dean of Insead, put it: *Leading business schools need to reach out for a global audience, and thus will increasingly belong to worldwide networks of alliance.*

Source: Les Echos

education. In this scenario, ICT and e-learning fall short of disrupting this newly organized competitive arena where traditional players win through strategic manoeuvres.

The Wharton-Insead alliance in research, the ESCP-EAP model with 5 integrated sites (Paris, London, Berlin, Madrid and Turin), the Essec or Insead creation of a site in Singapore, the (failed) discussions between Bocconi and the Politechnico di Milano to enter an alliance, indicate what this scenario could look like.

Scenario V: "Reactive adaptation"

In this scenario, business schools are struggling to transform themselves, in search of performance (typically through ranking), but find it extremely difficult as they lack resources while facing inertia in their environment. Yet, progress is being made, step by step: the system slowly adapts. European management education is now better recognized, while not fully bridging the gap with, nor clearly differentiating from the US.

Business schools (and to some extent the universities as a whole) fight on many fronts. They increase tuitions and fees, develop executive education, build ad hoc programs in cooperation with Industry, create foundations and collect donations, and call upon local governments to fund their local initiatives. Some restructuring also takes place as a way to share costs and gain visibility. The key driver in this scenario is a systematic, multi-channel hunt for additional funding.

Commercial thinking slowly becomes dominant although traditional public institutional logic still remains alive. While close cooperation between universities and companies is normal practice in this scenario, public bodies – particularly regional and local players – support their local business schools as instruments for regional economic development.

In this context several leading business schools design packages to attract faculty. They offer reduced teaching loads, research grants, and salaries and bonuses which make the career fairly attractive. As a result, professors are expected to publish and promote the name of their business school, and contribute to attracting good students because their excellence in teaching becomes visible, while at the same time performing well in executive training. They thus feel a very strong pressure to excel in all aspects of their professional tasks. They are also asked to accept a strict exclusivity, asking for written permission before considering accepting any outside teaching engagement.

Some of the researchers play it mainstream, competing to access the best ranked international journals, and the best among them do succeed in becoming members of the academic closed networks of elite research. These happy few are invited to stay on campuses abroad, which in turn helps them publish more at the highest level. As a result, European management research makes visible progress in the rankings, although most strategic issues remain: the rules of the game and the preferred types of research published are under North American leadership.

In this scenario, new entrants on the European market can make it in but face fierce opposition from incumbents fighting for survival on the core business of their home market. Some players attempt to promote e-learning as a way to differentiate but this does not significantly affect this scenario.

This scenario is driven by the capability of business schools and universities to imagine a complex array of ad hoc means to collect additional funding. The Trium program (NYU-HEC-LSE) or the institutional transformation of the Paris Dauphine university, now being allowed to select their students, are typical examples of how this scenario may appear.

Trium
The Trium Global Executive MBA, is offered by HEC, the London School of Economics and Political Sciences and the Stern Business School at New York University. Trium charges 105 000 $ per participant for a 12 weeks program taking place in Paris, London, New York, Shanghai and Sao Paolo. Remote internet coaching takes place in between sessions during the overall 18 month curriculum. Georges Blanc, who launched the program, observes that each participant spends 15 to 20 hours per week on work for Trium projects during the whole program.

With about 50 participants per session, such a program has been designed to generate operating profit for the institutions capable of marketing and implementing it.

Source: interview

New regulatory framework for Paris – Dauphine
The Dauphine University in Paris is no longer a traditional French university. In Feb 2004, Dauphine obtained a specific autonomous public status.

This was a pre-requisite to allow the university to select students according to their own criteria (with 5000 applicants for 800 seats in the undergraduate program). Under French law, universities cannot select students who successfully passed the baccalaureat exam at the end of High School.

In addition this specific position allows the university board to raise fees and tuitions apart from national standards.

Source: Herbillon report, 2004, p. 50

Table 4.1   Key features of the five scenarios

	1-Drifting away	2-European management stands up	3-Unbundling: BS as vendors	4-M&A's	5-Reactive adaptation
Funding	Mostly public and insufficient	Awareness about the financial issue : EU invest + national public resources + Foundations + companies	Diversified sources of funding Payment for services	Combining public and private resources, including from local/ regional governments	Public basic funding, some foundations, executive education, local and regional additional fundings
Attractiveness of careers for faculty	Low. 60% only of retiring baby-boomers are replaced. Quality of recruits is mediocre	Significant upgrading of careers attractiveness Good level of recruits	Clear segmentation of career paths	Segmentation of careers	Faculty produce to generate/ reinforce institutional visibility. Importance of Executive education
Alliances and mergers	Limited deals, ad hoc. Essential in best Business Schools	Promoted by EU A European job market emerges for business professors	The value chain breaks; Some professors create, exploit and maintain their own brand	Exclusive Alliances; Search for critical mass, or geographic coverage	Some deals, some go for volume, some for quality
Role of market	Increasing for the few who decide to go for it	Strong but kept under control	Dominant	Complementary to the dominance of institutional logic	Increasing
Role of institutions	Dominates in universities	Positive dynamics of universities with some autonomy	Weakened Universities as distribution channels	Still strong	Status quo with margins of manoeuvre Local pressures and incentives
New entrants	Corporate universities; Consultants	Limited role of new entrants as incumbents are in better shape	Many new entrants in opening spaces of the value chain	Limited; Incumbents institutions control the market	Moderate involvement
Management as a science ?	A widening gap with practitioners	European social sciences are mobilized. More clinical/ project research.	Debated; Consultants and practitioners sell their best practices as theories	Business seen as a science	Bipolarity: researchers who publish/teachers who train
E-learning	Limited development, lack of resources to invest	Some initiatives	Makes it possible to distribute same content in many class rooms at once	Institutions remain the dominant design	Some initiatives
Foreboding/ signaling examples	Some European universities in bad financial trouble	Germany creating business schools; CEMS Program	Strategy Academy, Theseus, Univ. Phoenix	Insead-Wharton, Essec or Insead Singapore; ESCP-EAP: 5 sites	Trium (NYU-HEC-LSE); Dauphine

Table 4.1 above summarizes the five scenarios according to the main variables identified throughout the analysis of the system of management education. Figure 4.2 presents the same scenarios graphically as a diagram using two key variables (the Business schools' capacity for action – horizontally; and the market vs institutional dominant thinking – vertically).

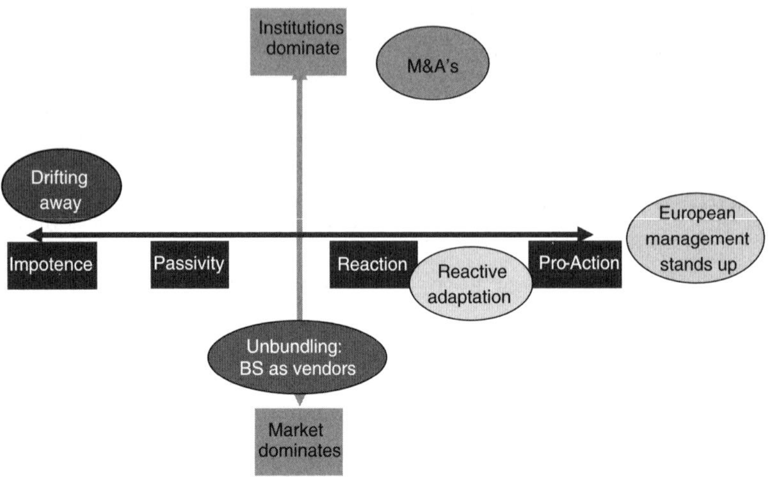

Figure 4.2   Mapping of the 5 scenarios

This is a journey in the land of Business Schools.

We questioned the future of management education.

Recognizing the dominance of the US model of business and business education, we started with a review of that model, thus creating the baseline for our Foresight.

We further chose to use the case of Europe as a case study, and our European lens as a way to discuss the system of management education and its dynamics.

We started by describing the situation as it is across different European countries, with their similarities and specificities. Along the way, we identified 10 families of players in a typical management education system. We then identified nine challenges affecting the system from within. Further, we identified seven exogenous pressures affecting the system from the outside. This was summarized graphically as Figure 4.1.

On that basis, we built five scenarios aiming at representing the diversity of the possible futures we could envision for business schools, given the players, the challenges and the pressures at hand in the system. These scenarios were documented and illustrated using a set of key variables stemming from the analysis. The scenarios were also represented as Figure 4.2.

In a way, the Foresight exercise started with the building of a complete descriptive representation of the system as it is today (Figure 4.1), which most observers would already be familiar with, at least in part. It then aimed at transforming Figure 4.1 into Figure 4.2 as a way of gaining more insight into possible outcomes for Business Schools in 2020 or so.

Our aim was not to tell the reader what the future (singular) will be, nor was it to recommend a specific strategy to a specific business school. The issue was to identify key drivers in the system, understand the underlying motivations of the many players taking part in the system, and build some understanding of what the futures could look like, as a way to bring more light on our actions today.

When looking at the five scenarios, the objective is not for the reader to pick the "best" or most "suitable" or most "convenient" This is not about hoping for the best scenario, nor choosing the most probable. The heart of the matter is to accept that the variety of potential futures described by the scenarios hopefully gives a sound representation of what future outcomes (plural) could look like.

Once again, we need to stress that we used Europe as a case study to imagine Foresight scenarios for the future of business schools. We believe that our five scenarios can be **adapted to other regions of the world.** Typically, we feel that four out of the five (Drifting away, M&A's, Unbundling, Reactive adaptation) can be easily transposed to fit contexts other than the US and the EU. And the one remaining (European management stands up) can be treated in two ways: it may be kept as such to indicate a major change appearing on the international stage of management education, as Europe would much more pro-actively and openly offer the world a differentiated model, challenging the US model of management and management education. Or this scenario may simply be adapted to become something like "the regional management stands up," meaning a similar pro-active move organized in that region on the theme of management and management education as the one described for the EU in our scenario.

In the case of the US (and to some extent Canada), we feel that our scenarios can be used as well. Two (Unbundling and M&A's) can be directly transposed. Two more (Drifting away and Reactive adaptation) should be interpreted as dealing with the posture of business schools outside North America or those US business schools trying to compete with the first league. Finally, the remaining scenario (European management stands up) may be adapted to describe a situation where a region of the world (be it the EU or Japan or one of the BRICS, etc.) would position itself as a challenger to the US dominant model of management and management education.

This is the type of discussion which we now turn to as a way to conclude this first part of the book. We will then turn to Part II to present the details and specificities of the contexts of management education in a sample of countries or regions around the world.

5
Strategic Implications for the Main Regions of the World

Our aim was to provide some insight into the possible futures of business schools. This is what the five scenarios above are for, thus offering a Foresight contribution.

It then behoves each and every player in the system to construct strategies capable of accommodating most, if not all, of the scenarios put forward. This means that any strategic move should be put to the compatibility/adaptability test: "Should this scenario unfold, to what extent will my strategy be adequate?"; "Should that other scenario unfold, how could my strategy be adapted to fit that scenario as well?"

Granularity

Discussing strategies requires raising the issue of the entity for which the strategic analysis takes place. What level of analysis is relevant in this context? Should we look essentially at business schools, at departments within business schools, at individuals (faculty members or students)? Instead, should we look at clusters or categories of business schools within a country, at a country or even a group of countries or a Region of the world?

This is a difficult issue. Typically, business school deans would most probably wish to discuss strategic options for a business school. However, in the context of this book, we deliberately chose to address strategic implications of our analysis at the level of countries or groups of countries.

We indeed believe that cultural, social and political specificities attached to geography play a major role in shaping the systems of Management Education, in turn strongly influencing what business schools can do.

We cannot discuss here specific detailed strategies for all categories of players in the system and for all countries or regions of the world, not to speak about the "compatibility/adaptability test" of these strategies when faced with the five scenarios.

However we can do a little bit of that here, at a level of analysis compatible with the scope of this book. Here is how we do it:

First, we sum up the business model of a business school.
Second, we identify and discuss generic strategic "postures" available to the main regions of the world regarding the issue of management education and research.
Third, we face these strategic "postures" with the five scenarios.
Fourth, we recapitulate the strategic options remaining available against most scenarios, for some of the key players in the system (business schools, Governments, Industry), for the main regions of the world.

Finally, in the subsequent chapter (Chap 6), we go one step further, as Europeans, to recommend these key players within the EU to strengthen the system of management education and research in Europe.

A typical business model for business schools

The **mission** of a business school is to teach and train participants (undergraduate students, young managers and executives) in the most advanced knowledge in business theory and practice, while contributing to the development and dissemination of new knowledge through research.

In order to do so, business schools try to attract high level participants and excellent faculty. **Reputation and Funding** are thus two key self-reinforcing ingredients of the cocktail.

The business model of a business school is organized around a typical portfolio of activities:

Undergraduate programs tend to cost more than they contribute – through the tuitions and fees and the allocation per student paid by the State (if any). However JC Spender rightly points out that "business undergraduates take 50% of their credits outside their major, so the business enrollment is of huge importance," absorbing fixed costs in the liberal arts and science faculties who supply the supporting credits. Likewise, undergraduate business programs have a rather low impact on reputation and brand, but create a base of alumni who may subsequently contribute through company support in the short and medium term and, more importantly, individual donations in the long run.

Master's programs, including **MBA** programs, are more or less balanced as the fees paid by the participants usually cover the costs. There is a net contribution when attendance is high, but this is usually not where a significant net contribution can be made. MBA's have a strong impact on reputation as many rankings rely heavily on criteria attached to the quality of the MBA and the salary and positions subsequently held by the graduates.

Executive education is a clear cash generator. It also strongly affects the reputation of the business school in Industry through an invisible but concrete "word-of-mouth" type of dissemination process among managers. Exec Ed also makes it possible for faculty to touch base with reality and to hear about down-to-earth issues raised and discussed by executives in the classroom. (Exec Ed participants tend to increasingly demand professors who are active in research because they are looking for in-depth thinking about their practice. Yet, they do not necessarily realize that the way mainstream research is conducted usually does not really prepare academics to address the types of managerial concerns and expectations of an audience of executives. This is a major paradox which increasingly causes tensions within the business model).

PhD programs and **research** projects conducted by the faculty need significant investments. Some resources may be brought in through external research contracts and grants. Another form appeared recently, with professorships created with a primary focus on research, e.g. a bank funding a team of researchers under the leadership of a principal investigator to develop new models. This parallels what has been done for a long time in natural sciences, e.g. for biotechnology, drugs or food, at the interface between public and private research. Yet, the production of new knowledge through research activities is a money-burning activity. Research, through publications, is the critical means to build and maintain long term reputation via rankings. Research is also the best way to ensure that the faculty is involved in the latest development of the field, thus continuously updating teaching contents accordingly. Articulating research and teaching is not straightforward, however, with the underlying tension between rigor and relevance of research activities.

Alumni make **donations**, thus building up the **endowments** which in turn generate additional revenues. The virtuous circle is at work when reputation attracts good students among whom the most successful will end up donating significant amounts, while the financial resources made available will permit the recruiting of high level faculty, providing excellent teaching and cutting edge research. Another form of donation is the creation of professorships – sponsored by a company – or even by a wealthy individual. This form of private financial support usually aims at funding academic activities across the board: improving the quality of education, accessing good graduates, connecting with research in a specific field as a source for new ideas, contributing to entrepreneurship activities, promoting interactions with Industry at large, etc.

Activity in the portfolio	Net financial contribution	Impact on visibility/reputation
Undergraduate	–	Low to moderate
MBA and Master's	~ 0 +	Strong
Executive Education	+ +	Strong
Research and PhD prgm	– –	Critical
Donations, Endowment	+ +	Low

Two comments should be added regarding business models for business schools:

A – Some business schools have successfully chosen to focus on only part of the overall portfolio presented above. IMD in Switzerland is essentially an executive education place, plus an MBA program and some research, without a PhD program, with no undergraduates and no other master's program. INSEAD used to be a place with an MBA program plus executive education; they later chose to develop a PhD program to support the research conducted by their faculty. Instituto de Empresa in Madrid is on a similar mode with no undergraduate programs, no PhD program until 2004, and still a limited permanent faculty.

B – As Europe is not used to the idea of private donations, Europeans tend to misunderstand what it really covers. Most donations to universities in the US are made by individuals, not just companies. These individuals are alumni who *"want to give back what they received."* Some of them have done particularly well and choose to donate significant amounts of money. This is quite rare in Europe, apart from very specific cases such as the Wallenberg family in Sweden or some of the donations made at Oxford or Cambridge.

As some universities and business schools in Europe have created foundations as a vehicle to collect donations and manage the money, it is striking to see that the fund raisers have until very recently essentially targeted corporations, not alumni. In our view this is understandable in the short term as Europeans do not have a culture of donation, but it may be a mistake in the long run as this will not help increase the donation potential of individuals – mostly the alumni.

Generic strategic postures available to the players

We look here at each one of the three clusters of countries or regions that we identify in the world for the sake of our analysis. We first look at developed countries or Regions (typically OECD countries – except North America), then at North America itself, and finally at Brics (Brazil, Russia, India, China and South Africa) and developing countries (viewed typically through South America or Middle East and North Africa or other Asian countries).

Given the US dominance, we propose a set of three strategic postures or broad strategies for business schools in each of the three clusters of countries. We insist that this discussion relates to the international arena of management education and research. We thus look at what business schools around the world can do to position themselves, fitting in with their own market needs, while taking into account the current institutional structure and the dynamics of competition: as discussed so far, the influence of external players, especially the leading US business schools, is indeed very strong in management education and research in most markets.

Europe and other OECD countries – other than North America

Catching up

Today, most business schools' deans in developed countries are on a catching-up mode, either implicitly or explicitly. This is the imitation strategy by which business schools play it by the established rules to compete as runners-up or runners-up-to-be against the leading US players.

This is the natural way to go. The international academic community of management is open enough to allow potential participants to join in. While fierce scientific debates on concepts and ideas are common, courtesy and openness also apply, especially in the international academic arena. Yet, it is not an easy ride for the outsiders. English is the language. Many of the rules are in fact tacit. The reviewing process for publications uses implicit principles which may render things difficult for those who come from nowhere, i.e. who were not initiated within the proper tribes.

As a result, quite paradoxically, such a strategy of catching up is in fact likely to contribute to reinforcing the leadership of the US model of management education. Indeed, playing the game by the rules imposed both directly and indirectly by the dominant player, but without adequate resources in relative terms, is likely to help the dominant player remain dominant.

Ignoring the leaders

A second posture is to ignore the leading players. To some extent, this is what Germany has been doing quite successfully – at least until the reunification after the fall of the Berlin Wall – with no business schools in the country, and a German association of economics and management professors publishing mostly books in German and doing their research away from the English-speaking, US-influenced, research avenues. One should add another characteristic of the German system: many top managers hold a PhD. This is a concrete sign of the respect that German Industry has for academia. Obviously, over the recent years, there has been a growing influence of the non-German-speaking academic world as well. But we want to insist on this: Germany has been economically successful, with export industries shipping products and machines around the world, while its management education system was clearly running apart from the US dominant model.

In a way, Japan may be put in a similar category, as Japanese management methods were either house-made (e.g. Just in Time) or imported and then adapted, but with no or little input from US business schools (e.g. Juran on Quality after World war II).

This strategy of deliberately ignoring the leadership of the US on management and management education is a risky way to go. It may lead to some form of isolation. As an example, in a world where alliances or M&A's are increasingly common in Industry, this may render things more difficult when it comes to dealing with very different "managerial animals." Indeed, the dominant model of management is logically at work in those companies representing the economic super power on world markets, as discussed in the Introduction. Not being familiar enough with the dominant model may create problems.

Differentiating to compete by leveraging national or regional specificities

Beyond the imitation of the "catching up" mode and the risky approach of "ignoring the leader," we argue that there exists a third way to go. This is the differentiation posture, by which the game is played but with a different approach from what the dominant players have imposed so far.

In our opinion, this is in part what Scandinavia has been doing for years in management, building upon the specificities of their social and political model. This is also what Italy did – to a certain extent – to cope with the specific needs of the Italian Industry, made up of a multitude of small entities (a mix of companies, family businesses and cooperatives) linked together through ad hoc contracts and social networks. There is probably a similar need in China where business is intricatedly connected to the Communist Party, thus requiring a combination of political, entrepreneurial and managerial skills to succeed, at least for the time being. Most of the typical US business schools case studies dealing with large multinational corporations are of limited relevance in such contexts. This point is clearly made by Mezghani in his chapter about Middle East and North Africa or by Koenig and Tapie on Asia (see Part II).

This third posture not only facilitates a better fit with the needs of the local businesses, it may also attract other regions of the world interested in finding another source of knowledge in management, away from the dominant model. But this path has its own risks as well, especially that of being pushed aside in the worldwide competition of management education if your business schools are not recognized as teaching established concepts (what is an established concept, if not a concept approved by the bandwagon through their review process?), or producing mainstream new knowledge (what is mainstream, if not what the bandwagon is telling you it is?).

These three postures obviously apply to potential challengers of the US model of management education – Europe, as we argue, being one of them. Two other specific contexts are worth examining here, that of North America itself and that of non-immediate challengers.

North America

We believe that the dominance of the US model allows North American business schools three typical postures.

Forging ahead

A first natural posture is to keep going as a leader, forging ahead along the same path, as a way to reinforce dominance. This bets on a self-reinforcing mechanism which relies upon existing structural advantages: the gap in resources available, the strength of existing brand names for leading US business schools, the control – both indirect and direct – of the rules of the game (defining what mainstream research is, *de facto* deciding which journal is leading or not via the citation index – when the bulk of publications in English stems from the US simply due to relative mass –, directly influencing the explicit and tacit criteria of what a good paper is in leading journals, etc.), the importance of the American corporation and the dynamism of the US economy, etc.

However, this straightforward strategy may in fact ignore what potential challengers might be preparing. Introspection due to fierce competition among business schools at home, and most remaining attention paid to continue imposing the existing model elsewhere, may lead North American Business Schools to disregard otherwise significant moves in Higher Education in other parts of the world.

Penetrate to influence

A second posture is to use a well-established dominance to infiltrate the main potential challengers as a way to control their dynamics from within, in turn reinforcing the dominance. In a way, the strong implication of the US management academic community in Europe may lead to some of that. This may not result from a strategic intent. First, there are clearly strong personal and intellectual links across the Atlantic Ocean, with some European management faculty having been trained and/or having taught in the US – and vice versa, although to a lesser extent. Second, there are North American professors, US or Canadian citizens, cultivating their cultural relation to Europe as a way to dig back into what they view as part of their own cultural heritage. Third, there is the emergence of a globalizing market of management faculty with business schools eager to enroll international faculty in as a way to enlarge the international scope of their teaching and research. There is also the development of the existing market for students keen to study abroad, as well as for executive education programs with an international focus. All of the above explains the strong social networks which developed over the years between European and North American business schools. Yet, one may argue that the North American involvement in the academic community of management in Europe also leads to shaping the system of European Business Schools and influences where it is heading to. Without necessarily an explicit or even implicit intent, such a process seems to be at work here, the effect of rankings having probably the strongest influence on the European system of Higher Education in management as it contributes to aligning European business schools on the US model. One might argue that the above analysis also applies to the influence of the US business schools in other regions such as Japan or China, for example.

This posture of *de facto* infiltration may however lead to some form of myopia, paradoxically, as the dominant player is so convinced of its own strength that it may in fact ignore the benefits which could stem from learning from the others.

Recognize and compete

The third posture for the North American business schools would be to recognize the potential emergence of other ways to train managers around the world, accepting that the rules of the game of the business of business schools might evolve in unexpected and possibly less controllable ways – at least to some extent. This remains to be seen, but that posture would probably be the healthiest for all parties. This would mean that US business schools would realize that they will eventually have to compete not only among themselves, i.e. against their US peers in the US and abroad, but also against players based in other countries, thus in other managerial contexts and cultures.

This may happen one day, but one might expect that even if a new player starts operating as a challenger – offering a differentiated model in the way Europe could do it, as we argue – it is unlikely that the US model will really feel challenged within the limits of our Foresight horizon, namely 2020.

Brics and developing countries

Again, here, we see three strategic postures specific for these countries.

Import from the leader

This is the natural way to go: learning from US business schools and sending students and faculty to the leading business schools in the US as the Mecca of management. This is what several European countries did in the 60s and 70s and what China has been doing heavily since the 80s. This is an import strategy, trying to access knowledge as it is, from where it is available, hoping for some form of local adaptation along the way.

The risk is in the potential misfit between the managerial knowledge that is being imported and the local specificities of the economy and the way companies operate in the local political, regulatory and social environment.

Yet, this is the most common strategic posture encountered around the world. This contributes to reinforcing the dominance of the US model.

Diversify sources

While still importing management training and knowledge from the outside, this second posture aims at accessing alternate sources as a way to avoid some form of dependence on a dominant supplier. Typically some countries in the Middle East chose to turn to Europe as a second partner in Higher Education in management. So did China to a certain extent. A similar orientation exists in South America where reinforcing historical relations with Europe, even in management education and research, is seen as a possible way to counterbalance what is perceived as a traditional strong influence of North America on the subcontinent.

Conversely, North African countries turn to the US or Canada as a way to open up beyond the historical quasi exclusive influence of France in most areas, including in management training.

However, this second posture may not be enough to ensure that these countries will truly benefit from managerial education fitted to their specificities. To what extent would an MBA degree from Stanford or Harvard really help run a family business in Tunisia today? Some of it may certainly help; some other parts may be irrelevant.

Blend and cross-sell

A third strategy for these countries is to move firmly towards customization of management knowledge imported from elsewhere, while at the same time progressively constructing a capacity to create local knowledge as well. This obviously requires a firm and long-lasting commitment to research and investment in the local development of teaching material (case studies, if not text books). In turn this strategy may lead to offering some expertise to other regions of the world, from a clearly differentiated base. This is, for example, the case when a Brazilian business school specialized in Executive Education such as the Fondation don Cabral enters the Chinese market to provide a unique experience of a developing country – another Brics, as a matter of fact – faced with a complex socio-political context, with very poor regions (the North East) and quite advanced urban centers (San Paolo, Rio de Janeiro, Belo Horizonte) with strong internal pressures from migrants coming into the cities, and corruption as part of business life, etc. All of this is likely to ring a bell in China.

Where else but in a similar socio-political context can you find family-owned companies diversifying into as many opportunities as the founding entrepreneur can leverage locally from his or her social network backed by political connections? This is not what standard managerial textbooks will teach you. This is where exchanges of experience of such specific business issues can take place between non-dominant players of the business schools arena.

In a way, this recalls the third posture identified for potential European and other OECD Challengers (*Differentiating to compete by leveraging national or regional specificities*). Again, the risk of this strategy is that of being pushed aside from the world competition of management education as the knowledge is developed at the periphery of the international management community centered on the dominant US leader. That specific knowledge may thus be ignored or regarded with contempt. Yet, this is probably a reasonable way to go for business schools in the zone, eager to find their own path while building an international reputation from a different angle.

Confronting the three postures to the five scenarios for each geographic cluster

We now turn to see how the strategic postures identified may fit in with each of the five scenarios we built. In other words, this is the "compatibility/adaptability test" of these strategies when confronted with the five scenarios for each of the three clusters of countries retained for our analysis.

Table 5.1   Europe and other OECD countries – apart from North America

	Drifting away	European management Stands up	M&A's	Business schools as vendors	Reactive adaptation
Catching up	Failure due to lack of resources and no political will. – A few EU BSchools may compete successfully.	Despite the thrust, EU BS bound to remain followers due to resource gap.	Can preserve identity and choice of partners; - may bring size & visibility but EU BS are followers.	-Risk of further domination with more contents imported from the US, - the "stars" are still trained in leading US BS.	May be seen as the current situation; with low resources, EU BS are bound to remain followers.
Ignoring the leader	Industry support and confidence in existing BS are insufficient.	Probably too late. This posture is no longer an option in Europe.	Risk of missing the boat.	EU faculty are not part of the market; US faculty promote their contents easily.	A non starter. Too late; and not desirable.
Differentiating	- Not enough; -Yet, some EU BS compete.	**Opportunity:** **see our call –** **Chap 6**	M&A can go both ways.	EU faculty can sell their content worldwide.	May not be enough to compete fully.

Tables 5.1, 5.2 and 5.3 present the summary of the "compatibility/adaptability test". How effective is each strategic stance when faced with each of the potential futures described in the five scenarios?

Each table covers one of the three clusters. The five scenarios are shown in columns. Each of the three possible strategies identified for the business schools of the countries within the cluster is checked against each of the scenarios: Is the posture compatible with the scenario? Can it be adapted to better fit the scenario? Could the strategy achieve anything if this scenario were to become reality?

A few comments stem from these tables:

US dominance in the field is bound to last, whatever the strategy adopted by US BSchools

For Europe – and most of the rest of the world – "ignoring the leader" is a non starter, to put it simply.

Table 5.2 North America

	Most others are drifting away	European management stands up	M&A's	Business schools as vendors	Reactive adaptation
Forging ahead	US BS dominate the market of management education.	Risk of ignoring the challenger(s), and losing full supremacy.	Preferred way to access campuses abroad; risk of misunderstandings with partners.	US faculty sell their content successfully worldwide.	Few non US BS may find local niches & meet some MNCs needs.
Penetrate to influence	US BS both dominate the market and control its dynamics, with no real competition.	As US BS influence, they are influenced in return; may in fact lead to "recognize and compete."	Domination via alliances with unbalanced resources; give visibility to foreign partners.	US faculty promote their content via partners; some inputs from other regions too.	US BS still dominate the market while supporting active players in other regions.
Recognize and compete	Although desirable, not really needed to remain dominant.	Worldwide competition where US BS still likely to have the lead.	M&As go both ways; alliances may become more balanced.	Market for contents is open to all, under US leadership.	Some non US BS are active around the globe as well.

Table 5.3   Brics and other developing countries

	Drifting away	European management stands up	M&A's	Business schools as vendors	Reactive adaptation
Import from the US leader	Failure due to lack of resources	Sustain the competitive advantage of US BS; risk of missing a new potentially relevant supplier.	May bring more visibility to local BS but US BS still dominate.	-Risk of further domination with more contents imported from the US, - the "stars" are still trained in leading US BS.	May be seen as the most likely situation; with low resources, Brics BS are bound to remain followers.
Diversify sources	Government and industry support and confidence in existing BS are insufficient.	Promote a worldwide competitive market; tap a variety of management models.	May help preserve identity and free choice of partners.	May help create a competitive market for scholars from which to recruit.	Will strengthen market competition; but not enough to "change the world."
Blend and cross-sell	Failure due to the lack of resources and confidence in regional BS.	As a third new competitor, speed up the development of a global competitive market; EU support is very likely.	M&A can go both ways, at least in principle.	Regional scholars may try to sell their own contents worldwide.	May not be enough to compete fully; some real opportunities to find market niches, though.

The "catching up" strategy is, we believe, the strategy currently implemented
  in leading EU BSchools
The "European Management stands up" scenario is more relevant and
  likely if Brics and RoW countries go for a "diversify sources" or "blend
  and cross-sell" strategy.

This means that there are interdependencies between strategies
adopted in the different geographic zones and the likelihood of
scenarios.

We now extract from the results of this analysis the strategic options
which we view as the most relevant for each zone, given their capacity
to cope or not with the variety of scenarios.

Strategic options remaining available against most scenarios

We choose here to select a limited number of specific players per zones of the world to recapitulate which reasonable strategic options remain available after the confrontation of the three main strategic postures discussed with the five scenarios resulting from the Foresight exercise.

We choose to retain the same three groups of countries: The US; the EU plus other OECD countries, except the US; the Brics and RoW (Brazil, Russia, India, China and South Africa and the rest of the World).

We choose to focus on four main families of players (Business Schools, Governments, Firms and Individuals – students, teaching staff and managers). We further choose to segment the business schools into two sub-categories which, for the sake of simplicity, we label first league and second league business schools, even though we would have difficulty in defining a clear-cut boundary between the two categories in each country. Under the "Firms" category, we also distinguish the multinational Corporations (MNCs) and the SMEs wherever appropriate.

We discuss below the strategic options which we view as reasonably relevant for each of these four families of players in the three groups of countries. We start with the US, then the Brics and RoW before introducing the case of the EU and other OECD countries – which is then developed further in Chapter 6.

The US

Our interpretation is that the leading US business schools are, we believe, currently trying to combine a strategy of "forging ahead" together with an implicit *de facto* move to "penetrate to influence" management education elsewhere in the world. This makes sense for the first league North American business schools. The strategy of influence means choosing the best potential players in some target countries, helping them upgrade their teaching and research while *de facto* influencing their policies if not their governance. This strategy is relevant as long as the resources available are sufficient – and the leading US players can typically afford it. This strategy is probably more appropriate than investing head-on into fully-owned new campuses abroad, which has proved difficult, if not unsuccessful, on many occasions. In addition, the "penetrate to influence" part of the strategy helps cope with some form of limited adaptation to local specificities, via exposure to international business and foreign faculty as well as foreign students and executives. This strategy may thus continue to fit the needs of the

American multinational corporation which keeps imposing its managerial model where it operates, accepting some local customization when needed – but only when needed.

Second league US business schools could play it the same way, using the overall "management made in America" umbrella brand name. Yet, the risk for them is paradoxically to become more insular in the process if they were to use their managerial model as the one and only reference both in training their audience in international business and in cooperating internationally, not properly listening to and learning from their international partners and markets. A more relevant strategy may be for them to recognize that there are other ways to conduct business due to local cultural and political specificities, to learn from these and adapt accordingly as a way to stick to market needs abroad. This is in part what some of these business schools did in the US in the 20s and 30s, i.e. focusing on the specific requirements of their local industrial environment. For these business schools active in training for international business, e.g. for their local client companies going abroad, this thus means developing research on multicultural, international contexts, e.g. studying how Chinese entrepreneurs deal with the Communist Party in China or how industrial districts operate in northern Italy.

In this context of overall leadership in management, the US Government may seem to have little more to do on the matter than it already does. The funding mechanisms for research via federal agencies are at work. It might be relevant to direct some of the grants to better understand the various business contexts around the globe, and provide international exposure to more management faculty, in turn contributing to both the "influence" strategy and the "recognize to compete" strategy. It might also be appropriate to encourage young Americans to study foreign languages and geography more systematically.

Yet, beyond this "business-as-usual" type of support, we feel that a much more fundamental question needs to be addressed. The "American way of running business" is bound to face difficulties around the globe when America's foreign policy is difficult to understand – and at times difficult to accept. We are back to the discussion we had in the introduction of the book about the rise and fall of empires. Leadership is a strong and powerful but difficult position to hold. As an example, when the US legislation goes for "SOx" (Sarbanes Oxley), it affects large companies around the world – both directly and indirectly. If, as we believe, the law went too far, due to some form of over-reaction in addressing an otherwise real and important issue about governance and control, then the US leadership position is weakened and its overall model of management is questioned. Very concretely some non-US companies are considering leaving the NY stock exchange as a response to that legislation, and some have already decided to withdraw. Another example has to do with the visa policy for foreign students and faculty. When the US immigration policy makes it significantly harder for foreign students to study in America and for foreign professors to join American universities for short stays or longer involvements, the entire US system of education and research suffers, and this affects business schools as well.

As far as American Firms are concerned, they may want to tap additional sources of talents beyond the US, thus either relying on the partners of the US business schools they work with, or on their own connections with local business schools if they feel a need for alternative sources. They may also want to support management research, directing their funding to topics which are not sufficiently explored, especially in managing across borders in complex, evolving new settings (alliances or acquisitions in multicultural settings, starting new businesses in uncertain regulatory and political contexts, sourcing from low cost countries where gaps in the labor laws may in turn hurt the firm's reputation as a boomerang, etc.). Along these lines, it may be appropriate for the US-based MNCs to facilitate the extension of private Foundations in different countries, in particular those where they are interested in promoting management education and research.

As a matter of fact, we believe that one of the important drivers of the American system of management education and research may in fact be Industry. More specifically, in the context of the world market for business schools, we believe that US-based MNCs play a key role in shaping the strategies and the overall dynamics of the sector. MNCs are continuously confronting the reality of world markets and contexts with their managerial model. They are thus in the best position to feed back whether the "forging ahead" posture and its "penetrate to influence" variant are the most relevant ways for US business schools to position themselves internationally. They might be the players who will eventually persuade US business schools to move towards a "recognize and compete" strategic stance as a way to cope with the world diversity and the emergence of management models designed and promoted in other countries.

The last family of players worth mentioning here are the individuals (students, faculty, managers). No strong point needs to be made apart from drawing the attention of individuals to the importance of opening up to the outside, learning foreign cultures and languages, choosing a school opened to international business, questioning the paradigm of the American way of doing business as any other emerging management paradigm, being ready to work in different regions of the world, confronting the experience gained abroad to the existing models of management in a reflective mode and bringing back to the US business schools some of that learning for experience sharing. As a matter of fact, many American individuals already manage to gain considerable international exposure and some do take the time to re-think that experience over. What may still be insufficient are the conceptual feedbacks from these individuals on to the US Business School agenda and strategy.

All in all, we feel that US business Schools are bound to remain leaders in management education and research for a long time even though one of our claims here is that new competition is building up, especially in Europe. We also believe that the best long term strategy for US business schools is to "recognize and compete" – recognizing the emergence of competing approaches to management as a way to prepare to compete. We acknowledge, however, that a simpler short term strategy is to "forge ahead" and "penetrate to influence" emerging competitors.

Brics and RoW

Traditionally, the best talents and the children of rich families were sent abroad to study – often in the US when it comes to management. However, this flux turned out to be insufficient to meet the numerical needs, especially in Brics where successfully growing local companies have been progressively demanding an increasing number of well-educated managers.[1] The lack of resources to fund scholarships together with the fear of the brain drain effect, (as many graduates would not return after completing their studies), often led local politicians to establish management education institutions locally. As a result, leading business schools have emerged in most countries of the zone, especially in Brics, with a clear intention to better supply the local managerial needs.

The current strategy of the business schools in the zone is a *de facto* to "import from the leader," namely from the US. English as the *lingua franca* of business, existing text books and case material, the contribution of local subsidiaries of MNCs are complementary explanations of this strategy. It makes a lot of sense. The current strategy is also to "diversify sources" as well, at least in some countries and only to a certain extent. Europe is a typical second source of management education. Note in passing that this may explain why one of the most famous university ranking, the Shangai ranking, came from a Brics. This illustrates how much some form of "references beyond borders" was needed – and still is – for such countries to sort out the traditional tacitness of higher education and research. This holds true for management education and research as well, especially since Brics and RoW business schools are to diversify their sources of imports on these matters.

Second league business schools in Brics and RoW simply follow that import path as well.

Yet, the most advanced institutions, those which we call here the first league business schools of the zone, have learned that this import strategy is not fully adequate for the needs of indigenous companies. We believe that a potentially more appropriate strategy is to "blend and cross-sell." This means that these business schools should keep importing management knowledge from the leader and other sources, including Europe, but with some significant investments in building a local capacity. By this, we mean not only case study material and textbooks but also specific concepts and models, if not theories, addressing the specificities of the local economy with specific management issues such as running family-owned businesses, operating in non-mature social contexts, growing diversified middle-size conglomerates, entering alliances with powerful MNCs, etc. In turn, beyond the blending of imported and home-made concepts and models, these business schools may offer their contents to similar institutions in other developing countries facing equivalent issues, although in not fully identical contexts. This is the cross-sell part of the strategy beyond the blending. This means entering the competitive arena of management education and research in a clearly differentiated mode, by leveraging the specificities of both the institutional, social and political context, and the managerial issues faced. As discussed earlier, a leading Brazilian business school may have a lot to bring to management education in China or India – and vice versa.

One additional way to compete may also be to follow the national champions as they go abroad. Huawei from China in the Telecom equipment business, Embraer from Brazil in aeronautics or Mittal from India in the steel industry are all operating beyond borders and may be efficient vehicles to promote business schools from their homebase. Along the same lines, international relations and spheres of influence may also be leveraged. Typical examples would be Africa, where China invests heavily, or the Muslim world for the emerging Middle East business schools.

Governments in the corresponding countries may logically adopt a mirror strategy: funding scholarships for the best students to study abroad, if resources permit, while putting in place incentives in order for these to return upon graduation; building solid academic institutions in management education and research with faculty properly trained and capable of conducting their own research, to go beyond the managerial models imported from the outside; ensuring enough funding for the faculty to keep in touch with the international academic community (via international conferences and the invitation of foreign faculty into the local business schools); directing grants to support research projects addressing local managerial issues – including cooperation with researchers working in similar contexts elsewhere; etc. This strategy requires a long-lasting political commitment, as academic capacity tends to build up slowly.

A key condition for the success of such a strategy of blending and cross-selling is that local firms play the same game. If they openly treat young talents equally, on the basis of competence, even if their business degree comes from a local institution, the overall strategy may work. However, if they give too much preference to diplomas from abroad, especially those from the leading western business schools, things will be much more difficult. They also need to support the system of education and research by recruiting the graduates, collaborating to define the curricula, contributing to some of the teaching, opening their doors for researchers to build case studies, funding some research projects, calling upon the local resources to train their executives, etc. Although this may not be a natural way for them to go, this "blend and cross-sell" strategy requires an active involvement and participation of local firms.

Finally, the individuals need to buy the strategy. Students going to study abroad should return after graduation, talented busy managers need to contribute some of their time to teach in local business schools, professors need to behave as entrepreneurs despite a potentially bureaucratic environment to develop new programs with local contents as discussed above. They need to be both visionary to envision the future of their domain at the business school, and down to earth to provide pragmatic answers to concrete short term challenges. As an example, the rigor vs relevance dilemma would lean towards relevance (obviously with as much rigor as possible) even if this may be done at the expense of international publications in leading journals, at least in the short term.

All in all, our view of the most appropriate strategy for players in Brics and RoW countries is to work together for a "blend and cross-sell" strategy to rethink managerial issues in the light of the specificities of the local context. We believe, however, that this is neither a natural nor an easy way to go.

Europe (and other similar OECD countries)

Most European business schools from the second league are simply incapable of competing in the international arena of management education and research. They cannot even consider ignoring the US leaders in management education because this is where most of the new knowledge in the field is being produced. These institutions are dominated, with insufficient resources to do anything else but import whatever is made available in the dominant literature. They conduct some research, most often published only in their own language, with little international dissemination, if any. In other words, these institutions are falling behind in the world competition of management education and research. Some of them, however, try to exist internationally by addressing the needs of developing countries, where they bring the flavour of Europe. But their competitive position is weak, if not marginal, with little hope for improvement.

The first league European business schools have a clear "catching up" strategy. They send their doctoral students abroad, especially to the US, to prepare them for the rules of competition in research via publications in top-ranked journals. They try to hire young faculty from the international market, with a strong emphasis on publications in "A" level journals. (As a matter of fact, in several instances they end up hiring nationals who have been trained in PhD programs in the US, thus unintentionally sending a negative signal to local PhD candidates). They offer packages to attract and retain the most promising talents, with limited teaching load, significant research money for the first years and a combination of a good salary plus bonuses per publication. In other words, these first league European business schools allocate all the resources they can collect to play the game by the rules, i.e. those which were progressively established by the US academic community over the last decades. As a result, these rules are now viewed as the standards of excellence not only by the North American world of business schools but also, to a large extent, in Europe.

This strategy proves to be fruitful as an increasing number of European researchers do get published in the very best journals, and some of the European business schools have made significant progress in the rankings. In other words, the "catching up" strategy seems to be paying off. We argue, however, that this may be misleading. Indeed an imitation strategy may win, but only if the imitator has enough resources against the incumbent. It is very clear that the existing business model of business schools will not permit European business schools to access the level of resources which their North American counterparts have and will have in the years to come. This clearly implies that even the first league European business schools are bound to remain followers, behind their US competitors. In other words, we argue that the strategy currently implemented by European leading business schools is inadequate, despite the short term improvements which it brought about in the rankings – and will continue to bring in the coming years. We claim that this strategy is logical in the short term, and necessary but insufficient in the long run.

Ignoring the leader, as Japan and Germany have done to a certain extent is not possible any more. This is too late as the managerial culture in most of Europe and the rest of the world, including in Germany – and in Japan, although to a lesser extent – has been penetrated and influenced by the American way of managing.

We thus argue that a better strategy for Europe would be to combine the "catching up" mode with a "differentiating" strategy.

This dual strategy needs to be further clarified, developed and discussed. This is done in the next chapter. Indeed, should Europe want to move in that direction, the major EU players would need to join forces to create the conditions for the "European Management stands up" scenario to occur. Such key EU players include business schools and universities, national governments and the EU (typically both the EU Commission and the Parliament) and Industry (large European firms as well as SMEs).

This is what we, as Europeans, advocate in the next chapter, through a Call to European stakeholders and leaders to strengthen management education and research in the EU.

The content of this dual strategy is thus developed and discussed in Chapter 6 as part of the call we send to EU leaders.

6
Strengthening a Management Education System: Back to the EU Case

Throughout Part I, we used Europe – in reference to the US baseline – as a case study to conduct a Foresight exercise to build scenarios for the future of business schools. We indicated that these scenarios could in fact be adapted to other countries and regions of the world. But we also indicated that our analysis suggested that Europe might be on the verge of becoming a credible challenger to the current dominance of the US in the field of management education and research. In the last part of Chapter 5, we further suggested that a dual strategy combining an active "catching up" strategy on the one hand, plus a dedicated "differentiating" strategy on the other, could be the best way for Europe to compete in the international arena of business schools.

As Europeans, we take the liberty in this chapter to go one step further. We feel that there is a strong need for European policy makers to open their eyes on the issue of management education. We send them the following messages and recommendations. (Along the way, the dual strategy which we recommend to the EU in management education and research is developed and discussed).

1   Management Education is an extremely important matter for the competitiveness of firms and more generally of organizations – public or private, for-profit or non-profit- operating in Europe and thus for the competitiveness of the European economy.

2   The current situation of management education and research in Europe is that of a fragmented juxtaposition of national systems caught in a race to follow the dominant US model of business schools, mainly through imports and imitation. Most of the European universities are

simply unable to compete in that race and may actually be falling behind. Some others are engaged in an impressive effort to compete, sometimes with some success.

3   As a result of this "catching up" strategy, a limited number of European business schools may progressively gain some visibility and recognition internationally. This is already the case, at least to a certain extent. Yet, quite paradoxically, such a strategy is in fact likely to contribute to reinforce the leadership of the US model of management education. Indeed, playing the game by the rules imposed (both directly and indirectly) by the dominant player, but with significantly fewer resources than the leader, is likely to help the dominant player remain dominant.

4   Some of the traits of the US model of management education are worth importing, obviously with some form of adaptation along the way. Others traits are very specific to the US context. For these, Europe ought to leverage its own specificities. More specifically, Table 6.1 summarizes what we suggest should be retained / not retained from the US model. The discussion of the items displayed in the table will lead us to present and clarify what we call the dual strategy which we recommend for European management to stand up: a combination of "catching up" and "differentiating."

Table 6.1   For a dual strategy in management education in the EU

What to retain from the US model	Which European specificities to leverage
–Job market for business faculty across the EU –Reducing the entry barriers for non nationals –University Governance: --autonomy and initiative –Business model (form & structure of revenues): --including fees and donations	–Leverage social sciences and humanities –Conduct systemic studies of complexity to produce holistic knowledge as well; teach more transverse managerial issues dealt with in their full interfunctional complexity –Study management in all types of organizations, including the public sector and the non-profit – non-governmental organizations –Leverage the intercultural variety of the EU –Promote other epistemic postures as well as qualitative, in-depth case study research, e.g. in-company clinical research –Leverage public sector involvement in Education: --combine market logic with public involvement

5   The EU needs a "Bologna for professors," i.e. a "Bologna agreement"[1] to promote mobility for university professors across Europe. More specifically, the business schools throughout Europe need a job market for business faculty across the EU. Europe needs something as efficient as the US job market for business faculty. This is a clear factor of dynamism of Business education and research in the US.

We urge the EU Commission to remove entry barriers for non-nationals who apply for business faculty positions. We also suggest addressing the difficult issue of tenure systems and compatibility of retirement plans as they widely differ across member states (see Chap 1).

Yet, the most important pre-requisite for the creation of a job market for business faculty in Europe is to harmonize PhD's and the conditions of eligibility for faculty positions in business schools and universities. (The current trend to favoring joint PhDs between universities goes in the right direction but will not be enough to fully address the issue).

Creating a job market for university professors is an immense task. But we believe that the European tradition of public involvement in university matters may in this instance prove to be a good lever, as paradoxical as it may sound. In a context of public universities often seen as bureaucratic, the Bologna agreement was implemented very quickly, we argue, because once the agreement was reached between governments and the EU Commission, then change could be driven centrally and deployed at record speed. We argue that a similar effect could operate on the initiative we recommend for a "Bologna for Professors."

6   Governance of most EU universities needs more autonomy. Again the US mode of governance for academic institutions is worth studying. Three major issues are at stake:

autonomy to manage resources locally: operating budget, investments, and above all, human resources and their career paths.

This would prove more efficient than that which prevails today in several countries where a ministry is trying to manage several dozen universities from the center. We insist that more autonomy to run the resources does not mean privatization.

autonomy to select students. This would be a good way to improve the control of student motivation and capacity to complete the studies they are about to start.

autonomy to set up fees and tuition locally, possibly within predefined limits.

These are issues for universities at large, not just business schools. Nevertheless, as BSchools often generate revenues in a context of scarce resources, the overall context of governance and funding in which they operate may make a significant difference.

As an example, when competition among business schools is fierce to attract and recruit the best available talents from the international job market, it is difficult for a BSchool dean to compete if tight administrative national rules constrain the offers too much. The same applies if university rules impose too high an internal tax on the revenues generated from market activities such as Executive Education. With the best intentions, e.g. imposing an "overhead tax" in the name of solidarity with other academic disciplines which have no or limited market opportunity, or deciding on a single pay structure for faculty across the university departments to ensure equitable treatment through uniformity, university governance may in fact severely handicap their business school. Management education and research may bring external revenues but do operate in a very competitive arena, thus requiring a specific treatment within the university system, and in our opinion, some form of autonomy as well.

Both the autonomy of universities in managing their resources and the autonomy of business schools within universities are the responsibility of national governments and related stakeholders. This is a prerequisite for any significant progress in the future.

7   The business model of management education and research is another area where the US model may be worth imitating. The business model is summarized in section 1 of Chapter 5.

A sensitive topic in Europe is the fee level for undergraduate studies. Europeans have been used to free education, even at university level. Concretely this led to yearly fees of a few hundred euros, while the cost per student in universities is of the order of 8,000 to 12,000 € according to disciplines, institutions or countries. Yet, recent years have seen a trend in Europe to raise the fee (4,500 Euros in the UK, 1,000 in Germany, 600 in Portugal, etc.). It may be politically and socially difficult to align the fee in EU universities to the level of fees and tuitions prevailing in the US but this matter is of importance to make sure that business schools can compete on comparable grounds. Obviously, any significant fee increase should be done with the provision of setting up scholarships for students from economically disadvantaged families as well as a system of bank loans to help cover the costs.

A second interesting feature of the business model of US business schools has to do with donations. This is a cultural trait of the American culture which Europe does not have. Yet, we urge business schools to reconsider their targeting when they set up Foundations to collect donations. Targeting companies is fine in the short run as this is where some money can be made available, but we suggest initiating the process of asking individuals, in most instances alumni, for donations as well. The fiscal systems of most EU member states already offer significant compensation for generous donors. This means that the only real obstacle is the lack of a tradition of donating. Although changing behavior and culture on such matters will take decades, action should start immediately to trigger the process of change.

In any case, both Industry and the public sector have a key role to play to make sure that EU business schools are funded well enough to be in a position to compete with their US peers, if not on an equal footing, at least on similar grounds. This will require a massive effort.

8   We argue that a relevant strategy for Europe would be a dual strategy combining a "catching up" mode with a "differentiating" strategy.

This means playing the competitive game of management education and research by the rules which the leading players established over the last 50 years (after the Foundation report of 1959). Playing that game means adopting a "catching up" strategy. But it also means calling upon some of the most interesting specificities and assets available in Europe to differentiate from the dominant US leaders.

More concretely, this means conducting mainstream research as well as pursuing differentiated strands of work with non-purely positivist and overly quantitative methodologies. This means teaching the usual functional knowledge produced by sub-disciplines in the departments typically found in business schools, but it also means teaching more transverse contents, adopting a holistic view of managerial problems as well. This means covering business studies, but also managerial issues in other organizations which are important and lively in Europe (the public sector or non-profit organizations). In addition, as discussed in Section 3 of Chapter 5, the differentiation part of the strategy will bear fruits if it is capable of attracting Brics and similar countries interested in diversifying their source of management knowledge. In this sense, entering alliances with such countries, especially the Brics, including to help them "blend and cross-sell," is thus of strategic importance for EU BSchools.

This dual strategy is not easy to design and implement. This is what the next items clarify and discuss.

9   We claim that Europe has a long tradition of **social science and humanities** which may be called upon to address management issues from a different, complementary angle. This does not mean that we ignore the quality of social sciences in North America, nor some of the past attempts to draw from that body of literature in business studies. However, we mean to point out that there are strong biases in the way the US research in management is allocating its resources and energy today. It belongs to Europe to mobilize its resources and talents in different though complementary ways, in order to bring a specific, differentiated contribution to management research.

10   Similarly, we argue that Europe has a tradition of **systemic thinking** which may help address holistic managerial issues across the traditional functional silos of management science. Various business schools' deans have repeatedly expressed concerns about the lines of divide which separate departments and sub-disciplines in business studies. Yet, much remains to be done in management research and teaching to adopt a broader view of management issues. Alexis de Tocqueville had pointed out the pragmatism, action-oriented behaviour, practical and common sense orientation of the culture emerging in North America at the time of his visits there. Strangely enough, although these are still distinctive traits of the American culture, the two subsequent centuries have seen an additional element coming in: America now believes in specialists. This can be seen in many aspects of US universities. Paradoxically, while students are asked to gain credits from departments and schools other than those where they major – and they indeed do so to a large extent -, the underlying rationale of the academic legitimacy in the US is expertise through specialization. Excellence would seem to equate with narrow bandwidth, but really deep. We would not argue that academia does not require specialization. This is what science supposedly demands. Yet, from our European perspective, we feel that there is still, rooted deep in Europe's culture, the idea that knowledge is also holistic. We feel that departmental or functional bits of knowledge in isolation are like orphans looking for the overall picture, where only a broader form of integrated knowledge can help sort things out and give additional usable meaning. This is typically why we argue that today's management curricula, divided up into functional silos mirroring the departmental organizations of

business schools, and of the research community as a matter of fact, is at fault. As in the old Indian tale of the blind men facing an elephant without being aware of it, we argue that a global systemic understanding of the whole beast is as important as, if not more important at times than, the detailed reports about the leg, the tail or the trunk of the animal – not knowing what the whole thing exactly is. Business studies badly need to complement the analytical partial views with a more global, transverse, integrated perspective. Here again, Europe may usefully contribute.

11   Another way for Europe to differentiate while addressing important managerial issues that have been largely neglected so far by business studies is to deal with **public** bodies and **non-profit organizations**. (In this context, Howard Thomas suggests that "management" is a broader and thus better wording than "business studies"). There is a considerable amount of work to be done in management, both in research and education, on the way to modernizing the public sector and even more so on non-profit organizations which are still seen as some form of alien in the world of business studies. Europe has a strong public sector and has neither distrust nor disdain for it. There is thus a real opportunity in Europe to study public organizations from a managerial standpoint, complementary to the tradition of political science. Similarly, non-profit organizations are a domain of their own, representing a third pole away from the usual public / private tension. This is somehow analog to strategic alliances which may be studied either as a hybrid form between markets and hierarchies or as a third modality of their own: non-profit organizations may be viewed as a hybrid between the public and private sectors, or as a third pole of their own. In any case, these alien organizations are worth investigating as they represent a significant share of social and even economic activities in many countries.

12   Europe has inherited a **variety of cultures and languages** from its long history. In this context, this is an asset which renders management education in Europe attractive to both EU and non-EU students and executives. William Parrot from AACSB captured this idea very clearly: "The ability of European MBAs to deal with business across a variety of cultural contexts adds significant value." This is thus a natural way for EU BSchools to build some additional form of differentiation.

13   A more fundamental question is that of positivism as the US dominant epistemic stance in mainstream management research. In this epistemology, business research mimics hard science where general rules have to be "discovered" through a process of observation, description, hypothesis generation and empirical "validation" via statistical samples

and rigorous testing. This may be seen as the result of the influence of economics on the field, away from anecdotal research – the infamous nickname used today to label research that does not comply with the dominant positivist view. In contrast, we argue that **clinical research** may also contribute to producing useful and relevant knowledge through more qualitative case study methods, adopting a more **constructivist** or interpretativist stance. Again, we are fully aware of the qualitative research conducted in the US using such approaches – in many instances this work is quite remarkable – we simply want to stress that this way of conducting research may be in excellent fit with some of the European research tradition and could be a powerful way of complementing the US production of knowledge in management, in turn helping to differentiate the corresponding contributions from Europe.

This strategy would clearly reinforce the position of Europe as a second supplier of management knowledge worldwide, offering an alternate source of management education and research to business schools around the globe. Yet, as JC Spender points out in his discussion of the business schools in the US, such a strategy clearly leads to questioning the "overly rational and quantitative" approach of management which prevails in North American business schools. In other words, this form of differentiation may mean not only complementing but also fundamentally challenging the current dominant US business school model.

As discussed earlier, however, this path is risky, as the established rules in the worldwide competition of management research may not easily cope with non-mainstream ways of producing knowledge: Again, what is an established piece of knowledge here, if not knowledge approved by the bandwagon through their review process? What is mainstream, if not what the bandwagon is telling you it is? This is why we suggest that this "differentiating" strategy should build upon the platform provided by the "catching up" strategy which, we believe, is the current strategy implemented in first league EU BSchools. This combined or dual strategy will help secure a legitimized position to challenge the dominant player both on its own ground (playing by its rules) and from a different chess board (via differentiation).

We recognize that this dual stance is not easy to hold, as it will introduce a permanent, structural epistemic debate within the European management research community itself. All things considered, we feel that such a debate, although possibly tense at times, should be manageable among Europeans as variety is already part of what the EU is made of. The major risk of this strategy would be that those European management researchers trained in the US and keen to excel in positivist, quantitative research may *de facto* ally with their North American peers. To a certain extent, this is what is already happening but, again, we believe that this risk, if properly identified and monitored, may be managed. The key point of this strategy is in fact to obtain benevolence and understanding on the part of these researchers to allow enough space for the other forms of management research which we recommend is promoted in Europe.

14   All in all, the dual strategy which we recommend requires a **balanced dynamic portfolio over time**:

Firstly, the EU business schools need the publications in A journals right away to gain visibility. For that, they thus need to invest in mainstream research, with strong US ties. This corresponds to the "catching up" part of the strategy. It will help EU business schools gain visibility, credibility and legitimacy in the international arena. Very concretely, this will help going up the ladder of international rankings from poor (or fair) to good. This will require time, dedication and resources. This is in most part underway for the first league EU institutions. But this will not be enough.

Secondly, in fact at the same time, EU business schools also need to blend some of the specific assets which are accessible to them: the richness of intellectual academic work in humanities and social sciences in European universities, some of the research tradition in cybernetics, system analysis and the science of complexity, the philosophical tradition in epistemology to clarify what exactly are management researchers doing when they try to create knowledge about how companies emerge, get organized, build cultures and strategies, enter alliances or acquire other firms, live and die. This will re-open a fertile research agenda which, quite sadly, we feel has been *de facto* abandoned over the last 25 years in the US – and thus elsewhere, given the US decisive influence in the field.

Thirdly, EU business schools need to ensure that their "catching up" stars, especially those with strong US links, will not condemn the second part of the strategy, in the name of their research ideology, to put it simply. This means repeated efforts to explain why the dual strategy makes sense, why there is a window of opportunity for European business schools to complement the US seam of knowledge production in management and thus an opportunity for differentiation in the world arena of management education and research. At the same time, the "softer" researchers should be invited to respect and recognize their colleagues who fight for the same business school flag, but in playing a slightly different game, following the dominant rules.

Fourthly, and as importantly, this strategy means that EU business schools need to clarify how they can capture the dual strategy into the curricula of the various programs offered. Here also, the strategy is systemic and needs to be deployed for the entire portfolio in an integrated, consistent way. If European management is to stand up, it means that the program contents at undergraduate or graduate level, for MBAs and for Executive education, are consistent with the research claims.

15   If nothing is done, while leading EU business schools are doing their best to compete internationally with limited resources, Europe runs the risk of a long-lasting North American domination in management education and research, a field of utmost importance for the EU economy. Our hope is that EU key players will listen to our call, think about it and act. Higher education in Europe combines the public and private sectors. Europe has a wide continuum from large MNCs operating worldwide, to local SMEs. This is an asset. Yet, one problem is that governments face significant funding problems for the university system as a whole and thus tend to count on Industry to complement business schools' funding. And Industry is not so keen on paying for what they view as the governments' responsibility. A second problem is that industrial leaders tend to have limited knowledge of, if not explicit reservations about, research activities in management in general and in business schools in particular. They tend to expect BSchools to focus on quality teaching to provide well-trained young talent to Industry plus relevant executive education programs for their managers. These are two serious problems. Yet, we believe that public and private leaders can join forces and interact with the stakeholders of the emerging EU system of management education and research.

It is matter of awareness, to which this book aims at contributing, and political will.

The business of business schools is doing fine in North America. It is up to EU leaders and stakeholders to act in order for European Management to stand up. The EU would benefit from such a move; other regions of the world, in particular the Brics, as well; North America would also gain from a refreshing competition from Europe. And management knowledge and practice would also benefit from a wider array of perspectives, ideas, methodological approaches, concepts and theories, leading to enriched forms and contents of curricula in business schools.

Part II

Current Situation and Trends in Management Education in Various Countries and Regions

7
U.K. Business Schools

Howard Thomas

Introduction and background

Business schools have gained strong recognition in the higher education landscape over the last one hundred years. Indeed, over the last twenty to thirty years, business schools and, particularly, M.B.A. programs have been among the fastest-growing segments in higher education worldwide. Despite the fact that earlier European traditions of training for commerce (e.g. the German Cameralist school and the French Grande Ecole and Ecole Superieure systems) provided the catalyst for the development of leading US business schools such as Harvard and Wharton, the US business school has become the dominant, global model for management education and gained fast institutional standardization with the establishment of the A.A.C.S.B. (Association to Advance Collegiate Schools in Business) International in 1916.

In the UK, for example, there was little, if any, development of business schools following the foundation of schools of commerce at the universities of Birmingham (1902) and Manchester (1904). The post-World War II recommendation of the British Institute of Management (B.I.M., founded in 1947) that business schools should be created was not implemented, but independent, private executive education institutions were set up to provide leadership and management training at Henley Management College in 1945 and Ashridge Management College in 1957 as a result of their championing by the B.I.M. and industrialists. It was only in the 1960s that the business school model was accepted, after the Franks Commission report, which endorsed the findings of the Ford and Carnegie Foundation reports on management education in the US in 1957, advocating the movement of business schools from trade schools (largely professionally oriented) to a more research- and discipline-based academic tradition. Franks integrated many strands in the UK policy debate, including interventions from the National Economic Development Office and the UK Robbins report on UK higher education, which both promoted the idea of one or two elite schools similar to Harvard and M.I.T., and stressed the importance of business schools to the development of the UK economy. In this vein, UK business schools were seen as instrumental in the development of well-trained managers, who would become the much-needed leaders and "captains of industry" cherished by leading executives and industrialists. Thus, London Business School and Manchester Business School were born in the mid-1960s with elite full-time M.B.A. programs similar to the two-year, full-time, US-based model. Subsequently, newer business schools, such as Cambridge (Judge), City (Cass), Cranfield, Henley, Lancaster, Nottingham, Oxford (Said) and Warwick (W.B.S.) have developed M.B.A. programs of an increasingly diverse character but, primarily of a one-year, full-time duration.

Currently, in the UK, according to the Association of Business Schools (A.B.S.), there are now over 100 M.B.A. programs offered by over 100 business schools (there are, in fact, 102 UK business schools which are now members of A.B.S. (see Table 7.1).

They offer a wide range of different models and approaches to business education. The London Business School and, to some extent, the Said Business School at Oxford model themselves closely on the elite US model (e.g. Harvard, M.I.T., etc.). Stand-alone, private schools, such as Ashridge and Henley, have a professional focus on practically-oriented programs and research (such as M.B.A.s and executive programs). Other professional schools, including former polytechnics such as Oxford Brookes, Kingston and Surrey, place great emphasis on pedagogy and high teaching quality in undergraduate, graduate and post-experience programs. Newer universities, such as Bath, Lancaster and Warwick, on the other hand, combine strong undergraduate and graduate programs with an emphasis on grounded, disciplinary-oriented, social science-based research. The Open University, Henley and Warwick have pioneered distance learning M.B.A.s and management programs, whereas schools such as Leicester, with its focus on a critical school of management, stress the linkages between management, the humanities and social science research. The Tanaka School at Imperial College has adopted a technology and science-based focus for its school, stressing research on technology-based management. And, the Cass School at City University has an emphasis on finance and insurance, reflecting its close proximity to the City of London. The evidence, therefore,

Table 7.1   List of UK business schools

A	Aberdeen Business School – The Robert Gordon University
	Ashcroft International Business School Ashridge
	Aston Business School of Management and Business – The University of Wales, Aberystwyth
	University of Aberdeen Business School
B	Bolton Business School – The University of Bolton
	Bournemouth University, The Business School
	Bradford University School of Management
	Bristol Business School – University of West of England
	Buckinghamshire Business School
	Business, Computing & Information Management – London South Bank University
	Faculty of Business, University of Brighton
	University of Bath, School of Management
	University of Birmingham – Birmingham Business School
	University of Bristol, Department of Management
	The School for Business and Regional Development, University of Wales, Bangor
	University of Bedfordshire Business School
C	Cardiff Business School
	Cardiff School of Management, University of Wales Institute, Cardiff
	Cass Business School, City of London Coventry Business School
	Cranfield School of Management
	University of Cambridge, Judge Business School
	University of Central England Business School
D	Durham Business School
	The Derbyshire Business School
	University of Abertay Dundee – Dundee Business School
E	Department of Business, Management and Leisure, Edge Hill University
	ESCP-EAP European School of Management, London European Business School, London
	The East London Business School
	The University of Edinburgh Management School
	University of East Anglia, School of Management
	School of Business and Economics – University of Exeter
G	Glasgow Caledonian University – Caledonian Business School
	University of Glamorgan Business School
	University of Glasgow – The School of Business and Management
	University of Gloucestershire Business School
	University of Greenwich – Business Faculty

Continued

Table 7.1   Continued

H	Henley Management College
	Huddersfield University Business School
	University of Hertfordshire Business School
	University of Hull Business School
	Business, and Management – Liverpool Hope University
I	Imperial College London, Tanaka Business School
K	Kent Business School
	Kingston Business School
	The Department of Management, Keele University
L	Lancashire Business School
	Lancaster University Management School
	Leeds Business School
	Leicester Business School – De Montfort University
	Leicester University Management Centre
	Lincoln Business School – University of Lincoln
	London Business School London Metropolitan University – Department of Business and Service Sector Management
	Loughborough University Business School The School of Management – Liverpool John Moores University
	The University of Liverpool Management School University of Leeds,
	Leeds University Business School
M	Manchester Business School
	Manchester Metropolitan University Business School
	MMUCheshire @ Crewe and Alsager
	Middlesex University Business School
N	Napier University Business School
	Newcastle Business School – University of Northumbria
	Northampton Business School – University College Northampton
	Nottingham Business School – Nottingham Trent University Nottingham
	University Business School University of Newcastle upon Tyne Business School
O	Open University Business School
	University of Oxford, Said Business School
	Business School – Oxford Brookes University
P	Paisley Business School – University of Paisley
	Portsmouth Business School
	The Plymouth Business School
Q	Queens School of Management, Queens University, Belfast
R	Reading University Business School
	Royal Agricultural College – School of Business

Continued

Table 7.1   Continued

	Royal Holloway, University of London – School of Management
	The School of Business and Social Sciences – Roehampton University
S	School of Management – Southampton University
	School of Management at the University of Surrey
	Sheffield Hallam University – School of Business and Finance
	Southampton Business School – Southampton Solent University
	Staffordshire University Business School
	Strathclyde Graduate Business School University of Sheffield – Management School
	University of St. Andrews – School of Management
	University of Stirling – Faculty of Management
	University of Sunderland Business School
	University of Salford, The Management School
	Swansea Business School
T	Teesside Business School
	Thames Valley University – Business School
U	University of Ulster – Faculty of Business and Management
W	University of Wales Newport – Newport Business School
	University of Westminster – Westminster Business School
	Warwick Business School
	Wolverhampton Business School
Y	Department of Management Studies, University of York

Source: A.B.S.

suggests greater diversity, entrepreneurialism and niche behaviour in the UK business school marketplace. As a result, the UK market demonstrates that a range of strategic types and styles thrive in the market, including quasi-US-model schools, professionally-oriented schools, social science-based schools, specialist schools with niches in marketing, finance, etc. and humanities/social science-based schools.

This chapter builds on this background and reviews the UK evidence on the funding sources, supply and demand patterns for business school education, the issues facing management education, including the regulatory environment, and the challenges and future strategies facing business school administrators.

Funding and supply and demand problems in the U.K.

By way of introduction for readers not familiar with the UK higher education environment, a typical student enters university at c.17–18 years of age (after twelve years of formal education) and completes an undergraduate degree in business (or any other subject) after three years. He/she may then enter postgraduate education and complete a specialist or research master's degree in a further one-year period. Generally, doctoral education in business requires at least three years after a first degree or master's degree. Professional postgraduate education, such as an M.B.A., is taken four to five years after undergraduate education, following the acquisition of relevant managerial experience in business or industry.

Funding

As noted by The Economist ("The Brains Business", September 2005), UK universities which are virtually all state-supported and regulated,[1] were subjected to a major shake-up in their environment during the reign of Prime Minister Margaret Thatcher in the early 1980s. She instituted a regime which sought to expand the availability of higher education for all qualified people but, simultaneously, neglected to provide adequate resources for this expansion. According to The Economist, the main problem has been the "relentless financial squeeze" which has led to a clear erosion of quality. They also note that, in the 1990s, expenditure per student fell by a third and the student-teacher ratio doubled from 9:1 to 18:1. In addition, as has been clear from the recent strike and work-to-rule of university teachers in the UK, academic salaries have become increasingly less competitive with a fall of c.2 percent per annum in real terms over the last two decades. The consequences of the continued inadequate funding and under-investment in universities are the increasing use of part-time faculty, the relative unattractiveness of academic careers, an increase in government micro-management and bureaucratisation in their university relationships, and strong evidence of financial failure in universities (with half of the over 100 universities facing financial deficits). Even world-class universities such as Oxford are not immune to this trend. The Economist reports that, in 2005, Oxford is running an operational deficit of £20m per year, and an accumulated deficit on teaching and research activities of £95.

Clearly, as The Economist notes, the UK universities "bargain with the state has turned out to be a pact with the devil." In essence, UK universities have been squeezed of funds, have had to survive with less resources, despite the recent advent of "top-up" fees for undergraduate courses of £3,000 per year (a figure much below the true economic cost of undergraduate education), and have increasingly been held accountable for their quality, performance and productivity to the detriment of their overall intellectual activity and quality. For example, the recent Shanghai Jiao Tong University survey of the world's top universities has only two U.K. universities in the top 20 (Cambridge at No. 3 and Oxford at No. 8 – and very few in the top 100), which is dominated by US universities which exhibit a much wider, more market-oriented set of funding and business models.

It is important to pose the question of how this overall funding regime, in essence with the UK government as the basic funding and regulatory body for the sector, has affected the growth and development of the UK business school sector which, as noted earlier, has over 100 legitimate UK-based competitors.

As noted by both A.B.S. (the Association of Business Schools) and the Council for Industry and Higher Education (C.I.H.E.), it is clear that the greater majority of UK business schools receive some level of grant financial support for teaching and research activities, primarily in the area of undergraduate and postgraduate programs. However, no business school relies on that government provision as the sole source of revenue and, typically, schools enhance their income by charging premium, market-based fees for certain postgraduate programs (e.g. M.B.A. programs or specialist Masters programs in finance) and, for their executive education services and offerings. Gradually, therefore, over time most business schools have adopted business models which have a strong commercial orientation, in order to generate the operating surpluses necessary to fund faculty, research and a whole host of facility and technology improvements. The differences between the funding models of purely private business schools (such as Ashridge and Henley) and the university-based business schools (such as London, Oxford, Cambridge, Warwick and Lancaster), therefore, narrowed and converged. It has also been the case with the university-based schools that their positive financial performance has attracted the attention of their university administrators and has resulted in many universities using their business schools as "cash cows" to fund other programs and activities on campus.

However, the main difference in the funding models of the UK business schools and their US counterparts lies in the successful fund-raising activities of the latter, which have allowed them to tap very carefully into the "culture of giving" in North America. In essence, the best US business schools (virtually all private) have raised vast sums of money and have "moved mountains" in building strong financial bases for business schools, thus allowing them to construct the best facilities, attract the best faculty and develop the most innovative teaching and research programs. In fact, of the top 20 business schools over the last six years of the Financial Times global business school rankings (see Table 7.2), 17 are US based and only three (Insead, I.M.D. and London Business School) are

Table 7.2 F.T. Rankings of M.B.A. programs

Business Schools	Governance	2005	2004	2003	2002	2001	2000	1999	Average ranking
Harvard Business School (US)	Private	1	2	2	2	2	1	1	2
Pennsylvania/Wharton (US)	Private	1	1	1	1	1	2	4	2
Columbia Business School (US)	Private	3	3	3	3	5	5	2	3
Stanford Graduate School (US)	Private	4	7	4	4	3	3	3	4
Chicago GSB (US)	Private	6	4	5	5	4	6	6	5
INSEAD (EU)	Private	8	4	6	6	7	9	11	7
London Business School (EU)	Private/Public	5	4	7	9	8	8	8	7
MIT/Sloan (US)	Private	13	9	10	7	6	4	5	8
Northwestern/Kellogg (US)	Private	11	11	9	10	9	7	7	9
NYU/Stern (US)	Private	9	8	8	8	10	13	17	10
Dartmouth/Amos Tuck (US)	Private	7	10	11	11	13	15	9	11
IMD (EU)	Private	13	12	13	14	11	11	13	12
Yale/SOM (US)	Private	9	13	12	12	20	18	20	15
Duke Fuqua (US)	Private	18	20	15	19	18	17	15	17

European – and it can be argued that all three European schools are, essentially, privately-funded.

The leading UK schools have recognised this fact and are actively developing fund-raising programs but have some considerable distance to make up in order to emulate their US counterparts.

Supply and demand patterns

It is important to recognise that UK business schools have a product line and portfolio that can encompass a broad range of programs. These include undergraduate programs, specialist and research Masters programs, M.B.A. programs, doctoral and research programs, executive programs and multiple modes of delivery from on-campus to distance learning activity. However, not all schools have a broad product line. Typically, the university-based schools are more likely to offer a broad product line but the private schools, such as Henley and Ashridge, generally focus more closely on professional programs such as the M.B.A. and executive education, which allows market-based tuition fees to be charged.

In demand terms, over the last twenty years, business and management education has been a major growth area in higher education in the UK (up by nearly one-third over the last ten years).

C.I.H.E. quoted figures from H.E.S.A. and A.B.S. for the years 2003–04 showing that 221,664 F.T.E. (full-time equivalent) students enrolled for business and management education courses in higher education. In essence, 13.6 percent of all higher education students were in the business and management area in 2003–2004.

Of the 221,664 business and management students in 2003–04, there were 140,935 at the first degree level, 27,555 students at the sub-degree level (doing either foundation degrees or courses such as the Higher National Diploma) and 49,649 postgraduate students (representing 21.6 percent of the total postgraduate population in higher education). It is important to note that a significant and increasing proportion of these students come from overseas, making the UK second only to the USA in attracting students from overseas (Source: The Economist, 21st September, 2005). In specific terms, the overseas students' distribution for 2003-04 comprised 12,656 EU students and 43,287 from the rest of the world, with China alone sending 19,012 students to the UK.

C.I.H.E. also provided clear evidence that the full-time M.B.A. market has grown by over 50 percent over the last ten years, with an 86 percent increase in M.B.A. students from overseas. And, part-time and distance learning variants of the M.B.A. have grown by c.20 percent and 30 percent over the same period.

In summary, therefore, the demand pattern for business and management education in the UK is very strong and the supply of business schools is such that there are well over 100 providers supported by public money, alongside private schools such as Ashridge, Buckingham and Henley. In addition, a range of foreign schools such as ESCP-EAP from France and Chicago from the US offer niche programs, such as Executive Education in the UK marketplace. Further, there is also clear evidence from the Lambert Report on Business-University Collaboration in 2003 that business, the customer of management education, is generally satisfied with the quality of the graduates that they recruit from business schools and higher education.

Despite the evidence of the strong success pattern of UK business schools, nevertheless, there is a range of issues and challenges that need to be explored and solved over the next few years. We now turn to an examination of the more important issues and challenges.

Issues and challenges facing management education in the U.K.

The main issues and challenges explored in this section are:

The regulatory environment and the impact of regulation

Faculty recruitment, development and retention

The role of research and knowledge development

The effects of globalisation and competition

The positioning of business schools

Regulation and its impact

What is abundantly clear from any analysis of the UK political environment is the reduction in real terms of government and public funding for higher education. Yet, it is equally clear that the amount, and extent, of involvement of the government in regulation of higher education is ever increasing. The determination and political drive of governments to demonstrate improvements in the productivity of higher education has led to a strong focus on the measurement and assessment of academic productivity by agencies such as H.E.F.C.E. (the Higher Education Funding Council for England), Q.A.A. (the Quality Assurance Agency), R.A.E. (the Research Assessment Exercise) and O.F.F.A. (the Office of Fair Access).

H.E.F.C.E., like parallel agencies in Scotland, provides both the funding stream to universities and a range of policy guidelines for their implementation. In addition, it audits annually the financial plans and accounts of those universities in order to monitor, control and provide feedback on financial performance. It also creates competitive initiatives for new developments in higher education and tries to encourage universities to embrace new strategic directions.

Q.A.A., the Quality Assurance Agency, monitors and assesses the pedagogical framework of each university. Through peer site visits and study reports, it examines curricula and teaching quality for every department in the university (including business schools). It provides an output score, which judges the schools' teaching quality as excellent, very good, etc. and provides a comparative measure of quality.

R.A.E., the Research Assessment Exercise, is administered by H.E.F.C.E. to provide a peer-based assessment of research quality. Faculty research publications in every area are assessed by a panel of peers and assessments of excellence (on a scale of excellent to poor) are provided as outputs. The last R.A.E., in 2001, created a ranking of business schools by research quality (5* is excellent, 5 is very good, etc.) as shown in Table 7.3. The next R.A.E. is scheduled for 2008 but with an amended rating scale and changes assessment criteria. The R.A.E. is very important for the research finances of universities in general, and business schools, because the higher the R.A.E. score, the greater the research funding awarded.

O.F.F.A. (the Office for Fair Access) was created recently, following the adoption of university top-up fees, to ensure that fair access to higher education is available to all strata of society. Thus, a balanced social class profile is a goal which each university, elite or not, must seek to achieve.

The invasive role and style of these regulatory agencies has led some critics to accuse the government of meddling with, and micromanaging, the university sector. Stable funding, less regulation and a more laissez-faire attitude, has been the clarion cry of those educationalists who would like to encourage an entrepreneurial and diverse landscape in higher education.

It should also be noted that business schools can also voluntarily engage in strategic and operational review of their programs by engaging accreditation agencies such as the US A.A.C.S.B. (Association to Advance Collegiate Schools of Business) International, the European EQUIS (European Quality Improvement Systems) administered by the European Foundation for Management Development and the UK A.M.B.A. (Association of M.B.A.s) for accreditation reviews. Such reviews generate useful critical feedback but, more importantly, attest to the international quality of programs and enable schools to build their brands in an increasingly global and competitive market.

Table 7.3 Analysis of UK schools (R.A.E., 2001)

5*	London Business School		
	Lancaster		
	Warwick		
5	Aston	Imperial	
	Bath	Leeds	
	Cambridge	Manchester	
	Cardiff	Nottingham	
	Cass	Oxford	
4	Birmingham	Heriott Watt	Royal Holloway
	Bradford	Hull	Sheffield
	Brunel	Keele	Southampton
	Cranfield	Loughborough	Stirling
	Edinburgh	Portsmouth	Strathclyde
	Exeter	Queen's Belfast	Surrey
3	Aberdeen	Hertfordshire	N/cle Northumbria
	Aberystwyth	Huddersfield	Nottingham Trent
	Bournemouth	Kent	Open University
	Brighton	Kingston	Plymouth
	Bristol	Leicester	Salford
	Caledonian	Lincoln	Sheffield Hallam
	De Montfort	Liverpool	South Bank
	Dundee	L'pool John Moores	Staffordshire
	Durham	London Metropolitan	Swansea
	East Anglia	Luton	Westminster
	Glamorgan	Manchester Metropolitan	
	Greenwich	Middlesex	Wolverhampton
2	Anglia Polytechnic	Northampton	
	Central England	Oxford Brooks	
	Coventry	Paisley	
	Derby	Queen Margaret, Edinburgh	
	East Derby	Southampton Institute	

Continued

Table 7.3   Continued

Unclassified		
	Buckinghamshire	Schiller International (U.S.)
	Dearne Valley	Suffolk College (U.S.)
	Henley	Sunderland
	Gloucestershire	Swansea
	Lancashire	Teesside
	Napier	Thames
	Ruffey Park	Univ. Wales, Newport
	Royal Agricultural School of Business	Univ. Wales, Cardiff

Faculty recruitment and retention

Recent reports (e.g. A.A.C.S.B. Doctoral Commission, A.B.S., 2005) point out clearly that recruiting top faculty is a strategic concern for UK business schools. A gradually aging faculty – with many top faculty set to retire over the next decade – and the lack of sufficient graduates from doctoral programs point to a big gap between the supply of, and demand for, quality business school faculty. The A.B.S. and C.I.H.E. point out (C.I.H.E., 2006) that, historically, UK schools have recruited up to half their faculty from non-traditional sources, i.e. from young managers, experienced business managers, etc., who have much less formal exposure to research training of the doctoral variety. In part, this shortage of doctorally trained faculty is because UK academic salaries have been declining relative to similar jobs elsewhere, and to those offered by competitive schools. In essence, academic careers in UK business schools are seen to be unattractive relative to either business careers or careers in US and Canadian business schools.

At the current time, UK business school academic salaries follow the schedule below:

Post	Range	Mode
Lecturers (Assistant Professor)	£25,000–£40,000	£33,000
Senior Lecturers/Readers (Associate Professors)	£40,000–£50,000	£45,000
Professors (Full Professors)	£55,000–£90,000	£65,000

Although these are suggestive ranges, schools are offered some flexibility to "sweeten the pot" slightly but salaries are strongly regulated (because of national union bargaining) and show little evidence of the use of performance-related pay, except perhaps for the more highly-rated UK business schools, which must compete in an international salary marketplace.

The role of research and knowledge development

Although, as noted earlier, business management education has grown rapidly and is now the largest single subject area in UK higher education, with c.14 percent of the students and 7 percent of the staff, research in the area has not progressed at a similar pace in quality terms. Some of this must be explained by the fact that business school faculty are often employed to man "teaching factories," not "research factories." C.I.H.E. (2006) notes that staff : student ratios in UK business and management in 2003/04 were reported as 26:1, compared with the average higher education sector ratio of 13:1. Such a huge imbalance means that business school faculty have to focus more on teaching and students to the obvious detriment of developing their research competences and research publication profiles.

Somewhat belatedly, this imbalance between teaching and research has been recognised by government and, more importantly, by the E.S.R.C. (the Economic and Social Research Council) in the UK This has led to the establishment, and funding to a current level of £20m, of A.I.M. (the Advanced Institute of Management) in 2001/02, with the goal of improving the quality and quantity of management research and of building research capability and capacity for management education. An important A.I.M. initiative has been the appointment of c.20-30 A.I.M. Fellows, who are drawn from the UK business school community but who are "bought out" from their current universities to focus entirely on management research. Fellows are encouraged to work as individuals and teams to build up research capability and knowledge transfer across all areas of management research. Not only have they generated good research output but they have disseminated this through seminars held across all regions of the UK. They have also stressed the need to balance rigor and relevance in management research so that the results of academically rigorous management research can be translated effectively and in simple terms to the wider management audience.

The effects of globalisation and competition

A.I.M. also stresses the need to build up the capacity for world-class management research in the UK. This is critical because the best UK business schools want to be regarded as both "national champions" and important players in the international business school marketplace. Globalization and the global economy are facts of life ("The World is Flat" according to Thomas Friedman) and, increasingly, business school students are drawn from all continents. Their careers require them to be global citizens, since they will work for multiple organisations and multi-national corporations over the time-span of their career profiles. This places strategic requirements on business schools that they are able to provide students with a flexible and culturally diverse program. Further, through such strategies as alliances with other major schools or the creation of additional campuses in other countries (e.g. Insead in Singapore, ESCP-EAP in European cities, Chicago in London, etc.), they can develop a range of potential international experiences during their degree curricula. However, for a UK business school to be regarded as a top international school, it must enhance its reputation by building top quality curricula and hiring the best faculty in order to attract high-quality students who regularly judge and compare league tables and rankings (such as the Financial Times) as strong evidence of the reputational quality and strength of a business school.

Business school positioning and funding

Building a strong international reputation and position requires a business school to have access to a strong resource pool. It is clear that governments, and universities themselves, are (and will continue to be) parsimonious in their provision of resources and, consequently, have allowed business schools to charge market-based fees for externally-oriented programs and executive education activities. However, there is increasing price pressure from competitor business schools and commercial education providers, so that the richness of the "cream" of the business school "cash cow" is being eroded somewhat. New initiatives and new programs can alleviate this competitive portfolio risk to some extent. However, the long-term solution must be to create an environment in which the business school is granted more entrepreneurial freedom in governance and program development, has enhanced ability to retain surpluses, and is encouraged to undertake and develop professional fund-raising programmes. While the UK lacks the North American corporate culture of giving, UK business schools must educate their alumni and friends to the pressing need for flexible funds to facilitate strategic investments in R.&D., faculty and facilities, in order to promote and enhance the quality of education. It should be argued that these investments are also critical in reputation and brand building activities, and absolutely essential to positioning the business school as a key player in the global marketplace.

Summary and conclusions

This review has surveyed the background of UK business schools, their funding, their demand and supply patterns and their current challenges. Over time, UK business must continually build upon the diversity of mission and values provided by the wide range of over 100 schools. As noted in the introduction, the U.K. already has examples of a wide range of schools, including elite schools such as London Business School; professionally oriented research schools such as Cranfield, Ashridge and Henley; social sciences oriented research schools such as Lancaster and Warwick; niche schools such as Cass (finance) and Imperial (technology); and humanities oriented schools such as Leicester. In time, we expect to see a cadre of five to ten schools (including London, Oxford (Said), Cambridge (Judge) and Warwick) being recognised as being significant international players with a parallel improvement in the quality of schools throughout the business school sector.

The following business schools appeared in the top 20 positions at least in one year of the period:

6 times:	UC Berkeley (Haas) and Virginia (Darden)	[Public schools]
5 times:	UCLA (Anderson)	[Public school]
4 times:	University of Michigan	[Public school]
3 times:	University of Western Ontario (Ivey) and University of North Carolina (Kenan-Flagler)	[Public schools]
2 times:	Emory and Cornell (Johnson).	[Private schools]

(*Source*: Antunes and Thomas, 2005)

References

A.A.C.S.B., Doctoral Commission Report, 2004, Tampa, Florida.

C.I.H.E. (Council for Industry on Higher Education) and A.B.S. (Association of Business Schools), UK National Forum for Employers and Business School Deans, February, 2006, Report, London.

Lambert Review on Business – University Collaboration, 2003, London.

The Economist, "The Brains Business", 10th September, 2005.

8
Management Education and Research in Germany

*Kathrin M. Möslein and Anne Sigismund Huff**

Historic roots and current status of German Betriebswirtschaftslehre**

> The system of education embodied in the German business schools (originally Handelshochschulen) has distinct historical origins and differs significantly from the system of higher education in business economics and management sciences that developed in other European countries.
>
> (Robert R. Locke, 1985)

The key term "Betriebswirtschaftslehre" describes the discipline of business administration and management – a discipline that did not emerge before the end of the 19th century. Usually the year 1898 is seen as the starting point of the discipline in German-speaking countries; this is the date when the first Handelshochschulen[1] were founded as educational institutions in Aachen, Leipzig, St. Gallen, and Vienna. Additional Handelshochschulen were founded after the turn of the century in Cologne and Frankfurt/Main (1901), Berlin (1906), Mannheim (1907), Munich (1910), Königsberg (1915) and Nuremberg (1919). These institutions were later extended to full universities (Cologne, Frankfurt, Mannheim), integrated in state universities (Aachen, Berlin, Munich, Nuremberg), or re-established as private institutions for higher management education (Leipzig).[2]

A few scholars, like Eugen Schmalenbach (1873–1955), Heinrich Nicklisch (1876–1946) and Fritz Schmidt (1882–1950), strongly influenced the field by establishing the first academic journals for the German-speaking research community.[3] These journals have remained the key publication outlets and are still the dominating journals in the German-speaking research community.

Similarly, today's dominating scholarly associations were all established in the early years of the discipline. The *Schmalenbach Gesellschaft (SG)* describes itself as a "Forum of Dialogue between Science and Business" – following the early commitment of Eugen Schmalenbach to develop business economics into an applied science by creating a close link between theory and practice.[4] SG represents both management researchers and executives. Its membership and executive board represents both, and each of its 25 committees is presided over by both a university teacher and a representative from industry. Currently SG counts about 1600 individual members and roughly 350 corporate members. Almost all of the 100 largest German companies are represented in the Schmalenbach Gesellschaft. It is a registered institution, non-profit oriented, and politically independent.

The *Association of University Professors of Management* (VHB – Verband der Hochschullehrer für Betriebswirtschaft e.V.) had its first meeting in 1914 and was formally founded in 1921 in Frankfurt/Main. It has more than 1500 members today and a clear focus on professors and research associates at research universities. This organization is generally considered to be the most influential academic association for higher management education and research in the German-speaking countries.

The development of Betriebswirtschaftslehre as an academic discipline has so far been a strong success story in Germany. Research and teaching staff in the academic system have more than tripled since the early 1980s. Even greater than the rise in employment, is the increase in student numbers. There were more than 160,000 students registered for Betriebswirtschaftslehre in 2004, compared to less than 40,000 in the early 1980s (see Table 8.1).

Table 8.1   Development of German Betriebswirtschaftslehre[5]

	Research and teaching staff	Professors	Students
1938		15	3,297
1953		26	11,223
1970		128	22,755
1982	2,193	646	36,016
1986	2,689	799	92,409
1995	5,402	1,170	139,209
2004	7,308	1,826	162,608

The rise in numbers depicted in Table 8.1 goes hand in hand with a process of diversification in terms of players involved with management education. As a next step we therefore look at the range of supply-side institutions, academic roles and other types of employment within these institutions, and the unique characteristics of the German academic system.

Higher education institutions in the German academic marketplace

we cannot understand the rise of the US business school century without recognizing the dominance of the German, or rather the Prussian, administrative models. Ironically Wharton's personal fortune was the direct result of Bismarck's currency reforms. Wharton had cornered the nickel market and made huge profits supplying this metal for the new German state's coinage (...) As a skilled metallurgist Wharton had learned to read and speak both German, the language of all scientific scholarship at that time, and French, the language of diplomacy and politics. (J.C. Spender, 2000)

To understand supply-side institutions of German Betriebswirtschaftslehre, we have to distinguish between educational actors that are in public or private ownership and indicate whether they are at university-level or at the level of a university of applied science. In the following discussion, we will look at these supply-side actors and mention exemplary German institutions that offer higher management education in each of these different institutional formats.

Currently more than 80 university institutions and more than 140 institutions at the level of university of applied sciences offer Betriebswirtschaftslehre as a study program. Out of the university-level institutions, less than 10 percent are privately held, while roughly 20 percent of the institutions of applied sciences are in private ownership. Table 8.2 provides examples of institutions in each category.

An important distinction between university-level institutions and universities of applied sciences is that only the former are allowed to enroll doctoral students, offer doctoral programs, award doctoral degrees, and also offer the "Habilitation" degree that is the traditional career path for future German professors. A strong research orientation and research-based study programs are part of their typical profile. Professors at university-level institutions on average have a higher salary and lower teaching load than their counterparts at the universities

Table 8.2　Selected institutions in the German academic marketplace

	University-level institutions (*"Wissenschaftliche Hochschulen"*)	**Universities of Applied Sciences** (*"Fachhochschulen"*)
Private ownership	EBS – European Business School Oestrich-Winkel HHL – Leipzig Graduate School of Management WHU – Wissenschaftl. Hochschule für Unternehmensführung Koblenz-Vallendar	Fachhochschule für Ökonomie und Management (FOM) Hamburg School of Business Administration (HSBA) Munich Business School (MBS)
Public ownership	Dept. of Business and Economics, FU Berlin (FU) Munich School of Management at Universität München (LMU) TUM Business School at Technische Universität München (TUM)	Fachhochschule München (FHM) Fachhochschule für Wirtschaft, Berlin (FHW) Hochschule Reutlingen – European School of Business (ESB)

of applied sciences. While 8 to 9 hours teaching per week during the semester is the common teaching load for university professors, 16 to 18 hours is a typical teaching load for a professor at a university of applied science.[6] As the German term "Universität" is restricted to university-level institutions, universities of applied science are not allowed to use the term and are called "Fachhochschulen" in German-speaking countries.

Both types of institutions traditionally offer a *Diplom* program in Betriebswirtschaftslehre, but only participants in programs at university-level institutions and outstanding candidates in programs at universities of applied sciences can qualify for writing a doctoral thesis. While this can be a disadvantage for those wanting to continue academic work, the corporate sector sometimes prefers graduates from Fachhochschulen as their study programs are seen to be closer to business reality and the entry-level salary of graduates from Fachhochschulen is usually lower than salaries for university graduates.

Traditionally there has been a very clear distinction between these two types of institutions and the professors working for them. This clear distinction, however, is now blurring. Most Fachhochschulen have been much faster in switching to study programs and outside communication in English than university programs; one advantage of the language switch is that it is has been possible to present themselves as "universities". Fachhochschulen have also been fast and effective in moving from the traditional German *Diplom* to the Bachelor and Master degree structure required by the Bologna process – a switch that allows them to award degrees that qualify for doctoral studies.

Traditionally there also has been a clear distinction between universities in public and private ownership. State universities were and still are the dominant players in the German-speaking world. They account for more than 80 percent of the institutions and for more than 90 percent of all business graduates. However, public universities are currently faced with the fact that private sector institutions dominate quality rankings. As private institutions raise tuition fees and state universities have not been allowed to do so (though it appears they will be required to do so in the future), it is the private sector institutions that usually offer much better service quality for students and by doing so allow for shorter study times as well as superior salary levels and higher satisfaction levels of their graduates – all important criteria in business school rankings.

On the other hand it is still hard for institutions in private ownership to retain faculty in competition with the public system that is typically seen as more prestigious by the public, has a higher reputation within the German academic community, and can offer life-time positions as civil servants often with a strong resource base that is guaranteed for a life-time (or at least long term), independent of performance measures.

Currently this traditional distinction between public and private institutions is also blurring. Some state universities are setting up separate private institutions parallel to their departments of business administration and economics, which serve as umbrella organizations for MBA and executive offerings. The Mannheim Business School gGmbH,[7] for instance, provides MBA programs and customized company programs on offer from the University of Mannheim's faculty for business studies. This non-profit organization has limited liability – the typical legal form chosen by institutions of higher-education in private ownership.

University-level institutions in private ownership[8]

The smallest category of university-level institutions in private ownership comes closest to the common international understanding of a Business School or Graduate School of Management. These private schools usually offer an MBA, part-time MBA and/or Executive programs. Many also offer the traditional German *Diplom* program in Betriebswirtschaftslehre. According to the Bologna process they now often offer Master of Science programs as well (and sometimes Bachelor programs for undergraduate students). As university-level institutions they typically offer the doctoral degree level as well as the Habilitation process for future professors. Table 8.2 shows the European Business School Oestrich-Winkel (EBS), the HHL – Leipzig Graduate School of Management, as well as the WHU – Wissenschaftl. Hochschule für Unternehmensführung Koblenz-Vallendar, as exemplary top-University-level institutions in private ownership.[9]

University-level institutions in state ownership are usually departments of larger multi-disciplinary universities. These university departments, however, are not the lowest operating unit within their universities. The organizational structure of a German university is based on the chair (Lehrstuhl).[10] Muller-Camen & Salzgeber (2005) have discussed in depth the specifics and consequences of the chair regime and point to its potentially "profound effect on change in academia" (p. 274). A chair holder in the German academic system is usually a civil servant with a tenured position. In addition to the chair holder, who concentrates responsibility and power, a Lehrstuhl usually supports one or more secretaries and some number of research and teaching associates. On average, chairs in Germany have about four or five junior or senior associates, but especially in technology-related fields of management research (like innovation management, information systems, production management, logistics or supply-chain management) teams of up to 50 researchers can be employed by one chair. In 1998, there were 633 chairs in the field of business administration and management in Germany (580), Austria (39) and Switzerland (14).[11] This kind of professorship exists only at university-level institutions. In addition, there are non-chaired professorships – usually members of a chair at university-level institutions or faculty at universities of applied sciences. As Muller-Camen & Salzgeber (2005) note, a chaired professor is guaranteed maximum freedom in teaching and research by the German constitution.[12]

> German professors still operate within a reputational-based work organization (Whitley 1984), which is controlled from within its own rank and which resembles the traditional British system before the advent of managerialism and the increasing marketization of higher education in the UK. Chairs have a wide discretion as to how they fulfil their job and have full responsibility for research and teaching. Management is absent and there is almost complete autonomy from external, non-collegiate influence. Financial certainty and complete job security are guaranteed by the tenure system.[13]

Universities of applied sciences in state ownership

Within the German higher education system universities of applied sciences (Fachhochschulen) are the largest and youngest organizations. Representing a new type of higher education institution, they were initiated via a Basic Declaration of Minister-Presidents of the Länder (States) in 1968:

> In establishing Fachhochschulen, the Länder responded to new challenges in the workplace – resulting from scientific and technical progress – and pertinent new training requirements. The Fachhochschulen in western Germany, most of which were established between 1969 and 1971, have their roots in the area's former engineering schools, academies and higher technical schools for design, social work and economics. The new Länder began establishing Fachhochschulen in 1991. From the outset, they profited from experience gained throughout the 20-year history (at the time) of Fachhochschulen in the old Länder.[14]

Complementary to research- and teaching-oriented universities, the new universites of applied sciences have a clear teaching orientation and provide educational programs that combine higher education qualifications and practically oriented training. Currently German universities of applied sciences offer *Diplom*, Bachelor and Master programs, train almost all of Germany's social workers and social educators, some two-thirds of all its engineers and about half of its students of business administration, management and computer science.[15] That means that of 21,750 business management graduates in Germany in 2004; 11,756 graduated from a German Fachhochschule.[16] This highlights the special importance of universities of applied sciences within the German higher education and employment system.

Universities of applied sciences in private ownership

Recently a number of private institutions at the level of Fachhochschule have emerged. The Hochschulrektorenkonferenz (HRK)[17] currently lists 46 of them. Table 8.2 shows the Fachhochschule für Ökonomie und Management (FOM), the Hamburg School of Business Administration (HSBA) and the Munich Business School (MBS) as selected examples. As for universities of applied sciences in general, the programs they offer usually lead to the degree of a Bachelor of Arts (not Bachelor of Science) and

Master of Arts or Master of Business Administration (not Master of Science) and do not automatically qualify for doctoral studies in Germany.

Today, the traditional negative image of universities of applied sciences, especially from the perspective of university professors, is more and more often challenged. In 2006 the CHE, a think tank funded by Bertelsmann Foundation,[18] teamed up with dapm, a professional association of leading German corporations that focuses its activities on HR development and marketing, and started the first ranking for Bachelor programs in business administration in Germany.[19] Fachhochschulen turned out to be the clear winners in this ranking that rated programs in terms of their expertise in teaching methods, people skills, practical orientation, and degree of internationality. The rankings also revealed that while universities of applied sciences have quickly moved towards offering Bachelor programs, most universities are still hesitant. Most of the 100 programs rated less than 20 percent are in university level institutions. This fits with the suggestion by some leading visonaires in university management who have postulated for some years that clear division of labour is desirable. The suggestion is that universities of applied sciences focus on bachelor education, while university-level institutions provide the post-graduate range of educational programs including Master of Science, MBA, part-time MBA and Executive programs. It goes without saying that this proposition is not easy to accept for policy makers and many professors at universities of applied sciences. The current tendency therefore is not to push for distinctive profiles within all four types of institution but to blur institutional boundaries even further, with representatives of the universities of applied sciences frequently claiming the right to award doctoral degrees in the future and some private institutions at the level of Fachhochschule applying and sometimes qualifying for being accredited as "wissenschaftliche Hochschule" (scientific university), in order to acquire university-level status and academic reputation.

Higher-education programs offered in the German marketplace

> To understand knowledge it is necessary to understand the institutions in which it is produced. (Gibbons, et al. 1994)

In the field of business administration and management the key programs offered in higher education in German-speaking countries are: the *"Diplom* program" in Betriebswirtschaftslehre, the Bachelor of Arts and Bachelor of Science, the Master of Arts and Master of Science, the MBA and part-time MBA, Doctoral programs, and Executive programs.

The Diplom program in Betriebswirtschaftslehre

Up to now, the *Diplom* program was chosen by the majority of students enrolled in Germany. It is subdivided into three or four semesters of undergraduate courses followed by graduate courses, which should be finished in four to five additional semesters. The emphasis of undergraduate courses is usually on the acquisition of basic knowledge in business administration, economics, statistics, and law as well as examinations (Propädeutika) in subjects such as information systems and programming, mathematics, and techniques of cost accounting.

During the graduate courses, specialization takes place and students typically have to decide for two electives from a broad range of possible specializations, while also taking additional coursework in general business administration and general economics. In addition students have to prepare and often also to defend a diploma thesis that is usually written over a three to six month period. Some institutions, like HHL and TUM Business School, also include an intense "practical project" as a mandatory module of the study program, which requires that small teams of four to six students address a focused problem posed by an external organization. The project is completed under the supervision and guidance of a university professor as mentor and a high-level representative of the external partner organization (either a private business or a public sector organization) as tutor of the project. These practical projects usually take three to six months and can be the starting point for an academic challenge that is subsequently addressed in the diploma thesis.

Bachelor and master programs in Betriebswirtschaftslehre

Most higher education institutions have or are about to set up bachelor and master program offerings according to the Bologna standards. The shift from the traditional German *Diplom* program to the new Bachelor-Master structure has to be implemented by 2010 according to the Bologna agreement. This shift not only implies a major change for higher education institutions in Germany, but also a significant change for students and their future employers as well. There is no shortage in publications about this change, and therefore we do not have to go into detail here.

We would add just one comment: Within the German and even international market place the intended "transparency" of the Bologna process has definitely not been achieved. Instead, a vast range of programs has been newly established, with different foci, depth and breadth. The situation currently leads to much confusion. Even accreditation is not a solution to this problem. While traditional diploma programs had to be set up according to clear standards and accredited by the ministry of science and education of the German Länder, the accreditation process for the new bachelor and master programs provides minimum standards. The range of national, European, and international accreditation bodies adds further confusion in the market place.

In our opinion, the strongest immediate impact of the Bologna process is not the intended supply-side transparency, but an enforced institutional change in the German higher education market, for the first time since WWII. All higher education institutions have to rethink their offerings, their profile, role and positioning. Some are taking the Bologna process as an opportunity for strategic thinking and strategic decision-making, a number of others appear to be caught in political turmoil or are proceeding with un-reflected actions. As a result the Bologna process is strengthening the move to differentiate the higher education institutions that have so far been formally defined as being "equal" with little chance for quality distinctions.

Doctoral programs in Betriebswirtschaftslehre

Independent (course-based, full time or part-time) doctoral programs doctoral programs are not common in the German academic system. Usually doctoral candidates are fully employed as research and teaching staff at a chair and work under the supervision of the chair holder. They have typically been trained in a *Diplom* program and sometimes have already worked for a chair as research assistants during earlier studies. While doctoral students they assist the professor in his or her teaching and research activities and are also involved in administrative duties. In parallel they work on their doctoral thesis which ideally is linked to key questions of a research project they are involved with. As part of the chair's research team they are part of a constant exchange of ideas, especially in chairs with a large research effort they have a natural group of counterparts with whom candidates can discuss their academic ideas and the progress of their doctoral research.

This approach to doctoral education is based on a "learning on the job" model of academic socialization. It naturally fits with the research funding approach of the German government which through its ministries (e.g. the German Federal Ministry of Research and Education) funds large scale projects that typically run in a three-year timeframe and usually have a research budget that allows employment of perhaps three or four doctoral candidates at one or more chairs. Many chair holders also supervise so-called "external doctoral candidates." These are not employed at the chair, but typically work in the corporate sector. These doctoral candidates add practical knowledge and experience to the research pool. The fact that they are often not closely integrated in the chair's research team and also do not get additional education in research methods, however, often leads to a relatively negative assessment of the work by the academic community despite their strong grounding in managerial problems and often excellent organizational data.

Recently – and further encouraged by the Exzellenzinitiative of the German Federal Government – many university-level institutions have started doctoral schools and programs to provide substantial additional research training for doctoral candidates. Among the early players in offering a formal doctoral program are the Universität München, HHL – the Leipzig Graduate School of Management, and FU Berlin. Each program has a distinctive profile and the three therefore can be used as examples of a broad range of approaches in this relatively young segment of the German academic marketplace:

- The Universität München offers a postgraduate three-year program that leads to a Master of Business Research (MBR). Within the 24-month program internal and external doctoral candidates are trained in research methods, philosophy of science, and specific content areas of business administration and management. The focus of the program is more on internal than external candidates. The results of the MBR program plus a doctoral thesis lead to the doctoral degree of a Dr. rer. pol.
- HHL – Leipzig Graduate School of Management, offers an integrated postgraduate three-year program for their internal and external doctoral candidates. The program includes course work and seminars on research methods and approaches as well as an international summer school. It is offered in a part-time mode and requires a doctoral thesis. The primary target group of this program is external candidates with solid management experience. Building on and in cooperation with the FENIX program that was successfully established in the late 1990s by academics of the Stockholm School of Economics, the Chalmers University of Technology in Gothenburg, the Ecole des Mines de

Paris, and the Institute for Management of Innovation and Technology (Imit in Sweden), the HHL program aims to provide an education that is more academic and reflective than existing leadership development programs and more focused on knowledge for practice than a traditional PhD education. The multi-institutional program with FENIX and the Institut für Wirtschaftsforschung Halle (IWH Halle) in Germany, aims to create a cross-border environment for industry and academia. The objective is to achieve research-based knowledge of both scientific and practical value.[20] The results of the course work, the research colloquia, the summer schools, as well as the doctoral thesis and its defense, lead to the doctoral degree of a Dr. oec.

- At FU Berlin we find a third and again distinctive form of doctoral program. This effort is purely topic-focused and funded by the Deutsche Forschungsgemeinschaft (German Research Foundation). The emphasis is on "Research on Organizational Paths," and the program explores the processes of path dependence, path breaking, and path creation in and between organizations. While in the first two doctoral programs described there is a broad range of disciplinary research foci within the field of business administration and management ranging from accounting, auditing and controlling to marketing, finance, and strategic management, the FU Berlin doctoral school is a focused research and teaching program for about 15 to 20 doctoral candidates concentrating on a specific research area under the supervision of 8 to 10 professors.

The three examples of clearly distinct doctoral programs show the range of offerings in this fast growing market segment. Only the future will show which type of program will gain the most widespread dissemination.

Career steps in the German academic marketplace

Scholars and educators who create and disseminate management knowledge through their writing and teaching, regardless of where they are located, need perhaps to recognize that no divine rule or secular scientific law exists that dictates what constitutes management knowledge or who should shape this discourse. (Stuart R. Clegg and Anne Ross-Smith, 2003)

Advancing in the German academic hierarchy is typically a well organized, closely mentored, but still challenging process. If we briefly compare the system with the US-based career model, we would notice the absence of formal doctoral programs, publication output in international academic journals, formal evaluation systems, and career path definitions. The German academic system and its community as a whole is much more rooted in the medieval guild model, as Clark (1983) pointed out. Socialization is the driver of knowledge creation and transfer rather than formalized departmental evaluations focused primarily on double-blind peer reviewed academic output. Further details are provided in the following discussion of steps in the academic career ladder.

The doctorate as a first step into the academic or business community

Pursuing a doctorate in Betriebswirtschaftslehre is seen as a quite attractive option in German-speaking countries. In 2004, 463 scholars were awarded a doctoral degree in Betriebswirtschaftslehre in Germany. The acquisition of a doctorate requires handing in a doctoral thesis (Dissertation) and an oral exam (Rigorosum) and/or a critical academic discussion (Disputation) as part of a public defense. The doctoral thesis has to be published and made widely available and visible to the community. Most successful candidates do not plan to stay in academia; rather the doctorate is seen as a good first step towards top level management positions. There is an ongoing discussion in Germany about the merits of an MBA as an alternative way to improve career prospects and raise salary levels. There is obviously a fashion cycle supporting the MBA, but the doctorate in Germany still seems to be a reliable foundation for a career in management practice. The positive role of the doctorate for individual candidates as well as firms can also be seen in entry positions that guarantee some kind of "sabbatical" arrangement to pursue a doctorate in parallel with the corporate assignment. These are quite common in top consultancies, as well as many industrial firms.

As mentioned above, internal as well as external doctoral candidates are always linked to a full professor at a university-level institution who serves as supervisor, mentor and first examiner. Integration with the lehrstuhl or chair system is usually a close one, which not only determines the disciplinary focus of the dissertation, but also socializes the candidate into a specific school of thought with associated theoretical and methodological foundations. Quality therefore depends on the culture, norms and values of the chair. Up to now the German academic community in Betriebswirtschaftslehre and related associations like the Association of University Professors of Management (VHB) and the

Schmalenbach Gesellschaft have not offered any systematic platform or format for academic discussion, training, or exchange at the doctoral level. While academic associations like the Academy of Management, the European Academy of Management, and the British Academy of Management (as well as German academic associations in fields like engineering and computer science) have membership open to doctoral students, there has not been an equivalent academic association in the field of German Betriebswirtschaftslehre. In 2007, however, VHB will for the first time offer pre-conference workshops for doctoral students and early-career scholars.

As part of the research team of the chair, doctoral candidates in the role of research associates are primarily socialized by their more experienced colleagues, senior associates, and the professor. Larger chairs support seminars and international exchange. Through growing international connections and networking within the German academic community, the lack of systematic training at a local, regional, or national level is motivating ambitious individuals to participate in international conferences and workshops. In addition, the implementation of more formal doctoral programs at some universities is compensating for the fact that the switch from the German *Diplom* to the Bachelor means a lower entry-level qualification for candidates pursuing a doctorate.

The habilitation as the traditional qualification step for a tenured professorship

After finishing the doctorate, the next qualification step towards a tenured professorship is the Habilitation (from the Latin word "habilis" or "adequate"). While the PhD is the highest academic degree and considered proof of the ability to carry out independent research, the Habilitation is a qualification step that does not lead to a degree but to the title of "Privatdozent," which opens the way for a full professorship at a university-level institution. The result of the Habilitation process is a simple "passed" or "not passed." In order to pass the Habilitation process and to obtain the "venia legendi" in Betriebswirtschaftslehre the successful candidate has to show that he or she can represent a broad field in research and teaching. The Habilitation thesis (Habilitationsschrift), is expected to draw upon a broad review of the literatures in multiple fields that relate to the chosen topic. The document, the candidate's CV, a full list of publications, and evidence of experience in academic teaching, are the key elements for the first formal evaluation step in the Habilitation process, which is carried out by a committee appointed by the faculty consortium. A candidate who successfully passes this step is invited to prepare an oral Habilitation Colloquium as the final step of the evaluation process, which is on a topic assigned by the faculty consortium that is typically not related to the subject of the Habilitation thesis.

The real Habilitation process, however, starts much earlier than the formal process of document preparation and colloquium. Usually candidates for a Habilitation are fully employed senior associates for a chair. This allows them to learn what it means to be a chair holder, and step by step to get involved in all the tasks and duties that are linked to the role of a chair holder. Habilitands usually have four to five hours teaching responsibility per week during winter and summer semesters, are responsible for writing research proposals and acquiring research funding. They are involved in the academic administration of the chair (which includes HR issues, accounting, controlling, and design of the research and teaching strategy of the chair). The Habilitand is likely to be involved in the chair's connections with an academic department (e.g. participation in professorial selection committees) and the university as a whole (e.g. involvement in strategic initiatives of the university and cross-departmental task forces). They also would replace the chair holder during their sabbatical or on shorter absences. The chair holder decides how much freedom and space for independent decisions is given to the Habilitand. Therefore the educational process depends very much on the individual chair holder and the relationship between the Habilitand and the chair holder. At its best, the Habilitation is an incredible chance for mentored individual learning, personal growth, and maturation.

In order to make the process less dependent on the individual discretion of chair holders, two innovations have recently been established in the German academic system. First, the alternative path of "Junior Professorship" has been established, which is discussed in more detail below. Second, Habilitation regulations have been revised to add some structure to the early phase of the Habilitation process. A team of mentors is put in place to guide the process and evaluate the candidate and his or her achievements, usually after two or three years of the four to six years typically required to complete a Habilitation. In addition, the new Habilitation regulations usually allow for a cumulative Habilitation thesis based on a more or less coherent bundle of published journal papers as an alternative to the integrated monograph traditionally required for a Habilitation. It is still too early to fully assess the advantages and disadvantages as well as the career implications of these new paths.

Junior professorships as a recent alternative step towards a tenured professorship

The so-called junior professorship was introduced in 2002 by the social-democrat government under the German Federal Minister of Education and Research, Edelgard Bulmahn. It is an attempt to abolish the seemingly old-fashioned Habilitation and to renew the academic system. The intention was to replace the Habilitation with a new model following the idea of the American tenure track system and to no longer require a successful Habilitation as the qualification and prerequisite for obtaining a tenured professorship. Following the American model of assistant and associate professorships, the appointment of a junior professor in Germany requires a formal position announcement and a selection process through an appointment committee. The idea is to offer a tenure track for those who are appointed as Junior Professors. Today a small number of junior professorships are in place, but they have not replaced the Habilitation model. Less than 10 percent of all current junior professor positions have a tenure option in their contract. Their salary level is set at W1, which is compared to other levels in further discussion below.

Despite strong support and funding by the Federal Government, with the declared goal of implementing up to 6,000 junior professorships by 2010 across all disciplines and universities, the introduction of the new model is currently not seen as a success story. From 2002 to 2006 only about 1,000 of the intended 6,000 junior professorships were implemented. At the end of 2006, there were not more than 10 position openings per months across all disciplines and all universities in Germany.[21] While the model seems to work well for some disciplines (including engineering and some natural sciences) it is far less accepted by others (especially in the humanities and social sciences). The junior professorship comes with a teaching load that is slightly higher than the teaching load of a traditional Habilitand and does not provide the very personal and responsible one-to-one mentorship of a chair holder. It offers, however, more rights for the individual to apply for research grants. So far, the model is widely rejected by universities and senior professors and also by potential candidates themselves. Today, some junior professors even pursue a Habilitation in parallel with their professorial role in order to improve their chance when applying for a tenured professorship at a later point in time. Despite the small numbers, low enthusiasm, and unclear career implications of the model, most individual junior professors who successfully pass the necessary evaluations as part of their qualification process, are well qualified and thus are strong candidates for a tenured professorship.

Tenured professorships and the German chair regime

In Germany there are two key categories of tenured professorships at university-level institutions: first, professors as chairholders (salary levels C4 or W3; see Figure 8.1) and second, professors with similar rights and duties but a lower salary level and usually no research and teaching staff (salary levels C3 or W2; see Figure 8.1).[22] The different salary schemes are described below. Both groups are formally called "Universitätsprofessoren." Their appointment requires a Habilitation or equivalent outstanding scientific achievement in addition to a PhD. There also are professors at universities of applied sciences. Their appointment usually requires on top of the PhD a minimum of five years practical work experience (out of which at least three years should have been spent outside the university system). In addition they should show special achievements in the application or development of scientific insights and methods. Their usual salary level is C3 or W2. In general the German system prohibits a candidate from receiving a first appointment at the same institution that provided

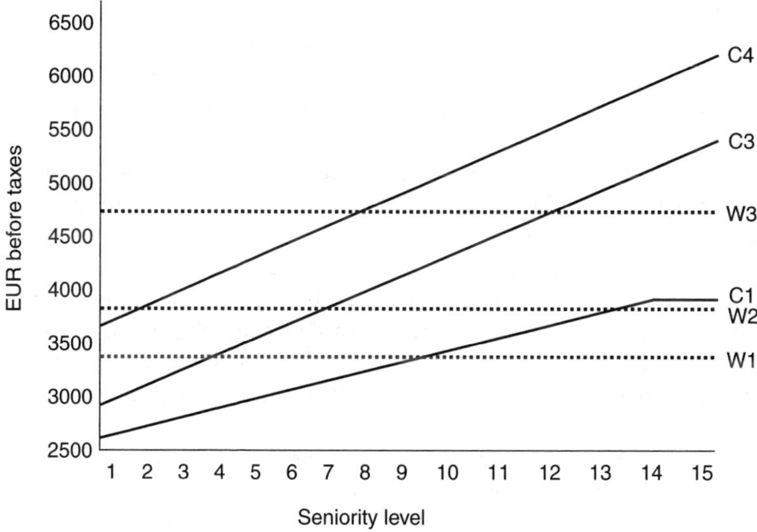

Figure 8.1   The German academic C and W salary scheme

him or her with the qualification for a professorship (this rule is called "Hausberufungsverbot").

The traditional academic C salary scheme differentiated between C1 (Habilitand), C3 (professorship without chair), C4 (full chaired professorship) and linked salary increases to seniority levels (see Figure 8.1). The new academic W salary scheme differentiates between W1 (junior professor), W2 (professorship without chair) and W3 (full chaired professorship) and tries to link salary increases solely to performance instead of seniority. Figure 8.1 shows the base salaries in the C as well as the W salary scheme. Figure 8.1 also shows the seniority based increase in the C scheme in comparison to the fixed base salary in the W scheme. The key question is what kind of performance based add-ons professors in the W salary scheme can expect. It turns out that this depends very much on the employment negotiations with the president (or rector) and the chancellor of the university that runs the appointment process. Universities have to make sure that their overall spending for salaries does not exceed their former average spending. Given the on average higher salaries of the older colleagues appointed under the C scheme, there is usually not much room for negotiating add-ons for newcomers. On the other hand, the W system definitely allows for unequal salaries and in certain cases even a young newcomer might negotiate a high surplus.

As pointed out earlier, the add-ons in the new salary scheme are meant to be performance based. Based on initial experience, however, it seems that the most attractive and relevant "performance aspect," is the performance to accept a position. For this single aspect of convincing a promising candidate to join the university, it is now possible to add a fixed sum on top of the monthly salary for a lifetime (irrespective of the performance on job). As a rule, this fixed add-on can increase the monthly W3 salary up to an overall maximum amount of 10,004.01 EUR before taxes, which would lead to an annual salary of a little more than 126,000.00 EUR per year. This amount can be seen as the theoretical maximum of professorial salaries in Germany. For strong research-active professors in the core fields of management at the leading schools of the country an average salary of 100,000 EUR per annum is not uncommon.

Table 8.3 shows the growth in the key professorial categories C4/W3 and C3/W2 over time. It is also interesting to have a look at the relatively late emergence of female professors in German Betriebswirtschaftslehre and their small representation at about 7 percent of the C4/W3 category of chair holders shown on this table.

Table 8.3 Development of German professorships in Betriebswirtschaftslehre[23]

	Professors in Betriebswirtschaftslehre at Germany			
	C4/W3	Female professors among C4/W3	C3/W2	Female professors among C3/W2
1982	124	–	297	8
1989	232	1	359	10
1994	263	8	502	28
2004	429	31	770	80

Demand for German Betriebswirtschaftslehre

So far we have looked at the institutional supply-side of German business administration training, including the programs offered and the academics providing management education. We will now briefly sketch two demand side issues: sources of revenue and the impact of regulatory bodies, before confronting the input dimension of third party research funding using the output indicator of publication intensity.

The demand for educational programs

In winter term 2004/2005 in Germany 22,986 prospective students applied for 10,084 available university places in Betriebswirtschaftslehre.[24] At that time the central distribution office for these university places (Zentralstelle für die Vergabe von Studienplätzen, ZVS, www.zvs.de) had the unique and Germany-wide responsibility to match individual applications against state administered supply. Students who were unable to secure a place in business administration usually started their studies in economics hoping to switch to business administration at a later point of time in their studies. Beginning in 2005 the picture has slightly changed. University places for Betriebswirtschaftslehre are no longer centrally managed for all universities across Germany and students are in most cases allowed to directly apply to the university of their choice. However, the supply side is still subject to governmental capacity regulations that try to provide as many university places as possible with current public funding. As of October 11, 2006 the Senate of the German University Presidents Conference (Hochschulrektorenkonferenz, www.hrk.de) publicly proposed changing the current university capacity regulations along the following lines: (1) introduction of target setting processes between the German Länder and their universities for determining the number of university

Table 8.4   Degrees awarded in "Betriebswirtschaftslehre" in Germany (1989-2004)[25]

| | Degree awarded | | | | | |
Year	Total	Bachelor	Master	Degree at Univ. of Applied Science	Diplom (and equiv.) at university-level inst.	Doctorate
1989	11.538	–	–	4.945	6.359	226
1994	18.419	–	–	6.688	11.356	362
1999	17.940	–	–	8.543	8.869	510
2004	21.750	457	340	11.756	8.702	479

places offered, (2) confirmation of the result by the Länder Parliament, (3) guarantee by the universities to provide at least the minimum quality standards recommended by the German Science Council (Wissenschaftsrat, www.wissenschaftsrat.de) for the capacity defined through the target setting process, (4) optional additional provision of university places or higher quality standards by the universities with additional funding from third parties and future tuition fees.

Given that capacity regulations are still valid as we write this chapter, we can best assess the overall situation in the German educational "market" for Betriebswirtschaftslehre by looking at the outcome of the degrees awarded across the different programs offered (Bachelor, Master, *Diplom*, Doctorate). Table 8.4 gives a rough overview of degrees awarded over the 15 year time span since the German reunification.

Sources of revenue and the distribution of third party research funding

State universities in Germany can still in many ways be described as "nachgeordnete Behörden" – substructures of the public administration. Basic funding for research and teaching is therefore public funding that usually covers the overall institutional structure as well as the employment contracts of faculty and staff. Berghoff et al. (2005) reviewed additional third party research funding spent by individual institutions between 2001-2003. They found that the top institutions listed in Table 8.5 raised more than 1 Mio EUR of additional third party research funding per year. The average third party research funding spent by individual researchers ranges from less than 13,000 EUR per annum up to more than 65,000 EUR per annum per person for the top institutions listed.

Table 8.5   Third party funding spent in the field of Betriebswirtschaftslehre at research oriented universities[26]

University	Third party funding per annum (in TEUR)	Avg. third party funding per researcher per annum (in TEUR)
TU München (TUM)	3,558	64.1
Univ. Frankfurt/Main	2,535	27.1
Univ. Oldenburg	2,343	65.7
Univ. Saarbrücken	2,232	28.5
Univ. Mannheim	2,189	21.7
TU Dresden	1,496	34.7
Univ. Hohenheim	1,435	39.9
Univ. Trier	1,408	40.8
Univ. München (LMU)	1,359	12.6
Europ. Univ. Frankfurt/Oder	1,184	37.8
Univ. Köln	1,077	12.8
EBS Oestrich-Winkel	996	15.5
HHL Leipzig	972	33.5
Univ Duisburg-Essen	951	18.9
TU Chemnitz	873	28.5
HU Berlin	829	19.5

Where does this funding come from? Figure 8.2 shows the sources of third party funding for Betriebswirtschaftslehre in German research universities. The German Federal Government (Bund), industry, and foundations are the three main sources of additional funding for business and management research, followed by funding from the German Research Council (DFG) and state governments (Länder). As we can see from Figure 8.2, federal government funding and funding from the regional state governments account for more than 32 percent of overall additional research funding. Foundations (16,4 percent) and the corporate sector (17,4) add another 33 percent to the overall cake. The German Research Council (DFG), which is seen as the most prestigious funding institution for management research, however, contributes less than 10 percent to the overall picture.

The impact of regulatory bodies

The German education system has a tradition of governmental accreditation. Historically the Länder governments were responsible for approving all

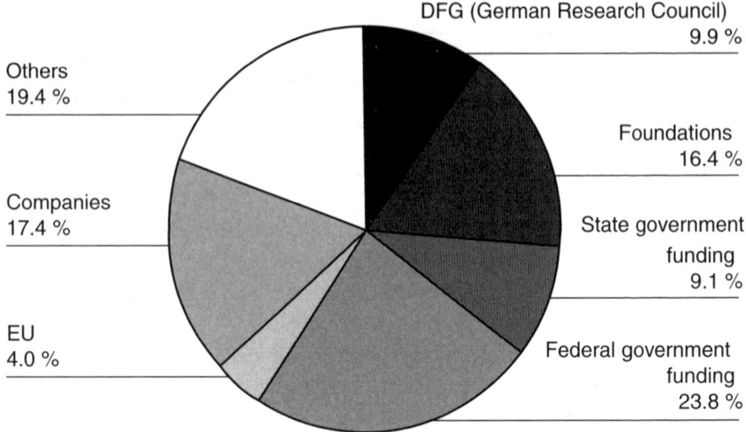

Figure 8.2   Sources of third party research funding for Betriebswirtschaftslehre[27]

kinds of study and examination regulations for study programs offered by German universities. Recently however, a broad spectrum of accreditation agencies has emerged. For the purpose of approving ("accrediting") these accreditation agencies, in 1998 the German Accreditation Council was established. Currently four accreditation agencies carry the quality seal of the German Accreditation Council and are formally accepted as accreditors of business school programs: AQAS (Agentur für Qualitätssicherung durch Akkreditierung von Studiengängen), ACQUIN (Akkreditierungs-, Certifizierungs- und Qualitätssicherungs-Institut), FIBAA (Foundation for International Business Administration Accreditation) and ZEvA (Zentrale Evaluations- und Akkreditierungsagentur Hannover). In order to fulfill students' expectations, business schools also have a growing interest in acquiring additional accreditation by international accreditation bodies like: AACSB (Association to Advance Collegiate Schools of Business) and EQUIS (European Quality Improvement System).

The diversity of regulatory bodies currently creates high uncertainty for all players in the German management education market – students and institutions as well. The dominant and formally accepted players (like ACQUIN) accredit individual programs instead of institutions (as does AACSB). The large top-class universities in Germany that in some cases would have to run more than 200 accreditation processes for one single institution therefore sometimes are resisting this kind of accredition on the level of individual programs. It would require an investment that is hard to accept given the fact that the accreditation bodies can only certify the accordance of study programs with existing minimum standards and also would not necessarily approve innovative programs with a profile off the beaten track. Therefore, universities of applied sciences which have a clear incentive to carry the quality seal of the German Accreditation Council are currently far ahead of state institutions in terms of accreditation of their study programs.

Third party research funding and publication intensity

An important evaluation criterion for academic research institutions is the publication intensity of its members. In its research ranking of German university-level Betriebswirtschaftslehre institutions for 2005, CHE reviewed this issue in detail.[28] The basis for their bibliometric analyses was four public databases.[29] For the years 2001-2003 the publication output of all professors employed in the top 17 institutions was reviewed. The identified publications were weighted based on the number of pages in the publication divided by the number of authors involved.[30] "Publications per year" in Table 8.6 indicates the cumulative weighted number of publication points for each respective school or department. "Publications per professor" shows the average weighted publication points for individual professors at this school or department.

In a recent study, Klaus Macharzina, Joachim Wolf and Anne Rohn did a journal-related quantitative evaluation of German research output in

Table 8.6 Top institutions rated by publication intensity per year[31]

University	Publications per year (weighted publ. points)	Publications per professor (avg. weighted publ. points)
WHU Vallendar	218	40.9
Univ. Mannheim	159	23.8
Univ. München (LMU)	144	28.8
Univ. Münster	139	19.9
TU München (TUM)	128	15.4
Univ. Saarbrücken	124	24.9
EBS Oestrich-Winkel	117	18.5
Univ. Erlangen-Nürnberg	113	22.5
Univ. Duisburg-Essen	106	19.9
FU Berlin	105	24.3

business administration.[32] Their study spans a time frame from 1992 to 2001 and focuses on the six major German-speaking journals, replicating and extending an earlier analysis conducted in the mid-nineties. In sum, their analysis shows that (1) the overall ranking of business schools in terms of their publication intensity has not changed very much and (2) the percentage of full professors and practitioners who contribute to these journals has decreased while the share of junior researchers has increased compared to the time period of the earlier study.[33]

Based on the study by Berghoff et al. (2005), Figure 8.3 compares the input dimension of third-party funding with the output dimension of publication intensity for university-level institutions in Germany. The highlighted triangle symbols add "high reputation of the business school" as a third dimension. Reputation in this case was assessed using a survey among German university professors that aimed to evaluate which universities are the leading institutions in terms of research in business administration and management. (Ranking one's own institution was not an option.) The top rated group was made up of those institutions that attracted at least 5 percent of the votes: University of Mannheim, University of Munich (LMU), University of Cologne, University of Münster, University of Frankfurt/Main and Humboldt University Berlin.

Though there is clearly not a great deal of consensus, all top-rated institutions in terms of research in business administration and management are traditional multi-disciplinary research universities in public-ownership. The top three (Mannheim, Munich and Cologne) are a well-established triangle where many of the founding fathers and leading thinkers of German Betriebswirtschaftslehre in the last century were based, including Eugen Schmalenbach (1873–1955), Erich Gutenberg (1897-1984) and Heinrich Nicklisch (1876–1946).

Figure 8.3, however, also shows two atypical "newcomers" in the German business school scene. WHU Vallendar, one of the few single-disciplinary, university-level institutions in private ownership, is the leading star by far in terms of publication output. TU München, with its newly founded TUM Business School, shows up as the outstanding institution in terms of third-party research funding. Both institutions are usually also top rated when students or company representatives are involved in ranking. It might take some time until they show up in the subjective reputation rankings by university professors in Germany. What we see already today, however, is the emergence of new and strong competitors in the German higher-education market for business administration and management.

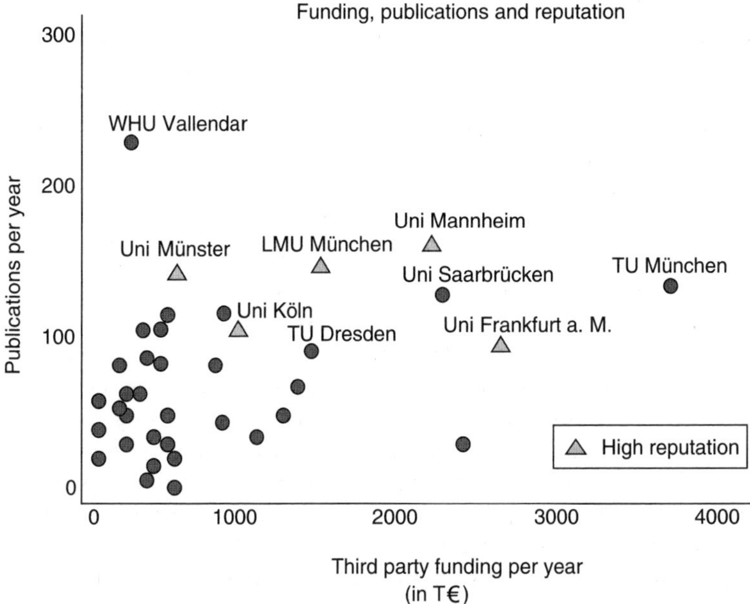

Figure 8.3 Confronting third-party funding and publication intensity in German Betriebswirtschaftslehre[34]

Institutions with a clear business school mission, international outreach, and a strong unique profile like WHU as a focused private institution or TUM Business School with its distinctive focus on linking management research and teaching to technology-related developments might be the precursors of change in the German academic institutional landscape for Betriebswirtschaftslehre.

Outlook for the future of German Betriebswirtschaftslehre

The authors of this chapter have an interest in the global development of business education and research and have some experience in US, UK, and German universities. The German system of chairs with life-time employment is comparable to arrangements in most university systems around the world, but its implementation is closer to that seen in science and engineering in the US and the UK than in business. German professors also tend to be more closely connected to companies than most of their US or UK counterparts. We believe the scale and scope of the

Betriebswirtschaftslehre system is an important strength as business schools try to create knowledge about organizations that are increasing in size and complexity.[35] A further strength of the German system is that it has educated managers and consultants who have experience with research through the *Diplom* system, while a significant number also have PhDs. These practitioners are more likely to be interested in and appreciate interaction with their university counterparts, and a large number also sponsor student projects and give lectures in business courses. Business schools in the German-speaking system thus tend to have multi-layered contacts with companies that support meaningful exchange.

Of course, every system has its weaknesses. Most of the problems we see in Germany are shared by other programs around the world. For example, as the number of students has increased, class sizes have grown and there have been difficulties in adequately supervising individual student work, notably the theses required by the *Diplom* system. As with all tenure systems, there is the waste associated with professors who do not perform. More uniquely, the German system has also been relatively insular. After the early history of influence on US and European thinking about business education summarized by Spender,[36] in the Post WWII period most German professors have published very little outside of the German-speaking system. In comparison to the United States, there are also fewer connections among academic institutions within Germany that promote exchange. Participants in the German education system, especially newcomers, currently are confused about career paths and a significant number seem to be opting for employment abroad where advancement paths are more clearly defined.

A critical question for the future has to do with the theoretical and empirical foundation of research. We are very positive about increased awareness in Germany of business research in the English language, along with serious efforts to methodologically prepare students for independent research. But there is much of value in the German theoretical and empirical tradition as well. Relative isolation had an unanticipated plus: German business research and education developed a unique point of view. As the third largest economy in the world, these insights are important. A growing number of scholars are in the position to translate this knowledge into English-language publications.

In terms of research, one question is whether the introduction of assistant, associate and full professorships without research support will grow, and whether they will fragment attention. The current "Excellence Initiative" – a € 1.9 billion initiative set up by the German Federal and State Governments for the period 2006 through 2011 to promote top-level research in Germany – might add speed to the ongoing change in the German university system and offers the chance to make the current strengths of the German university system more visible. The initiative aims "to strengthen science and research in Germany in the long term, improve its international competitiveness and raise the profile of the top performers in academia and research."[37] The focus of the initiative is very much on technology, engineering and natural sciences. However, it also pushes the technology- and management-oriented type of Betriebswirtschaftslehre that is a relatively unique strength of the German business-school system. By selecting TUM with its concept "The Entrepreneurial University" as one of three Elite Universities in Germany,[38] the initiative further strengthens the technology- and management-oriented Betriebswirtschaftslehre with its focus on entrepreneurial innovation strategies in organizations and markets.[39]

References

Albach, H. (1990): Business Administration: History in German-Speaking Countries, in: Grochla, E. et al. (eds.): Handbook of German Business Management, Vol. 1, Stuttgart et al. 1990, S. 246–270.

Berghoff, S./Federkeil, G./Giebisch, P./Hachmeister, C.-D./Müller-Böling, D. (2005): Das CHE-Forschungsranking deutscher Universitäten – BWL 2005, Auszug aus dem Arbeitspapier Nr. 70 vom 11. November 2005, Centrum für Hochschulentwicklung, 2005.

BMBF (2003): Universities of Applied Sciences in Germany, report published by the Federal Ministry of Education and Research (BMBF), Bonn, Germany, 4th revised edition, August 2003.

Bradley, L./Gregson, G./King, Z./Pate, J./Möslein, K./Neely, A. (2004): The Challenge of Business-University Collaboration – Context, Content and Process, Summary Report from an AIM/SMI Management Research Forum, Advanced Institute of Management Research (AIM), London, May 2004.

CHE (2004): Zwei Jahre Juniorprofessur. Analysen und Empfehlungen, Gütersloh, September 2004.

Clark, B. (1983): The higher education system. Academic organization in cross-national perspective, Univ. of California Press: Berkeley, CA.

Clegg, S.R./Ross-Smith, A. (2003): Revising the Boundaries: Management Education and Learning in a Postpositivist World, in : Academy of Management Learning and Education, 2003, Vol. 2, No. 1, pp. 85-98.

dapm/CHE (2006): Employability Rating BWL (Bachelor) 2006, der arbeitskreis personalmarketing (dapm) & Centrum für Hochschulentwicklung (CHE), March 2006.

Dorf, Y.J. (1999): Der Universitätsprofessor: Hochschullehrer im Beamtenverhältnis – Selbstverständlichkeit und/oder Notwendigkeit, Peter Lang Verlag: Frankfurt a.M.

Engwall, L. (1999). The Carriers of European Management Ideas, Department of Business Studies, Uppsala University, Uppsala, Sweden, CEMP Report No. 7, December 1999.

FSOG (2006): Statistik Betriebswirtschaftslehre, publicly available data provided by the Federal Statistical Office of Germany, Statistical Information Service, Wiesbaden, March 2006.

Gibbons, M./Limoges, C./Nowotny, H./Schwartzman, S./Scott, P. and Trow, M. (1994): The New Production of Knowledge. The Dynamics of Science and Research in Contemporary Societies, London u.a.

Hartung, M.J. (2006): Ein letzter Gruß. Sie sollte die angestaubte Berufungspraxis an den Universitäten verändern. Jetzt steht die Juniorprofessur vor dem Aus, in: Die Zeit, 13th July 2006 (accessible online via: http://www.zeit.de/2006/29/C-Juniorprofessur?page=1).

Huff, A.S./Huff, J.O. (2001): Re-Focusing the Business School Agenda, in: British Journal of Management, Vol. 12, Special Issue, December 2001, pp. S49–S54.

Ivory, C./Miskell, P./Shipton, H./White, A./Möslein, K. and Neely, A. (2006): UK Business Schools: Historical Contexts and Future Scenarios. Summary Report from an AIM/EBK Management Research Forum, Advanced Institute of Management Research (AIM), London, UK, 2006.

Locke, R.R. (1985): Business education in Germany: Past systems and current practice, in: Business History Review, 59 (summer), pp. 232-253.

Macharzina, K./Wolf, J./Rohn, A. (2004): Quantitative Evaluation of German Research Output in Business Administration: 1992-2001, in: Management International Review, Vol. 44, No. 3, 2004, pp. 335-359.

Möslein, K. (2005): Der Markt für Managementwissen. Wissensgenerierung im Zusammenspiel von Wirtschaftswissenschaft und Wirtschaftspraxis, Gabler-DUV: Wiesbaden 2005.

Muller-Camen, M./Salzgeber, S. (2005): Changes in Academic Work and the Chair Regime: The Case of German Business Administration Academics, in: Organization Studies, Vol. 26, No. 2, pp. 271-290.

Oechsler, W.A. (1999): Entwicklung von Professuren und Habilitationen im Fach Betriebswirtschaftslehre 1998-2001, Forschungsbericht der Fakultät für Betriebswirtschaftslehre, Nr. 9905, Mannheim.

Reichwald, R. (2007): Technologieorientierte Betriebswirtschaftslehre, in: zfbf – Schmalenbachs Zeitschrift für betriebswirtschaftliche Forschung, special issue 56/07, pp. 112–139.

Rühli, E. (2002): Betriebswirtschaftslehre nach dem Zweiten Weltkrieg (1945–ca. 1970), in: Gaugler, E./Köhler, R. (eds.): Entwicklungen der Betriebswirtschaftslehre, Schäffer-Poeschel: Stuttgart, pp. 111-133.

Schneider, D. (2001): Betriebswirtschaftslehre, Band 4: Geschichte und Methoden der Wirtschaftswissenschaft. München, Wien.

Spender, J.-C. (2000): Underlying antinomies and perpetuated problems: An historical view of the challenges confronting business schools today, New York Institute of Technology, Old Westbury, NY 11568, February 2000.

Starkey, K./Madan, P. (2001): Bridging the Relevance Gap: Aligning Stakeholders in the Future of Management Research, in: British Journal of Management, Vol. 12, Special Issue, December 2001, pp. S3-S26.

Whitley, R. (1984): The intellectual and social organization of the sciences, Clarendon-Press: Oxford.

Witte, E. (2003): Betriebswirtschaftliche Forschung im technisch-naturwissen schaftlichen Kontext, Manuskript zum Vortrag anläßlich der Verleihung der

Ehrendoktorwürde an der Technischen Universität München am 15. Januar 2003.

ZVS (2005): Angebot und Nachfrage nach Studienplätzen in bundesweit zulassungsbeschränkten Studiengängen zum Wintersemester 2004/2005, ZVS-Daten, Informations- und Pressestelle der ZVS, Dortmund, 2005.

9
Management Education and Research in France

Stéphanie Dameron and Thomas Durand

Compared to other social sciences, the science of management is a rather new field in France. The first major schools of management appeared between the nineteenth century and the early twentieth with the creation of ESCP in 1819, HEC in 1881 and ESSEC in 1907. These business schools were created primarily by the Chambers of Commerce and Industry (CCIs). CCIs are public institutions created by Napoleon in 1803 to sustain regional development through the emergence of private companies. Until the early 1960s, business was not considered as an academic discipline to be taught at universities, and knowledge about management remained solely in the hands of experts and consultants. It was only in 1955 that the first Master's degree in management was offered by a public university, followed by Pierre Tabatoni's creation of the first institute for business management (Institut d'Administration des Entreprises, IAE).

The late sixties brought a public policy of strong development of higher education in management, with typically in 1968 the creation of the Paris-Dauphine University, which would focus on organization management, and the French foundation for management education ("FNEGE"). The latter played a leading role in the creation of a corps of business professors through the financing of French students going to the United States for a PhD in management.

The institutionalization of management as an academic field within the French higher education system can be dated as of 1969, when France created its own national academic committee for management education and research, with corresponding curricula and degrees. From then on, business schools and universities experienced a continuing rise in the number of students enrolling in management programs. Today, according to FNEGE, 17 percent of all higher education students in France study business and management (FNEGE, 2003). As a result, this sector of education has gained very high social visibility.

While the label "management education" in fact covers a variety of offerings and structures, the French institutional setting of business management studies is still very much evolving.

In our first section, we describe the main suppliers of management education and their strategies: the so-called Grandes Ecoles (or GE-business schools) are the main players at the Master's level while traditional public universities have a legal monopoly on PhD programs. The next section deals with an analysis of the profession of business professors, its attractiveness and the challenges it will face in the coming years. We then consider the demand side of the system, looking at students', executives' and firms' expectations and demands on business schools and universities. We conclude with an analysis of the role played by quality assessment bodies.

The supply of higher education in business in France

There are two main families of suppliers of business education in France: the "GE"-business schools and the universities. GE-business schools clearly have the lead. They are the main suppliers of Master-level programs and Executive Education; they select students from among the best talents; their alumni hold key positions throughout Industry; the salaries offered to young graduates are high. Fees and tuitions are significant, the resources available per student are significantly higher than those found elsewhere in higher education in France. These are elite schools and their prestige within the French society is quite high.

In contrast, management programs at universities tend to be less prestigious; students cannot be selected on the same basis; tuitions and fees are minimal and resources available are lower; companies tend to offer lower salaries to university graduates and social prestige is more limited. However, universities still have a monopoly on the Doctoral degree. As a result, the social status of a university professor in management remains significant, although declining in recent years.

The "Grandes Ecoles" business schools – the GE-business schools

At the beginning of the 19th century, neither engineering nor business was considered as a discipline to be taught at universities. As these two fields were becoming instrumental in the rising of industry throughout the 19th century, France created specific Engineering schools and Business schools apart from universities. These were soon known as the "Grandes Ecoles." As their alumni became entrepreneurs and leaders in Industry, the GE gradually became elite places where ambitious parents would send their talented children. This is still the case today.

Today GE-business schools are the first suppliers of a structured education in management. Like most engineering schools in France, they select their students from a national competitive examination. In order to prepare for this selection process, students spend two to three years of preparatory classes after high school. For the best among the GE-business schools, the admission process is highly selective. This is the classical virtuous loop by which the prestige of the elite place attracts the best talents which permits visible and successful careers, in turn reinforcing the prestige of the school.

Table 9.1 presents a ranking of the leading French GE-Business Schools. (This list does not include Insead which is of a different breed. Insead may not be considered as a French GE-business school. Insead started more as a US spin-off, built from the American business school model and implanted in Europe. Created in 1957, it is dedicated to offering MBAs and Executive Education. A PhD program was created in the early 90s. Today Insead is a European key player in management education, claiming global reach with its Singapore campus plus its Wharton

Table 9.1 Rankings of the 12 leading French business schools (2005)

Ecole	Ranking by French newspaper (L'Express, 2005)	Number of new students (first year-2005)
HEC	1	380
ESSEC	1	365
ESCP-EAP	3	356
EM Lyon	4	355
EDHEC	5	485
ESC Grenoble	6	365
ESC Toulouse	7	345
Audencia	8	365
Euromed Marseille	9	205
ESC Rouen	10	265
ESC Reims	11	275
ESC Bordeaux	12	230

Own construction based on L'Express (www.lexpress.fr) and www.prepa-HEC.org

agreement on research. Insead is based in France but does not view itself as a French business school. Nor does the French academic community in management view Insead as a French institution).

Most GE-business schools essentially deliver Master's degrees and Executive Education. They do not deliver Bachelor's degrees nor PhDs. The Doctoral degree still remains, by and large, the monopoly of public universities, with the exception of HEC which obtained the right to award Doctorate degrees in 1985. Some GE-business schools have entered alliances with a public university in order to offer a Doctoral degree, while some others have even launched their own PhD outside the publicly regulated setting, notably ESSEC and INSEAD.

Business schools offer three kinds of Master's degree:

a general Master's degree, which takes three additional years after the two to three years spent in preparing the competitive examination at entry: this is called the *"Grande Ecole" program* and the reputation of the school is based mainly on the quality of this program (and the strength of the network of alumni).

several *specialised Master's* degrees, called *"Mastère"*, which take one or two years after a Bachelor's degree: students for these come mainly from engineering schools or public universities. For these, the selection is based on academic records.

MBA offered to young managers with a few years of work experience (Some also offer Executive MBA , e.g. on a part time basis, as part of their Executive Education programs).

This 2005 ranking of business schools, produced by French newspapers, reflects the accumulation of points obtained by the schools on a range of criteria: salaries after graduation, student selection, level of research, language skills, international network of partners, etc.

As a result of this multi-layer offering at Master's level, there tends to be a misunderstanding, internationally, of what a Master's diploma from a French business school in fact is.

The traditional diploma of a GE-business school is awarded after successful completion of the "GE program." By and large, it corresponds to the new European Master degree established through the Bologna process. Yet, the strong difference between this "GE diploma" and the other Master's degrees awarded within the same institution has to do with the prestige attached to the highly selective process to enter the GE program.

The wording "Master of Science in Management" is increasingly used to name the Master's degrees in Business which are not MBAs.

As an attempt to highlight the distinction between the two first types of Master's degree, the ESSEC business school chose to claim the MBA label for their "GE program." This was intended to pinpoint the specific value of their "GE program." However by using the concept of MBA which usually applies to programs for students with some significant managerial experience, this move obviously introduced another layer of confusion. As a result, this decision may have consequences for the international visibility and rankings of the Essec business school.

The French business schools are members of the "Conférence des Grandes Ecoles" (CGE) which brings together 226 members, 181 of which are both engineering and management "Grandes Ecoles", nine are foreign universities, and 36 are institutions of higher education. Founded in 1973, the CGE society plays an important role in the management education sector. Most notably, it aims to promote the "Grandes Ecoles" system, at both a national and an international level, and to act as a voice with government policy-makers and the research community. Of the 71 business schools recognised by the state, 32 business schools are active members of the association of the "Grandes Ecoles" and award a "Mastère" degree (Conférences des Grandes Ecoles). However, within CGE, some engineering schools are also listed under the field of management, and the frontiers between engineering and management schools are blurring at the Master's degree level.

Nonetheless French business schools play the principal role in delivering management education in France, and they dominate the rankings of the European market for the Masters of Science degree in Management (Appendix 1). They offer a diploma recognized by the Ministry for National Education, and they account for 43 percent of the postgraduate students in management in France (FNEGE, 2003). However, the sector is more divergent than it might seem. There are too many French business schools for the French market and many must grapple with the challenge of insufficient demand for the supply. Their reputation depends in large part on the selectiveness of their admissions process. In 2004, 7,900 candidates sat the nation-wide examination and 6,366 students were admitted to a business school. With the exception of the very best, most of the French business schools have difficulty maintaining a highly selective process.

On average, a student in a business school costs more than €10,500 a year (Conférence des Grances Ecoles). Unlike universities or engineering schools, business school is not state-funded in France. Business schools have three sources of revenue: Firstly, the main source of income is the tuition fees from students and Executive Education; on average, these come to about €7,000 per year for students in leading business schools; secondly, as the main business schools are "consular" schools – this means they are part of, or under the control of, a Chamber of Commerce – subsidies from the Chambers of Commerce and Industry account for approximately 20–40 percent of the operational budget; thirdly, companies contribute funds in various forms: donations, material gifts, gifts from foundations, and some contract research, etc.

To secure the necessary financing, the leading business schools pursue two main business strategies: developing a name internationally so as to broaden the recruitment base for both students and teachers, and identifying new sources of financing. The schools pursue these strategies in a variety of ways.

The leading French business schools mobilize in three ways to meet international standards:

1. Obtaining international accreditation, both American and European.

Most of the leading business schools have EQUIS accreditation. However, some French business schools have followed different strategies to ensure international visibility for their different programs. Some, like ESSEC or Audencia, have chosen to label their "Grande Ecole" programs an MBA, while others, like HEC or ESCP-EAP, have chosen to label their program "Master of Science", following the Bologna process, and to launch a full-time MBA for practioners. Time has yet to tell which approach will turn out to be more successful.

The classification chosen by a business school for its offerings can have a significant effect on international rankings.

2. Implementing an international network more than bilateral alliances.

The leading French business schools are negotiating exclusive relationships with competitors in order to offer multinational diplomas. For instance, ESCP-EAP has developed a trans-national model of education management called "the European tracks." This is a three-country program with one year spent on three of the five campuses in Paris, London, Berlin, Madrid and Turin. Depending on the track chosen, graduates can receive up to three degrees among a Grande Ecole degree (France), a European MSc in Management (UK), a Diplomkaufman (Germany) and a Laurea Magistrate (Italy). ESSEC offers a European MBA in association with Manheim University (Germany) and Warwick University (UK), and has created a campus in Singapore in 2004.

3.   Launching full-time MBA programs in order to develop an international reputation and Executive MBAs to secure new revenue.

HEC offers a full-time MBA in addition to the "Grande Ecole" program. ESSEC calls its "Grande Ecole" program an MBA and has launched executive MBA: ESSEC's Executive MBA was ranked 10th by the Financial Times among European Executive MBAs in 2006. However, it should be noted that French MBAs are sometimes more sector-oriented than in the US, for instance dedicated to the luxury sector or to the information and communication technology (ICT) sector, or even specialised in one discipline.

In order to meet international standards and to implement their strategies of international recognition and new revenue identification, French business schools must ensure the visibility of their research. The new trend, due mainly to the role played by accreditation agencies like EQUIS, is for business schools to hire professors who can publish in the best journals. However, international research professors are rare, and thus expensive. The leading business schools try to be more attractive by improving salaries and work conditions. Their new professors can dedicate more time to research during the first few years, and sometimes these new stars can be better paid than their older colleagues, who, ironically, are those in charge of hiring them.

The difference in available resources forces business schools with otherwise identical strategic objectives, and with very similar business portfolios (Master's, MBA, Executive Education, research) to implement their business strategies in different ways, which in itself leads to a differentiation between their offerings. Some schools are focused on their region, others have a national presence, while only the leading ones can make a claim to being international.

In their pursuit of new sources of revenues, the business schools have four primary strategies:

Development of Executive Education: INSEAD has recently launched an Executive MBA.

Reconsideration of tuition fees: the association of "Grandes Ecoles" has recommended an increase in fees, and the development of a system of loans.

Increased support from corporations, especially through the creation of foundations: certain schools have developed structured fund-raising programs created to request funds from corporations, like the ESCP-EAP European Foundation launched in 2005.

Increased support from alumni: some, like ESSEC, have begun large campaigns to raise funds through alumni donations, using strategies very similar to those used by American business schools. Yet, those campaigns are targeted mostly to companies, less to alumni.

The schools would like to strengthen their links with companies. They hope to make the corporations feel a sense of responsibility for the current problems of education management, in order to encourage them to take an active role in the financing of the schools. Certain schools, such as EM Lyon, Bordeaux EM and also ESC Rouen, have reformed their structures to give companies direct involvement in the decision-making process.

The universities

Universities in France are public and deliver all the education management degrees at a very low price. However, the particular situation of each university varies considerably and the structure of education management differs greatly from one university to another.

Three modes of organisation can be combined:

The teaching of management can be the responsibility of a department of the university which itself runs programs such as a Master in Management.

The teaching of management can be done by an institute, such as an IAE, which is relatively autonomous within the university. IAE's network is composed of 29 institutions, which form a body of nearly 25,000 students per year.

Management can be taught in an alternative program, not dedicated to teaching management, such as economics or pharmaceutical programs.

French universities deliver national diplomas, meaning that the curriculum and thus the diploma are approved and recognized nationally. Undergraduate degrees can be specialised in management or, more often, are combined with other disciplines, frequently those related to economics. Moreover, universities basically have a monopoly on doctorate programs. The universities are represented through their faculty within the national regulatory authorities, and thus can have very strong lobbying capabilities.

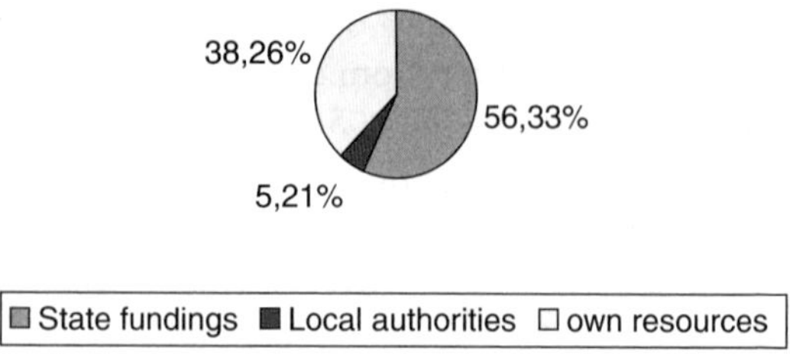

Figure 9.1   The operational budget of universities in 2004*

* Not included salaries of civil servants (all professors and administrative staff).

Sources: Conférence des Présidents des Universités/les Echos.

A business student at a university in France costs an average of €8,800 per year (this figure takes into account the cost of students in hard sciences where education cost are higher than for management), slightly less than the €10,500 cost at a GE-Business School, and considerably less than the approximately €20,000 for an American business student.

Universities secure funds in three ways. State grants make up the majority of the university's funding. Some of their resources come from student registrations fees (on average 150 to 190 euros per student per year !) and other profitable university programs. It should be noted that publicly owned establishments are still not free to raise their registration fees, despite the 2007-reform of their governance. Finally, funds are sometimes provided by local governments and communities.

Traditionally, universities had been more active than Grandes Ecoles in management research. They had the largest faculty, controlled the PhD degree and benefited from a good research reputation attached to tradition.

However, since the mid 90s, the situation has changed considerably, and some of the best young French PhD graduates have begun choosing job positions at GE-business schools. While the latter have an attractive recruitment policy in order to meet international standards, PhD graduates can be discouraged from entering the public system due to wage policies, working conditions and lack of international visibility. As a result, French public universities face considerable challenges.

The 2007-reform on French universities governance is a clear step to address the issue of funding ("Libertés et Responsabilités des Universités" – LRU Act). The reform allows Deans to raise new sources of revenue, and to attract and/or keep talented faculty with more flexible financial incentives. The creation of foundations at public universities is facilitated and tax exemptions for donating firms are made more attractive. However, tuition fees are still regulated and remain quite low in France: €150, €190 and €290 per year for Bachelor's, Master's and Doctorate's degrees respectively. To generate additional resources for public universities, some strongly recommend increasing tuition fees, especially at Master's level.

Following the GE-business schools' strategy, some universities have chosen to develop continuous education, like the MBA or Executive Master's degree, to increase their financial resources and so to improve the financial compensation of their faculty. For example, Paris Dauphine University has launched an Executive MBA in partnership with UQAM University in Montreal (Canada). A debate is currently taking place in France on the autonomy of the universities to manage their budget, charge higher fees, collect external funds, and freely appoint their faculty.

The universities also face the issue of a lack of international influence. In the face of competition from French GE-business schools and an increasing number of other universities in Europe, the French universities need to establish their legitimacy in management education and widen their base for enrollment. This implies attracting both French and foreign students. Broadly speaking, the French universities still lag the GE-business schools in their internationalization. Moreover, with the exception of some institutions, like the IAE of Aix-en-Provence, public universities have not chosen to pursue international accreditation yet.

However, the implementation of the Bologna process – signed in 1998 and 1999 by 38 European countries with the aim of harmonizing European educational offerings in line with the 'Bachelor-Master-Doctorate' standard – has brought French universities increasingly into competition with other European degrees in management, despite their lack of international influence in the management field. In itself, this has increased both the visibility of their diplomas and their rankings, most notably the ranking produced by the University of Shanghaï. This in turn is compelling the universities to conform in some way to accreditation standards. This push towards international visibility increases the pressure to publish in the best international journals, but the lack of monetary and even career incentives for professors still remain. Nevertheless, this is a relatively new trend with consequences to be seen only in a few years.

The universities do not promote a global brand to establish their reputation and international visibility. The first explanation for this is that French professors and deans are not used to "selling" their own institution, an example of this being of the Sorbonne brand which, while being internationally well known, is not actively exploited. Moreover,

Table 9.2   Structure of the higher education system in management

	Entrance in higher education – requirement: +2	+3	+4	+5	+6	+7	+8 (or more)
University			License	Master 1 (formerly Maîtrise)	Master 2 (formerly DEA or DESS)			Doctorate
GE-business schools	Baccalauréat Age: 18	Entrance exam after 2 to 3 years (Limited number of seats)	Program Grande Ecole: Labeled "Master of Science" (or "MBA" in the case of ESSEC)				
			Specialised "mastère"				

contrary to the model of American business schools, which centers on a prestigious MBA supporting a global brand, management education at French universities is a juxtaposition of various short programs, and specialised Master's programs. This situation makes it difficult to develop a global brand. Paris Dauphine University is perhaps the one exception to this, but real visibility mostly within the country.

Finally, compared to business schools, public universities have little or no control over the quality of the new students whom they enroll. Except, again, for Paris Dauphine University, which has a special status of "Grand Etablissement," there is no specific selection for entry into the French university system. As long as students have passed the national examination called "baccalauréat" at the end of high school, they can then enter whichever public university they wish. With the important exception of medical schools and GE- engineering and business schools, universities can select students only at the entrance into the second year of a Master's program (Table 9.2).

The faculty

The faculty is both a key resource and a key player in higher-level management education. Professors can have their own agenda and strategies.

There are three levels of tenured position at public universities: full professor (professeur), associate professor (maître de conférences with Habilitation à Diriger des Recherches), assistant professor (maître de

Table 9.3   The increase of tenured position in management, economics and law in public university

	1984	1995	2001	2004	Increase between 1984 and 2004
Management Professors	111	259	293	358	+ 322%
Assistant and associate Professors	192	543	1001	1185	+ 620%
Economics Professors	288		543	569	+198%
Assistant and associate Professors	236		1080	1189	+503%
Law Professors				1104	
Assistant and associate Professors				1880	

Sources: F. Pavis (2003) and Direction des Personnels Enseignants, www.education.gouv.fr

conférences). The difference between associate professor and assistant professor is that the former has the right to supervise PhD students. The leading business schools use the US model for tenured positions, which is significantly different from the French university model, as discussed below. The number of tenured positions in management has increased significantly over the last twenty years, following the growth in demand for business education (Table 9.3). Yet, there is still a strong inertia in the system. While students were moving away from studying economics towards business education, new positions continued to be given to departments of economics. To make a long story short, one might view this as the result of Law and Economics still dominating over the field of Management within academic circles in France.

There has been a relative decline in recruitment of new professors since 1998, but this has been less significant than the decline experienced in other disciplines (Table 9.4).

However, despite this relative decline, the number of PhDs interested in academic career at universities is still too low to provide enough new applicants for tenured positions. With only 83 percent of assistant professorships filled for the 2003 period, recruitment is a problem for the universities, particularly for those that do not run doctoral degrees. The capacity of the system to renew the supply of teaching staff is in question, especially with the massive wave of retirement that is expected in the coming years.

In-breeding, i.e. recruitment by universities of their own PhD graduates, is characteristic of the system. The emergence of a real "market" for

Table 9.4   Number of free positions in public universities

	1998	2000	2002	Reduction between 1998 and 2004
Management sciences	174	157	148	−15%
Assistant professors	(25)	(30)	(28)	
Economics Assistant	107	70	61	−43%
professors	(13)	(6)	(7)	
Law Assistant	278	168	181	−35%
professors	(24)	(17)	(35)	

Figures in brackets indicate the number of positions provided by transfers.

Source: Direction des Personnels Enseignants, www.education.gouv.fr

management professors remains to be seen. The system limits mobility between institutions. As an example, a newly recruited assistant professor is asked to remain at least four years at the same university. Any exception requires a formal written permission from the university president. In this context, requests for transfers are rare. In addition, after the first two years in a position, the appointee automatically receives tenure (but this is a tenure in the position held at that point, i.e. assistant professor). The logic of the internationalization of faculty is in conflict with the domestic system's disincentives to mobility: a professor recruited by a foreign university and asking for a leave of absence will be asked to give up tenure after three years. The domestic regulations significantly limit the opportunities for international mobility unless one gives up job security.

To become an associate professor in a public university, an assistant professor has to pass the "habilitation à diriger des recherches." The "habilitation" is a qualification step that does not lead to a degree but rather qualifies the candidate to supervise PhD students. The successful candidate has to demonstrate the interest, the consistency and the scope of his research activities and must already have published. The habilitation thesis is presented and defended orally in front of a jury composed of full professors coming from at least two different universities. The process is easier and simpler than the German habilitation and does not have the same prestige.

The most prestigious way to become a full professor (professeur agrégé) for an assistant professor or an associate professor is to pass the university "Agregation," a competitive national exam that takes place every two years. This process lasts about a year, and the jury consists of seven members, five "professeurs agrégés" representing different disciplines of management and two other members, typically practitioners.

There are about 90 candidates every two years and 20 to 25 are awarded the title of full professor and a position somewhere in France in a list of job positions offered.

The first step is to deliver a document similar to the habilitation thesis and to defend the research works orally in front of the jury. Second, the candidate draw a subject from any topic relating to management, has eight hours to prepare it and must then analyse it orally in a structured way for 30 minutes: the aim is to show a general knowledge of any management field, such as finance, marketing, human resource management and so on. The final step involves drawing a case from their field, and, with eight hours of preparation, discussing it in a 30 minute discourse: the aim is to evaluate the teaching ability of the candidate. Each step is pass or fail: the candidate must pass each step to move forward. The candidates who pass all these tests are ranked by the jury. The list of the universities offering positions is published by the ministry before the end of the process. The best ranked candidates choose first from that list.

The pay of associate and assistant professors is primarily linked to seniority. The salary rises every 34 months, as the professor climbs the levels within his grade. For university professors, the evaluating committees within the university or at a national level (the "national commission for universities" or "CNU") are involved in the decision to allow a professor to move up a grade (Table 9.5).

The pay scale within the university system does not compare favourably with the GE-business schools (Table 9.6). At a GE-business school, a professor's salary at the start of a career is generally higher than that at a university, even if it is still below the level of those at North American

Table 9.5 Monthly salaries (net, after health insurance and pension, but before income tax)

Net monthly pay	Assistant and associate professors	Professors	Class room Teaching
Start of career	€1 991	€2 888	
After 2 years	€2 242	€3 222	128 to 192
Last level, "normal" rank (MCF) or the "first" class (PR)	€3 604	€5 112	hours per year
End of career	€4 229	€5 798	

Source: Teaching personal administration, November 2007 (http://www.education.gouv.fr/cid2638/devenir-enseignant-du-superieur.html#carriere-et-remuneration).

Table 9.6 Monthly salaries of assistant professors in business schools before income tax

Assistant professor	Net monthly starting salary (approximate)	Class room teaching obligation
Paris business schools (HEC, ESSEC, ESCP-EAP)	€3000	150 hours
INSEAD	€7500	80 hours

Source: Basso *et al.*, 2004.

universities, particularly those of the best among these latter. Moreover, a professor's teaching duties can vary in relation to the individual's activities and aims, as negotiated with the institution's management.

According to Basso *et al* (2004), the system is marked by greater opacity and is determined largely by individual negotiations with the GE-business schools, while within the universities it is still largely determined by seniority. If, until now, the prestige of a full professor enabled a university to defend its position, it seems that several of the best young doctors about to start an academic career are now heading towards GE-business schools. This is a recent and very clear signal of a shift that may well be long-lasting.

Thus both the pay and teaching load gaps for job offers have increased between:

on the one hand, an assistant professorship at a "grande école" (GE-business school), with a negotiated package that reduces the teaching burden and offers travel and research expenses, thus making it more favourable to research work and thus publications;

and, on the other hand, an assistant professorship at a university where, to advance, it is necessary to prepare for the competitive examination, the "agrégation," to put up with transfers to institutions in which one may not have wished to work and where the teaching load of the most junior professors is both heavy and only loosely focused on their core interests, and without necessarily giving them access to the best students who tended to be attracted by the prestige of Grandes Ecoles.

The demand for higher education in business

Demand for graduate and post-graduate degrees

Early-stage management students form an extremely heterogeneous group, with diverse social backgrounds. This heterogeneity is perceptible in the knowledge to which they have access and the professional opportunities that they expect. In 2003, almost 360,000 students pursued management education (in the broad sense of the term) at the entry level Bac+2 (baccalauréat, or high school diploma level, plus an additional 2 years of study, be it a Bachelor's degree or preparatory classes of further education). This represented 17 percent of all higher-level education. The number of management students has been growing since the beginning of the 1990s. However, the number of new students taken into the first year has not increased. If the total number of management students is nonetheless growing, it is due to the success of the Master's degrees in management, and the growing length of studies.

The mechanisms for financing study are increasing. The access to loans is made easier by banks anxious to attract this promising client base. Internships in management are generally paid. As mandatory internships as part of the training curriculum are now standard, and their number and duration are increasing, they can be a significant new source of revenue. The system of apprenticeship is growing in certain educational courses and is becoming another significant source of funding. Hence, at ESSEC, 35 percent of students of the ESSEC-MBA are apprenticed. One year spent in industry is included in the HEC curriculum, as it is at EM Lyon. Students are behaving less and less like unquestioning users of the educational system and more like clients or even consumers. They are demanding and want a good return on their investment. The nature of the teacher-student relationship is thus deeply affected.

As the length of study and the difficulties in securing employment increase, students prefer selective channels (the preparatory classes for GE-business schools) when possible. As a result, in the last six years, the proportion of young entrants into a university Bachelor's degree has dropped, from 57.4 percent to 52.4 percent. Students tend to increasingly ask for programs based on part-time apprenticeships in Industry.

French students are also sensitive to the international recognition of their diplomas, and expect some English-speaking classes. In Europe they are, just after German students, those who make most use of the Erasmus program: 21,521 students spent one year in another European country in 2004/2005, most (6,735) for management education, with Spain being their preferred destination (Eurostat).

Demand for continuous and executive education

According to the FNEGE's 2004 study, the global market for continuing management education in France is worth about 1.7 billion euros, of which 360 million euros goes to continuing management education for middle and senior executives.

In 2003, 1.34 million people pursued continuing education in management, that is to say 13.5 percent of all continuing education. The large majority of participants in continuing education programs offered by graduate schools of management are managers (83 percent). Those schools that have a turnover from continuing education of 3 million euros or more have the highest proportion of middle and senior level managers: 62 percent of participants, compared to less than 42 percent in other institutions. There is also a link between the turnover of the institution and the professional hierarchical position of the participants (FNEGE, 2004).

The participants in these continuing education programs constitute a considerable mass of people that directly affects the system. Firstly, as these participants buy an educational service, they demand, in return, a quality of service at the level of their expectations and the price paid. This includes not only course content and the perceived quality of the lecturers, but also the quality of services such as catering, accommodation, and logistical and administrative support. Furthermore, they bring with them corporate experience that can interact with that of other participants, but above all, with the knowledge of professors who can sometimes feel challenged. It is thus a source of potential enrichment for the latter, but it (also?) presents a significant risk of being destabilising or even "de-legitimising." Finally, the participants form a basis of evaluating the offerings presented by different institutions, in real time. This process can lastingly alter the image of these institutions in the corporate world.

Demand from companies

Corporations usually have an ambivalent attitude toward the management education system. In some ways they work closely with the educating institutions, for example in recruiting, while at the same time staying clear of any responsibility for policy making. Companies are significantly involved in the life of the schools: presence at recruiting fairs, donations to students, and scholarships. They also take part in teaching activities, including development of syllabi. The relationship between higher education institutions and companies is strongly determined by geography (FNEGE study, 2003). Hence, the Parisian business schools benefit significantly from their proximity to the headquarters of many large corporations. On the other hand, the regional branches of large national and international corporations often lack this ability to create contacts with the universities.

The actual monetary contributions from the corporations to the business schools come in many forms (Basso *et al*, 2004):

- There is a so-called "education tax," paid by corporations, which the institutions are competing to collect. Competition for the collection of this money exists not only between the institutions, but also within each institution. Post-graduate and research programs are the only ones that cannot apply for these funds.
- Any tax due but not claimed by a university is collected by the local Chamber of Commerce and Industry which allocates the remaining money to GE-business schools.
- Direct donations to the schools are rare and rather insignificant. This is not part of the traditions. Some exceptions are the financing of Chairs.
- Corporations will have a significant need for management in the coming years. The effect of demography alone started being felt from 2004, requiring the replacement of 89,000 managers each year from 2007, more than double the replacement rate of 2001, which saw only 47,000 managers retire (Basso *et al*, 2004). Companies' recruitment criteria are also changing, moving markedly towards experience rather than knowledge or know-how (FNEGE, 2003). The competencies sought by companies seem to combine multi-competence profiles and functional specialists. They would also like to see much closer links between technological education and management education, in order to bring closer together those who produce and those who manage. In the face of the coming need to recruit young graduates, certain companies are not hesitating to become directly involved in the educational process. Regarding companies' demand for continuing education (FNEGE, 2004), corporations do not want to increase their continuing management education budgets. However, it is possible to imagine an increase in the part financed directly by the participants, as certain institutions have already seen. According to the same study, in the next five years, the courses that will see a rise in demand are:

  - tailor-made programs
  - inter-company courses
  - coaching and personal development
  - English-speaking international educational courses

According to this study, courses will become shorter, while "blended learning," linking on-site and distance learning may develop.

The regulatory bodies

Regional, national and supra-national regulation

The chambers of commerce and industry (CCI)

Generally speaking, the GE-business schools are not independent, as they are controlled by the CCI. Most of the schools depend on the CCI not only for their budget, but also for their administrative staff. The CCI therefore plays a central part in the structure and governance of the schools. Founded by Napoleon Bonaparte in 1803, the Chambers of Commerce and Industry are made up of publicly owned institutions. They fall under the supervision of the Ministry for Industry and Trade. Their role is "analyzing economic fabric, supporting the corporations, taking part in regional planning, and managing developments" (www. cci.fr). The initial and continuing training of administrative workers is a priority for the CCI and accounts for 25 percent of their total budget on average.

The CCI have seen their financial resources decrease over the past ten years. One of the main sources of revenue for the CCI is a specific tax on companies-professional tax (IATP). This tax is growing below inflation. The CCI are no longer allowed to collect the training tax that they had been collecting up until March, 2004. Understanding the high demand on financial resources, the CCI have significantly limited the growth in subsidies for their institutions.

Ministries

Business schools and universities are controlled by two separate ministries. The GE-Business schools are under the supervision of the Ministry for the Industry of the Economy and Finances, while the universities depend on the Ministry for National Education. In the new "Bachelor-Master-Doctorate" structure, the GE-business schools have to have their diploma accredited by the State to label them "Master's" while the universities award state-recognized diplomas. The relationship between the GE-business schools and the universities is thus closely tied to this question.

The question of funding remains key. The experienced within the field of public research in France was highlighted by the protests, in the spring of 2005, when French researchers complained about the lack of public support for research projects and decent salaries for public research staff. A national research agency was then created in order to fund selected research projects from all disciplines, at least in part. This new source of finance may prove to have a significant impact on university research in the coming years. However, the public authorities will have difficulty making any further financial commitments, notably in terms of salaries. At the same time, the CCI will be limiting the growth of their subsidies to institutions. Certain schools will have to finance new programs themselves over an extended period of time. In order to help diversify funding sources, the 2003 rules on the creation of foundations have been eased: companies can contribute up to 5 percent of their turnover and receive a tax break of up to 60 percent of the contribution.

Quality assessment

Management education in France is more and more subject to heavy quality regulation. The weight of the regulators and the definition of common European and/or global standards tend to bring schools and universities together, at least to a certain extent.

There are several players involved in quality assessment. Besides the regulatory authorities, the Chambers of Commerce and Industry and the governmental ministries, there are additional families of bodies which contribute to quality assessment:

- Academic societies and journals. These societies are involved in the creation of standards. Most of them tend to reward the best papers of their annual conference and the best theses of the year. They are backed by the review committees of journals, which precisely define their editorial line. In 2004, the economy & management section of the national evaluating committee for scientific research, related to the CNRS, clustered these magazines under four categories; this classification echoes the American standards and was started after French institutions did poorly in the Shanghai ranking. Francophone publications are basically in the fourth and least category. This clustering of journals is likely to have strong implications on researchers and their future publishing strategies.
- The public press also plays an important role in making the business schools attractive. The Financial Times's international ranking of MBAs is certainly the best known and the one that has the greatest influence.

For the moment, only a handful of French programs find their way into this ranking: only three French MBAs were ranked in the hundred listed in 2006: INSEAD's MBA took 8th place, HEC, the 22nd and ESCP-EAP the 99th, while ESSEC or ESCP-EAP or EM Lyon's were unranked. However, the good results achieved in the recent ranking of Masters of Science in Management, again produced by the Financial Times, highlighted French business schools' offerings internationally, thus encouraging further competitive positioning strategies by the "Grand Ecoles" programs (Appendix 1). French magazines also publish annual rankings of business schools and French university programs.

- The international accreditation authorities play a relatively new but increasingly significant role, notably to develop the international visibility of the institutions. The accreditation process is initiated by a request from the institution, which then itself pays for the process. Three main groups share the accreditation "market:"
  - The Association to Advance Collegiate Schools of Business ("AACSB") is an American agency that accredits management education institutions. Created in 1916, the organization is made up of 452 accredited members. At the end of 2004, five business schools had received the AACSB accreditation: ESSEC, HEC, ESCP-EAP and the ESC Toulouse and ESC Grenoble groups.
  - The European Foundation for Management Development ("EFMD") offers the EQUIS standard, created in 1997. The Equis label is awarded for a five-year period. Its main aim is the improvement of the quality of management education. At the beginning of 2004, 13 French institutions had been accredited and five others were in the process of evaluation.
  - The Association of MBAs ("AMBA") is the accreditation created in the United Kingdom in 1967. The association certifies only MBA programs and not the institutions themselves. It is mostly influential within the UK, slightly less so in the rest of Europe.

As a result, the competition between institutions is in large part mediated by these regulating authorities (journals and academic societies, the press, accreditation agencies) that help to legitimize reputations and therefore to direct demand towards the more visible, award-winning, ranked and accredited institutions.

Conclusion

The growing recognition in Europe of the French Masters of Science in Management, the increased flexibility to leverage private funds made possible by the 2007 reform, and the creation of public funds aimed at financing research projects may give a new impetus to management education and research in France. In addition, due to the pressure of international standards, the French market for management education is segmenting. There are basically three groups: those that have the means to compete in the international arena, about five players or so (HEC, ESSEC, ESCP-EAP, EM Lyon, Paris Dauphine university and obviously INSEAD); those who play a role at the national level, a dozen or so; and finally those with primarily local influence. In sum, the French system of management education is undergoing a major transformation. While the best French Business Schools are improving their standing in the international rankings, the other players struggle to compete in their global, regional, national and local arenas.

Appendix 1

The top 10 European master's in management programs (*The Financial Times*)

Ranks in 2007	Ranks in 2006	School name	Country	Program name
1	1	HEC Paris	France	Master of science in Management (Grande Ecole Program)
2	2	Cems	The Cems programme is taught in 17 countries	Master in International Management
3	8	London Schools of Economics	U.K.	Master of science in Management
4	3	ESCP-EAP	France, UK, Italy, Germany, Spain	Master in Management (Grande Ecole program)
5	6	ESSEC business schools	France	Master in Strategy and International Business
6	5	EM Lyon	France	Master of Science in Management (Grande Ecole program)
7	4	Grenoble Graduate School of Business	France	Master in International Business
8	10	Audencia	France	Master in management (Grande Ecole program)
9	8	Stockholm Schools of Economics	Sweden	Master of Science in Economics
10	13	RSM Erasmus University	Netherlands	Master in Management

(http://rankings.ft.com/masters-in-management)

References

Studies

"Attraits et qualité des études scientifiques universitaires", Porchet report, 2003.

"Bilan des campagnes de recrutement dans le supérieur", Ministère de l'Education Nationale, 2001.

"Bilan des campagnes de recrutement dans le supérieur", Ministère de l'Education Nationale, 2002.

"Bilan des campagnes de recrutement dans le supérieur", Ministère de l'Education Nationale, 2003.

"Bilan des campagnes de recrutement dans le supérieur", Ministère de l'Education Nationale, 2004.

"Etude sur la participation des étudiants aux élections universitaires", Rapport Cidem, 2004.

"La coopération européenne en matière de garantie de qualité dans l'enseignement supérieur, proposition de recommandation", P. Navatte, CPU, October 2004.

"La formation continue en gestion: états des lieux et perspectives", Bertrand Moingeon, FNEGE study, 2004.

"L'éducation au management en France entre traditions nationales et concurrence internationale – Cinq thèses sur les conditions d'un redéploiement des formations intiales à la gestion", Jean-Pierre Nioche, Symposium of 25th anniversary of FNEGE, 1993.

"La notion de PRES, texte sur la structuration de la recherche et de l'enseignement supérieur en France", text adopted by the conférence des présidents d'Université (CPU) of 21 October 2004.

"Nouvelle définition des tâches des enseignants et des enseignants chercheurs dans l'enseignement supérieur français", Esperet commission report, 2001.

Observatoire des formations à la gestion, FNEGE, 2003.

"Ouverture et développement à l'international des grandes écoles de gestion", Study by the Ministère de l'Industrie, de l'économie et des finances, novembre 2002.

"Professeur de management en France: une communauté? Quelle(s) communauté(s)?", David Courpasson and Zied Guedri, FNEGE study, 2006.

"Proposition pour une modification du décret 84–431 portant statut des Enseignants chercheurs", Rapport Belloc, 2003.

"Prospective 2015 des établissements de gestion. Cinq scénarios pour agir." Thomas Durand, with the assistance of Stéphanie Dameron, FNEGE study, 2005.

"Que deviennent les bacheliers après leur baccalauréat?", France, portrait social, Insee, 2004. www.lesechos.fr

"Rapport d'information sur l'enseignement supérieur en Europe de la délégation de l'Assemblée Nationale pour l'union européenne", Michel Herbillon (coord.), November 2004.

"Relations entre entreprises et établissements d'enseignement supérieur de gestion, bilan et perspectives", Christian Marmuse (coord.), FNEGE study, 2003.

"Scenarios 2003–2012", The Open University, internal report kindly provided by Brenda Gourley, Vice Chancellor, The Open University, Milton Keynes, UK.

Books

Basso O., P.-P. Dornier & J.-P. Mounier (2004), *Tu seras patron, mon fils, les grandes écoles de commerce face au modèle américain*, Village Mondial.

Pavis F. (2003), *Sociologie d'une discipline hétéronome. Le monde des formations en gestion entre universités et entreprises en France. Années 1960–1990*, Doctor of Sociology these for the Université Paris I-Panthéon-Sorbonne, 6 January.

10
Higher Education in Business: The Case of Spain

Isabel Gutiérrez and Jaime Ortega

This chapter provides an overview of Spanish undergraduate and graduate business education, and includes both the public and private educational systems. In Section I we describe the main suppliers of business education. We show that while public universities dominate the undergraduate and PhD levels, private business schools make up the main player at the master level. Section II describes business faculty with a particular emphasis on the public system. We provide an overview of salary and promotion systems. In Section III we describe the demand side, paying special attention to the demographic trends which affect the level of demand for all degrees and the specific demand for business studies. Finally, Section IV describes the role of the three main regulatory bodies.

The supply of higher education in business

Two main suppliers of business higher education can be differentiated in Spain, the universities and the business schools. These two types of educational institutions do not really compete at the same level of business training. While the universities are mainly devoted to the provision of undergraduate and doctoral degrees, business schools are the main suppliers for master and executive education in Spain. In this section we briefly describe this duality.

The universities

Public universities

The emergence of formal education in Business Administration (BA) in the Spanish context can be dated back to 1897 when the Schools of Commerce were founded by Royal Decree and set up in the main Spanish cities. The most prestigious Schools were those of Madrid,

Barcelona and Bilbao. Studies in these Schools were distributed over three levels: *peritaje mercantil* (elementary), *profesorado mercantil* (intermediate) and *intendente mercantil* and *actuario de seguros* (advanced). The curriculum emphasized accounting and management, but also covered law and general economics. The training provided in these schools was practitioner-oriented and the degrees were highly regarded socially. In contrast, research activities in the business field were neglected and professors usually combined their teaching duties with professional practice.

In 1943 the first *Faculty of Political Science and Economics* was founded in Madrid. This governmental decision attempted to fill the significant lag in the field of economics education in comparison with other countries in Europe. Ten years later two new Faculties were created in Barcelona and Bilbao due to the fast economic development of both Catalonia and the Basque Country. However, the early curricula of the Faculties did not cover business administration subjects. The Faculties largely ignored the Schools of Commerce with respect to syllabus design and the provision of teaching staff. Training in BA remained the responsibility of the Schools of Commerce.

In 1953, as a result of the absorption of the advanced courses of the Schools of Commerce, these Faculties were transformed into *Faculties of Political, Economic and Commercial Sciences* with specific branches in Economics, Business Administration and Actuarial Sciences. The amount of teaching in business administration became more important, but still had a reduced share of the curriculum in comparison to general economics and law subjects. In parallel, the faculty body was differentiated by introducing the specific fields of Accounting and Business Economics. This reform had a deep effect on the Schools of Commerce, since their advanced courses were absorbed into the teaching of the Faculties and the greater prestige in teaching within the subject areas of Accounting and Business Economics moved from the Schools of Commerce to the Faculties.

In 1971 the name and the teaching profiles of these Faculties were again modified, and since then the *Faculties of Economics and Business* are responsible for delivering two separate undergraduate degrees, one in Economics and another one in Business Administration. In 1972 the Spanish government decided to integrate the Schools of Commerce into the university system. From that year the studies for the Licentiate degree in BA (4–5 years) and the Doctorate in BA were offered in the Faculties of Economics and Business, while the Diplomas in BA (3 years) were delivered in the Schools of Commerce within the corresponding

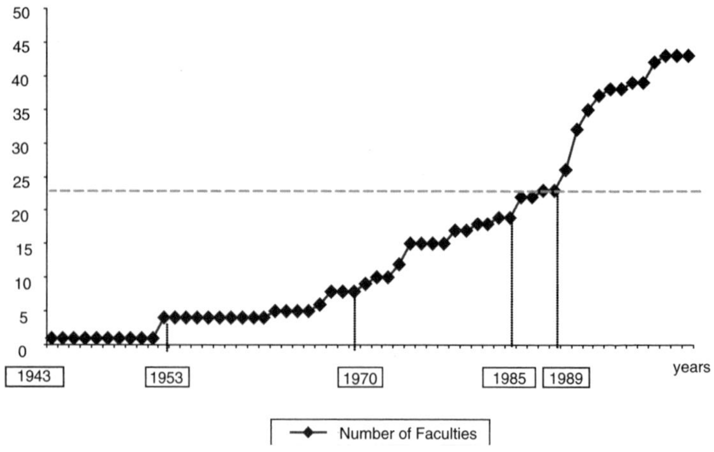

Figure 10.1   Growth of faculties of economics and business per year of foundation
Source: Own Elaboration.

university. Despite this process of integration, while economics studies concentrated tradition and prestige, business studies were generally viewed as secondary and less rigorous. In fact, the majority of business degrees were offered with several years of delay with respect to the Degrees in Economics in the Faculties of Economics and Business.[1] Both the creation of a new and specialized type of Faculty and the integration of Schools of Commerce in the universities contributed to a process of expansion that accelerated in the 1980s and 1990s. Figure 10.1 illustrates that the growth of Faculties of Economics and Business started around the mid seventies and that the number of faculties doubled in the mid eighties. For the most part, however, this should not be interpreted as an increase in the supply of business education, but rather as a reorganization process whereby some campuses or pre-existing faculties were segregated in order to create new universities. In total, eighteen public universities were created after 1989, but only five (Carlos III, Pompeu Fabra, Jaume I, Rey Juan Carlos, and Pablo de Olavide) were strictly new.[2] Moreover, supply of business education by these five schools is relatively small.

In addition, some subjects related to BA are also included to some extent in the curricula of other university centers with different scientific or professional orientations, such as Industrial Engineering. Table 10.1 shows all undergraduate degrees related to business education

Table 10.1   Official undergraduate degrees narrowly related to BA

Diplomas (three years of training)	Licentiate (four or five years of training, depending on the university)	Specialized degrees (Two additional years after bachelor or diploma)
*Business Administration (DE) *Tourism (DT) *Public Administration (DGAP)	*Business Administration (LADE) *Economics (LE)	*Actuarial Sciences (LCA) *Market Research and Marketing Techniques (LITM) *Industrial Organization Engineering (IO)

Source: Own elaboration Degrees in color are more strictly related to business administration.

Table 10.2   Structure of the higher education system

Degrees of higher education in Spain (before the Bologna agreement)				
Entrance into higher education	+3	+4	+5	+6	+8 (or more)
Entry examination (*Selectividad*)	Diploma	Licentiate degree	Licentiate degree		Doctoral degree

Degrees of higher education in Spain (after the Bologna agreement)				
Entrance into higher education	+3	+4	+5	+6	+8 (or more)
Entry examination (*Selectividad*)		Undergraduate degree	Master degree (Master of Science-professional)	Master degree (Master of Science-academic)	Doctoral degree

Source: Own Elaboration.

as they are currently offered, and Table 10.2 shows the changes to be introduced as a result of the Bologna agreement.

The Spanish university regulation changed dramatically after the University Reform Act (LRU) of 1983, but the structure described remains the same as far as the BA education is concerned. The reform affected mainly the research incentives, the definition of the fields of research and teaching, and the corporate governance of universities, among other characteristics of the system. A new reform was enacted in 2001, and a new one is currently in the Spanish Parliament. The latter has to face the big challenge of adapting Faculties' curricula to the European Space of Higher Education.

As opposed to undergraduate curricula, which are regulated by law, doctoral curricula are quite freely designed by the universities. They typically comprise one or two years of course work and a thesis-writing period. There is great variety in such programs: while some of them are full-time programs, others are designed as part-time programs; some of them are very wide in scope, but others are very specialized. As shown in Figure 10.2, research in business administration has been traditionally weak in Spain and has only very recently increased. The number of PhD theses in business administration has greatly increased in the last twenty years according to the official data source *Teseo*. Before the mid-eighties PhD theses were extremely rare (ten or fewer per year), but have significantly increased since the mid-nineties. It should however be noted that the large increase experienced in 2000–2002 and the subsequent reduction in 2002–2004 are largely due to the Law of 2001. The law established more centralized rules for hiring and promotion (see section below) and led many doctoral students to finish their theses earlier. It may also have led some of the departments to lower their thesis requirements in order to be able to hire their own doctoral students under the old (pre-2001) system's rules.

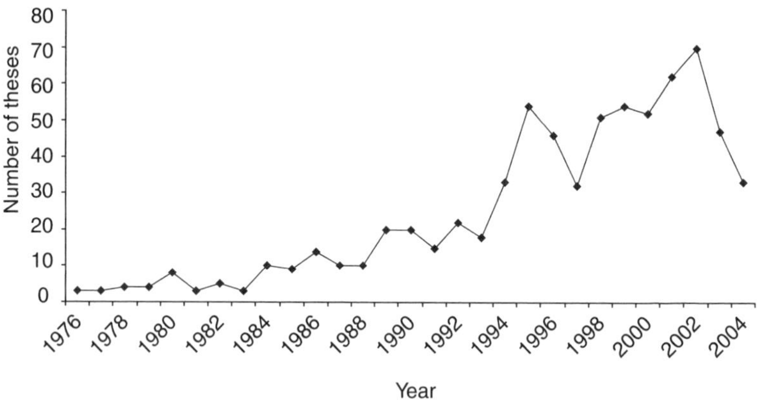

Figure 10.2   PhD theses in business administration (all universities)

Source: http://www.mcu.es/TESEO/

Catholic church universities

Currently existing Catholic Church universities are shown in Table 10. 3. As in other European countries, the Catholic Church had originally played a crucial role in the creation of the first universities, which in some cases (*e.g.* Palencia and Salamanca) were born from the schools of the cathedrals. The history of Spanish universities is beyond the scope of this paper, but it should be noted that the first universities were created in the 13th century: specifically, the Universities of Palencia was created between 1208 and 1214, the University of Salamanca was created around 1218, and by 1300 there were already four universities in Spain (the two above-mentioned universities and the universities of

Table 10.3   Spanish catholic universities

Traditional Church Universities

	Year of foundation	Year of official recognition by the Spanish government	Official degrees in BA since	Governance and/or ownership
Universidad de Navarra	1952	1962	1987	Opus Dei
Universidad de Deusto	1886	1963	1973	Jesuits
Universidad Pontificia de Comillas	1904	1977	1981	Jesuits
Universidad Pontificia de Salamanca	1940	1970	1997	Spanish Episcopal Conference

New Catholic Universities

	Year of foundation	Year of official recognition by the Regional government	Official degrees in BA since	Governance and/or ownership
Universidad Católica de Valencia	2004	2004	2004	Catholic Foundation-Archbishopry of Valencia
Universidad Católica de Murcia	1996	1999	1999	Catholic Foundation
Universidad Católica de Ávila	1996	1999	1999	Bishopry of Ávila

Source: Own elaboration.

Valladolid and Lérida). The role of the monarchy, which contributed with funding and official recognition, was also very important. In fact, the first universities had to have both royal and pontifical recognition.

Historically, with the separation of Church and State the only old universities which remained completely governed by the Church were the pontifical universities. All other universities, which were public, lost their Catholic identity, first informally through the increasing separation between academic work and the Church, and then formally with the separation of Church and State. During the Franco dictatorship (1939–1975), because Catholicism was the official religion, all the public educational system was formally considered by the government as "Catholic," and the degrees granted by the pontifical universities were not even officially recognized. This lack of official recognition ended in April 1962 with a general Agreement between the Vatican and the Spanish State (the so-called *Concordato*). The *Concordato* included among others issues, the official qualification of the degrees delivered by the Catholic Universities, namely the University of Deusto, the Pontifical Universities of Salamanca and Comillas, and the University of Navarra.

Although these four universities had a long history of higher education in several fields, mainly philosophy and divinity studies, none of them included business or economics undergraduate degrees. The first Università Cattolica del Sacro Cuore that included BA as a Licentiate degree was the University of Deusto, located in Bilbao. The University of Navarra also included studies in BA in its center in Barcelona, IESE, but only at the master level. Later on, these Catholic universities started to create their own Faculties of Economics and Business.

However, it should be noted that some Catholic institutions were already offering business education before the pontifical and public universities introduced these studies in their curricula. Such parallel educational system consisted of a large number of smaller professional schools which were not recognized as universities and, in order to gain official recognition for their undergraduate degrees, had to sign so-called "ascription agreements" with officially recognized (public or Catholic Church) universities or integrate themselves into Catholic Church universities. The need for such "ascription agreements" ended with the Royal Decree of 1991 which allowed for the creation of private universities (see below) and led many of these schools to acquire a university status as private universities (see below).

The pioneers in the creation of professional schools of higher education were the Jesuits. In 1908 they had founded ICAI (*Catholic Institute for Arts and Industry*) which in 1950 built up a well-known School of

Industrial Engineering. ICAI expanded its scope in 1960 by founding ICADE, a specialized school for higher education business and law. Both ICAI and ICADE were integrated into Pontificia de Comillas in 1978. In 1964 the Jesuits founded ETEA in Córdoba as a school specialized in agriculture-oriented business education and in 1983 the school signed an "ascription agreement" with the University of Córdoba. ESADE was founded by the Jesuits in 1959 as an independent school and, although its degrees were not officially recognized until the mid-seventies (with the agreements between Spain and the Vatican) the institution had a strong reputation and acceptance in the job market. Differently from ICADE and ETEA, ESADE is a school which provides education in all the educational levels (undergraduate, master and doctoral). Nowadays, ESADE is a part of the private university Ramón Llull.

In addition to the four older Catholic universities, three new Catholic universities were more recently created and include business studies in their scope. The Università Cattolica del Sacro Cuore of Valencia originated from pre-existing schools that belonged to the Archbishopric of Valencia and used to be "ascribed" to the University of Valencia or to University Miguel Hernández. In contrast, the Catholic Universities of Ávila and Murcia did not originate from previously existing Faculties.

Private universities

Up to 1991, only the public universities and the Catholic Church universities were officially recognized as centers of higher education. In 1991, a Royal Decree regulated the conditions for the creation of private universities and since then several have been created, mostly in Madrid and Barcelona. The types of degrees that these universities can offer are the same as those offered by the public universities. Currently, there are sixteen private universities legally recognized in Spain, twelve of which are offering Licentiate degrees in Business Administration, and ten of which offer the Diploma in Business.

There is some variety within the set of private universities. A half of those universities are in fact Catholic, although they are not subject to the *Concordato*: the CEU universities (which include the Universities Abat Oliva, Cardenal Herrera and San Pablo) belong to a Catholic Foundation and originate from several schools which before 1991 were "ascribed" to public universities. University San Jorge belongs to a Catholic Foundation and the University of Mondragón belongs to the Mondragón Cooperative holding. Both originate from previously existing professional schools founded by Catholic priests. The Universities Francisco de Vitoria, Ramón Llull and SEK are also Catholic. The remaining private universities are not Catholic. Both

Catholic and non-Catholic private universities have a strong emphasis on teaching, close ties with the business environment, and relatively poor research records. The Catholic universities have stronger academic values whereas the non-Catholic universities follow a more business-like model.

Overview of the university system

To sum up, the university system in Spain is currently composed of three types of educational actors: the public universities, the Catholic Church universities and the private universities (see Table 10.4).

Table 10.4   Universities in the Spanish higher education system

Type	No.	Name
Public universities	48	A Coruña; Alcalá de Henares; Alicante; Almería; Autónoma de Barcelona; Autónoma de Madrid; Barcelona; Burgos; Cádiz; Cantabria; Carlos III de Madrid; Castilla-La Mancha; Complutense de Madrid; Córdoba; Extremadura; Girona; Granada; Huelva; Illes Balears; Jaén; Jaume I de Castellón; La Laguna; La Rioja; Las Palmas de Gran Canaria; León; Lleida; Málaga; Miguel Hernández de Elche; Murcia; Nacional de Educación a Distancia (UNED)*; Oviedo; Pablo de Olavide; País Vasco; Politécnica de Cartagena; Politécnica de Catalunya; Politécnica de Madrid; Politécnica de Valencia; Pompeu Fabra; Pública de Navarra; Rey Juan Carlos; Rovira i Virgili; Salamanca; Santiago de Compostela; Sevilla; Valencia-Estudi General; Valladolid; Vigo; Zaragoza
Private Universities	16	Abat Oliba CEU; Alfonso X El Sabio; Antonio de Nebrija; Camilo José Cela; Cardenal Herrera-CEU; Europea de Madrid; Europea Miguel de Cervantes; Francisco de Vitoria; Internacional de Cataluña; Mondragón Unibertsitatea; Oberta de Catalunya*; Ramon Llull; San Jorge; San Pablo CEU; SEK; Vic
Catholic Church Universities	7	Católica de Valencia San Vicente Mártir; Católica San Antonio de Murcia; Católica Santa Teresa de Ávila; Deusto; Navarra; Pontificia Comillas; Pontificia de Salamanca

* Distance and on line Education.

Source: http://www.mec.es/educa/ccuniv/html/Registro_Nacional_de_Universidades_centros_y_ensenanzas/

Table 10.5   Number of centers offering higher education in business administration per universities and type of degree (year 2006)

	Degrees							
	Licenciate Business Admin	Licenciate Economics	Specialization Engineering in Industrial Organization	Diploma Business Admin	Diploma Tourism	Diploma Public Administration	Specialization Actuarial Sciences	Specialization Marketing
Public Universities (48)	46	33	14	45	41	24	11	15
Private Universities (16)	12	3	3	10	10	1	0	5
Catholic Church Universities (7)	7	1	3	3	2	0	2	1
Total number of Faculties offering BA Studies	65	37	20	58	53	25	13	21

Source: Own Elaboration (Columns in color indicate the degrees closer to business Education).

Table 10.6 Registered undergraduate students by degree and university status

Degree	Public		Catholic Church		Private		Total
	Number	Percent	Number	Percent	Number	Percent	
Licentiate in Business Administration (LADE)	86.618	88,67	6.160	6,31	4.908	5,02	97.686
Licentiate in Economics (LE)	35.785	98,31	481	1,32	135	0,37	36.401
Diploma in Business Administration (DCE)	73.326	89,58	577	0,70	7.951	9,71	81.854
Diploma in Tourism (RT)	27.170	91,98	1.089	3,69	1.279	4,33	29.538
Diploma in Public Administration (DGAP)	6.857	99,61	0	0,00	27	0,39	6.884
SD Actuarial Sciences (LCA)	1.671	96,48	61	3,52	0	0,00	1.732
SD Market Research (LITM) and Marketing Techniques	2.429	76,31	199	6,25	555	17,44	3.183
SD Industrial Organization Engineering (IOI)	3.422	78,58	511	11,73	422	9,69	4.355
Total	237.278	90,69	9.078	3,47	15.277	5,84	261.633

Source: http://www.mec.es/educa/ccuniv/html/estadistica/curso2003-2004/ESTADISTICA_UNIVERSITARIA_ALUMNADO_CURSO_2003-2004.pdf

Tables 10.5 and 10.6 indicate that the Spanish university system is dominated by public universities. This reality also applies to business education. From a total of 65 centers supplying the Licentiate degree in BA, 46 (*i.e.* 71 percent) are public Faculties of Economics and Business. Moreover, public universities are even larger in terms of students: as shown in Table 10.5, more than 90 percent of undergraduate students are registered in public universities (see Table 10.6). Even more dramatic are the differences in the Licentiate degree in Economics where only four Faculties are out the public system and 98 percent of students are registered in public universities.

In general, public universities have better reputations and quality than private ones at the undergraduate level. Often, private universities receive students whose academic records are not strong enough to be admitted into the public system. Some of the Catholic Church universities, particularly the older ones, have also better reputations and quality than private universities. Compared to public universities, they have a stronger emphasis on teaching and relatively poor research records.

Apart from some exceptions, the public university system is in general preferred by business students for both price and quality reasons: approximately 90 percent of all undergraduate students attend public universities.

The annual cost per student in the public university system varies from 3,200 to 4,000 euros, but the annual tuition fee is on average 800 euros per year, *i.e.* students only pay 20 percent of the cost of higher education. The remaining 80 percent is primarily funded by the Autonomous Communities (regional governments), which provide approximately 76 percent of total revenue through direct subsidies (see Figure 10.3).

Universities budget distribution in spain

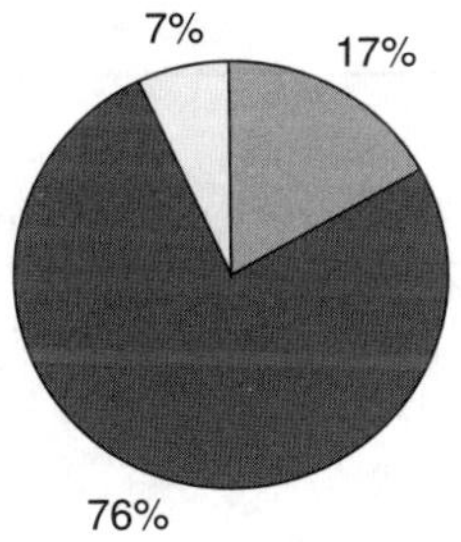

Figure 10.3 Public universities revenue

Regional Government Subsidies (76%), Students Fees (17%), other revenues (7%)

Source: Own elaboration based on the budgets of six public universities (budget year in parenthesis): Autónoma de Madrid (2006), Oviedo (2005), Sevilla (2005), Valladolid (2005), Valencia (2005), and Zaragoza (2005).

Catholic Church and private universities are much more expensive. In Catholic Church universities' fees vary from 3,500 euros for the new institutions (U. Católica de Ávila, U. Católica de Valencia, or U. Católica de Murcia) to approximately 6,500 euros for ICADE or ESADE; and in private universities' annual tuition fees increase to up to 6,000 euros.

Whereas undergraduate education is dominated by public universities, a completely different story happens at the master level. Before the early 1990s, the public universities neglected the education at the master level and were devoted to provide both undergraduate and doctoral training. Professional and executive education were in the hands of private institutions. At the beginning of the nineties this situation started to change when some public universities introduced the so-called "university master programs," a hybrid educational product oriented to young graduates with little or no professional experience. Nowadays, these university masters are commonly offered by universities (see Table 10. 7). In most cases these masters do not represent real competition for the Business Schools that operate in Spain and have a more limited impact on job market value: they target students with little or no professional experience, have weak links with the business environment and weak alumni networks, and do not seek accreditation from the standard international bodies.[3] The origin of these university masters is closely linked to the historically high Spanish unemployment rates. In the 1980s and early 1990s graduates with licentiate degrees would spend a long time looking for a job. University masters provided them with an opportunity to further their training while looking for a job.

Table 10.7 Number of master and graduate programs by university types (academic year 2005–2006)

	Public universities	Private universities	Catholic church universities
Full MBA	30	5	5
Specialized MBA (Finance, Marketing, and the like)	37	9	7
Specialized courses (short duration)	38	5	3
Executive MBA	9	2	3

Source: Own Elaboration from http://cv1.cpd.ua.es/EstudiosXXI/0ESTU0/SU2PPESII1EE2/ST6064/index.html

Although these masters provided a more market-oriented training than undergraduate degrees, they did not allow students to access jobs qualitatively different from the ones available to fresh licentiate graduates. In this sense they differed from MBA programs, which aim at providing a qualitatively important career move.

Tables 10.5 and 10.7 show that 65 percent of public universities offering a Bachelor degree in BA also offer an MBA program. This percentage goes up to 71 percent in the case of Catholic Church universities. The main difference is in the supply of executive education. While 50 percent of Catholic universities with an undergraduate degree in BA offer executive MBA programs, the percentage goes down to 19 percent for public universities.

The business schools

The first business schools emerged in Spain in the late 1950s as very active actors in both executive and MBA education and in parallel to the creation of Catholic schools of higher education referred to in section I. The three pioneers, EADA (founded in 1957), IESE (1958) and ESADE (1959), were located in Barcelona because of the relative prosperity of Catalonia at that time. Madrid's main school, Instituto de Empresa was founded much later, in 1973, with the purpose of covering an enormous void in executive education in Spain's capital city.

Due to the fast economic development of Spain in the last two decades, all business schools have significantly expanded their scope and geographical market. Today Madrid is the economic and financial capital of Spain and the Schools that were initially located in Barcelona have opened new educational centers in Madrid. For instance, IESE expanded its geographical domain by creating in 1982 a new campus in Madrid which is exclusively devoted to executive education. ESADE's Madrid campus is also specialized in executive and professional education.

Three of the Spanish Business Schools are listed in the Financial Times's ranking (see Table 10.8): Instituto de Empresa, IESE and ESADE. These schools are internationally oriented both in terms of faculty and students, and offer both regular programs (Full time MBA and Executive MBA) and executive education courses (in-company training, recycling functional executives, and senior programs, among others).

So far, international accreditation has played a modest role in Spain. Only four business schools (EADA, IESE, ESADE and Instituto de Empresa) and one university (U. Carlos III) have gained at least one of the three international accreditations (AACSB, AMBA or EQUIS), and

Table 10.8 Main business schools and MBA programs: international rankings and accreditations

Business school	Year of foundation	FT ranking		University dependency	Accreditation		
		Global MBA 2006	Executive MBA 2005		AACSB	EQUIS	AMBA
Escuela de Alta Dirección y Administración (EADA)	1957	–	–	NONE	NO	YES	YES
Instituto de Estudios Superiores de la Empresa (IESE)	1958	13	–	U. Navarra	NO	YES	YES
Escuela Superior de Administración de Empresas (ESADE)	1959	27	–	U. Ramón Llull	YES	YES	YES
Escuela Superior de Gestión Comercial y Marketing (ESIC)	1965	–	–	U. Rey Juan Carlos U. Miguel Hernández	NO	NO	NO
Instituto de Empresa (IE)	1973	12	4	NONE	YES	YES	YES

Source: Own Elaboration.

only two business schools (ESADE and Instituto de Empresa) have gained the three accreditations. Although accredited schools have gained great international visibility and acceptance, most business schools and universities are not applying for accreditation. This is largely due to the segmented nature of the Spanish system, where business schools are the main suppliers of MBA programs, and universities are the main research actors. Most business schools lack the research records that are needed for accreditation, and most universities offer Master's programs that do not conform to the student selection, quality of delivery and placement records required by international accreditation bodies.

To conclude, the market for education in BA is totally segmented in Spain. The undergraduate (Bachelor and Diplomas) and Doctoral levels are mostly dominated by public universities, whereas the Master, Executive and professional education levels are dominated by Business Schools. Perhaps the only exception to this segmentation is ESADE, which provides educational service in all of the levels, but is not a leader in any of them.

The faculty

By law, all business-related faculty working in public universities are classified into three fields: "Finance and Accounting," "Management" and "Marketing." These fields are very broadly defined.[4] The definition of these fields is important mostly for job assignment and promotion reasons. First, all faculty positions have to be assigned to one field and only those faculty members who already belong to the field can apply to the corresponding positions. Second, and most important, the promotion committees are defined by fields: thus, a committee appointed to fill a vacancy in the "Finance and Accounting" field can only be composed of faculty members who already belong to the field. Changing from one field to another is relatively simple – it just requires an administrative request – but is rarely done, mostly because the fields are quite largely defined. In fact, a more important problem comes from the heterogeneity of the fields themselves: for example, the "Finance and Accounting" is particularly heterogeneous and so is, to a lesser extent, the "Management" field.

In public universities there are approximately two thousand tenured professors (see Table 10.9). More than a half belong to the "Finance and Accounting" field, a bit more than a third belong to the "Management" field, and only ten percent belong to the "Marketing" field.

Table 10.9   Public university tenured professors by field (2003)

	No. of professors	%
Finance and Accounting	1,107	54.48
Management	706	34.74
Marketing	219	10.78
Total	2,032	100.00

Source: http://www.mec.es/educa/jsp/plantilla.jsp?area=ccuniv&id=1031D

Table 10.10   Public university tenured professors by field and level (2003)

Field	TEU		CEU		TU		CU	
	No.	%	No.	%	No.	%	No.	%
Finance and Accounting	482	43.54	48	4.34	424	38.30	153	13.82
Management	240	33.99	47	6.66	302	42.78	117	16.57
Marketing	61	27.85	8	3.65	109	49.77	41	18.72

Source: http://www.mec.es/educa/jsp/plantilla.jsp?area=ccuniv&id=1031D

As far as job levels are concerned, tenured positions can be of four types: "Profesor Titular de Escuela Universitaria" (TEU), "Catedrático de Escuela Universitaria" (CEU), "Profesor Titular de Universidad" (TU) and "Catedrático de Universidad" (CU). The CU and TU categories are equivalent to the Professor and Associate Professor categories. The CEU category is equivalent to a full professorship and the TEU position is a tenured professorship which does not require a PhD degree.[5] Table 10.10 shows the number of tenured professors of each type by field.

According to Table 10.10 (Figure 10.4), the ratio of associate professors to full professors (TU/CU) is very similar across fields: 2.77 for "Finance and Accounting", 2.58 for "Management", and 2.66 for "Marketing".

Remuneration in the public university system depends upon job level, seniority and research output. Table 10.11 and Figure 10.5 show gross monthly remuneration for an associate professor (TU) and a full professor (CU) as a function of seniority. "Minimum salary" refers to all pay components that are independent of performance, i.e. the basic salary plus all seniority-based supplements. There are two such supplements: one of them is added every three years (around 40 monthly euros) and

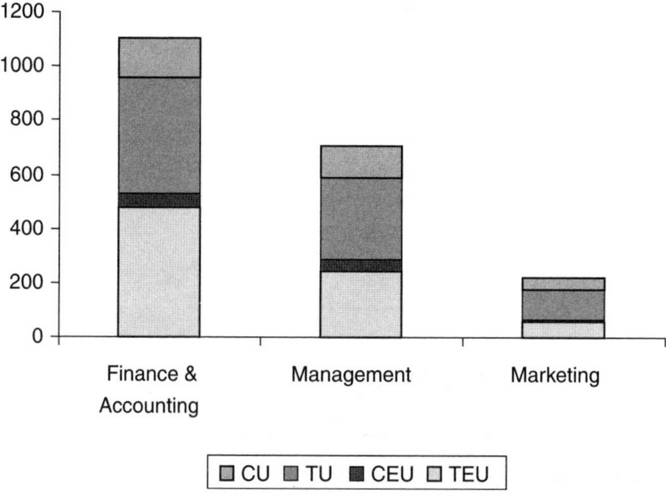

Figure 10.4   Public university tenured professors by field and level

Table 10.11   Gross monthly salaries of tenured professors (in euros)

Years of tenure	TU		CU	
	Minimum	Maximum	Minimum	Maximum
1	2,284	2,284		
11	2,641	2,966	3,477	3,621
21	2,998	3,556	3,888	4,320
31	3,395	4,187	4,340	5,061

Source: Own elaboration.

the second one is added every five years (around 115 monthly euros). "Maximum salary" refers to the minimum salary plus the maximum research bonus that a professor can earn at each stage in his or her career. The research bonus is granted every six years if the faculty member receives a positive research evaluation. Such evaluations are conducted by the National Research Activity Evaluation Commission (CNEAI) and are based on publication records (see below).

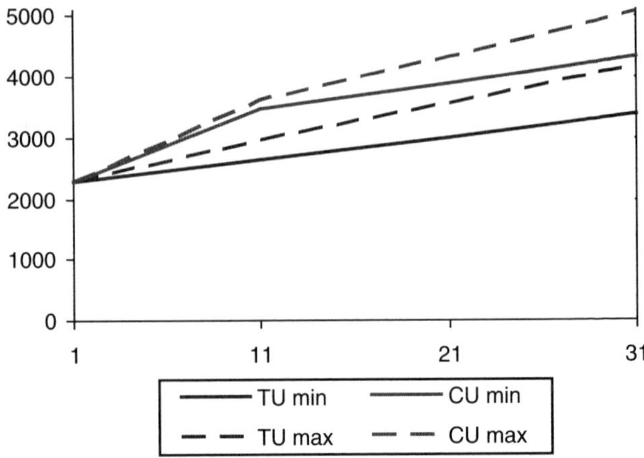

Figure 10.5   Gross monthly salaries of tenured professors as a function of tenure (in euros)

The table shows that, for an associate professor, basic remuneration increases by 48.64 percent over a 30-year career and maximum remuneration increases by 83.32 percent over the same period. Assuming the associate professor is promoted to full professor after ten years, which is a reasonable assumption for Spanish standards, the maximum increase over the 30-year period would be 121.58 percent. There are two important conclusions to be derived from these figures. First of all, career opportunities are extremely modest when remuneration is considered: professors who would pursue their careers over a 30-year period and who would have good research records would only be able to double their salaries over their careers. The best full professors in terms of research output would multiply their salaries by only 2.2 over a lifetime career and, by the end of their careers, their research bonuses would represent only 14 percent of total remuneration. For associate professors at the beginning of their careers, the maximum research bonuses would be even smaller (between 5 and 10 percent).

Such weak incentives for research are one of the reasons why research output in Spain is low. A large number of professors little by little abandon research and focus on activities that yield much higher monetary payoffs, such as consulting, management and Master-level teaching. As far as Master-level teaching is concerned, it must be noted that so far (before the Bologna agreement was implemented in Spain) all Masters degrees offered by public universities have been offered at market prices. Since instructors are not allowed to reduce their undergraduate teaching in order to increase their Master-level teaching, and universities must finance Masters degrees with tuitions, professors teaching at the Master-level are usually rewarded at market prices. This introduces very negative incentives for research. To take a realistic example, suppose a professor teaches a 20-hour MBA course every year and is paid 150 euros per hour, which is a reasonable and perhaps conservative estimate. This would increase his salary by 250 euros per month. For an associate professor, this would be equivalent to obtaining two positive research evaluations, for which he would have to wait twelve years.

Promotion rules for permanent positions are currently made in two steps. The first step is a national accreditation which is organized by fields. Candidates are evaluated by an assessment committee whose members are randomly chosen from a pool of professors of the relevant fields with a minimum number of positive research evaluations. At the second step, universities can post vacancies for associate or full professorships. Only those professors who have already passed their accreditation can apply to these positions. This second step is decentralized: each university can select the candidates it prefers.

In Catholic and private universities, faculty salaries are normally slightly higher than in public universities, but monetary incentives for research are usually non-existent and teaching loads are higher than in public universities. All in all, only the most important Business Schools offer salaries which are competitive at the international level.

The demand for higher education in business

Demand for bachelor degrees

A vast majority of undergraduate students come straight from High School and have to take a set of university entry exams called *Selectividad* which are common to all universities and are administered by the government. The *Selectividad* includes several exams, some of which correspond to core courses while others correspond to elective courses. The *Selectividad* grade is combined with the average High School grade to obtain a final grade which is used to assign universities and degrees. For the public university system, once they have completed their *Selectividad* exams and provided that their final grade is greater than 5, applicants fill in a list with the degrees and universities to which they would like to apply, by order of preference. Applicants are then mechanically assigned, starting from those with the highest grades and going down to those with the lower grades. Private and Catholic universities do not follow this mechanical system but the *Selectividad* grade is still usually considered an important factor.

Ex post, the Ministry of Education publishes the minimum entry grades for each university and degree, i.e. the lowest grade among all students who were accepted for that degree in that specific university. Table 10.12 shows these grades for a sample of undergraduate degrees.

Minimum entry grades can be viewed as prices, which depend upon the supply and demand of education. A grade equal to 5 denotes that the number of student "vacancies" offered by the system is larger than the number of students whose final grade is at least 5 and who would like to study for that particular degree. In contrast, a grade higher than 5 denotes that some students whose final grade is greater than 5 and who would like to study for that degree are not allowed to. For the two main degrees in business administration (the Licentiate Degree and the Diploma in Business Administration) minimum entry grades are greater than 5 and are greater than the entry grades of other traditionally important degrees such as Law or Economics.

Table 10.12   Minimum entry grades: comparison with selected degrees (2005–2006)

Degree	Supply	Minimum entry grade
Civil Engineering	1,356	6.86
Licentiate in Biology	4,946	5.51
Industrial Engineering	4,713	5.42
Licentiate in Business Administration (LADE)	14,360	5.34
Telecommunications Engineering	3,419	5.29
Diploma in Business Administration (DCE)	12,827	5.18
Licentiate in Economics (LE)	5,344	5.14
Licentiate in Philosophy	923	5.04
Licentiate in Law	8,643	5.03
Licentiate in Hispanic Philology	1,532	5.03
Licentiate in Physics	1,169	5.00

Source: http://apliweb.mec.es/notasweb/jsp/compBdDo.do

Table 10.12 also shows that for most degrees, the minimum entry grade is quite low. In fact there are very few degrees for which it is above 6 and for most degrees the entry grades are very close or equal to 5. The public university system has been steadily increasing its capacity since the early 1980s in order to accommodate the Spanish baby boom cohorts, who started their undergraduate studies in the 1980s and early 1990s. However, due to a sharp decrease in natality, the baby boom cohorts have been followed by much smaller cohorts who have been starting their undergraduate degrees in the last ten years. Despite the reduction in cohort sizes, the supply of public universities has continued to increase in these years, thus leading to the current situation whereby for most university degrees a very modest grade is sufficient for an application to be admitted.

Figure 10.6 illustrates the reduction in natality, which took place from the mid-1970s to the mid-1990s. The cohorts that will be entering the undergraduate degrees in the next ten years (2006–2016) are those born between 1988 and 1998. The average annual size of these cohorts is 385,252. Taking into account that the average size of the 1978–1988 cohorts was 505,272, we can estimate that the total number of undergraduate students in the next ten years will be 24 percent lower than the number of undergraduate students in the last 10 years (1996–2006). With respect to the number of undergraduate students who started their degrees between 1986 and 1996, we estimate that the number of

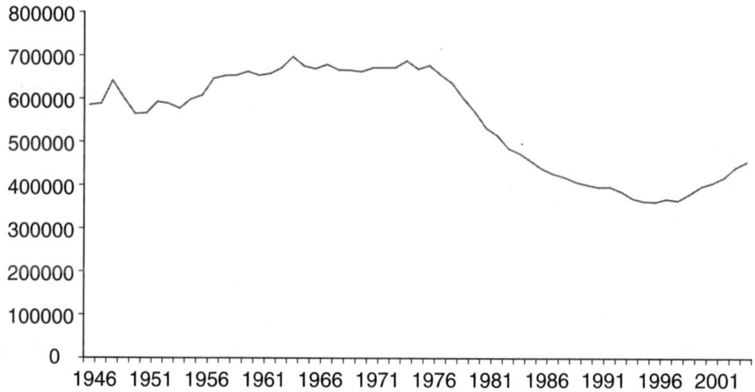

Figure 10.6   Number of births (1946–2004)

Source: http://www.ine.es/inebase/cgi/um?M=%2Ft20%2Fe245%2Fp05&O=inebase&N=&L=

undergraduate students who will start their degrees between 2006 and 2016 will be 42 percent lower.

Demand for continuous and executive education

Although there are no national data, the demand for continuous and executive education appears to be relatively small in Spain, for two main reasons. First of all, the Spanish labor market has experienced very high unemployment rates in the 1980s and 1990s, and even in the last decade unemployment rates have been above the European average. Second, the labor market relies to a large extent on informal networks. For these two reasons, it is still very costly for employees to change jobs and, to the extent that continuous and executive education aim at providing a career change, interest for such courses remains relatively small.

Demand from companies

Overall, there has been little communication between Spanish companies and universities, which has made it difficult for universities to adjust their degrees to the human resource needs of companies. While companies are typically satisfied with the academic level of graduates, they consider that undergraduate degrees lack adequate training in work skills. The fact that such skills are not very well developed at the universities partly explains why the Spanish MBA degrees that are most demanded are those offered by private business schools, which have a strong focus on skills development.

The distance between the business and academic worlds in Spain explains why most businesses view undergraduate degrees as selection and signaling devices. The demand for engineers is very strong, even for management-related positions, because entry into engineering schools is more difficult and thus provides more guarantees about the candidates' abilities. In fact, as shown in Table 10.13, only a minority of IBEX-35 CEOs has an academic background in Economics, and almost a half are Engineers. Among those engineers, approximately a third have pursued an MBA degree.

Given the reduction in the number of students, it is expected that in the next ten years many Engineering degrees will have low (close to 5) entry grades. As a consequence, the advantage of engineering schools in terms of selection will gradually diminish and business degrees might be in a better position to compete against engineering degrees.

Table 10.13   Academic background of IBEX-35 CEOs

Degree	CEOs (%)
Engineering	45
Licentiate Degree in Economics	29
Licentiate Degree in Law	19
No degree	7
Total	100
MBA degree	26
Engineers with MBA degree	36

Source: Own elaboration from the web site of companies listed in IBEX35.

The regulatory bodies

Regional, national and supra-national regulation

The Spanish educational system has become increasingly decentralized in the last few years. However, the central government still retains important responsibilities, such as the definition of student selection requirements, curricular requirements, promotion rules, fees and salaries. Regional Governments are essentially responsible for the funding and have less regulatory power than the central government. They decide how much to invest in different universities and can also establish extra compensation for faculty members.

Student selection is mechanically determined according to the rules that we have outlined above. Before 2003, the Spanish market used to be segmented: by law, High School graduates could apply only to the public universities located in their area of residence. Since 2003 this regulation is no longer in place and all students can apply to all public universities. As far as curricular requirements are concerned, the Ministry of Education establishes minimum requirements that have to be met by all degrees and then universities have some freedom to implement such requirements. Specifically, the Ministry establishes how credits have to be distributed across the various fields, and the universities can decide which subjects are offered within each field.

As far as promotion requirements are concerned, regulation has increased in the last few years. Before 2002, the system was more decentralized: there were no national habilitation exams; there was one ad-hoc selection committee appointed for each position at each university; and finally, two out of five members of the selection committee would be appointed by the university that had posted the vacancy. After 2002, a more centralized system was put in place (see above). The Spanish Parliament is now discussing a deep reform of the Law of Universities enacted in 2001 and it is expected that universities gain more autonomy and the system become more decentralized again.

Quality assessment

Besides the regulatory role of the central and autonomous governments, there are three important national agencies that play an important quality assessment role: CNEAI, ANECA and ANEP.

CNEAI

CNEAI (National Research Activity Evaluation Commission) was created by law in December 1989 and its role is to carry out the six-year research evaluations that have been mentioned in Section II. CNEAI objectives are twofold: to selectively increase researchers' salaries (i.e. an economic motivation), and to officially improve the publication patterns of Spanish researchers into line with the patterns followed by the rest of the Western countries. The ultimate objective of this agency is to foster university professors' research productivity and improve the diffusion of this research both nationally and internationally.

CNEAI is organized in eleven expert committees that include the fields of Mathematics and Physics, Chemistry, Cellular and Molecular Biology, Biomedical Sciences, Life and Earth Sciences, Engineering and Architecture, Social/Political/Behavioural/Educational Sciences, Economics and Business Studies, Law and Jurisprudence, History and Art, and Philosophy/Philology/Linguistics. CNEAI members are university professors and are appointed by the government on an annual basis. Evaluations are based on publication records provided by the researchers themselves, and specific criteria are defined for each field. CNEAI evaluation system involves only tenured staff at research centers and universities.

This peer review evaluation system is fairly similar to the systems used in other countries such as the USA, The Netherlands and Australia. In particular, there are clear similarities between the Spanish system and the Research Assessment Exercises used in the UK since the beginning of the 1990s. However, there are specific features of the Spanish system. First, in most countries evaluation is carried out at the level of the institution or research group, but in Spain evaluation is carried out at the level of the individual researcher. Second, whereas the criteria used by the panel of reviewers to determine research quality are, in most countries, fairly diverse and more or less generic, in the Spanish case they are fairly explicit. Criteria by field have evolved over time and different standards have been approved in 1994, 1996, and 2005, and in general the changes introduced have sought to make the Spanish requirements more similar to the international scientific standards of each field.

In 2001 and 2007 the new Laws of Universities reinforced the role of these evaluations for pay and promotion purposes and, as a consequence of that, the CNEAI has become a crucial player in the higher education system: six-year evaluations are little by little being considered as a very important determinant of peer recognition; even though their economic impact on salaries is still very modest (see Section II). CNEAI has significantly contributed to the improvement of research productivity in Spain. The number of publications in international journals has greatly increased in all fields, including the field of Economics and Business, although research productivity still remains lower in comparison with the average across fields (see Figure 10.7).

Figure 10.7   Evolution of percentages of positive evaluated period by CNEAI

Source: http://www.mec.es/ciencia/cneai/files/Memoria%201989-2003%20-%20 UNIVERSIDAD.pdf

ANECA

The second key agency is ANECA (National Quality Evaluation and Accreditation Agency). It was created in 2002 and is responsible for certifying the quality of graduate and undergraduate programs as well as for accrediting professors. As far as programs are concerned, ANECA runs an Institutional Evaluation Program aimed at evaluating the quality of official undergraduate degrees; and a quality landmark program that provides accreditation for doctoral programs. Accreditation of doctoral programs is particularly important because it is a requirement for some public grants. As far as the accreditation of professors is concerned, ANECA primarily takes into account research records.

ANEP

La ANEP (National Agency for Evaluation and Prospective) was created in 1986 and its main role is to evaluate applications for research grants and other research-related funding. Evaluations are peer-based and anonymous. ANEP has played a very important role since its creation because it has contributed to introducing research-excellence criteria into public funding. In the business and economics fields, the main research funding program (the Ministry of Education's National R&D Plan) has granted approximately 4.6 million euros in 2004 (for approximately 75 research groups) and 5.6 million euros in 2005 (for approximately 100 research groups). Taking into account the number of applications, this means that approximately 35–45 percent of research projects are funded. In addition, ANEP also evaluates applications to some of the Regional Governments' research grants.

Conclusion

In the field of business administration, higher education is provided by four different actors in Spain: public universities, Catholic Church universities, private universities, and business schools. The system is highly segmented: whereas universities (particularly public) are the main players at the undergraduate and doctoral levels, business schools have stronger reputations at the masters level. In addition, it is a highly regulated system: private universities were only very recently allowed (in 1991), and the public system gives universities little discretion on budgetary matters, particularly faculty pay and tuition fees.

The high level of regulation hinders public universities' initiatives towards more active research and higher-quality teaching, and has contributed to build an organizational culture that does not foster academic excellence. Recent legislative changes have also brought considerable instability to the public university system: after the Law of 1983 a new Law was passed in 2001 and is in the process of being considerably changed again. This uncertainty, together with poor monetary incentives, is particularly detrimental in the business fields. The opportunity cost of an academic career is larger than in other academic fields and has increased in Spain due to the large economic growth and the business schools' increasing focus on research.

Business research has grown significantly in the last decade and has narrowed the gap with economics research, which had a longer tradition in Spain. However, there are still some important weaknesses. Although the number of international publications has greatly increased, publications in top journals are still rare. In addition, most high-quality research is concentrated in a few public universities and some business schools.

Universities and business schools face different challenges. As far as public universities are concerned, the main challenge is to change from a low-cost to a high-quality model of education. The public system has been traditionally designed to offer low-cost undergraduate education and to provide comparable standards of teaching quality throughout Spain. Although the system has been relatively successful in these respects, it has failed to foster academic excellence. Both in terms of teaching and research, the challenge for the coming years is to introduce greater accountability for quality so that public universities wishing to follow a high-quality strategy can receive adequate resources. As far as Catholic Church and private universities are concerned, we think that the main challenge will be to move from a teaching-based strategy towards a strategy that places a greater emphasis on research. This challenge is particularly important for some of the non-Catholic private universities that have adopted business-like models with relatively weak academic values.

On the business schools' side, there are in our view two related challenges. The first one is research. Being aware that international accreditation requires good research records, some of the business schools have improved their research, but this tendency needs to be consolidated. The second, related challenge concerns the composition of faculty. Traditionally, Spanish business schools have relied quite heavily on adjunct faculty and full-time faculty has often played a minor role.

Although adjunct faculty can help fill certain gaps in business education, a permanent, research-active body of full-time faculty is necessary to guarantee high academic standards in both research and teaching, and to guarantee homogeneous standards of delivery throughout the various academic programs.

Data sources

ANECA. http://www.aneca.es/
EADA. http://www.eada.edu/
ESADE Business School. http://www.esade.edu/
ESIC-Business and Marketing School. http://www.esic.es/
ETEA-Córdoba. http://www.etea.com/
ICADE. http://www.icade.es/
IESE Business School. http://www.iese.edu/
Instituto de Empresa. http://www.ie.edu/
Instituto Nacional de Estadística de España. http://www.ine.es/
  Indicadores demográficos básicos.
Ministry of Education of Spain. http://www.mec.es/
  Base de Datos de tesis doctorales: TESEO
  Datos y Cifras del Sistema Universitario Español
  Estadística del Alumnado.
  Estadística Universitaria
  Guía de las Enseñanzas Universitarias
  Informe del profesorado funcionario de las Universidades Públicas Españolas y la actividad investigadora. CNEAI
  Memoria de los resultados de las evaluaciones realizadas de 1989 a 2003 (profesores de universidad). CNEAI
  Precios Públicos universitarios para cada Comunidad Autónoma
Universia. Portal de Universidades Españolas y Latinoamericanas. http://www.universia.es/
Web sites of Spanish universities.

11
Management Education in Italy[*]

Donatella Depperu

The competitive system in the field of management studies

In Italy there are 92 universities, almost 70 percent of which have a faculty of economics and/or management, where it is possible to get a Bachelor's degree in Economics or Business Studies.[1] Just two universities have more than one faculty in the field of economics or management (the Università Cattolica del Sacro Cuore and the University of Bologna). Table 11.1 shows how many universities offer degrees in management and in economics.

The number of these faculties has increased a lot in the last 30 years as a result of the increasing interest of students for the topics dealt with in these faculties and the chances to get a job after graduation. In the last five years it has slightly increased.

The total number of university students in management or economics was around 225.000 in the academic year 2004–05.

It is possible to access economics and management faculties after completing any kind of secondary school. Some universities require students to pass a test before enrolling and often some of them take into consideration the marks students got in their secondary schools in order to make a ranking and select those to enroll.

In the following pages the main players are described.

Competitors

To get a bachelor degree in Italy it is necessary to attend courses run by universities. No other institution is allowed to award such a degree.

The Italian University system has been restructured a few years ago through a reform (end of year 1999) and a new reform has been approved

Table 11.1   Number of universities that offer a degree in management

Years	Number of universities that offer degrees in management	Number of degrees in management
2005	59	165
2004	57	175
2003	57	179
2002	57	180
2001	56	185

Source: Miur – Banca dati offerta formativa.

Years	Number of universities that offer degrees in economics	Number of degrees in economics
2005	46	95
2004	45	98
2003	45	99
2002	45	105
2001	46	117

Fonte: Miur – Banca dati offerta formativa.

by the Italian Parliament in October 2005. While in the past most universities used to have 4-year courses, at the end of which students could get their degree (called *laurea*) now, according to the Bologna process, there are:

- Three-year courses to get the first level degree (the equivalent of a bachelor degree), called *laurea*;[2]
- two more years courses to get the second level degree (called *laurea specialistica or magistralis*);
- Ph.D. courses, accessible after the second level degree;
- Master courses. There are two kinds of master courses: first level master course (defined *master universitari di primo livello*) and second level master course (called *master universitari di secondo livello*). The first level master course can be taken after the bachelor degree; the second level master course can be attended after students have already got their *laurea specialistica*. First level master courses can share some courses with the *laurea magistralis* ones or be totally independent from them. The basic idea is that master courses should be more

Table 11.2 Structure of the education system in Italy

Degrees in higher education in Italy (before the reform of 1999)

Entrance into higher education	+2	+3	+4	+5	+6
Maturità		Diploma universitario	Laurea (economics, management, Italian literature, foreign languages, law, ...)	Laurea (architecture, engineering)	Laurea (medicine) Dottorato di ricerca

Degrees in higher education in Italy (after the reform of 1999)

Entrance into higher education	+2	+3	+4	+5	+6	+8
Maturità		Laurea triennale	Master universitario di primo livello	Laurea magistralis	Laurea (medicine)	Dottorato di ricerca

practical than the *Laurea magistralis* is. But those that share some courses with the *Laurea magistralis* are welcome as they give master students the opportunity to get also the *Laurea magistralis* in less than two years.

Table 11.2 shows the structure of the education system in Italy before and after the reform.

All the above degrees are recognized by the Ministry of Education.

Not all universities have Ph.D. courses and master courses. A few of them don't have any *laurea specialistica* course, but most of them offer a range of *lauree specialistiche* in the business or economics field (from a minimum of 2–3 to a maximum of 15–16).

Most Italian universities are state-owned, even though the few private universities in Italy are relevant for management studies. Table 11.3 shows the list of Italian universities (both state-owned and private) that offer degrees in economics and management. Around 15 percent of them are private.

State-owned universities

Italian state-owned universities are very diverse: some of them are rather small, local and concentrated on a few faculties; others are very large (some established many years ago, some recently), with a lot of

Table 11.3 Italian universities that offer degrees in economics and management

Degrees offered by economics and management faculties by University – 2005

University	Number of faculties of economics and/or management	Laurea triennale (management)	Laurea triennale (economics)	Lauree magistralis (economics, management, economical statistics)	First level masters	Second level masters
Politecnica delle Marche	1	3	2	4	2	2
Università degli Studi di Bari	1	4	2	4	6	0
Libera Università Mediterranea Jean Monnet	1	1	0	1	3	1
Università degli Studi di Bergamo	1	3	1	3	4	3
Università degli Studi di Bologna	3	10	8	14	26	2
Libera Università degli Studi di Bolzano	1	1	1	1	0	0
Università degli Studi di Brescia	1	3	1	3	0	0
Università degli Studi di Cagliari	1	2	2	2	1	1
Università della Calabria	1	2	0	3	7	
Università degli Studi di Cassino	1	3	1	2	2	0
Libero Istituto Universitario "Carlo Cattaneo" di Castellana	1	1	0	1	3	5
Università degli Studi di Catania	1	3	1	4	0	0
Università degli Studi "G. D'Annunzio" di Chieti-Pescara	1	3	4	6	1	0

Libera Università della Sicilia Centrale "Kore" (ENNA)	1	1	0	0	0	0
Università degli Studi di Ferrara	1	1	1	2	0	1
Università degli Studi di Firenze	1	5	1	14	7	2
Università degli Studi di Foggia	1	2	2	2	3	0
Università degli studi di Genova	1	4	1	5	4	1
Università degli Studi dell' Insubria	1	1	1	2	2	0
Università degli Studi dell'Aquila	1	3	0	1	2	0
Università degli Studi di Lecce	1	3	2	3	n.a.	n.a.
Università degli Studi di Macerata	1	3	0	2	3	0
Università degli Studi di Messina	1	2	3	3	1	0
Università degli Studi di Milano – Bicocca	1	3	3	4	2	0
Università Commerciale "Luigi Bocconi" di Milano	1	5	3	10	14	2
Università Cattolica del "Sacro Cuore" di Milano	3	7	2	11	12	2
Università degli Studi di Modena e Reggio Emilia	1	3	1	9	4	0
Università degli Studi del Molise	1	1	0	3	0	0
Università degli Studi di Napoli	1	2	3	7	2	2
Seconda Università degli Studi di Napoli	1	2	1	2	1	0

Continued

Table 11.3 Continued

University	Number of faculties of economics and/or management	Laurea triennale (management)	Laurea triennale (economics)	Lauree magistralis (economics, management, economical statistics)	First level masters	Second level masters
Università degli Studi di NAPOLI Parthenope	1	6	1	3	2	0
Università degli Studi di Padova	1	1	3	3	2	0
Università degli Studi di Palermo	1	2	2	3	3	0
Università degli Studi di Parma	1	4	1	4	5	0
Università degli Studi di Pavia	1	2	1	6	2	0
Università degli Studi di Perugia	1	6	0	6	3	1
Università degli Studi del Piemonte Orientale "A Avogadro"	1	2	0	2	5	0
Università degli Studi di Pisa	1	3	3	n.a.	n.a.	n.a.
Università degli Studi di Roma "La Sapienza"	1	6	6	16	21	
Università degli Studi di Roma "Tor Vergata"	1	3	3	3	11	9
Università degli Studi ROMA TRE	1	0	2	7	0	9
Libera Università Internazionale di Studi Sociali "Guido Carli" – (LUISS) di Roma	1	2	1	4	1	0

220

Libera Università degli Studi "S. Pio V" Roma	1	0	0	1	2	0
Università Telematica Guglielmo Marconi	1	0	1	0	5	1
Università' Telematica TEL.M.A.	1	1	0	0	0	0
Università degli Studi di Salerno	1	1	1	2	0	3
Università degli Studi del Sannio	1*	3	0	2	1	0
Università degli Studi di Sassari	1	2	1	2	0	0
Università degli Studi di Siena	1	3	5	8	6	3
Università degli studi di Torino	1	5	4	10	2	0
Università degli Studi di Trento	1	2	2	5	4	4
Università degli Studi di Trieste	1	3	2	4	3	0
Università degli Studi della Tuscia	1	2	0	2	0	0
Università degli Studi di Udine	1	3	1	5	2	1
Università telematica internazionale UNINETTUNO	1	1	1	0	0	0
Università degli Studi di Urbino	1	3	0	3	2	0
Università degli Studi "Ca' Foscari" di Venezia	1	5	3	14	3	2
Università degli Studi di Verona	1	3	2	7	9	1

Source: Miur – Database Offerta Formativa; Siti delle singole Università.

221

faculties, located in the largest towns of the country. The largest of them is La Sapienza University, that is located in Rome, with 21 faculties and more than 139.000 students.

In the North of Italy there is a high concentration of both state-owned and private universities (in Milan, for example, there are three private universities in the field of economics and management – Bocconi, Catholic and IULM), but also in Bari, Bologna, Napoli, Padova, Torino, Roma there are very large institutions: Bari University had almost 55.000 students in the academic year 2005–06, Bologna almost 92.000, Napoli more than 91.000 in the largest of its 5 Universities (the "Federico II" University), Padova more than 61.000, Torino more than 65.000, while Roma has 11 Universities . In the South of Italy there is a much lower number of Universities, some of which are rather recent.

Chart 1 shows the distribution of Italian universities (both state-owned and private) in all fields.

Fees to attend state-owned universities are rather cheap, even though in the last years they have increased. Usually the fees are related to the personal or family income of students and in a state-owned university they can range from 250 € to 3500 € per year. On average, a student in a state-owned University pays 803 euros a year.[3] The cheapest universities are those located in small towns in the South of Italy, while the most expensive ones are located in large towns (Milano, Torino, Napoli) or, even though located in small or medium sized towns, have a good reputation (perhaps because they are among the oldest ones). The fee paid by the richest families can be 2–3 times higher than those paid by students whose families have a low income. For those students whose income is very low and who get very good marks, there is the possibility to get some financial support through a scholarship.

State-owned universities sometimes make a selection of candidates at the entrance, enrolling just the number of students they want to accept. This process is not compulsory. Selection is realized in different ways: in some cases students have to pass a test on specific subjects, in others they need to have got a minimum mark at the end of their secondary schools, sometimes there is a ranking done through a combination of tests and previous marks. Not all the universities have introduced a selection system. Recently, however, the Ministry of Education has asked every faculty to establish the maximum number of students to enroll in the following year, given the number of teachers they have. If the number of students enrolled exceeds the limit defined the previous year, the faculty has to be enlarged. This number for some universities represents a constraint, but for others is just an eventual limit.

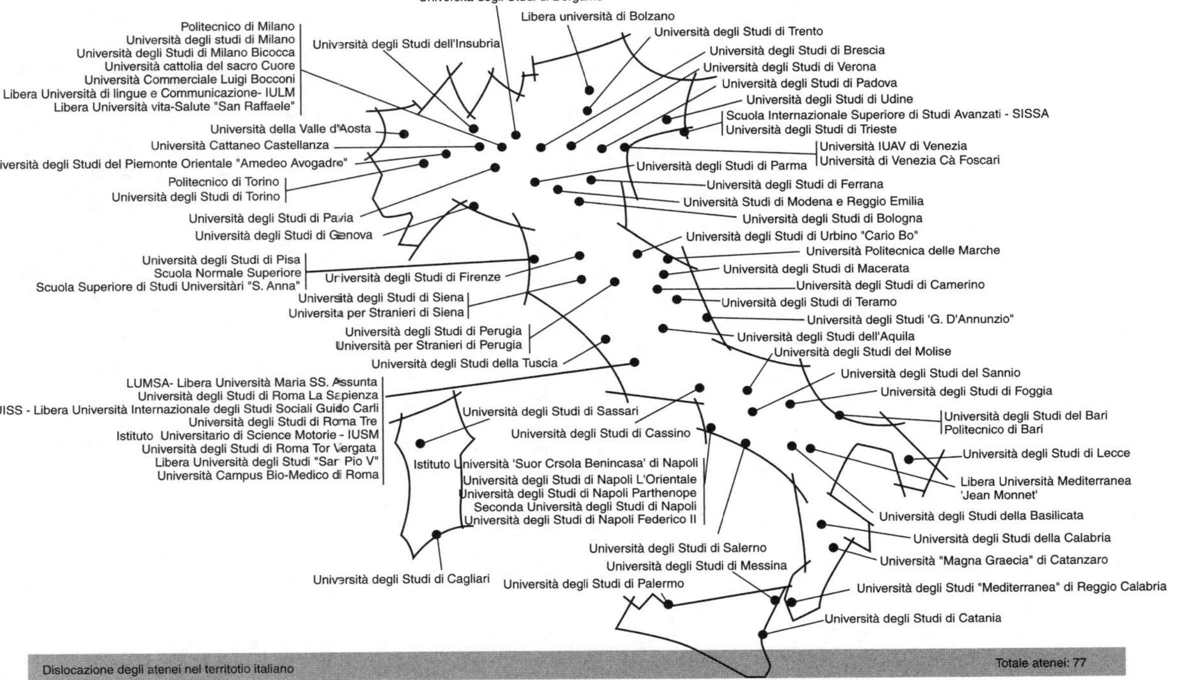

Chart 11.1   Geographical distribution of Italian Universities

Source: www.crui.it

Universities every year have to define:

- the maximum number of students they will enroll,
- the mix of topics they will teach,
- the size of the faculty.

As a consequence of the reform process:

- universities are responsible for the coverage of their costs, even though some of the costs they face are not under their control. The most important of these is the cost of their faculty members, whose wages are the same all over the country and regulated by the Ministry of Education;
- funding from the State is related to the results of their research and teaching activities, which are assessed on a three year basis.

The large number of economics and business faculties has led students to choose close-to-home faculties, mainly for their first level degree (*laurea triennale*). This trend is probably due on the one hand to the fact that the job market for business graduates is still quite dynamic; on the other hand a typical business faculty needs less funds in comparison with others like: medicine, biology, engineering, etc. (whose technologies and equipment are much more expensive): hence, it is quite feasible to support business and economics faculties in many different universities. (Note that this does not facilitate reaching critical size, e.g. to gain international visibility, but it provides some capillarity to bring close-to-home business education to students).

Private universities

In Italy there a few private universities and almost all of them have a faculty of economics or management.

Out of these, two are very big: Bocconi University and the Università Cattolica del Sacro Cuore.

Bocconi University is focused on management studies and economics and is located in Milan; besides the University there is a School of Management (SDA Bocconi), that runs MBAs and other master courses and plays a key role in executive education in Italy. SDA Bocconi, in fact, was the first and still is the most important business school in Italy, competing internationally and ranked in international rankings.

The Università Cattolica del Sacro Cuore is very large, has many faculties and different campuses: Milan, Rome, Piacenza and Cremona, Brescia, Campobasso. Business studies within the Università Cattolica del Sacro Cuore are relevant as the number of students is high; there are three faculties of economics and business, two of which are located in the campus of Milan (some courses are run also in Rome) and one in that of Piacenza and Cremona.

Other private universities are much smaller and often closely related to enterprise associations (national or local). Some of them are also involved in the executive education. One example is represented by the LUISS, which is located in Rome.

The fees to attend private universities are much higher than those of state-owned universities and sometimes depend on the student or student family income. They can range from 2,000–3,000 to 9,000–10,000 € per year. Private universities can get also some financial aid from the State.

Private universities tend to have a good reputation in the business community. The reasons for that are different for each university, but the main factors can be listed as follows:

- good organization;
- closeness to the business community;
- range of courses offered;
- facilities.

In some cases, the reputation comes also from the fact that top managers of relevant firms are alumni from such universities.

Other competitors and new entrants

The most relevant competitors of economics and business faculties are the *technical universities (politecnici)*, some of which around 20 years ago started to introduce engineering degrees with a focus on managerial topics. In Italy there are 8 (out of 53) faculties of engineering oriented to management. Technical universities have a good reputation and in some cases, as for the Politecnico of Milano, they also have their own business school.

Business schools in Italy are not as popular as they are in other European countries or in the US.

As already mentioned, there is a very large school of business that is part of Bocconi University; other schools exist, that run executive courses or master courses, but they are small and often local. Some of these schools have been established by entrepreneurial associations (an example is CUOA, located in the North-east of Italy), or by the Chambers of Commerce. In the latter case, the courses they run are short executive courses, sold at rather low prices. They never are competitors of Universities. These schools can't be seen as competitors of Universities because they are focused mainly on executive education and sometimes are very local.

In the executive education and only for the top customers, the competition comes from **foreign business schools**, both European and American. Usually, they don't have subsidiaries in Italy, but they attract Italian students to the US or to their European home countries; in some cases they also have some agreements with Italian institutions (for example for exchange of MBA students). Among them are some US business schools and some European (for example, INSEAD or London Business School).

Maybe in the future even some foreign universities will try to enter the Italian market directly, even though the many constraints and regulations, together with the language barrier, make it difficult for a foreign player to compete directly against local competitors. What is happening as far as universities are concerned is a trend to making **alliances** with Italian universities in order to offer "double degrees" or at least exchange programs for undergraduate and graduate students.

In the executive education sector, we also have to consider the role played by **corporate universities**.

First of all, they usually address their courses to their employees only. A second important factor is that in Italy almost 98 percent of firms are small and medium sized, which means:

- they can't have any corporate university;
- most of them are "afraid" of approaching the executive education and don't have such a big interest in courses run by corporate universities, business schools or universities.

Small and medium sized firms' entrepreneurs and managers often prefer to attend short courses run by associations or by their consultants.

Consultants are very active in managerial education, both for large sized firms and for SMEs. Executives, young talents, high potential employees of large companies often attend "tailor-made" courses run by large sized consulting firms, most of which are international; SMEs, instead, also buy consultancy services that include a sort of managerial education, often run by small consultants, generally local consultants.

We can map "strategic groups" of the industry in different ways, as shown in Figure 11.1 and 11.2.

Strategic group A – State-owned universities, that are the most relevant players of the industry in terms of number of students. They do research and offer Lauree triennali, Lauree magistrali, Master universitari, in some cases Ph.D. courses.

Strategic group B – Private Universities, that are relevant for the reputation they have and the strong links with the business community. Two of them are large and attract students from all the country, while all the others are rather small and mainly local. They do research, offer Lauree triennali, Lauree magistrali, Master universitari, in some cases Ph.D. courses and MBAs or executive courses.

Strategic group C – belonging to this strategic group are the schools of the chambers of commerce (local schools) that are characterized by very low prices, not comparable with those of private business schools. They do not do research, their degrees are not recognized by the Ministry of Education.

Strategic group D – Belonging to this strategic group are both large and small consultancy firms. They usually do not do research and are concentrated on the executive education only.

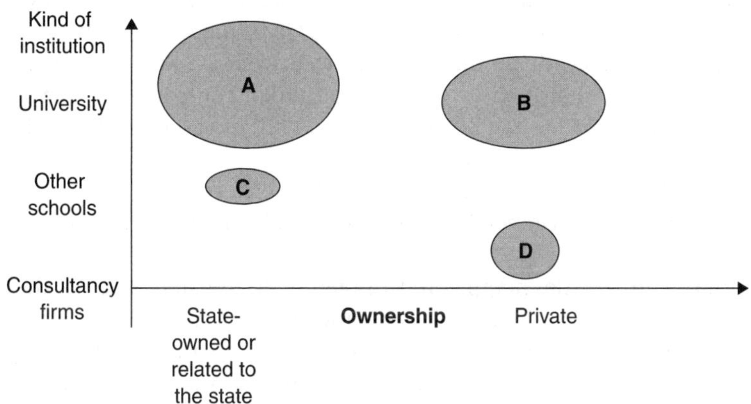

Figure 11.1   Strategic groups in the management education sector

Strategic group A – belonging to this group are some very large state-owned universities located in the largest towns. They have many faculties and thousands of students in different fields.

Strategic group B – belonging to this group are two Universities: Bocconi University (specialized in management and economic studies) and the Università Cattolica del Sacro Cuore (very large and diversified). If we con-

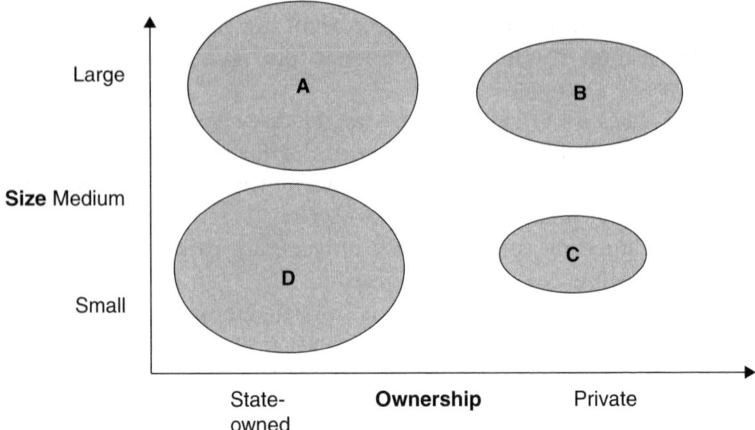

Figure 11.2   Strategic groups within the university sector

sider also executive education, to this strategic group also belong large con-sultancy firms.

Strategic group C – small private Universities are part of the strategic group C. In many cases they are supported by some associations. Luiss, for example, is a private university located in Rome and is owned by Confindustria, that is the association of Italian companies; LUMS is a private university located 30 km away from Milano and is supported by the association of local firms.

Strategic group D – belonging to this strategic group are many small sized State-owned Universities, often located in small or medium sized towns.

All the universities mapped in this picture do research: some of them are already internationally oriented, and compete in the international arena for publications; some are in the first phase of their internation-alization and some others are more domestically oriented. The general trend, however, is towards the internationalization of faculties, also because the Ministry of Education in year 2005–06 has for the first time ranked the universities according to their publications, involving domestic and foreign reviewers. For the first time, great relevance has been attributed to international publications.

Students

In the academic year 2003–04 (see Table 11.4), around 45,300 students were enrolled by business and economics (or statistics) faculties vis-à-vis the 52,700 enrolled in academic year 1994–95.

Table 11.4   Students enrolled by field. Academic years from 1994/95 to 2003/04 (a)

Fields	1994/95	1995/96	1996/97	1997/98	1998/99	1999/00	2000/01	2001/02	2002/03	2003/04
Scientific	11.903	11.690	10.696	9.637	9.574	9.341	10.846	12.611	12.415	12.088
Chemical/pharmaceutical	10.020	10.162	11.277	10.936	10.708	9.538	9.130	9.796	11.350	13.044
Biological	17.116	17.040	15.029	14.963	14.792	13.266	12.914	16.097	17.914	19.585
Medical	13.167	13.336	15.624	15.909	15.984	17.687	19.558	21.696	24.516	25.514
Engineering	39.688	38.363	39.155	37.863	35.381	35.439	37.061	37.178	37.193	36.864
Architecture	8.257	7.883	8.498	8.745	8.496	8.534	8.774	12.976	15.924	17.238
Agricultural	8.116	8.490	9.839	8.774	7.904	6.922	6.364	7.035	7.901	8.131
Economics, management, statistics	**52.749**	**50.369**	**50.562**	**46.323**	**45.211**	**44.534**	**43.405**	**45.665**	**45.886**	**45.332**
Political-social	34.827	35.707	35.425	32.295	32.386	30.416	31.933	46.731	47.245	45.676
Law	66.505	62.029	57.399	50.689	45.158	42.099	38.874	38.105	39.627	40.965
Literature	33.275	34.851	31.593	33.072	31.219	27.690	26.200	29.105	32.232	32.224
Languages	17.965	17.767	17.779	18.135	18.187	16.907	17.622	18.882	20.572	20.139
Teaching	14.064	15.890	17.843	18.324	19.791	17.348	16.649	15.970	17.763	18.758
Psychology	8.420	8.105	7.776	10.723	11.285	11.636	12.119	14.547	11.218	11.832
Sport	3.497	3.666	3.723	4.028	3.951	4.475	4.077	4.511	5.071	5.513
Defense	–	–	–	–	–	–	–	383	333	216
Total	**339.569**	**335.348**	**332.218**	**320.416**	**310.027**	**295.832**	**295.526**	**331.288**	**347.160**	**353.119**

(a) From the academic year 2000/01 data refer to those students that enter the University for the first time. Previous data include students that are enrolled at the first year even though having being students at the University in a different field.

Source: Istat, Rilevazione dell'istruzione universitaria fino all'a.a. 1995/96, MIUR-URST per gli a.a. 1996/97 e successivi.

Table 11.5 shows the number of students enrolled in the economics and management faculties by University in academic year 2003–2004 and 2004–05.

One of the problems that still affects Italian universities is the number of students that leave the university after the 1st year. The average percentage of students that leave the university after the first year was around 22 percent for Management and Economics faculties in academic year 2003–04. In part, this is due to the fact that there are people who

Table 11.5 Number of faculties of economics and management and of students enrolled by university

University	Number of economics and management faculties	Number of students enrolled in academic year 2004/2005	Number of students enrolled in academic year 2003/2004
Politecnica delle Marche	1	832	0
Università degli Studi di Bari	1	1997	2085
Libera Università Mediterranea Jean Monnet	1	324	32
Università degli Studi di Bergamo	1	834	493
Università degli Studi di Bologna	3	2318	1868
Libera Università degli Studi di Bolzano	1	165	64
Università degli Studi di Brescia	1	910	444
Università degli Studi di Cagliari	1	670	558
Università della Calabria	1	1599	1488
Università degli Studi di Cassino	1	531	550
Libero Istituto Universitario "Carlo Cattaneo" di Castellanza	1	289	255
Università degli Studi di Catania	1	1952	1893
Università degli Studi "G. D'Annunzio" di Chieti-Pescara	1	486	733
Libera Università della Sicilia Centrale "Kore" (ENNA)	1	np	Np
Università degli Studi di Ferrara	1	346	262
Università degli Studi di Firenze	1	1431	1435
Università degli Studi di Foggia	1	500	455

Continued

Table 11.5   Continued

Università degli studi di Genova	1	827	524
Università degli Studi dell' Insubria	1	450	506
Università degli Studi dell'Aquila	1	323	382
Università degli Studi di Lecce	1	771	758
Università degli Studi di Macerata	1	209	231
Università degli Studi di Messina	1	896	868
Università degli Studi di Milano – Bicocca	1	1744	1330
Università Commerciale "Luigi Bocconi" di Milano	1	4339	2525
Università Cattolica del "Sacro Cuore" di Milano	3	1954	1471
Università degli Studi di Modena e Reggio Emilia	1	847	718
Università degli Studi del Molise	1	688	754
Università degli Studi di Napoli	1	1383	1235
Seconda Università degli Studi di Napoli	1	605	529
Università degli Studi di NAPOLI Parthenope	1	1703	1777
Università degli Studi di Padova	1	262	256
Università degli Studi di Palermo	1	1331	853
Università degli Studi di Parma	1	1180	1024
Università degli Studi di Pavia	1	535	444
Università degli Studi di Perugia	1	1060	980
Università degli Studi del Piemonte Orientale "A Avogadro"	1	629	563
Università degli Studi di Pisa	1	995	802
Università degli Studi di Roma "La Sapienza"	1	2156	2031
Università degli Studi di Roma "Tor Vergata"	1	1202	943
Università degli Studi ROMA TRE	1	950	816
Libera Università Internazionale di Studi Sociali "Guido Carli" – (LUISS) di Roma	1	242	465
Libera Università degli Studi "S. Pio V" Roma	1	63	63

Continued

Table 11.5   Continued

University	Number of economics and management faculties	Number of students enrolled in academic year 2004/2005	Number of students enrolled in academic year 2003/2004
Università Telematica Guglielmo Marconi	1	np	Np
Università' Telematica TEL.M.A.	1	np	Np
Università degli Studi di Salerno	1	1124	914
Università degli Studi del Sannio	1*	705	851
Università degli Studi di Sassari	1	429	457
Università degli Studi di Siena	1	760	675
Università degli studi di Torino	1	2522	2005
Università degli Studi di Trento	1	618	440
Università degli Studi di Trieste	1	422	321
Università degli Studi della Tuscia	1	300	361
Università degli Studi di Udine	1	661	443
Università telematica internazionale UNINETTUNO	1	np	Np
Università degli Studi di Urbino	1	359	250
Università degli Studi "Ca' Foscari" di Venezia	1	2094	1534
Università degli Studi di Verona	1	609	855

* Questa Università ha anche una Facoltà di Scienze economiche e aziendali

Fonte: Miur – Database Offerta Formativa. Il dato sul numero di studenti iscritti alle facoltà di economia deriva invece dal database "Anagrafe Nazionale Studenti."

enter the University while they are waiting for a job. When they get the job, they leave the university. Other students enrol when they are already working and they leave the university because it is too difficult to work and study.

The number of students that get a degree on due time is still very low, but increasing. It was equal to 17 percent in year 2000 and almost 27 percent in year 2003. The University-reform that introduced the 3+2 system (*Laurea triennale* and *Laurea magistralis*) seems to be one of the reasons why more students get their degrees on time: the *Laurea triennale* is one year shorter than the previous one and there is no need to write a dissertation in order to get the degree, which makes it easier for students to reach the goal on time.

On the other hand, as the Ministry of Education is introducing mechanisms that reward universities (in terms of financing) according to the percentage of students that get the degree on time, there is a good reason for universities to organize their courses in a better way, focusing on the objective to reduce the number of students who don't get the degree on time.

The State

The State plays a relevant role in the business education sector. This is not only because of the financial support to Universities, but also for the constraints to university decisions. We will analyze it looking at two factors:

- the university reform
- the financial support to universities

The University Reform

In year 1999 the University Reform was voted by the Italian parliament. A new change should have taken place because of the reform of October 2005. But, as the Government changed in year 2006, the 2005 reform has not been implemented yet.

According to the 1999 reform, the following were introduced:

- the 3+2+3 system;
- the financial independence of Universities.

The introduction of the 3+2+3 system has provoked many changes in universities. First of all, they had to revise their curricula and reorganize their activities.

The first problem was to figure out how many students would decide to stop studying after their bachelor degree and how many would keep on studying. Then, they had to decide what to offer and how to differentiate from their competitors.

The process has not finished yet, but a first result is the increase in the number of curricula offered at national level. Some second level degrees are so specialized that some faculties did not reach the minimum number of students to warrant them.

Financial support to Universities

After the reform, universities are responsible for their financial situations. This means that they have to cover their costs with funds they get from students' fees plus those they receive from the State. Until now most of the budget of state-owned universities is covered by the State and, according to some recent research, 12 percent is covered by students' fees. Students' fees have increased a lot in the last years whilst the State transfer to State-owned universities has decreased.[4]

The State is the main supporter for research activities and from now on the size of funds that universities get from the State will depend more and more upon their past results. To assess these results, every three years each department has to be evaluated by a commission nominated by the State. The objective is to distribute 30 percent of total funds from the Ministry according to the results of this assessment. Problems could arise for some universities as more than 70 percent of the state funds are used to pay faculty wages.

As already said before, one of the most relevant innovations is the increasing weight given to international publications. For this reason almost all universities and many faculty members are trying to make agreements with foreign institutions and colleagues.

Private universities rely mainly on students' fees (that can account from 50 percent to 80–90 percent of total revenues, see figure 11.3). However they get contributions from the State for research activities and they are subject to the same assessment of state-owned universities as far as research outputs are concerned.

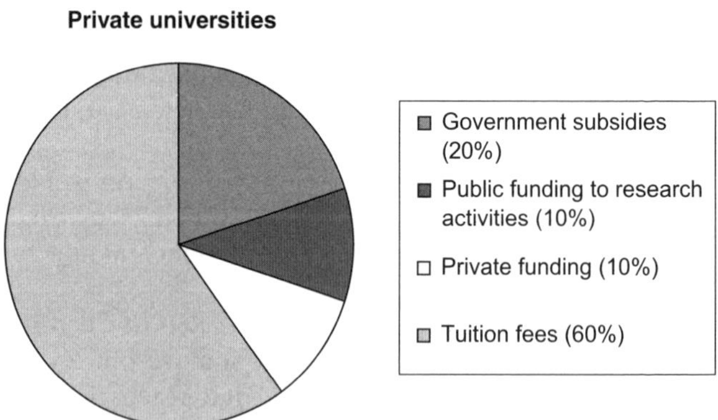

Figure 11.3 Distribution of revenues of public and private universities in Italy

A private university can get 20–30 percent of its budget from the Ministry of Education.

Professors

In Italy there is a total of 4,175 faculty members in the economics and management faculties, as shown in Table 11.6. Around 1,400 out of 4,175 are in the field of management.[5]

The most important changes introduced by the 2005 reform concern the career paths of faculty members. Until 2005 there have been three levels:

- researchers;
- associate professors;
- full professors.

Researchers are at the lower level. To become a researcher a person needs to pass a public examination, both written and oral. For the first three years researchers are full-time employees; after the third year they can choose whether to be full- or part-time employees. In theory they should not teach, but in practice many researchers have a work load that is not far from that of an associate or a full professor. Due to the reform, in the future there will not be researchers any more. After three years as a researcher, there is an assessment based on publications. If the result is positive, the person cannot be removed by the University forever.

Table 11.6   Faculty members of economics and management faculties

Faculty members – Academic years 1997–2004				
Year	Full professors	Associate professors	Researchers	Total
1997	973	890	1458	3321
1998	972	887	1463	3322
1999	970	1247	1328	3545
2000	1155	1176	1376	3707
2001	1322	1281	1317	3920
2002	1464	1343	1337	4144
2003	1470	1325	1290	4085
2004	1495	1321	1359	4175

Source: Miur – Banca dati docenti di ruolo.

Associate professors are selected through public examinations where they have to have a discussion on their publications, and a teaching exam (they have to present a lecture of about one hour on a subject that they select out of three extracted subjects in their field). Associate professors choose if they want to be full- or part-time professors and according to this choice they have a different workload. After three years from the moment they become associate professors in their university, there in an assessment based on publications of the last three years.

Full professors are selected through a public examination based just on the assessment of their publications. They can decide to be full- or part-time employees and after three years from the moment they are hired as full professors, there is an assessment (based on the publications of the last three years). After this assessment they get the tenure.

Until year 1999 the public examination took place at local level for researchers and at national level for associate and full professors: a commission was elected (on average every one to two years) for each field and it had the duty to select as many professors as necessary to fill the gaps in all the universities of Italy.

With the reform of year 1999 the system changed and all public examinations were to take place locally. For each chair there was the possibility to decide for a short list of two selected candidates. The one not chosen by the university could however be hired (in a period of two years) by the same or another university, meaning that he or she was considered as having taken (and passed) that other public examination.

The 2005 reform has changed the system again. From 2006 on, there will be just national public examinations and the number of people who pass the examination getting the habilitation will be equal to or 40 percent over the number of chairs that universities estimate will be necessary for their development in a three-year period.

Besides, because of the reform, the position of "researchers" will not exist any more. Universities will have the possibility to have assistant professors without hiring them forever, but just signing a three-year contract and the chance to extend it to six years. After this period, assistant professors should be able to pass a public examination to get the habilitation as Associate Professors and then be hired from a university.

Faculty members of private universities follow the same career paths as the teachers of state-owned universities, as the public examination is the same. Also wages are similar, even though private universities have the chance to increase wages according to their needs. Until now this option has not been widely used (which means that faculty members of private universities are often paid exactly the same as their colleagues in state-owned universities). What private universities can do, however, is to sign contracts with teachers from other institutions, even paying them much more than their stable faculty. This is an advantage in their internationalization process as they have the possibility to attract foreign teachers that would not be willing to work for state-owned universities because of the low level of wages.

On average Italian universities are not concerned about quality insuring as they don't compete in the international arena yet. Business schools, instead, are much more sensitive vis-à-vis this issue.

As far as rankings are concerned, some Italian newspapers and journals rank universities according to their own variables. The Ministry of Education has just started to rank universities according to their research output and only a few Italian Universities are ranked in international journals.

The ranking of business schools at present is relevant just for a few schools, while other players are not interested in it as they compete just at domestic level.

Table 11.7 and Figure 11.4 show how much money researchers, associate professors and full professors get from the University. They have then to pay taxes over what they get. The costs for the University are higher than the gross wages as they also include social costs.

Table 11.7   Wages for researchers and professors

	Minimum gross wage	**Costs for the university (wage + social costs)**
Researcher (first 3 years)	21.000 €	30.500 €
Full-time researcher (after 3 years)	30.000 €	41.200 €
Full-time associate professor (first 3 years)	37.000 €	50.800 €
Full-time associate professor (after 3 years)	39.000 €	53.600 €
Full-time full professor (first 3 years)	49.000 €	67.100 €
Full-time full professor (after 3 years)	51.800 €	71.100 €

Source: http://www.unibo.it

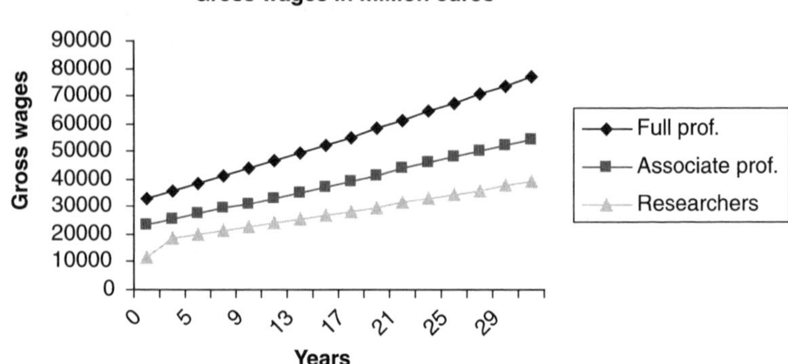

Figure 11.4   Gross wages received by full-time researchers, associate and full professors in a time span of 31 years

After the assessment of year-3, for full time faculty there is an increase of 8 percent every two years until year 15 and of 6 percent after that.

According to the 2005 reform, state-owned universities will also have the possibility to increase wages of their faculty according to specific activities performed. Besides, there will be no distinction between full- and part-time as all faculty members will be asked to teach for at least 120 contact hours.

Trends

Internationalization

Even though not really supported yet by some professors, the internationalization is a clear trend for many Universities. The internationalization process takes place in different ways:

- agreements with foreign universities to realize exchange of students and double degrees;
- Ph.D. students spend periods of time abroad;
- attention given to international publications.

There still are obstacles, the more important of which are:

- The academic career is related to national examinations where the international experience of candidates, at least until now, has not been considered that relevant;

- In the business studies field the most important publications are still books, not papers. As a consequence, Italian researchers who publish articles are not assessed as positively as those who write books. This creates a schizophrenic situation where researcher are required to write books to progress in their national careers and are required to write papers if they want to progress in the international academy;
- Because the degrees of universities are recognized by the State, professors must be selected through national examinations, and universities are not free to hire the teachers they want, according to an independent selection process. This implies that foreign teachers cannot get the tenure unless they pass the national examination.
- Universities – excepting a few ones – until now have not been that concerned about international accreditation and rankings, which were relevant just for business schools that deliver MBAs courses; now they are starting to be more and more conscious of the relevance that these things have.

Fragmentation

Another trend is fragmentation. As has been underlined before, many small faculties have been established in the last 10–20 years. This has led to a strong competition between universities and also some opportunistic behavior. Degrees are awarded in Italy through an "accumulation system": students can get their degree after they have got all the credits (180 for the first level degree, 300 credits for the first + second level degree, 60 for master degrees), and not necessarily in a predefined

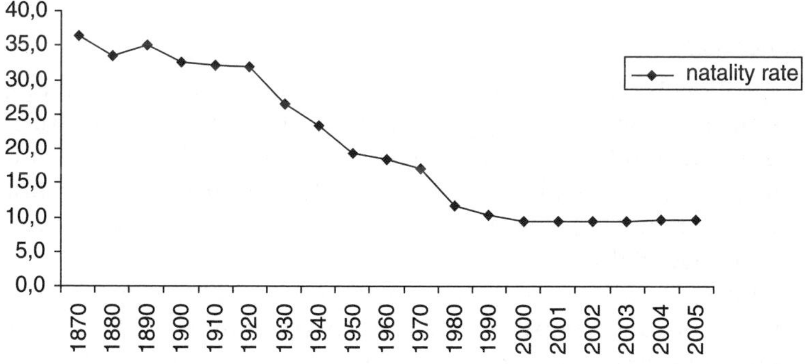

Figure 11.5   Birth rate in Italy

period of time. This has led to some problems as many students get the final degree after too many years. To solve this problem, the Ministry of Education has decided to relate funding to the universities to the percentage of students that get their degree on due time. This, according to some people, could be an incentive for universities to be less severe and enhance opportunistic behavior in order to get money, some universities could try to be less demanding. This risk could be higher for small universities which depend a lot on State funding because the fees they get from their students are not sufficient to cover their costs.

Market shrinking

The population of young people in Italy is decreasing as shown in Figure 11.5. Even though more and more people keep on studying after their secondary schools, the decrease of natality is provoking a shrinking of the market that is not counterbalanced by the increase of foreign students as yet.

These are increasing but not as much as necessary. To counterbalance the decrease in the number of native students it would be necessary to launch new courses run in English: just a few Universities have already started this process and the language barrier is still high.

Besides, some Italian students are starting to go and study abroad after they get their first level degree. There is an increasing attraction by foreign MBA courses, run by American and European business schools. This outflow is not compensated by the inflow of foreign students as not enough students in the world speak Italian, where very few Universities run courses in English.

There are no data available concerning economics and management faculties, but if we consider all fields, foreign students in Italy are only about 2 percent of total students.

Competition and cooperation

Competition is stronger and stronger, and universities are spending more and more on marketing, public relations and advertising to attract students. The result could be a divergence between small and large universities, where the small universities have the resources to attract just local students and the large ones compete nationally (and in some cases even internationally).

As it has already emerged in the previous paragraphs, in many cases management education is delivered by schools or universities that are the result of the cooperation with industrial associations, both local or national. This leads business and economics faculties to specialise also on research: small, local Universities are more concerned about the local economic issues, study local districts, do research on small sized companies, while faculties that are located in large towns have stronger links with large firms.

Cooperation with foreign institutions is also becoming more and more relevant: exchange programs and double degrees have increased a lot in the last years (not only within Europe and with US institutions); some institutions are trying to start up their own courses in the Far East or make joint ventures with domestic business schools.

12

Higher Management Education in the Netherlands

Niels Noorderhaven and Aswin Van Oijen

The context of management education in the Netherlands

Higher education in the Netherlands comes in two types: universities and universities of professional education. There are thirteen universities in the Netherlands, including three technical universities and the Agricultural University in Wageningen, but excluding the Open University. These universities are funded by the State, partly on the basis of performance indicators like the numbers of diplomas, first-year students and doctoral degrees. Universities may divide their state aid between "education" and "research" as they see fit. Each university bears the cost of its physical infrastructure.[1] Due to mergers, the number of universities of professional education (in Dutch: hoger beroepsonderwijs or *HBO institutions*) has decreased to 54. These universities are also funded by the State, according to comparable parameters. In addition to government grants, both universities and HBOs rely on tuition fees and revenues from contract research and contract education. Of the total state contribution, nearly 92 percent is made available in the form of a lump sum. Universities and HBO institutions independently decide on the most effective allocation of these funds to cover personnel and other costs. Starting in 2002, the Netherlands implemented a bachelor-master degree system in higher education. Universities offer bachelor's, master's, and doctoral degrees. HBOs offer bachelor's degrees under the State-financed system, and are permitted to offer master's programs if self-financed. Doctoral programs are restricted to the universities.

At the same time as the implementation of the bachelor-master structure, the Dutch government put into place an accreditation system for higher education, which took the place of the existing system of peer evaluation set up by the associations of Dutch universities and of HBOs. In the new system, there is a single accreditation organization, the Dutch-Flemish Accredition Organization (NVAO), which accredits higher education programs on the basis of external evaluations. These evaluations are not performed by the NVAO itself, but by third parties, the Examining and Evaluating Bodies (in Dutch: Visiterende en Beoordelende Instanties or *VBIs*). The VBIs apply the criteria set by the NVAO.[2] If an educational program is not accredited by the NVAO, the consequence is that graduates will not receive the official educational degree, and the educational institution will not receive state funding for the program. In the field of business administration, a growing number of Dutch universities have acquired international accreditation by the AACSB or EQUIS, on top of the national accreditation granted by the NVAO.

Admission to Dutch universities and HBOs is on the basis of formal qualifications. Students with a diploma from the prerequisite Dutch school type (or the international equivalent) have the right to be admitted to a bachelor's program, provided they have chosen the right

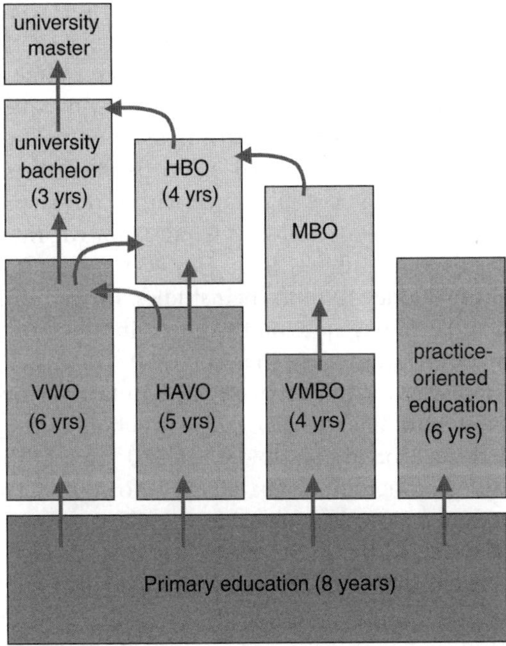

Figure 12.1   The Dutch Education System[3]

profile of course subjects, fitting the requirements of the particular bachelor's program. In the Dutch system, selection takes place mainly in the final year of primary school, thus around the age of 11–12, when the decision is made as to what type and level of secondary education a pupil is admitted. This selection is done on the basis of a national test and the advice from the primary school. Of the various types of secondary school, only one grants direct access to university bachelor programs, the VWO (preparatory scientific education). Access to bachelor programs from HBOs is on the basis of VWO or HAVO (higher general secondary education). Dutch institutions for higher education are not permitted to select students, other than on the basis of these formal qualifications. An exception is Nyenrode Business Universiteit, an institution with university status but without state funding. Selection at the master's level is possible, within certain restrictions. Students with a bachelor's diploma from an HBO institute can access university master's programs after a preparatory program of about one year. Figure 12.1 provides a complete overview of the Dutch system of education.

Almost all students studying in the Netherlands who are nationals of one of the European Union member states are entitled to funding from the Dutch State. Funding can come in several parts.[4] First of all, students can receive a basic grant. Besides, they are entitled to free public transportation, within certain limits. Students with low-income parents can obtain an additional grant. All these parts hold for only a limited number of years. They are not necessarily gifts, but depend on the student's performance. If a student has not graduated within ten years, everything has to be repaid. Repayment is always required for the final part of the funding, which is a low-interest loan. However, students are still very hesitant to borrow money to fund their studies. Instead, almost seventy percent of the students have jobs on the side.[5] Since students can use the funding to pay for the tuition fee, the Dutch State finances higher education not only directly, but also indirectly. The tuition is currently bound to a maximum of almost 1,500 euros per year. Schools are already free to decide on the tuition for students older than 30 years (at the beginning of the educational program), for students who follow a part-time or dual program and for students outside the EU, Norway, Iceland and Liechtenstein.

After many years of budget cuts, funding of education by the Dutch State has increased again in recent years, although it must be said that, in terms of funding per student, the level in real terms today is lower than some decades ago. Cancelling budget reductions decided upon earlier causes part of the increase.

Apart from the direct funding of education and research by the State and the indirect funding through student grants, the Dutch universities also receive government funding specifically for research through various channels. The three most important are KNAW, NWO and Bsik. The KNAW (Royal Dutch Academy of Sciences) and NWO (Netherlands' Organization for Scientific Research) fund selected high-calibre research projects on a competitive basis.[6] There is an emphasis on fundamental research, and business administration projects are not very frequently successful. Bsik is a scheme for strengthening the knowledge infrastructure in the Netherlands. The current, third program has a budget of around 800 million euros for a five-year period. Funds are allocated to thematic subprograms, and within these subprograms projects are funded only if the private sector also funds at least 33 percent of the cost. The largest subprograms in terms of budget are in the natural sciences, and not very interesting to business administration scholars. However, some of the other programs are relevant, and management scholars perform many applied research projects under the aegis of Bsik.

Recently, a number of the basic rules of the game in Dutch higher education became the subject of increasing political discussion. One very important topic is the distinction between universities and HBOs. The shift to the bachelor-master structure has muddled this distinction, since both school types can now offer bachelor's as well as master's programs. One university of professional education, Fontys Hogescholen, is even hiring PhD students.[7] However, cooperation with a university is required for this, since only universities have the formal right to grant doctorate degrees, and their reactions vary from reserved (e.g., the University of Tilburg) to hostile (e.g., the University Utrecht).[8] On the other hand, obstacles to mergers between universities and universities of professional education were removed recently. The Vrije Universiteit Amsterdam and the Hogeschool Windesheim have already merged. Finally, there is continuous pressure from the side of the HBOs to receive a share of the research funds distributed by the government.

Other topics that are the subjects of discussion are the level of tuitions and the freedom of universities and HBOs to vary tuition levels. Also, the selection of students entering bachelor's and master's programs is discussed. Starting in 2005, experiments with both higher tuitions and "selection at the gate" have been allowed by the State Secretary for higher education.[9]

Players in Dutch higher management education

In this section, we will briefly describe the main players in higher management education in the Netherlands.

Suppliers of higher management education in the Netherlands

The main university management education programs in the Netherlands fall under two labels: *Bedrijfskunde* (Business Administration) and *Bedrijfseconomie* (Business Economics). Business Economics is an offspring of the Economics programs originating from the 1930s. Originally, the Business Economics programs were strongly dominated by accounting; later finance, marketing and management were added. Business Administration has been offered since 1970, first at the technical university of Delft, in cooperation with the Erasmus University of Rotterdam. In 1984, this program moved to the Erasmus University. The start of the Business Administration programs was a response to the perceived lack of a practical orientation and the one-sided reliance on the economics discipline in the Business Economics programs. By now, Business Administration and Business Economics programs have become more alike, and at the universities offering both types of programs the overlap is considerable.

The universities of Groningen, Tilburg, and Maastricht, and the Free University of Amsterdam, the Radboud University Nijmegen, and the Erasmus University Rotterdam offer the full range of Business Administration and Business Economics programs, at the bachelor's, master's and PhD level.[10] The other universities offer a smaller range of business-related programs, which are often specialized management programs, like Management of Technology at Delft University of Technology, or the International Management program at Leiden University. Economics programs, including Business Economics and Business Administration, are offered at 57 HBO institutions (including different local branches of large HBOs). Other suppliers are Nyenrode Business Universiteit (a specialized management institute with university status but without PhD programs), the Open University (distance learning), and branches of foreign universities, such as NIMBAS and Webster University. Furthermore, there are a number of institutes that provide post-experience and executive management education, like the Rotterdam School of Management (linked to the Erasmus University), TIAS (linked to Tilburg University), and the IBO institute for business administration. By far the largest suppliers in the university sector in terms of students are the Erasmus University, Maastricht University, Tilburg University and the University of Groningen.

Faculty at Dutch universities have the following ranks: assistant professor, associate professor, and full professor. Within these ranks some sub-distinctions exist. An earned PhD is an entry requirement for the rank of assistant professor, but in some cases this requirement is waived temporarily or even permanently; for example, when an individual is indispensable for teaching. At the associate and full professor levels an earned PhD is mandatory. Although the picture varies between the faculties of Business Economics and Business Administration at the Dutch universities, typically the proportion of time spent on research moves up with the ranks. The extremes are assistant professors with no research time, and full professors with no teaching tasks at all, but these are exceptions. In general, faculty members have a mix of teaching and research tasks, but the proportions vary. At HBOs there are two main ranks: docent and lector. Employees in the rank of docent concentrate mainly on teaching. Lectors also have a task in the field of (applied) research. Salaries at Dutch universities vary from 2700 euro/month for a starting assistant professor to 8000 euro/month for a senior full professor. Universities have leeway to pay bonuses for exceptional achievements.

The demand side of higher management education in the Netherlands

In 2004/2005, the total number of students in higher education was about 543,000.[11] The distribution between universities and universities of professional education came down to approximately 37 and 63 percent, respectively. The largest number of students, 133,800, could be found in Business Administration. Another 52,900 students were enrolled for programs in the social sciences, including Business Economics. Based on our estimate of the number of students in Business Economics, the total number of students of Business Administration and Business Economics is around 150,000. Again, roughly one third are enrolled at universities, while two thirds can be found at universities of professional education. The vast majority of these students participate in full-time programs. For example, only about 15 percent of the total number of business students at universities of professional education follow part-time programs. For universities, this percentage is even lower. Part-time students can be found in programs offering initial degrees and in executive or post-experience programs. Participation in executive or post-experience programs is usually sponsored by the employers of the students. Students who quit a job to follow this kind of education to improve their chances on the job market are still rare. Consequently, schools that are active in this area closely follow the cycles of the labor market. The numbers of students participating in business programs have increased over the past decade, both absolutely and relatively. For example, while total enrolment in higher education has risen by almost 22 percent between 1995/1996 and 2004/2005, the number of students of Business Administration has increased by approximately 41 percent.

Generally, graduates from Business Administration programs and from Business Economics programs compete for similar jobs, although companies seem to prefer graduates from Business Economics for positions in the area of finance and accounting. HBO graduates typically apply for jobs at a somewhat lower level. This is one of the reasons for substantial numbers of HBO alumni to pursue a university degree on top of their HBO degree. In 2003, for example, 21 percent of all first year students at universities originated from HBO institutions.

More specific information on the positions that graduates obtain is hard to come by. Nevertheless, we have gathered data on the educational background of the top management teams of 32 randomly selected large Dutch listed firms, like AkzoNobel and Heineken. Of the 116 top managers we evaluated, 58 percent had a background in business and economics, 47 percent had more of a technical background, 16 percent had a law degree, and 9 percent had a different educational background.[12] Prospects seem rather bleak for those graduates from HBO institutions who want to become a top manager in a listed firm. Only 4 percent of the top managers obtained their highest degree from these schools. In contrast, 90 percent graduated from a university. For the remaining cases, the school type was either unknown or the managers had only passed secondary school.

Both universities and universities of professional education perform research for third parties, like government institutes and firms. The absolute and relative importance differs significantly, though. In 2003, for example, revenues for this type of research constituted 567 million euros, or almost 12 percent of total revenues for universities, while, for universities of professional education, they were only 9 millions euros, or about 0.4 percent of their total revenues.[13] Figures that would allow a breakdown over business and other disciplines are not available.

Regulators and quality monitoring actors

As already suggested, Dutch universities and universities of professional education are independent organizations. They decide, for example, on the teaching methods, the spending of funds and the infrastructure and housing. The Dutch Government is responsible for issues that concern higher education as a whole. Thus, it ensures the quality of higher education, the efficient spending of public funds and the accessibility of higher education, mainly through the study funding system.[14] The most important institution is the Dutch Ministry of Education, Culture and Sciences (in Dutch: Ministerie van Onderwijs, Cultuur en Wetenschappen). The governments of the Dutch provinces have no role in education. The general goals of the Ministry, at least with respect to education, are that everybody follows good education and that everybody prepares for independence and responsibility. It is headed by one Minister and two State Secretaries. One of the State Secretaries is specifically responsible for higher education. The Ministry contains 25 units or "directies". The three units involved in higher education, research and science policy and study funding policy are particularly relevant for higher education.[15] All three together are headed by one Director General.

A number of separate organizations are involved in the responsibility of the Dutch Government with respect to quality of higher education. We have already mentioned the NVAO (Nederlands-Vlaamse Accreditatie Organisatie), the Dutch-Flemish Accreditation Organization. Every six years, educational programs are evaluated by the VBIs (Visiterende en Beoordelende Instanties) or Examining and Evaluating Bodies. The VBIs are hired by the schools, but have to be on a list of NVAO-approved organizations. For 2006, six VBIs were on the list, including, for example, the QANU (Quality Assurance Netherlands Universities), which stems from the VSNU (Vereniging Nederlandse Universiteiten or Association of Dutch Universities) and the NQA (Netherlands Quality Agency), which stems from the HBO-Raad (the council for universities of professional education), but also international organizations, like the German ASIIN (Akkreditierungsagentur für Studiengänge der Ingenieurwissenschaften, der Informatik, der Naturwissenshaften und der Mathematik e.V.) and the Norwegian DNV (Det Norske Veritas bv).[16] Based on the reports that are prepared by a VBI, the NVAO can decide to accredit an educational program. The performance of the NVAO and the accreditation system in general is monitored by the Inspectie van het Onderwijs (Inspectorate of Education), which is placed under the Ministry.[17]

Strategies in Dutch higher management education

For an insightful description of the strategies of players in Dutch higher management education we cannot rely only on the institutional websites and published mission statements, etc. We have to construe the strategies followed by players in Dutch higher management education by observing their actions. What follows is an analysis of the situation which is unavoidably coloured by the experiences of the authors at one particular provider of higher management education, viz., Tilburg University.

Starting with the universities, most of these prominent players in the field of higher management education have in our view so far not really developed differentiation strategies. All university faculties of economics and business administration nowadays emphasize quality of teaching and research. The University of Maastricht is unique in its teaching approach of problem-based learning. In general, the Anglo-Saxon, and more particularly the American model of university education is making headway in the Netherlands. The restructuring of all programs into a bachelor-master model is but one indication of this trend. Another sign is the rise of broad multidisciplinary bachelor's programs modelled after those in the UK and the USA. The bachelor's program of University College Utrecht is an example.

In schools of (business) economics and business administration the top-tier American institutions serve as a role model. This is reflected among other things in an increasing focus on publications in international top journals. The school of Economics and Business Administration of Tilburg University around ten years ago as the first university faculty adopted the Anglo-Saxon style tenure-track system. This example is being followed by some of the other universities, albeit slowly. Another innovation adopted at Tilburg University around ten years ago that is increasingly adopted at other places in the Netherlands is the competitive allocation of research time. At Tilburg, the teaching load (and thus research time) of faculty members depends on past research performance, as reflected in the impact-weighted number of publications in the past five years and the number of citations in the past ten years. This system is independent of rank, meaning that it is entirely possible (and indeed it happens quite frequently) that a productive assistant professor has more research time than a senior full professor. Faculty on tenure-track at Tilburg University have guaranteed research time.

Whereas other universities in the Netherlands have adjusted their ambitions upwardly, no faculty of Economics and/or Business Administration so far seems to have adopted the Tilburg model completely. A reason may be the strong emphasis on consensus decision making,[18] which is difficult to reconcile with a system of clear winners (faculty receiving tenure and research time) and losers (faculty denied tenure and/or research time).

In the emulation of the American model, the Dutch universities focus on the top universities in the USA. However, this model is not so easy to transplant to the Netherlands. Obvious impediments are the very limited possibilities for student selection and the fixed tuition fees. These factors make it very difficult to enter into the positive spirals of quality improvement and increase of income that are typical of US top institutions. Also, the Netherlands lacks a tradition of corporate and private donations to universities. Companies and other organizations do sponsor chairs to a certain extent, but donations for, for example, buildings or other facilities are extremely rare. This means that the adoption of the US model by Dutch universities must always remain partial.

Universities of professional education

Looking from a distance, the complementarity of HBOs and universities in Dutch higher management education is undeniable. Management jobs exist at various levels, and graduates from the universities and HBOs have comparative advantages for different types of positions. For instance, HBO programs in Commercial Economics provide students with hands-on knowledge of sales and marketing, while university programs in Marketing provide a strong background in the foundation disciplines (e.g., psychology, statistics) necessary, for instance, for the design of new marketing research programs, but not for day-to-day activities within a marketing department.

But there are also growing tensions between the two sectors of Dutch higher education. The HBOs consistently try to downplay the difference between themselves and universities. They adopt a strategy of gradually upgrading the quality of faculty and educational programs, and building a basis in research. The addition of the rank of "Lector" to the HBO faculty should be seen in this light. Increasingly, "lectors" are positioned as comparable to university professors. As already indicated, Fontys, one of the largest HBOs, started 25 PhD projects. The PhD students do their research at the HBO and are supervised by HBO faculty, with a university professor acting as promoter. As a result of this strategy of HBOs the relationships between universities and HBOs are regularly somewhat tense. A recent example has been a proposal by the chair of the council of HBOs to the Minister of Education to raise the prices of university master programs (apparently to improve the competitive position of HBO master programs) and the negative response of the association of universities to that proposal.

In terms of research output, HBOs are a long way from closing the gap with the universities. Research activities, up to the present, are still strongly concentrated on applied research. In fact, given the increased pressure on university faculty to publish in international top journals, and the by-and-large successful response to that pressure, the gap in terms of fundamental research output is only getting bigger. However, university boards fear that policy makers at the Ministry of Education may have a "research is research" perspective, that is, count numbers of publications rather than look at quality indicators like journal impact factors. If this is true, it is possible that HBOs in the future may share in research funding.

Other suppliers

The bachelor-master structure (as the new structure is commonly referred to in the Netherlands) seems to offer new opportunities for less conventional providers. The traditional Dutch degrees were strongly protected, but this seems to be much less the case with the new, internationally more recognizable degrees. It will be more difficult for Dutch universities to distinguish themselves clearly from nonconventional providers who, superficially seen, offer the same final degrees as they do. Occasionally, politicians voice the opinion that government funding of higher education should not remain restricted to the officially recognized universities and HBOs, but should in principle be accessible to any provider that meets the quality requirements. So far this has not led to a policy change, however.

The introduction of the bachelor-master structure has not led to the dramatic changes in the landscape of higher education expected by many. For most students the new structure seems to mean little more than a new way of ordering the programs. The bachelor's degree is not seen as a final degree by university students, the great majority of whom continue to pursue a master's title. But there is little doubt that over time a growing proportion of students will leave the universities with a bachelor's degree, to return (either full-time of part-time) for a master's degree later, after having gained work experience. The big difference will be that then they are not captive customers of the established universities and HBOs any more, so they can be expected to be more open for other options, like foreign universities or their branches in the Netherlands, and new and existing commercial providers of higher management education.

Students

Dutch students in higher management education are at present quality-conscious only to a limited degree. Probably the most important criterion in choosing a university or HBO is the geographical location. This attitude has been reinforced by the fact that the quality differences between Dutch universities and between Dutch HBOs are perceived to be small. If we look at particular disciplines, however, quality differences as expressed, for example, in student and alumni polls, are clearly present, and these differences persist over time. But so far there seems to be hardly any relationship between the choice for a certain university or HBO and these quality scores. Also, Dutch employers do not really give a premium for having studied at a particular institution. A positive exception is maybe Nyenrode Business Universiteit (mainly for commercial positions). Also, students with a degree from a top university from the USA are more sought after.

Employers

So far, employers and their associations have demonstrated limited interest in higher management education. Also their influence remains rather restricted. The most important employers' associations from time to time try to exert influence on the Ministry of Education if certain developments are seen as contrary to the interests of their members. In recent years this was, among other things, the case when universities and HBOs were accused of unfair competition with commercial providers of contract research. Overall, the gap between both universities and HBOs and the private sector remains relatively large.

Regulators

The Dutch Ministry of Education is officially pursuing a policy of decentralization, but it seems that politicians and administrators alike have problems to contain their reflex to micro-manage education. Still, progress has been made, in particular concerning the budgetary freedom of Dutch institutes of higher education.

NVAO seems to be positioned as a guardian of the general minimum level of quality for higher education. One problem of NVAO may be the draconic nature of the consequences of refusing accreditation. The approach is rather formalistic.

International accreditation organizations (AACSB, EQUIS) are gaining importance, if not for other reasons, then at least because the NVAO accreditation offers no distinction.

Conclusions

In conclusion, the field of higher management education in the Netherlands is quite dynamic. Two partially opposite tendencies can be detected in the manifold changes of the past few years. On the one hand, there are clear developments in the direction of more quality in education and (especially) research. Research output of Dutch universities in the field of business and management has increased dramatically, both in terms of quality and quantity. Initiatives in the direction of a stricter selection of students entering the programs are sanctioned to a certain extent by the Government, albeit so far only under the label of "experiments". On the other hand, there are also forces that work in the direction of homogenization that threaten to drag high-quality Dutch providers of management education down. In the first place, the system of fixed tuition fees and the lack of awareness of quality differences by both students and prospective employers make it difficult to earn a return on investments in quality improvement. Secondly, the emancipation of the HBOs may be at the expense of the universities if a fixed research budget would be spread out among almost 70 recipients instead of the present 13 universities. This would probably be most detrimental for those university departments aiming at publications in top journals, for this strategy requires heavy investment but results in smaller numbers of publications. A third development with a possibly important impact in the longer run is the shift to a bachelor-master structure. As mentioned above, this may open up a large market for higher management education at the master's level, as in the system students with a bachelor's degree are no longer captive customers of the universities. Commercial providers and branches of foreign (mainly US) universities may make important inroads into the Dutch higher management education market in the future.

13
Management Education and Research in Sweden

Bengt Stymne[1]

Challenges facing management education in Sweden[2]

The evidence and analyses presented in this report can be summarized as four challenges:

Financial Challenge. Academic education in Sweden has to be provided free of charge. However, the money furnished by the Government is not enough to uphold the quality of the all existing business study programs. One way out of this dilemma for the individual regional college or university is to out-compete others to which students otherwise would have gone. What strategy should it choose to obtain faculty and resources necessary for developing a program that attracts more students?

Challenge of Inadequate Knowledge of High-School Graduates. High schools provide students deemed ill-prepared for the business study programs. The leading schools are avoiding this problem by attracting the best students. But how should the other programs adapt their educational goals and pedagogical methods in order to deliver training adequate for their students?

Challenge of the gap between business studies and needs of practice

- Similarly to the American MBA, the present business study programs in Sweden usually consist of an amalgamation of rather technical sub-disciplines like accounting, finance, marketing and organizational behavior, plus some more or less perfunctory courses in leadership. Is there room also for an integrated program that trains the students to become general managers and business leaders in the way Academies of War train young officers to become generals?

- Business graduates and managers are increasingly working in non-Swedish firms, partly as a result of mergers and acquisitions. Also, many business graduates seek jobs abroad. How shall business study programs respond to the need of training students for working under foreign management regimes that are operating with quite different values and norms from those in Sweden?
- Business studies have focused on the management of large firms. How shall business study programs respond to the growing economic importance of managing networks, entrepreneurship, innovation, new ventures and small growing firms?

Challenge of faltering demand for continued management training

- Management training institutes are good at delivering standard courses in different management fields. Firms, however, rather need frequent updating and retraining of their staff in connection with reorganization, adopting new products, entering new markets and meeting novel types of competition. The firms' experiences from organizing this training in-house are mixed. How could this window of opportunity be exploited by management training institutes to integrate the training they offer with the firms' own change programs?
- Top executives of leading companies go abroad for short courses and seminars rather than to Swedish continued education. How could Swedish management training providers act in order to become involved in training that attracts an international clientele of top managers?

The Swedish academic system[3]

Admission to academic studies

To be eligible for academic studies a student should have high school competence in a number of topics depending on the type of program aimed at. For the applicants fulfilling the basic requirements, admission to academic studies is based on competition. The competition is based on high school grades, a national entrance test or a combination of both. Individual programs are allowed also to require the fulfillment of special requirements and may give credits for outstanding professional, artistic and athletic achievements.

Table 13.1   Degrees and diploma as of July 1, 2007

English translation	Swedish term	Minimum length of study
Basic degrees	**Grundnivå**	
College exam	Högskoleexamen	2 years
Bachelor	Kandidat	3 years
Advanced degrees	**Avancerad nivå**	
Master	Magister	3+1 years
Advanced master	Master	3+2 years
Professional degrees	**Yrkesexamen (examples)**	
Nurse	Sjuksköterska	3 years
Business economist	Civilekonom	4 years
Engineer	Civilingenjör	5 years
Physician	Läkare	5.5 years
Research Degrees	**Forskarnivå**	
3:e cycle	Licentiatexamen	5+2 years
PhD	Doktorsexamen	5+4 years

Degrees and diploma

The diploma from the Swedish academic system will from July 2007 conform to the Bologna Protocol (see Table 13.1).

Changes from the earlier system from 1993 are minimal. The universities will continue to provide two "Basic" diplomas: *College exam,* requiring two years of study, and *Bachelor's,* requiring three years of study. On the "Advanced" level there will, as before, be a *Master's,* requiring another year of study on top of the candidate exam. A new *Advanced Master's* requiring 3 + 2 years of study will be added. Like today, there will be more than 40 different professional exams requiring from one to five-and-a-half years of study.

Students interested in management have generally been studying for four years to obtain a master with a specialization in business administration (ekonomie magister). In the future they will have the choice of either studying for a four-year professional degree as "business economist" (civilekonom) or go on to an advanced master requiring five years of study.

Graduates who have wanted to engage in research have mostly aimed at a doctoral degree. Formally, a PhD requires four years of study on top of a master exam but often takes the double. On the average, the new PhDs in 2005 were 35 years old and had started their doctorial studies 6 years earlier. There is also a another research-oriented degree called *licentiate* which either can be passed as a station on the road toward the doctorate or can be used as an exit for those who cannot, or do not want to, obtain the more advanced degree. The required time for the two research-oriented exams will remain unchanged.

Providers of academic level education (see Table 13.2)

There are 21 organizations in Sweden that can issue diplomas both on the basic and doctorial level. Fourteen of these organizations are state-owned universities. The remaining seven are Superior Schools (hög-skola). Four of them are state-owned and three private. The universities have a faculty that represents broader and deeper research competence than the state-owned superior schools.

Twenty-seven colleges can issue only professional and basic diplomas (Bachelor and Master). Of the eighteen state-owned schools in this category, nine can be characterized as regional colleges and nine as

Table 13.2   Classification of providers of academic level education

Research oriented providers of academic education	State-owned	Private	All
Universities	14	0	14
Superior Schools	4	3	7
Total	18	3	21
Providers of basic academic education			
Regional colleges	9		
Teacher college		1	1
Forestry college		1	1
Art colleges	7	1	8
Health colleges	2	3	5
Theological colleges		3	3
Total	18	9	27

professional schools for teachers and artists. The private colleges train artists, foresters, and clergy.

History of the Swedish academic system

Two of the universities were founded before the industrial revolution. They became the hubs of the university towns of Uppsala (1477) and Lund (1666) that for centuries dominated academic life in Sweden. Many students traveled to them from rural areas to be trained to join the clergy. In the period after the Napoleonic wars, the demand for university-trained labor increased in the two main cities of Sweden. In addition to the two old provincial universities, two new ones were therefore founded in Stockholm, 1878, and Göteborg, 1891.

Following the lead of the German *Hochschole* and the French *Grand Ecole*, five autonomous academic level professional schools called *högskola* were started before World War II. The first was Karolinska Institutet that was founded in Stockholm in 1810 for the training of surgeons and medical doctors. It was followed in 1827 by the Royal Institute of Technology in Stockholm for the training of engineers. Engineers became trained also at the Chalmers School of Technology that was founded in Göteborg in 1829. A School of Commerce for the training of businessmen was set up in Stockholm in 1909 and was followed by a similar school in Göteborg in 1928. These professional schools are still regarded as the leaders in the Swedish academic system and are below referred to as "the Elite Schools."

Three new universities were founded after World War II to meet the increasing demand for academic level education from students as well as from industry and the public sector. Umeå University became the first in 1964. It was the first university in the vast northern part of Sweden and built on the model of the two oldest universities. Like them it became the center of a university town. The two other universities were set up in the industrial towns of Linköping in southern Sweden and Luleå in the very north. Both have a special emphasis on the training of engineers.

From the 1980s onwards, government educational policy has aimed at providing academic education to half of each new generation of the population. Many vocational types of post-high school education, like the ones for nurses and artists, have been elevated to an academic status. The creation of regional university colleges has been the main means for this expansion. As these colleges gather

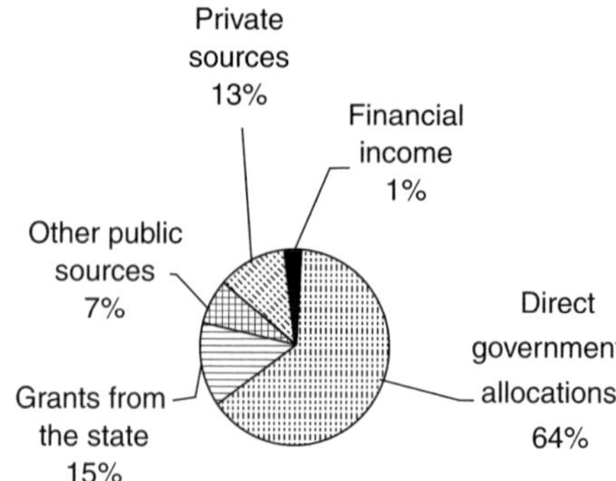

Figure 13.1   Sources of the 5 billion Euros income of the Swedish Academic System in 2005

experience and develop their resources, they can achieve the status of universities.

Financing of academic education

All academic education in Sweden, be it provided by the Government or by private sources, has to be free of charge. The academic system spent the equivalent of 5 billion euros[4] in 2005, which corresponds to 1.7 percent of the BNP. Figure 13.1 shows the sources of income.

Direct government budget allocations and grants from national research funds dominate. Of the 5 billion euros, 2.7b. are used for research and research education, and 2.3b. for basic education. In addition to what it allocates to the academic system, the Government pays 1.2 billion euros per year in economic support to the students. This means that each student on an average gets 4,000 euros in economic support per year.

A part of what the Government allocates to the academic system is paid as incentives to the course provider based on how many credits that each student actually obtains. In the humanistic and social sciences (including business studies) a university gets on the average 1,830 € per year for a student that obtains the normal number of credits. In comparison, 4,625 € is obtained for a science students and 28,390 for an opera student. The amount being paid for each student has been decreasing during the last ten years.

Contrary to the Government's goal that academic training should increase, to be provided to 50 percent of the population, the number of students inscribed in the academic system decreased in 2004/2005 for the first time in fifteen years. The decrease is due mainly to cuts in the Government's budget allocation to the university system.

The supply side

Background

Europe's fourth chair in the economic sciences was created at Uppsala University in 1741 in spite of strong resistance from the professorial bodies. The chair was inspired by Germany where similar chairs had been established in Halle 1727 and in Rinteln in 1730. The first professor dealt already then, according to Engwall (1992), with issues that today would be labelled as management.

As pointed out above, the first Swedish business school was set up in 1909. The name in Swedish is *Handelshögskolan.* Below, we will refer to this school as "Stockholm School of Economics" or "SSE" which is the English name the school has given itself. The initiative to set up a business school in Stockholm came from industry in the form of the Wallenberg banking family, the City of Stockholm and the Swedish Government.

An expressed aim of SSE was the advancement of the merchant's trade. The School was to make being a businessman an occupation that the best and brightest of the country's youth should aspire to. The teaching at SSE was to be built on a scientific base in order to distinguish it from the traditional European model of teaching trade practices. In 1928 a second business school was set up in Göteborg on the pattern established by SSE. The two business schools were yearly furnishing Swedish industry with about 300 accountants and general managers. An increasing number of the CEOs and leading officers of the large companies were drawn from these schools. Still today, a large proportion of such posts are held especially by alumni of SSE.

It was not until 1958 that business studies were taken up by the Swedish universities and the duopoly of the business schools was broken. That year, two chairs in accounting were established in the universities of Lund and Uppsala. Additional chairs and the creation of departments of business administration in the other universities followed in the 1960s (Engwall 2004). Later, the engineering schools have also included business administration in their programs. Since 1980, a very strong expansion has taken place. Business studies have become part of the curriculum at most of the new regional universities and colleges. The number of business students increased twenty times between the 1950s and 2005, and the yearly number of graduates with a specialization in business studies has increased tenfold.

Engwall (2004) demonstrates how the system of business studies in Sweden has developed from a German influence toward an increasingly stronger American influence after the Second World War. Many professors spent shorter or longer study periods in the USA. American literature, or Swedish literature based on American ideas predominates. Most schools provide executive MBAs. SSE started a full-time MBA program in 2004. The Americanization has meant a segmentation of business studies in sub-disciplines with little contact with each other. Management as an art that treats the system to be managed as a totality and integrates all the different sub-areas is not taught at all, or is at best relegated to a few odd courses on leadership and business policy.

Suppliers of business education

There are 22 academic institutions supplying business education. Below we have grouped them into four categories: The Leading Schools, the Engineering Schools, the Universities and the Regional Colleges. In addition we make some remarks on Distance Learning.

Leading schools of business studies

There are five organizations that we have grouped into this category. Only one of these, SSE, is an autonomous body. The other four are formally parts of universities even if their business study programs have been organized in a more or less business school-like fashion. *Göteborg School of Business, Economics and Law* is no longer an autonomous body but has been absorbed by the government-owned Göteborg University. *Jönköping International Business School* is part of the Jönköping University, which is owned by a foundation. The other entities that we have grouped among the Leading Schools are the *School of Economics and Management* at the University of Lund and *Economicum* at the *University of Uppsala*.

The leading schools are well-anchored in their regional environment and supported by their industry and local authorities. They have a good faculty/student ratio. Their faculty represents most different sub-areas of business studies. Many of the faculty have a good academic standing and publish in renowned international scientific journals. In addition to basic financing they attract a good deal of research grants from public and private research funds.

The leading schools compete for the best high school graduates. Even if most of the students come from each school's own region, the schools try to attract students from the rest of the country by having differentiated profiles. SSE, for example, runs a successful program in finance, while Uppsala cultivates an international orientation, and Jönköping an orientation toward entrepreneurship.

The students from the leading programs are in high demand on the labor market. In 2001, 85 percent of graduates from SSE had jobs before they finished their studies. The corresponding figure for the provincial Superior School of Kalmar was barely 18 percent (Ejnefält & Strådalen 2005).

Business studies in engineering schools

In the category of Engineering Schools we have grouped the business study programs from four universities and superior schools with a technical profile: Chalmers University of Technology in Göteborg, The University of Linköping, the University of Luleå, and the Royal Institute of Technology in Stockholm. Like the leading business study schools, they have a qualified faculty in business studies.

They all run programs that combine business studies with engineering. The "economy engineers" that they produce have a reasonably good labor market. In addition, the schools allow graduates from the different engineering disciplines to include business studies in their diplomas to become more attractive for management positions.

The business study faculty of the University of Linköping runs an additional program that results in a diploma in business studies. That university is striving for a cross-disciplinary orientation by organizing its research in the social sciences according to themes rather than according to traditional disciplinary divisions.

Business studies in universities

In this category have been grouped the business study programs of the Universities of Stockholm and Umeå. In particular, Stockholm has a large faculty but also a large number of students. Therefore the programs have had to accept the role of producing a substantial number of business graduates with limited resources.

Business studies in regional university colleges

Under this heading we have grouped fifteen regional universities, superior schools and colleges. Most of these academic education providers have been set up to strengthen the development of stagnating regions. The Superior School of the Mälar Valley is partially deviating from that model by being situated in an economically dynamic area in the middle of Sweden. The regional colleges did not originally have the status of universities and could not issue PhD diplomas. Business studies are not organized as a specific program. Usually business studies are but one subject of many that are offered by the department of social sciences. Many of the students that start their business studies in a regional college switch over to one of the older universities or business schools after they have passed a college exam after a couple of years.

Taken as a group the regional colleges have a dearth of qualified faculty in business studies. Some of their courses are provided by teachers from the established universities that they co-operate with. Their own faculty consists partly of graduate students at these better-resourced establishments. Because of their relative lack of resources and their dependence on the established schools, the regional colleges have difficulty in creating a vigorous local academic environment for education and research.

Role of distance teaching

The Authority for Web-learning reports that over 400 courses in the area of economy and administration are offered over the Web. Such courses are among others offered by the "Mid University" that co-operates with several other regional colleges and the educational channel of Sweden Radio in offering web-learning.

EF is one of the interesting new Swedish service companies growing fast internationally. Originally it organized language courses in Great Britain for Swedish youth. It is now delivering Web-supported language courses world wide. It claims to be the world's largest private educational company with 3,000 administrative staff and 23,000 teachers. It is the leading supplier of English courses in China by means of a franchising system. It is also aiming for the lucrative MBA market with a program based mainly on Web-based distance learning. As part of this strategy it has bought the already accredited Arthur D. Little Business School in Boston and renamed it the "Hult International School" after the founder of EF. That school runs the most internationally orientated MBA program in the US with over 90 percent of the students coming from abroad. The Economist ranks it as number 22 of the world's best business schools, just ahead of London Business School.

Supply of basic academic training

Business can be studied as a free-standing topic or as a four-year program leading to the newly institutionalized diploma of business economist (civilekonom). Table 13.3 shows the number of professional or semi-professional degrees produced by the university system in 2004/2005. Of about 25.000 graduates, 10 percent came from business studies.

Table 13.3 Number of professionally-oriented degrees granted by the Swedish academic system in 2005

	Number	Percentage
Teacher	8,424	33
Engineer, architect	4,594	18
Business graduate, civilekonom	2,593	10
Medical doctor, psychologist	1,105	4
Lawyer	949	4
Other master level education	7,700	30
Total four year professional degrees	25,365	100

Source: Högskoleverket 2006

The evaluation committee of the National Agency for Education (Högskoleverket 2002) predicts that the growing inflow of business students in combination with decreasing resources will lead to serious problems for the area. There is insufficient teacher time available for seminar type discussions and for supervising students working on their theses. More students are being accepted who have insufficient knowledge and study habits from high-school, especially their command of mathematics; English and Swedish is not up to par. The teaching has therefore to be performed more in a high-school fashion.

Graduate studies and research

The evaluation committee of the National Agency for Education found that the graduate programs in business studies vary a good deal in content and organization. It could be added that also the quality of doctoral dissertations varies considerably.

Since most doctoral programs have insufficient resources, the committee suggested that different universities should co-operate in providing graduate courses.

Suppliers of continued education

IFL (Swedish Management Institute) which is associated with SSE is Sweden's largest provider of continued management education with yearly sales of 30 million euros, which corresponds to about half of the market for continued business education provided by the academic system. The other leading schools run similar programs with participants from firms and public organization in the region.

The two main technical universities, The Chalmers University of Technology in Göteborg and the Royal Institute of Technology are building up units for continued management education. Their courses have an appeal to managers from technically oriented firms.

The leading business schools in Europe and the US – for example: London Business School, IMD, INSEAD, ENSADE, HBS, Wharton and MIT are serious competitors with the Swedish providers of management education, especially for higher level managers.

Faculty of business studies

Like all other university level education, business studies should be based on scientific principles. Therefore, all teachers should also be carrying out research. A sufficient number of PhDs are needed in each area in which an academic entity wants to carry out serious research. A group of at least 3-5 qualified scientists are probably needed for meaningful seminars and discussions around work in progress. Generally, only the leading schools, the engineering schools and the universities muster a reasonable number of teachers with PhDs.

The evaluation of the university level business education referred to above found that the quality, capacity and competence of the faculty were outstanding at SSE. It was found sufficient at the universities of Uppsala, Jönköping and Luleå, while it was seen as insufficient at the large university of Stockholm and in the regional establishments. Especially, there was not enough competent faculty in the areas of accounting, finance and marketing. The committee recommended that each regional college should specialize in one area rather than aiming to cover the whole field of business studies.

Remuneration of faculty

Wage setting in the university system is, as in the rest of the Swedish labor market, accomplished by negotiation at the local level. Employment conditions are usually regulated by collective agreements between the employer and the teachers' union. Also minimum wages are usually part of the collective agreements. However, wages above the minima are set individually and the unions may represent or assist the individual employee in the wage setting. Table 13.4 shows the wage structure for year 2005 for academic staff in the social sciences including business studies. The figures are monthly salaries translated to euros (1€=SEK 9.3). The variation within each category is considerable and it is interesting

to note that there is just a small difference in pay between the best paid
doctorial candidate and the worst paid professor.

Table 13.4   Gross monthly salary in Euros for male[5] staff at various levels in the
social sciences (including business studies)

Category	Lowest pay	Median pay	Highest pay
Doctorial candidates	1,871	2,183	3,226
Assistant researcher (post doc)	2,791	3,183	3,763
Lecturer	2,688	3,559	5,265
Professor	3,505	4,801	6,763

The figures show the gross amount on which the receiver will have to pay income tax.[6]
Source: SACO & SULF.

Table 13.5 shows the salaries of academic staff in social science including business studies compared to those of other disciplines. The
social science staff are on the whole better paid than their colleagues
from the humanistic field, they receive a salary more and less at par
with science and technology but have lower salaries than staff in the
medical area.

Table 13.5   Gross monthly salary 2005 for male social science (including business
studies) staff in relation to that of other disciplines

Position Discipline	Doctorial candidate	Assistant researcher (post doc)	Lecturer	Professor
Humanistic sciences	102%	107%	105%	112%
Technology and science	97%	100%	97%	99%
Medicine	99%	98%	88%	99%

Source: SACO & SULF.

Table 13.6 shows the pay of social science staff on different levels in relation to business graduates in private industry in comparable age groups
The table shows (the percentage marked in block figures) that a doctorial
candidate in the area of business studies can expect to earn 20 percent less
compared to his former study-mate in the same age group who chose to go
to industry directly after graduation. The assistant researcher can expect
to earn a little less than the study-mate who directly went to industry. A
lecturer would still not earn as much as his former study-mate in industry.
Only after having obtained a professorship, a teacher in business studies

could expect to earn clearly more, i.e. 22 percent than his average former study-mate who went directly to industry.

Table 13.6   Gross monthly salary for different categories of male social science staff in relation to business graduates working in industry

Position Category	Doctorial candidate	Assistant researcher (post doc)	Lecturer	Professor
28 year old business graduates in private industry	81%	118%	132%	179%
33 year old business graduates in private industry	65%	95%	107%	144%
38 year old business graduates in private industry	58%	84%	94%	127%
43 year old business graduates in private industry	56%	81%	91%	122%

Source: SACO.

Table 13.7   Gross monthly salary of different categories of male science staff in relation to different jobholders in industry

Position Category	Doctorial candidate	Assistant researcher (post doc)	Lecturer	Professor
Functional manager in industry	36%	52%	59%	79%
Nurse	66%	97%	108%	146%
Office Clerc	79%	115%	129%	174%
Skilled laborer	102%	148%	166%	223%

Sources: SACO and Statistics, Sweden.

Table 13.7 compares how much social science staff are paid in relation to different categories of posts in private industry. It can be seen that a doctorial candidate can expect to make about the same amount of money as the skilled laborer, who has been able to work and earn money during the years it took for the candidate to obtain his first academic degree. The assistant researcher could expect to earn a little less than a nurse, who has invested five years less than him on academic studies. Moreover, the table shows that if the professor had been bright and ambitious enough to become manager of, for example, an accounting department in industry instead of choosing an academic career, he could be expected to lift a salary more than 20 percent higher than his professorial one.

Our analysis above indicates that lower levels of the academic staff in business studies are underpaid in relation to the professor. This is, of course, a feature that is purposely built into the academic system. The system is designed to make members of the staff compete for the top job and to contribute important research findings to their science in order to qualify. But probably the salary of a professor is too low relative to a career in industry for attracting top talent business graduates to become researchers and to engage in the highly competitive game of scientific research and publication.

In order to counteract their competitive disadvantage on the labor market in relation to industry, universities allow their staff to earn extra income from consultation and teaching in continued management training. Two to five days extra engagement in such activities could contribute to a doubling of one's ordinary monthly salary. Such incentives may make people stay on with the university but it is doubtful if the possibility of moonlighting could lure good graduates to begin to study for a doctorate. The necessity to engage in extra-curricular activities may also have the adverse affect that the university or the business school cannot take full advantage of the staffs' skills in teaching managers and in collaborating with industry. If the staff had not felt the pressure to take on outside jobs in order to earn a decent income, their skills could have been better used instead to build up a stronger position for the school in continued education and collaborative research.

Demand for academic business studies

Demand for basic academic training

There were more than 300,000 (full year equivalents) students enrolled in basic university level education in 2004 (Högskoleverket 2005). This figure corresponds to roughly 40 percent of the batch of Swedes that are born each year. However, during the last few years the inflow of students has decreased. This sign of weakening in the demand could be related to the increasing unemployment among university graduates.

Business studies are, with the exception of mathematics, the subject attracting the largest numbers of students in Sweden. More than 10 percent or an odd 30,000 students are engaged in business studies, including those who aim at other degrees than business. The even higher figure for mathematics is due to that subject being mandatory for engineering students.

The demand for a certain program or topic can be estimated by the number of applicants for each available slot. The strongest demand from the students for university level education is in the health sector. The weakest is in the science area. In year 2005 there were 2.3 applicants per place in business studies, 9.8 for medical doctor studies, 2.0 for teaching and 1.6 for engineering. Competition is especially fierce for the elite schools. For example, in 2005, there were 12 applicants per available slot at SSE.

A business graduate could traditionally be sure to find employment rather quickly. Even if unemployment among business graduates has increased a bit during the first years of the twenty first century, they still have a relatively strong position on the labor market. Of the business administration graduates in 2003, about 15 percent had not got a regular job one and a half years later. Only graduates in the medical profession fared better, with just 10 percent without regular employment after one and a half years. Students in the humanistic area are in the toughest position. A third of them have not been able to find a regular job after one and half years.

Demand for the elite schools

The brightest of Swedish high school students aim to get into one of the elite programs rather than to a specific discipline. These programs are likely to attract the youngsters who have ambition and talent to become top level managers and business leaders. As was pointed out in the historic review above, the elite programs are found in the leading schools of business studies, medicine, and engineering (especially theoretical physics). The quality and image of the leading academic business study programs determine how well they compete with the elite programs in engineering and medicine in the fight for the best students. The success of the elite programs can be ascribed to first mover advantage, which has permitted them to assemble massive resources. Sons and daughters of successful alumni are likely to follow in their parents' foot-steps. Similarly, employers continue to recruit graduates from schools they know well. Only one of the leading programs of business studies is to be found in an organization founded after WWII. It is the *International School of Management* that was set up in Jönköping in 1994. Its success may be explained by the freedom it has got to innovate by being owned by a private foundation. In comparison with other academic establishments in Sweden it has actively been recruiting the best faculty from where it can find them and has paid them well. It has consciously projected a positive image of itself and has nurtured a profile of entrepreneurship.

Demand from women

The demand for university studies in Sweden is much higher from women than from men in all areas but engineering. Two thirds of all graduates are women. For business studies there is at present, however, more or less a balance between the sexes. If the trend continues a feminization of the area of business studies, too, can be expected, except for the elite programs.

Demand from foreign students

The darkness and harshness of the Swedish winter in combination with the scant international usefulness of the language serve as deterrents for foreign students to study in Sweden. In spite of these forbidding conditions there are quite a number of foreign students in Swedish business studies. Many come to Sweden as exchange students. Swedish business students are very keen on spending a semester during their training at a business school abroad. To fulfill this demand, exchange programs with foreign universities are set up by the Swedish schools.

One reason that foreign students are attracted, after all, by studies in Sweden is that university studies are provided free of tuition and other charges. Their studies are facilitated by the many courses that are given in English.

Industry's changing need for management competence

From the latter part of the nineteenth century until the 1960s Sweden was one of the fastest-growing economies in the world. The nation was transformed from an agricultural country to become highly industrialized. Mining, forestry and the exploitation of the country's vast resources of hydroelectricity provided the basis for the industries of steel, shipbuilding, matches, pulp and paper. In addition, product innovations gave birth to large engineering and chemical corporations like Alfa Laval (separators and heat exchangers, ASEA (electricity generation and transmission), Electrolux (household goods), Nobel (chemistry), SKF (ball-bearings) and Volvo (cars and trucks). Most of the production of the Swedish manufacturing industry was, and continues to be, exported. Many firms set up affiliates in foreign countries. Bankers and engineers were the architects of the industrial expansion. The content of studies at the two business schools in Stockholm and Göteborg was shaped in order to provide managers to the expanding industry. The curricula of these two schools have had a profound impact also on the business study programs that have been launched during the latter half of the twentieth century.

However, during the second half of the twentieth century and the first years of the twenty first, the Swedish economy has gone through a major re-structuring that has not fully been reflected in the curricula for business studies. In a crisis starting toward the end of the 1960s the country's raw material-based industries like shipbuilding and steel lost their competitive edge in relation to that of emerging low-cost countries, and shrank. Employment in the manufacturing industry was long maintained by a series of devaluations of the Swedish currency. This policy was abandoned in the beginning of the twenty first century and plants representing a substantial part of the employment in manufacturing had to be closed down. Also the Government policy of directly subsiding ailing industries was abandoned and regions were instead encouraged to take care of their own economic development.

The deregulation of the financial market that took place in the 1980's has given Sweden a vigorous financial industry. Likewise, the deregulation of the telecommunications sector has opened up the world market for mobile telephony, in which Ericsson has become a major player.

The service sector has expanded and absorbed some of the redundant labor from manufacturing. In the wake of deteriorating real wages that have weakened the buying power of the Swedish households, innovative retailers like IKEA (furniture), H&M (fashion), and Oriflame (cosmetics) have found ways to source and sell good products cheaply. These firms have, like services firms such as Securitas (security guards and services), Interum Justitia (debt information and collection), and EF (language training), obtained strong positions on the world market.

The ongoing globalization has meant that ownership of many of the old flagships of Swedish industry has fully or partly been taken over by foreigners. Examples are the pharmaceutical firms Astra and Pharmacia, the forestry giant Stora, the car makers Saab and Volvo, and the financial houses of Nordea, Skandia and Alfred Berg.

The export-oriented Swedish manufacturing company used to be the standard customer that the country's business study programs were designed for. Management education will, however, have to adapt to the changes in the economic landscape. The business graduates increasingly work for international companies based abroad rather than for just Swedish multinationals. The firm they are working for will often be one of the partners in an emergent international network rather than a free-standing entity. Business students will have to understand that they probably will work in service rather than in the manufacturing industry.

The present and future economic growth comes from small firms and ventures rather than from larger firms. Small firms have traditionally had few business graduates employed. Therefore business schools have to figure out how they could possibly provide managers to such small firms.

Competition on the global scene is fierce. In order to survive in this situation, firms have to innovate. This process can be managed. However, it is no longer enough to rely on the R&D departments for the necessary changes. In the competitive game of innovation, entrepreneurs, ventures and small firms play an increasingly critical role. Traditionally, the academic business programs are geared toward producing graduates who can work in larger companies. Nowadays, they are facing the challenge of offering programs for future entrepreneurs and still observe that business studies should stand on a scientific base.

Demand for advanced academic training

The 370 PhDs that received their diplomas in business studies between 1971 and 2000 were not, according to the National agency for Education report (Högskoleverket 2002), enough to meet the demand for qualified researchers and teachers. The Evaluation Committee concluded that the shortage of teachers was one of the most serious problems facing the area of business studies.

In the period that followed, the production of PhDs in the management area has increased considerably. As Table 13.8 shows, an average of 54 PhDs got their diploma each year during 2001–2005. All new doctors do not stay in the academic system, though. PhDs in management are increasingly sought by consultancy firms. They are also in demand

Table 13.8   Number of new PhDs in management per year 2001–2005

Supplier	PhDs
Stockholm School of Economics	11
University of Göteborg	9
University of Stockholm	7
University of Uppsala	6
University of Lund	5
Six others	16
Whole Academic System	**54**

in the area of public administration, e.g. for planning and for the government bodies responsible for the financing of research.

The unemployment statistics show that the demand and supply of PhDs in management have become more balanced. Of the PhDs in the area of business studies 4.5 percent were reported unemployed in 2005. This figure is close to the average for all subject areas. PhDs in medicine have the lowest unemployment rate (0.9 percent) and in those in biology have the highest (11 percent).

Demand for continued management training

At present the sales of continued management training from the academic system can be estimated at 55 million euros. The total demand for continued management training is many times higher. An interviewee from a Swedish multinational said that his firm in one year spent several hundred million euros on training activities (not including the salaries of the participants).

Most courses provided by the academic system are designed for individuals coming from different companies. There is a considerable demand for Executive MBAs, for example, from engineers who want to complement their basic degree with a business diploma.

There is also demand for freestanding courses in the various areas of business studies as well as in leadership. Employers often want employees who are being promoted to a management position, to prepare themselves by following a training program in management consisting of recurring sessions, each of a few days long, over a year or so.

Another area for continued management training is courses in specialized areas: for example, purchase management, or for special industries, e.g. real estate management. Firms also demand courses organized in-house, e.g. for all managers at a certain level. Such training used to be produced by the firm's training officer but is increasingly being outsourced. A representative for a large international firm guessed that the firm in the future would demand that such courses become integrated with ongoing organizational change programs.

There is also a market for usually shorter courses given by highly regarded experts on special management methods: for example on business process engineering. Sometimes such courses border on management entertainment that is also in high demand, for example, to enliven sales conferences and staff gatherings.

In addition, there is a demand for training to prepare persons who are promoted to top management positions. The cost of such training is not really a concern. Instead the training should be of short duration, be provided by highly reputed schools or management institutes and provide an international context where trainees would meet high potentials from other firms.

Rule-setters for management education

The Swedish Government calls the tune for academic business education since it pays the piper. It has stipulated that all education including academic studies has to be provided free. This stipulation of course poses problems especially for the three private schools for business studies. Also, it creates a bias so that students choose to continue studies in Sweden rather than go abroad.

As it becomes harder and harder for the Government to finance the academic educational system, the pressure mounts for allowing at least some fees. If fees are to be allowed, some type of system has to be introduced that prevents youth without an academic family back-ground from becoming closed out from academic studies.

A key goal for the Swedish Government has been to keep the unemployment figure down to four percent. Since it is comparatively easy for business students to find employment, the Government has permitted the area to grow. In this context it is an advantage that business education is cheap in relation to engineering education. A conservative government replaced the social democratic one in the autumn of 2006. The new government's goal for the labor market is to maximize the number of people employed, rather than to minimize the number of people unemployed. It is doubtful, though, if the new government will be able to stay long enough for the new policies to really have an impact on the educational system, because earlier conservative reigns have been only short-lived intermissions during 70 years of social-democratic domination. Also the unions of public sector workers, which wield strong power independently of the color of the government, are hostile to the labor market policies of the new government. With these reservations, some comments on these policies are made in the next paragraph.

In order to implement the new government policy, the educational system will probably be encouraged to become more responsive to market needs. Also, possibilities for getting a better return on the investments that individuals make in their own education will probably be improved; for example, by the encouragement of a wider spread in individual wages. The new government also favors more competition in the health sector, which hitherto has been controlled by huge public entities. All these possible measures would probably increase the demand for business education, especially such that attracts good students and is deemed to deliver useful training of high quality.

Another policy of the Government has been to stimulate regional economic growth. Therefore it has financed the founding of regional universities. A perverse effect of this policy is that qualified labor is supplied in areas where it is not demanded, whereas the schools in areas where demand is high do not have enough funds. The new government's interest in training that meets market demands and is of high puts on the regional colleges and universities. They can no longer expect preferential treatment. They will have to concentrate their resources in areas where they have, or could achieve, a distinctive competence that gives them competitive advantage. Many will have to merge with others.

In addition to the central government, the boards of the different schools and universities are important rule setters. The boards also contain local politicians and representatives from industry. Their role is especially influential in the private and the regional schools.

The Government's monitoring of the academic business education is made through a special agency called "Högskoleverket." One example of its monitoring is the evaluation that has been referred to above and which provided evaluation and advice to the different suppliers of business education.

Accreditation of business schools is carried out by the European Foundation for Management Development according to "EQUIS" (European Quality Improvement System). The accreditation process takes into account all aspects of a school's activities and requires that a school has achieved a high degree of internationalization. In Sweden SSE and the School of Economics and Law in Göteborg have been accredited.

The rankings provided by the Financial Times, Wall Street Journal, and Economist are, according to a recent doctoral thesis (Wedlin 2004), playing an increasingly important role as norm-setters for European business education. A high ranking on the lists signals that the school belongs to the elite business schools. The rankings contribute to the diffusion of ideas about what constitutes an excellent business school, that business schools are competitors in the international market, and that the MBA is a template for what a management education program should look like. For example, the possibility to be ranked was one reason for Stockholm School of Economics to start the first full-time MBA program in Sweden in 2004.

The strategy and interplay between the actors

Strategy of leading schools

Below follows a discussion based on the Stockholm School of Economics which can also be taken as indicative for the strategy of the other leading schools.

Basic business training

SSE aims at upholding its image as the leading Swedish school in the area of business studies. SSE's mission is to recruit some of the country's best and most ambitious students so that they, like generations of students before them, will become able leaders of Swedish industry. Therefore, the attractiveness of the school has to be upheld.

One main characteristic of the school is to base its teaching on research carried out by a number of research centers in, and institutes associated with, the school. Another way to become attractive is to allocate much teacher time to seminar discussions and to supervision of exercises and theses writing. A third characteristic is nurturing good contacts with industry. The good relations with industry make it possible to get leading business people as guest lecturers. Many courses use project work in companies as a pedagogical device. The good contacts also facilitate students to get access to firms for their thesis work.

A further feature much appreciated by the students is the opportunity to study abroad at a partner school. Moreover, the school gets a cosmopolitan touch by the exchange students that reciprocate by coming to SSE for study during one semester.

SSE wants to prepare its graduates for future jobs in the large international companies head-quartered both in Sweden and other countries. The CEMS-degree is a step on the road. CEMS is a common diploma for the leading business school from each of a number of European countries. A student can take courses from the other member schools in addition to his or her own. The mastery of three languages is one of the requirements for the degree.

An additional means for SSE to pave the way for an international career for its students is by conforming to the Bologna protocol by dividing the studies into a three-year basic program plus a two-year advanced program leading to a master. Students from other schools are admitted through competitive selection to the advanced two-year part of the program.

The school recognizes that it cannot develop all the competences in-house that are needed. Therefore alliances have to be formed with schools in other countries that could provide part of the needed training; at the same time, they expose students to another culture. The co-operation can be manifested in joint or double diplomas. For example, an SSE-student involved in such a scheme would be able to receive a diploma from an engineering school (perhaps abroad) in addition to the diploma from SSE. The additional diploma would require only limited extra studies for the student if the co-operating schools agree on recognizing a large part of the credits earned in the other school as valid in one's own school as well.

In addition to providing general management training, SSE has a specialized niche in the area of accounting and finance. It has provided the fledging finance industry in Stockholm with qualified labor. A large number of the graduates having specialized in finance are recruited every year by the finance industry in London. Many graduates are also recruited by the large international consultant houses. This trend opens the possibility of another niche that SSE could perhaps exploit: a professional program in consulting.

Swedish industry and Government see the Baltic States and the St Petersburg Region as important markets. SSE has therefore set up affiliate business schools in Riga and St Petersburg in order to respond to a strong demand for business studies in those regions, and for training managers that could be recruited to Swedish firms that have activities there.

Graduate training at SSE

In spite of SSE having only five percent of all business students in Sweden, it produces 20 percent of all PhDs in the field. However, the money available for research is becoming scarce. Therefore, the school is cutting down the number of professors, and tries to limit the number of graduate students that each professor supervises.

In spite of the financial difficulties, SSE wants to defend its position as the country's leading research organization in business studies and as the country's largest producer of PhDs in that field. In order to use the available resources better, SSE will organize courses jointly with other schools. Also, research projects may have to be carried out jointly with research organizations in Sweden and abroad.

Continued management education at SSE

The Executive Education arm of SSE has recently merged with IFL (the Swedish Management Institute). The strategy behind this move is to consolidate a dominating market share in Sweden in general and in the Stockholm area in particular. Seen from the perspective of SSE, continuing education is one of the ways to broaden the contacts with Swedish industry and, so to speak, keep alumni as partners and customers of the school. Also, continued education activities can generate resources for the research. It offers, moreover, a way for faculty at the school to develop contacts with practice. In addition, it is also a way for the faculty to improve their income.

Strategy and action of the regional colleges

Since the regional colleges have scarce resources, their business studies will have to specialize in areas which relate to regional strength. Examples are tourism in Östersund, which is located near the major winter resorts, and service management in Karlstad. Such specialized profiles can be reinforced by collaborating with foreign centers that have the same type of specialization. Synergies can also be won if research in business studies is aligned with the research goals of other disciplines. The regions where the colleges are located often have a weak labor market. It is therefore important to build links that strengthen the growth capability of local industry; for example, involvement in teaching activities, periods of practice, thesis work that addresses concerns of local industry, specially designed courses, workshops and seminars, and joint development projects. The local college should not content itself with educating labor for the local labor market. It should also do its best to support regional initiatives that could result in a growing demand for qualified labor, including management talent.

Strategy and action of industry

The Confederation of Swedish Enterprise represents employers and is also the spokesman for industry as a whole. Its general goal is to work for an improved state of affairs for business and industry. It wants Sweden, before 2015, to regain its former ranking as one of the most prosperous countries in the world. It sees education as a key factor in achieving better economic development. The Confederation puts special emphasis on improving secondary education. It also advocates more direct links between the secondary schools and local industry. It wants the schools to spread knowledge about the importance of entrepreneurship and make the pupils understand that being an entrepreneur is a possible choice for them.

The Confederation has not expressed a specific policy for academic business studies. Its policy is that labor market questions should be decentralized to the different employers' federations. Recruitment and training of personnel are seen as questions for the individual firm to handle.

Strategy and action of a Swedish multinational

To illustrate the strategy of industrial companies in the area of management training, one Swedish multinational will be used as an example. This example is based on an interview with a person responsible for management training during the period described. A radical change of the company's policy in this area took place in 2003. The change coincides with an economic crisis in the company which has now been over-come. The change was triggered by an analysis showing that the company spent 400 million euros on training activities in 2001.

Old policy   The firm's training policy was based on the conviction that competence development and investments in human resources could really contribute to competitiveness and economic success. To win, the firm had to engage in the "war of talent."

The company is very technology-oriented and recruits a substantial share of each year's output of graduates from the engineering schools. Business graduates were recruited to a lesser extent and mainly for the accounting departments.

Many expatriates were stationed at the different local units worldwide. It was said that the local units became like sites where the traveling circus of expatriates temporarily set up their tents.

Assessment centers were used to identify candidates for future management positions. The candidates with managerial talent were sent to tailor-made courses at business schools that had been picked for their excellence, e.g. LBS, Columbia, Duke, INSEAD, and ENSADE.

Talented employees identified by the local units around the world got training at local management institutes. Swedish management training institutes were not given any priority but were treated just as another local training. Frequent conferences built around business gurus were also arranged at different places in the world.

To be promoted to a top management position, the candidate would had to have served abroad in different positions. The managers that were considered as top talent in the company were initiated to high management positions through a specially adapted course in one of the best American business schools. The course consisted of three sessions of one week each.

A "Corporate University" was being built up. One idea behind the university was to consolidate various training activities. Another idea was to put much emphasis on learning by individual and collective re-flection over what is happening.

Emerging policy The emerging policy bears the mark of austerity made necessary by the economic crisis the company experienced during the first years of the twenty first century. A change in promotion policy has taken place. More recruitment is made locally and fewer Swedish expatriates are used. Business graduates are being promoted to top positions that used to be reserved for engineers. A special trainee program for business graduates has started. Management knowledge is slowly being recognized as a strategic resource, both internally and by the owners.

During a period of time, it was seen as an advantage to have both an engineering and business diploma when a promotion was contemplated. It does, however, no longer matter so much what kind of diploma one has. The main thing is the candidate's performance. Performance is evaluated in a yearly management planning process. The ones that are deemed suitable for promotion to a management position are given the opportunity to go to the "core management course."

Sending people off to external courses, which was common in the 1990s, has now stopped. Instead, the core management course is sourced from local consultants in different countries. The course has to follow precise guidelines developed by an officer placed at the central HRM-unit. The training uses ample Web-support.

The many conferences have been replaced by a course provided at one of the top European business schools. Even after the change, the top management training provided by the famous American business school remains intact.

Exit rather than voice In spite of its size, this multinational does not attempt to influence the educational system in the country or that of individual universities. Instead it chooses from among the available providers of training.

Summary of the firm's change in strategy Management is becoming more accepted as a strategic resource even in this technically oriented company. Management training has become much more standardized than it used to be. The purpose and content of the training has become more centrally controlled out from a clear idea of how what is useful for the company. More of the training is produced in-house and the amount of courses delivered at business schools is reduced. The in-house training staff is reduced and the training is sourced from consultants. Even if the cost for management training has been reduced, its value for the company is not necessarily less because the training is more aligned to the company's goals than before.

Concluding reflection

Our analysis has shown that business studies are among the areas of the Swedish Academic System for which demand is strongest. There are a fair number of highly-resourced leading schools that combine teaching and research that can meet some of this demand. On the other hand, there are numerous, less well-resourced regional colleges and universities that make it possible for a large number of students to pursue business studies close to home and in collaboration with local industry. These regional suppliers of business studies have to find a way to balance the task at hand with the resources they can muster.

Globalization and profound changes in the structure of Swedish industry require adaptation and innovation of business study programs. The different programs are, however, similar and more variation could be beneficial. The general trend in designing business study programs has been an Americanization that does not encourage an integrated view of management that might open up new opportunities for both management and practice.

Our material indicates that managements of business and government organizations are starting to think that reorganization can be combined with training of managers. If it is so, a new large market for continued management training could become available. That market could not be satisfied by courses provided on the premises of management institutes. It requires instead that academic staff work collaboratively with the managers in designing a process that integrates organizational and strategic change with training adapted to the specific situation.

References

Ejnefjäll, S. & Strådalen, M., 2005, *Den Attraktiva Civilekonomen*. Gotland University College, Magisteruppsats VT 2005.

Engwall, L., 2004, The Americanization of Nordic Management Education. *J. Management Inquiry*, Vol 13:2, 109–117.

Engwall, L., 1992, Mercury Meets Minerva: Business Studies and Higher Education: The Swedish Case. Oxford: Pergamon Press.

Högskoleverket (National Agency for Education), 2002, *Utvärdering av utbildning i företagsekonomi vid svenska universitet och högskolor*. Högskoleverkets rapportserie 2002:10R.

Högskoleverket (National Agency for Education), 2006, 2005, Yearly reports + various reports and statistics.

SACO (The Swedish Confederation of Professional Associations), Income statistics.

Statistics Sweden, Income statistics.

SULF (Swedish Association of University Teachers), Income Statistics www. lonesok.saco.se.

Wedlin, L. Playing the Ranking Game. Field formation and boundary-work in European Management education. University of Uppsala, 2004.

Interviews

Lars Bergman, Stockholm School of Economics
Jan Edgren, Högskolan i Halmstad
Peter Hyllman, PMO, Stockholm School of Economics
Peter Hägglund, IFL (Swedish Management Institute)
P.O. Nyquist, Cardo AB

14
Higher Management Education in Portugal

João C. Neves[1]

The context of management education in Portugal

The Public University started in the Middle Ages, founded by the Monarchs under the authority and supervision of the Catholic Church. For many centuries, there was only the University of Coimbra, founded in 1290 and transferred several times between Coimbra and Lisbon. Formal management education is dated back to 1759 when the Board of Trade, with the support of the Prime Minister, Marquis of Pombal, founded the School of Commerce in Lisbon. In 1869, the school merged with the Institute of Industry of Lisbon and in 1930 was integrated in the Technical University of Lisbon.

The present structure of Higher Education (HE) was mainly established between 1977 and 1980. Until 1979, all HE was public except for the Università Cattolica del Sacro Cuore, which has a unique status under the Concordat signed with the Holy See on 7th May 1940 and 24th May 2004.

The types of institutions that offer degrees in management studies are:

- Universities and Polytechnics;
- Public, Private and Cooperative Institutions, and the Università Cattolica del Sacro Cuore.

Presently it is hard to find any difference between the roles of universities and polytechnics but the latter are not allowed to offer doctorate degrees. The system is flexible as students may transfer from one system to another to continue their studies.

In the 1980's the network of Public HE expanded in number and size, as well as the Private sector, which had strong political support from its very beginning.

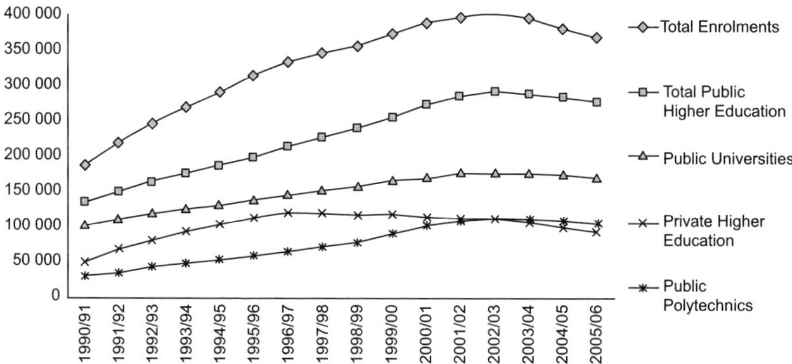

Figure 14.1   Total number of students enrolled in the higher education system
Source: Ministry of Science, Technology, and Higher Education, 2006.

The number of students in the HE system has increased considerably, essentially because the access requirements became less demanding. Medicine remains the most selective field of studies and students need to get very high grades in the national entrance exams and a brilliant curriculum in the secondary school.

The demand in the various fields of studies is as follows:

- Social Sciences, Business and Law (32 percent). Management is 8 percent of total undergraduates, and economics 3 percent.
- Engineering, Manufacturing and Building Industry (22 percent).
- Health and Welfare (16 percent).

The market share for undergraduate management studies is 20 percent for the private and cooperative sector, and 5 percent for the Università Cattolica del Sacro Cuore. i.e. 25 percent private. They had approximately 10 percent in 1983, growing to 22 percent in 1989, reaching a maximum of 36 percent in 1996.

At the master's level, the private and cooperative sector has a market share of 10 percent only, and the Università Cattolica del Sacro Cuore 14 percent.

In general, public universities and the Università Cattolica del Sacro Cuore have higher reputations and quality than the private and cooperative universities, which may explain the lower percentage of management students taking master's degrees in the private and cooperative sector.

Table 14.1   Number of institutions of higher education in Portugal

	University		Polytechnic	
	Universities	Other schools (not integrated)	Institutes	Other schools (not integrated)
Public	14	5	15	16
Private	13	35	2	60
Total	27	40	17	76

Source: Ministry of Science, Technology, and Higher Education, 2006.

There are several types of master's degrees in management, where 16 of them can be classified as MBA type. Only three are offered by the private and cooperative sector. The MBA programs have an average of 60 students enrolled, and the largest program is from the Università Cattolica del Sacro Cuore, with 25 percent of the total MBAs.

Table 14.1 summarizes the offer of HE in Portugal:

The structure of management degrees in Portugal

The organization of universities is by faculties, schools, and/or institutes. The management faculties are usually integrated with the faculty of economics in schools or institutes of economics and management.

Both universities (Schools of Economics and Management) and polytechnics offer HE in management. The universities offer *Licenciatura*, Master's, and Doctor Degrees in Economics and Management (Business administration and Public administration), and Mathematics Applied to Economics and Management. They also offer specialized master's degrees and post-graduation programs in management such as Marketing, Banking and finance, Information systems, Human resources, Transportation and logistics management, Real estate management and Actuarial sciences. Bachelor's and *Licenciatura* degrees offered by Polytechnics related to management are Commerce, Accounting and Tax, Hotel and Restaurant Management, Marketing and Advertisement, Transport and Logistics Management, and Tourism and Leisure.

After the implementation of the Bologna Accord the Polytechnics offer *Licenciatura* and Master's degrees.

The structure of management degrees in Portugal before the Bologna Accord and after its implementation is as follows:

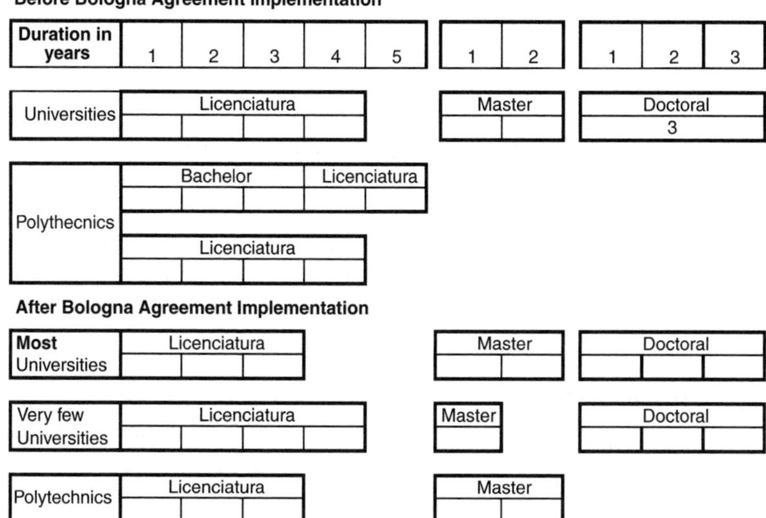

Figure 14.2   Duration of Degrees in Management in Portugal

Undergraduate studies

Undergraduates are selected on a basis of the weighted average of the grades obtained at upper-secondary school and the national exams. Each institution sets the examination required for each field of studies. Most schools of economics and management require Mathematics only, but others also require Economics or Portuguese. Several private schools of economics and management also accept exams of sociology, geography, psychology, or philosophy.

The entrance to each public HE institution and program is subject to a regime of quantitative limitations (*numerus clauses*). Applications for places in the public system are run through a national competition organized by the Ministry during July. A second opportunity exists by the end of September for leftover places.

Foreign candidates are subject to the same requirements including the Portuguese language. They must request to the Department of Secondary Education for the equivalent of their secondary studies based on their official certification, ratified by the Portuguese Embassy or Consulate in their home country.

Portugal has been very active from the beginning in the European mobility programs: Erasmus-Socrates, Tempus, and Leonardo da Vinci. The majority of incoming students are from Luxembourg, Switzerland, France, Belgium, and the UK.

Most HE institutions – private and public – offer *licenciaturas* in a full-time basis. In contrast, post-graduation and master's degrees are usually in a part-time basis to conciliate the studies with the jobs of the students. As the Bologna Accord is changing the number of years of *licenciatura,* the schools of economics and management will now offer master's degrees also in a full-time basis.

The number of students in management *licenciatura* is on Table 14.2:

Table 14.2   No. of students in licenciatura in management

Management	Women	Men	Total
Polytechnics	3,882	9,293	13,175
Universities	9,448	17,889	27,337
No. Of programs:			
Polytechnics			104
Universities			76

Source: OCES – Observatory of Science and Higher Education.

Table 14.3   Enrolment of management students in the largest universities

Faculties of Economics and Management	Women	Men	Total	%
Aberta (i.e. Open) University	1,041	1,591	2,632	9.6%
Technical University of Lisbon – ISEG	804	1,394	2,198	8.0%
ISCTE	499	969	1,468	5.4%
Nova University – Faculty of Economics	497	858	1,355	5.0%
Oporto University – Faculty of Economics	414	771	1,185	4.3%
Università Cattolica del Sacro Cuore – Faculty of Economics and Management – Lisbon	363	639	1,002	3.7%
Minho University – School of Economics and Management	299	594	893	3.3%
Università Cattolica del Sacro Cuore – Faculty of Economics and Management – Oporto	319	514	833	3.0%
Total	4,236	7,330	11,566	42.3%

Source: OCES – Observatory of Science and Higher Education.

In spite of the large number of schools and programs, the eight most significant faculties attract 42 percent of *licenciatura* management students (Table 14.3). The largest school in number is Aberta University because it is a distance learning HE institution.

Master's degree

There are 45 master's degree programs in general management and specialized fields such as Finance; Marketing; Information Systems; Human Resources; Operations and Logistics; Entrepreneurship, Innovation and Technology; Health Management; Management of Sports and International Management that enroll approximately 2,000 students, of which a third are women.

The MBA is the most popular, attracting 50 percent of the master's students of all management fields. Management of Sports and Public Administration follow with 11 percent and 10 percent respectively. The success of Management of Sports can be explained by the large number of people with *licenciatura* in Sports aiming to develop their own businesses or by their involvement in the management of Clubs, Federations or Associations.

As previously mentioned, the largest MBA program is the Università Cattolica del Sacro Cuore followed by Porto University, Nova University, and ISEG Technical University of Lisbon.

No Portuguese Management School has its MBA ranked internationally (such as by the Financial Times or The Economist) as they are nationally oriented. Nova started teaching courses in English, hired international faculty and was recently accredited by the AMBA and Equis. Beside this international achievement, the AMBA accredited Católica MBA and ISEG Technical University of Lisbon, and the Royal Institution of Chartered Surveyors (RICS) accredited the Master of Real Estate Management of ISEG Technical University of Lisbon. To our knowledge, international bodies accredited no other master's programs in Portugal until now, but other schools are likely to follow the path of these three leading business schools.

Doctoral degree

The total number of students enrolled in doctoral degree programs in management in 2005-2006 is 412. The Public system has 71 percent market share and the Università Cattolica del Sacro Cuore 5 percent.

It is worth noting that management schools do not need to offer formal courses to award a doctoral degree. Some schools award their doctoral degree based exclusively on the discussion of the thesis. In that case, a student may enroll in the degree as long as he finds a qualified supervisor interested in the project, and the Scientific Committee accepts the research project. This is the reason why so many of Portuguese Professors did their doctoral studies abroad.

The first Doctoral Program in management was launched by ISEG in 2001, followed by other schools such as ISCTE, University of Coimbra, University of Minho, University of Beira Interior and Lusíada University. It is expected that other schools will follow this path. For example, Nova University that has the ancient Doctoral Program in Economics has decided to launch a Doctoral Program specialized in Finance.

Non-academic courses and executive education

Three public universities (ISEG, ISCTE and Nova) and the Università Cattolica del Sacro Cuore offer most of the Post-graduate programs (no academic degree) and executive training. Private companies, including international consulting firms, also offer executive training. The other academic institutions have a very small market share.

Private institutions remained almost dedicated to undergraduate studies, with some exceptions.

Several factors may explain why private schools have so low a market share in post-graduation studies: they have less emphasis in full-time faculty, professors are less known, and they have a smaller proportion of teachers with doctoral degrees, and poor emphasis on research.

It is necessary to note the limitations on commenting on private institutions – because of the lack of publicly available information in this sector.

Research, size and quality

Among the biggest and most highly respected institutions are Nova University of Lisbon, ISEG – Technical University of Lisbon, ISCTE, University of Porto, University of Minho and Università Cattolica del Sacro Cuore. These five public institutions and the Università Cattolica del Sacro Cuore manage the biggest budgets for teaching and research, and have the largest number of enrolled undergraduate and post-graduate students. They are renowned in aspects such as faculty quality, publications that serve the student community, research & development production with internationally recognized papers, number of new applicants admitted as their first choice, nationwide and internationally recognized top-class infrastructures, renowned ex-students, robust and rigorous curricula, and extra-curricular programs and activities, including executive programs and studies for the industry and Government. Between 1970 and 2005 Porto University collected 1001 publications of

Portuguese authors and Portuguese institutions in 379 international journals indexed in the EconLit database, and find that Nova, ISEG and Università Cattolica del Sacro Cuore published 68 percent of the total Portuguese institutions.

Although generally smaller and younger, the other public universities and polytechnics are seen as regional powerhouses and contribute to the development of their regions. University of Aveiro, University of Minho and University of Beira Interior have been frequently referred to as the "new generation" of the Portuguese university institutions, renowned in general for its innovative methods and modernity.

The Polytechnics' offer in management is clearly excessive for a small country with 10 million inhabitants. They offer 104 programs in management, the 30 smallest institutions enrolling 669 students in total, averaging 11 students per class in the *licenciatura*. The small size of some schools offering management education in some private universities and some public polytechnics is a problem, because of the need for critical mass to generate financially viable schools that attract good teachers with specialized knowledge in particular areas, as well as generate research capabilities and raise funds for research.

The faculty

The career of faculty members in Universities had the following path:

- Trainee Assistant – the minimum entry requirement is the *licenciatura*;
- Assistant – a master's degree is the minimum requirement;
- Assistant Professor – requires a doctorate degree;
- Associate Professor – a doctorate degree and a minimum of five years' service in the category;
- Full Professor (catedrático) – requires the aggregation and a minimum of three years' service in the category after the aggregation.

Aggregation is a special public assessment, where a jury constituted by professors and/or associate professors with aggregation from various universities, evaluate the candidate – based on three papers – his CV, a class session and the organization of a course. If the candidate is accepted, there is a two-days' examination of two hours each session. On the first day, the candidate presents the organization of the course, followed by a discussion with the jury of his work and CV. On the second day, the candidate presents his class session, followed by a discussion with the jury.

Table 14.4 exhibits the structure of degrees hold by the faculty of management and economics:

Table 14.4 Faculty in Public and Private Universities

Holding degree	Public	Private
Doctorate	55%	27%
Master	24%	32%
Licenciatura	21%	41%

Source: Ministry of Science Technology, and Higher Education, 2006.

Mobility of professors in HE is very low, and mostly based on internal promotions. According to the law, the faculty is evaluated based on various capabilities: teaching, research, publications, service to the community and management of academy. Leading universities have additional requirements for faculty career development. For example, in some cases, Scientific Committees have approved internal guidelines requiring minimum levels of publication in international journals, students' assessments and so on.

It is possible to have a definitive contract at all levels of professorship depending on the curriculum vitae; however, this commonly occurs only at the Full Professor level or at the Associate Professor level after the aggregation assessment.

The career of faculty in the Polytechnics follows a similar path, although with fewer requirements: An Assistant (needs a *Licenciatura*); An Adjunct Professor (Master's degree of or DESE Diploma of Specialized Studies); A Coordinator Professor (Doctorate degree is not required and a minimum of 3-years' service as Aggregate Professor).

Professors and Associate Professors represent 23 percent of the total faculty in the university, and Coordinator Professors and Adjunct Professors represent 29 percent of the Polytechnic's faculty.

Public Universities show academic staff to have higher degrees than the private sector.

Smaller and regional universities do not present detailed information per school; therefore, we do not have complete information on economics and management faculties. However, our estimation is that 70 percent of the faculty of management and economics have full-time contracts, and teachers with the category of Full Professor are 4 percent of the total, and Associate Professors 12 percent.

The gross annual salaries of university professors with exclusive contracts are as in Table 14.5. In Portugal, salaries are paid (for all professions) in 14 fractions – one per month plus extra payments in the month of holiday and at Christmas). As can be observed in Table 14.5, the salary

Table 14.5   Gross annual salaries of University Professors in 2006

No. of years	Full Professor	Associate Professor		Assistant Professor	
		After Aggregation	Before Aggregation	After Aggregation	Before Aggregation
Year 1	61.245 €	52.649 €	47.277 €	47.277 €	41.904 €
Year 4	64.468 €	54.798 €	49.426 €	49.426 €	45.128 €
Year 7	66.617 €	56.947 €	53.724 €	53.724 €	49.426 €
Year 10	70.915 €	61.245 €	55.873 €	55.873 €	52.649 €

in each category is affected by the seniority in the category. Professors wishing to do independent consulting or executive training may sign non-exclusive contract with a reduction of one third of salary.

The personal tax rate in the country varies from 10.5 percent to 42 percent, depending on the salaries, marital status, number of children and deductible expenses such as health, housing, education, etc. A Full Professor with two children, for example, has approximately 27 percent deducted.

The leading schools also pay bonuses for published research, according to the category of the journal. An example could be 6,500€ for Alpha journals, 3,000€ for Beta and 2,500€ for Gamma. If this is the case, schools have to find money from private budgets; the leading schools have created Foundations or Institutes to research in cooperation with large companies in order to be able to give incentives to their faculty members. The bonus paid for each article published is limited by the amount of the budget available for the year, and a sum is paid pro-rata if the budget is insufficient for all research produced. Some of the leading schools prefer to reduce the teaching load of those who publish their research internationally, which is an additional incentive for doing and publishing the research.

Applied research for the industry usually pays a fee to the professor, depending on his involvement in each project. These projects are paid at commercial rates, and consequently they are financially more attractive than research for publication in academic journals.

Executive training and post-graduate programs are paid per hour in the range of 125€ to 250€, depending on the school, the level of the faculty and the type of program offered. As a result, a three-day executive course offers approximately one month's salary. It is obvious that the financial incentive to research is very small in comparison to executive training or consultancy to industry or government.

The required teaching loads are a minimum of 9 hours per week (and a maximum of 12). Considering that each semester has 13 weeks, a total

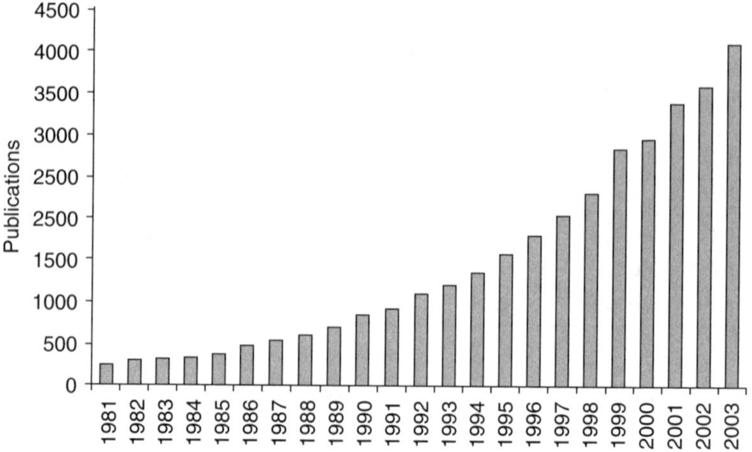

Figure 14.3   Evolution of the number of scientific publications by Portuguese institutions in ISI, 1980–2003.

Source: Ministry of Science, Technology, and Higher Education, 2006.

of 234 hours of teaching per year is required. It is common to count hours differently according to the degree. For example, in master's and doctorate degrees each hour accounts for 1.5 hours. In addition, it is common to see a policy of teaching-load reduction for faculty members with management positions in the school.

In spite of the impressive evolution of research in Portugal (Figure 14.3), the segment of management research is still in its infancy.

There is a lack of institutional organization of management research activities, and most of the management research is based on the initiative of individuals and their relationship with other individuals, frequently from the university where they studied abroad. The larger management schools already have their management research centers, which are usually financed by public funds from FCT – Foundation for Science and Technology. Some schools also have centers dedicated to applied research and community service which develop projects for a fee, for enterprises, industry associations or the Government.

FCT ranks the research centers using international expert panels. The rank has a five-degree scale from poor to excellent and the panel makes recommendations for strategic orientation, future investments, and activity plans of the center. Financing is discontinued to centers classified as poor. The others are financed under a multi-year program, and volumes of funds depend partially on the center's evaluation. Technical

University, Aveiro, Nova de Lisboa, Coimbra and Porto show the higher percentage of researchers classified as Excellent and Very Good.

Costs and finance of higher education

Costs of higher education

The author is not aware of any recent study concerning the costs and finance of HE in management in Portugal. The cost of HE can be addressed from three perspectives: the Student, the Government and the School.

From a student's perspective, costs include instruction and living expenses. For the *Licenciatura* the expenses of a student were estimated between 5,400€ to 9,500€ per year (Table 14.6).

Because fees are insufficient to cover the total costs of public universities, for the public system it is necessary to add the amount of public funds. The Budget of the Central Government to HE in 2006 was 1,222.4 million euros of which 154.7 million is for social support to students that may be used to pay housing, food, and scholarships. As a result, the public funds per student are approximately 3,813€ and the total cost of a student per year in the public system is estimated to be 9,200 €.

Table 14.6 Estimated annual costs for the family of an undergraduate student in 2005–2006

Items		Private	Public
Instruction Expenses	Up front fee	317 €	0 €
	Tuition fee	3.702 €	902 €
	Book and other educational expenses	799 €	619 €
	Subtotal	**4.818 €**	**1.521 €**
Living Expenses	Lodging	328 €	598 €
	Food	1.967 €	1.491 €
	Transportation	598 €	508 €
	Other personal expenses	1.809 €	1.269 €
	Subtotal	**4.702 €**	**3.866 €**
	Total	**9.520 €**	**5.387 €**

Source: Based on Cabrito (2002), and adjusted for inflation rates.

About 24 percent of students receive some direct public support. Loans for students with special benefits are also available. However, students from lower income brackets are averse to debt. Sixty eight percent of students that have benefited from these types of loans are from high or medium-high income brackets.

Tuition fees

The law determines the range of tuition fees for *licenciaturas* (undergraduate students), and for all other degrees, schools have freedom to set the fees: therefore they are at the market price.

The tuition fee for undergraduate studies established in 1941, was equivalent to 6.00€ and was kept constant until 1974. From then it rose very slowly until 1992 when the Government decided to increase it to 400€. The objection by students was strong and they organized demonstrations and strikes, resulting in confrontation with Police Forces. The tuition fee was back to 6.00 € with the socialist Government in 1996. In 2003, the Government decentralized the power to set the tuition fee to the universities in a range of 1.3 times the minimum salary (464 €) and the capitalization of the 6.00€ from 1941 to current prices. Tuition fees for 2005-2006 were in the range of 487€ to 902€ (Figure 14.4).

Universities with higher demand (Aveiro, Coimbra, Minho, ISEG Technical University, Porto and ISCTE) set their tuition fees at maximum level (900€ to 902€).

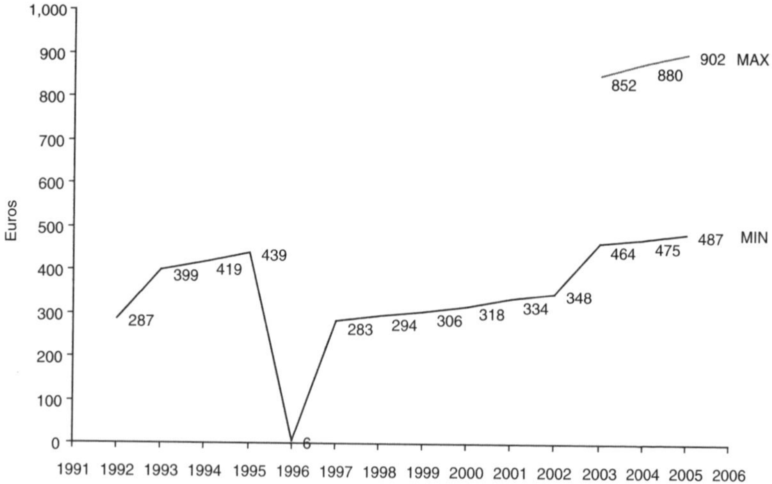

Figure 14.4   Evolution of Tuition Fees (€)

The regulatory bodies

The Ministry of Science, Technology, and Higher Education (MCTES) is the entity responsible for the policies concerning HE, innovation, and research.

The reform of Portuguese HE that took place in 1973 (Veiga Simão Reform) was largely influenced by the economic version of human capital theories and reports from OECD. The democratic revolution of 1974 changed the initial objectives because of the dispute with the capitalist ideology. By 1986, the binary system was consolidated and legitimacy to the management of public universities and polytechnics was supported by the principle of election of collegial bodies:

- The Scientific Committee that is concerned with the development of research, the quality of programs, and quality and development of faculty members;
- The Executive Committee whose role is the management of the institution;
- The Pedagogical Committee that is concerned with the quality of teaching and the overview of the students' rights.

The trend to give more autonomy to HE institutions started in 1994 with the financial management based on the accountability principle where financing should be based and conditioned to the evaluation of universities. In 1998, the autonomy of universities was reinforced, and the same happened to polytechnics in 1990. As a result, Public Universities and Polytechnics are autonomous and free to manage their academic, administrative, and financial affairs. There is, however, limited scope to decide on the size and structure of teaching staff at higher levels (Full Professors and Associate Professors) and the salaries that are exclusively decided centrally by the MCTES.

Pressures on HE institutions to be more connected with the industry, and criticism by entrepreneurial leaders in the 1980s and 1990s of the collegial forms of institutional governance and management have pushed for laws linking teaching and research to the economy and the evaluation of HEIs. In 1988, the Law 91/88 insisted on the need of transferring knowledge and technology to the industry. Public Universities and the Università Cattolica del Sacro Cuore through the Council of Rectors of Public Universities (CRUP) launched a public debate and initiated an auto-evaluation process. This pilot-evaluation was welcomed by the Government and the process of internal and external evaluation of HEIs was introduced in the law by 1994 (Law 38/94). The members of CRUP founded the Foundation of Public

Universities (FUP). The FUP was recognized by the MCTES as the entity that should develop the external process of evaluation of universities.

However, because of the need to enlarge the evaluation to other segments of HE, the CNAVES (National Higher Education Evaluation Council) was established in 1998 as an independent body responsible for external assessment of all HEIs. Evaluation Panels did evaluations of *licenciaturas* but there is not yet a general system of degree accreditation. The CNAVES is a member of the European Association for Quality Assurance Education (ENQA). There are still no direct links between the results of the evaluation and the financing of schools.

Professional chartered institutions (such as engineering, medicine, architecture, pharmacy, economics/management, law, etc.) run their own accreditation systems, starting in 1994 by the Engineers' Chartered Institute (*Ordem dos Engenheiros*). These accreditations follow essentially the guidelines of the ABET (ABET.org), examining specific programs at undergraduate level and concentrating mainly on the assessment of course curricula, education means and evaluation methods.

The criteria to evaluate the quality of programs and HEIs, based on the need of students' mobility, were published in 2003. There was also created the Consultative Council for Higher Education, which is responsible for giving views to the Minister in terms of the needs of HE per field of study, and the articulation between universities and polytechnics and private and public education, as well as the relations between the science policy and the industry.

More recently, the Government signed an agreement with ENQA and OECD to evaluate 10 HEIs. The objective is to evaluate the performance of these HEIs using international criteria and require the ENQA to give a proposal for a system of accreditation and evaluation of quality. This is expected have an outcome by December 2006.

As previously mentioned, management schools of higher quality are submitting themselves to international accreditation, and national accreditation has no impact on them.

The future of management schools and all HEI will be dictated by the new law approved on 10 September 2007 (Law 62/2007) that opens the options to transform HEI into foundations.

Concluding remarks

The relationship between teaching and research is still an on-going discussion in most schools of economics and management, and clearly the three main conceptual axes described by Santiago and Carvalho (2004) are under discussion:

- Research as a support to teaching – research is represented as a process that should be oriented towards teaching/learning, and makes no sense if it is absent from the process of learning;
- Research as the main conceptual activity vis-à-vis teaching – as a consequence research is seen as the privilege mission of HE, and the argument is that this is the function that distinguishes top universities from others;
- Partial or total separation between the two – in these discussions some argue that some basic units should assume a central role in teaching although supported by applied research, and others that institutions should be more oriented towards research activities.

Some entrepreneurs have also commented on the need for, or economic relevance of, HE. The arguments follow three fold: (1) HEIs should develop more services to society – providing consultancy and useful studies to governments, industries and other sectors of the society; (2) develop training programs towards the immediate needs of industries; (3) research should be oriented to the immediate knowledge and technology-transfer, improving the technology level and competitiveness of the economy. All these three axes are important means of getting additional funds when the expectations are for a reduction of public funding to HEI, and the number of students is declining. This approach is, however, unlikely to happen unless MCTES changes the collegial mode of governance, and substantially reduces the public funds attributed to HEIs, or there is a government decision to restructure polytechnics and universities, possibly including mergers and liquidations. These issues evidence the need for restructuring the governance of HEI.

In fact, the difference between the roles of the university and polytechnic are not clear, and they are becoming similar with the implementation of the Bologna Accord. The biggest difference is that universities may offer doctorate degree. The question is if the Bimodal system is dying, or is it viable, and on which terms?

The World Bank in the 1970s was critical of the erratic policies toward the existing polytechnics, and raised the issue of diseconomies of scale in the system, suggesting there were too many small institutions. In our view, this criticism is still valid. The larger schools of management have programs that need restructuring, and eventually merging with other schools would be beneficial for the country and the State Budget.

Instead of a decision on this matter, the government put a law in September 2007 that gives the option to the schools to transform into a new Juridical Status.

Besides the previous issues, globalization and new technologies are two other issues that in our view deserve discussion in the Portuguese Society.

In a global economy Portugal is one of the European countries that has no management school ranking internationally. There is no management school in Portugal aiming at the international market. CIFAG, an excellent executive training center, had such a project however it was liquidated by the Government in 1992, but it is better late than never. There are good management schools in Lisbon (Catholic, Nova, ISEG Technical University, and ISCTE) and in the North (Porto, Minho and Aveiro) that have the required capabilities, but probably what is lacking is vision and cooperation between universities and political power to make things happen The present collegial systems of governance of schools do not help.

The development of new technologies on the other side is almost ignored by management schools. The most well known program using distance learning and blended courses is Dislogo from the Università Cattolica del Sacro Cuore, addressed to executives. All management schools follow the traditional teaching in the class. Aberta University that was created to offer distance learning programs does not offer the quality required. It needs a profound restructuring on its courses and methodologies in order to become more accessible to students and facilitate the process of learning.

References

Bessa, D. (1998), "Profile of Scientific Research in Portugal: Economics and Management," Observatory of Science and Technology.

Cabrito, B. (2004), "O financiamento do Ensino Superior em Portugal: Entre o Estado e o Mercado," *Educ. Soc.* , Campinas, vol. 25, n. 8, 977–996, Especial October.

Cabrito, B. (2002), "O financiamento do Ensino Superior: Condição social e despesas dos estudantes universitários em Portugal," *Educa*, 180–181.

Cabrito, B. (2001), "Higher education and equity in Portugal," *Tertiary Education and Management*, 7 (1), 23–29.

Dima, A. (2005). "Higher Education in Portugal," Country Report, CHEPS Higher Education Monitor, Centre for Higher Education Policy Studies, February, 2005.

Eurydice (2006), "National summary sheets on education systems in Europe and ongoing reforms, European Commission," Directorate-General for Education and Culture.

MCTES (2006), "Tertiary Education in Portugal: Background report prepared to support the international assessment of the Portuguese system of tertiary education." Working paper 1.1, April 2006.

OECD (2005), Education at a Glance 2005.

OCES – Observatory of Higher Education System (2004a), Ensino Superior Público: Pessoal docente e rácio aluno/docente eti em 31-12-2004, Direcção de Serviços de Estatística e de Indicadores do Observatório da Ciência e do Ensino Superior, 6 December, 2005.

OCES – Observatory of Higher Education System (2004b), O Sistema do Ensino Superior em Portugal: 1993–2003, September 2004.

Orçamento Geral do Estado, 2006 – Annual Budget 2006.

Rodrigues, L., Craig, R. (2004). "English mercantilist influences on the foundation of the Portuguese School of Commerce in 1759," *Atlantic Economic Journal*, December.

Santiago, R. and Carvalho, T. (2004), "Effects of managerialism on the perceptions of higher education in Portugal," *Higher Education Policy*, 17, 427–444.

15

Business Education in Central and Eastern Europe

Jean-Paul Larçon and Nassef Hmimda

Context

During the communist era in Central and Eastern Europe, although theories of capitalist economics were relatively freely discussed in some of the countries' research institutes, the study of capitalist business methodologies was by definition excluded from the university curricula. The main effort was directed to the study of planned economy in economic departments, and operational management (Fayol and Taylor mode of organization) in some engineering institutions. What may have appeared as business studies at that time was in fact business studies in a non-competitive environment. The common legacy of communist rule across the region has left business educators with a shared set of problems, limiting their ability to adapt or play a role in the adoption of market-oriented principles. These problems include:

- a dogmatic tradition of higher education driven by political theory;
- a pronounced separation of business academics from business itself.

The transition to market economy

The transition to market economy at the beginning of the 1990s brought back the business studies into the university curricula. Szkoła Główna Handlowa (*Warsaw School of Economics*) in Warsaw, Poland, illustrates this pattern.

The rebirth of business studies in Central and Eastern Europe was mainly market driven. The job market was dramatically calling for well-trained managers after the fall of the Berlin Wall. Today the impact of business education on salaries may not be really important. Yet,

SGH – Szkoła Główna Handlowa (*Warsaw School of Economics*) in Warsaw, Poland – is the oldest economic university in Poland. It started its activities on 13th October 1906. After several designations (*August Zieliński Private Trade Courses for Men* from 1906 to 1915; *High School of Economics* from 1915 to 1933) it took the name of *Szkoła Główna Handlowa (SGH) in March 1933*. Following the political and socio-economic changes in the country after the Second World War, the school was nationalized and renamed *Szkoła Główna Planowania i Statystyki (SGPiS – Central School for Planning and Statistics)*. The teaching programs were adapted to the steering economy needs; they were also filled with elements of Marxist economics. In 1991, the school former name – *Szkoła Główna Handlowa* – was restored.

business graduates tend to find a job much more easily than graduates in economics, public administration or political science. Moreover, this shortage of business capabilities tends to ensure a better career for those with a business training.

The educational structure

In the 1990s, the educational structure is diverse across the region. So diverse, in fact, that some segmentation into strategic groups soon started to appear as a way to sort out the diversity.

The Latvian Ministry of Education has prepared a paper dividing its thirty one higher educational institutions into three very unofficial groups. In the first place come the traditional well-established institutions (Universities, Academies, Higher Educational Institutions, Higher Schools and Institutes). In a second group are a collection of recently established state-founded and state-financed institutions, which, although perhaps not yet having a proper statute or official accreditation, are still "unofficially recognised" by the State. In a third group are private institutions that have a license to begin higher educational activities, under the terms of the 1991 Education Act. Most of these were only granted licences in 1993 and in most cases their diplomas are still not accredited, and the State cannot assume responsibility for the quality of their education. Outside this, there is a smaller, but unspecified, number of private institutions, that have no license but which continue to operate outside the legislative framework.

In the business education field, virtually all the business academic programs have been either founded independently or spun off from existing economics, engineering, transportation, communications or agricultural programs since 1989–1990. In Poland, the Politechnika Warszawska (Warsaw University of Technology), created its own business school (following the model of MIT in the US and Imperial College in London).

On the one hand traditional institutions, mainly economics departments, started teaching business. On the other hand, new business schools, either private or public, were founded. In Poland there are now 140 non-state/ private institutions of higher education with over 250,000 students. Many of these are Business Schools, specialising in such areas as business administration, banking and management, which usually grant a professionally oriented bachelor-level degree.

The majority of the actual business curriculum is in fact a balanced combination of education in economy and management. With a few visible exceptions, however, formerly established so-called business schools inherited from the communist regimes have not responded much to the major change which took place in their environment, and continue to teach the same subjects in the same ways as they did before the demise of communism. In some ways this is not surprising, because most of these so-called "business schools" are actually economics schools, staffed with political economists for whom business subjects as taught in the West are unfamiliar. This soviet legacy is one of the prominent problems that face the business education in Central Europe: there is a strong and pressing need for well trained faculty in management and business sciences.

Foreign assistance for business studies in Central and Eastern Europe

There has been a virtual explosion of management education programs in Central and Eastern Europe since the transition, beginning in 1989, from the communist to a more capitalist economy and the collapse of the Soviet Union in 1991. This trend produced the opening of several business schools with an unequal quality, mainly financed by the European Union or local governments' subsidies. Once the subsidies ended, the sector suffered from a shake-out, and only well-managed business schools, with adequate faculty, remained.

Foreign assistance has become increasingly important in financing the administrative reorganisation needed to remove one of the major bottlenecks slowing down the momentum of the whole reform process. The role of the European Union's TEMPUS programme in this sphere has been very important. Set up in 1990, as part of the comprehensive PHARE programme, it covers everything from staff and student mobility, through curriculum and teaching material development to the purchase of essential equipment.

In the Czech Republic, the VSB-Technical University in Ostrava and the Silesian University in Opava have received TEMPUS support to create a master in "European Business and Management." Mendel Agriculture and Forestry University in Brno, the Technical University in Brno and the University of Pardubice used TEMPUS support to set up two-year postgraduate degrees in "European Studies in Business-Economics and Management" at all three universities.

Charles University and the University of Economics in Prague have received TEMPUS financing to look at the possibilities for developing an MBA programme at Charles University, Faculty of Social Sciences.

In some cases, American business schools have played a key role in disseminating modern management practices. In 1989, the US Congress passed a legislation known as the Support for Eastern European Democracy (SEED) Act. A year later USAID began providing grants to US universities to promote linkages with institutions in Central and Eastern Europe in order to develop their capability to provide management training and education. Hence, under the SEED Act, the USAID ran the Management Training and Economic Education Project (MTEEP). By 1997, there were 12 university-to-university linkage projects under the MTEEP in nine countries in Central and Eastern Europe. They prepared a broad mix of programs: Ph.D, MBA degree, certificate programs, short term seminars and workshops.

The Faculty of Economics at Tirana University already offers a master's level postgraduate program on Management and Administration, supported by the University of Nebraska, USA. This is a two-year program and the first group of students graduated in April 1998. All of the seven lecturers and the teaching material came from America, but it is planned to replace the lecturers with specially trained Albanians in the years to come.

A similar strategy has been followed by the Faculty of Business at Bulgaria's University for National and World Economy. In late 1992, it introduced a bachelor level degree in European Business Administration as a joint program with the University of Humberside in the United Kingdom.

Legislation

All the Central and Eastern European countries have by now passed Laws guaranteeing academic freedom, granting autonomy to their universities and defining the role that the government will play within the system. In Poland, where all of the country's post-communist governments have stressed the importance of education and training for the country's general strategy of integrating into western structures, a comprehensive higher education law was among the first enacted by the newly elected Polish Parliament in September 1990. Since then, the universities have been seen as independent, self-governing units, dependent on the state only where money is concerned and cooperating with the Ministry of National Education, through the General Council of Higher Education, the elected representative body of all higher schools, with wide constitutional and advisory rights.

In most countries too, the Ministry of Education has set up autonomous Evaluation and Accreditation Committees and Institutes for Educational Policy and Research. Several countries, having rapidly freed the university system from state control, have passed follow-up laws to both fine-tune the new system, to bring it more into line with developing

In Bulgaria, where academic autonomy had been granted in 1990, a more comprehensive law was passed in December 1995, which recognised and drew up regulations for non-state/private colleges and universities. These reforms allow the emergence of private, fee-paying universities and colleges of higher education in the region.

In Poland, the basis for the emergence of such a sector had already been laid by the September 1990 Higher Education Act, but this step was delayed in the Czech Republic until the autumn of 1998. By then, the Hungarian government's 1997 White Paper on Higher Education had already gone beyond just making a non-state tertiary education sector possible, and now assigned it an important role in the national strategy to expand student enrolments and to react more quickly to changing demands for courses.

EU norms, and to officially recognise developments that have run ahead of legislation.

In response, with the exception of the Czech Republic, there has been a quick growth of the private sector across the region. It is in this sector that some of the most innovative changes have been made in national educational systems since 1989.

Shrinking budgets have meant that State-financed institutions have found it exceptionally difficult to respond in an adequate way to the increasing demand for programs in management and business. It is here that the private sector has been able to play a role. The fact that these sectors offer higher-than-average starting salaries has encouraged students to enrol, despite lingering public attitudes of suspicion towards "buying" education.

Research in the business education sector

As part of the "sovietization" of the higher educational sector in the early 1950s, universities in Central and Eastern Europe became predominantly teaching institutions, with research being concentrated in autonomous institutes operating under the Academy of Sciences.

With this legacy, present business department and business schools have neither the adequate experience nor a sufficient budget for research. They have to reinvent a balanced research and teaching policy. They need to allocate time for research to professors who actually bear a significant level of teaching (an average of 200 hours/academic year), and career evaluation based on scientific publications. Research is not yet a predominant evaluation criterion for business schools and departments in the region. Most of the evaluation is made locally within the local boundaries, and operated mainly by business magazines, which primarily focus on salaries and careers of graduates.

Future trends

There seems to be now a period of consolidation with the emergence of major business schools in Central and Eastern Europe. In Budapest, the Karl Marx University changed its name in 1991 to Budapest University of Economic Sciences. In 2000, it became Budapest University of Economic Sciences and Public Administration (BUESPA, with the integration of the latter college); and finally, with the University of Horticulture joining in 2003, it became "Corvinus" after the king Matthias Corvinus of Hungary. In Czech Republic, VSE (Vysoká škola ekonomická) after the "Velvet Revolution" experienced a general reorganization and became a Business School following the HEC or ESADE model.

Major schools now aim at meeting the international standards in business education. This is widely observed through the rising demand for accreditation, and particularly for European standard EQUIS. The 3 major business schools in Central Europe (SGH, VSE, Corvinus) joined the CEMS (Community of European Management Schools and International Companies). But even here, as for most of the state university Business departments, the overall focus is upon broad business related programs that meet the market demand. The programs are mainly covering such areas as human resources, strategic management, accounting, finance, business communication, marketing and advertising.

In this consolidation period for business education, two main business school models are now emerging:

The research-based business schools, which rely on a faculty of researchers in business sciences, and which are mainly the historical institutions in the region;
The entrepreneurship-based business schools, which rely heavily on a faculty of professionals and practitioners.

In Russia, where the government wants to create world-class Russian business schools, two business schools were inaugurated in 2006, one research-based in St Petersburg and the other more entrepreneurship-based in Moscow.

Since 1990, there has been a region-wide move towards establishing a "short" degree in Business. Thus, instead of the first degree being awarded after five years of study at Master's level or the local *Magister*, the trend now is to break this down into a three- to four-year Bachelor's degree, and a one to two year Master's degree, followed by a two- to three-year Ph.D, thus somehow following the 3-5-8 model which the EU adopted. The intention is to produce less specialized graduates who can get a job after their bachelor's and hopefully prove more adaptable to changing labour market conditions than their "long cycle" predecessors.

All together, and despite the significant inertia attached to the legacy of the former communist regimes, the situation for higher education in Business in Central and Eastern Europe is changing. Strong entrepreneurial drives tend to create, develop and maintain western type business schools, either from adapting existing economics departments or growing them as private entities. There is still a long way to go, but the process is ongoing as the 3 major business schools in Central Europe (SGH in Warsaw, VSE in Prague, Corvinus in Budapest) lead the way.

16
The Business of Business Education in the United States

JC Spender

Introduction

In 2006, after some post 9/11 wobbles, the US BSchools are rolling and growing again.

The recent GMAC (Graduate Management Admission Council www.gmac.com) Corporate Recruiters Survey shows the Business Schools business recovering from the setbacks of 2004 and 2005 (GMAC, 2006b), though applications are still not at their 2003 level. Irrespective, the graduating students' prospects are improving rapidly. Average starting salaries for new MBAs have risen from around $64,000 p.a. in 2004 to around $92,000 p.a. in 2006. Of the new hires entering the larger US companies, around 40 percent held MBAs, and almost all of these companies offered these recruits substantial removal expenses and hiring bonuses (GMAC, 2006a).

As we write, most US employers consider the economy to be good, or at least sufficiently promising to support a further increase in MBA hiring. In spite of a slew of jeremiads, declaring the MBA process intellectually bankrupt, they are evidently happy with the BSchools' products (Fernandes, 2004, 2005). For their part the MBAs are overwhelmingly satisfied with their decision to pursue the degree, concluding it offers a substantial ROI as well as opening up new career opportunities (GMAC, 2006c).

The production of management education

There are thought to be around 7,600 academic business management programs world-wide. This number excludes, of course, the many

---

Please note that a specific chapter dedicated to the Business Schools in the US was used as the baseline just after the book introduction. The information provided below is essentially to complement the main points already presented in the "baseline."

professional management training and improvement programs delivered within organizations both public and private, and by the huge number of management training consultants and consulting firms. While the principal part of the business lies in the MBA programs, some of the strongest growth is occurring in "executive education." This is sometimes distinguished from the full-time and part-time MBA programs as higher-priced intensive non-degree work geared specifically to the higher executive. But the label is also used to designate part-time MBA programs designed for the student who works full-time in an executive role. According to IPEDS, the educational database maintained by NCES (National Center for Education Statistics – http://nces.ed.gov/ipeds), there are some 1,650 business programs based in the US offering PhD, MBA, Batchelor, and Associates degrees in various aspects of the business discipline.

The MBA is the core of the Nation's business school activity and 895 US schools graduated 10 or more MBAs. Some 445 of these had programs accredited by the AACSB (now known as the Association to Advance Collegiate Schools of Business – www.aacsb.edu). Accreditation is somewhat complicated by the US's federalized educational structure, each state controlling the granting of university and college degrees and so its own educational accreditation system. In practice the states have collaborated, creating the eight so-called "regionals" which accredit the educational institutions in each "region" (e.g. www.msache.org). AACSB accreditation is professional, of the MBA program offered, while the "regionals" accredit the school's host university. The AACSB also accredits accounting programs.

There are competing business program accreditation organizations such as the ACBSP (Association of Collegiate Business Schools and Programs – www.acbsp.org), focused on the undergraduate schools, and the IACBE (International Assembly for Collegiate Business Education – www.iacbe.org), which looks to the less prestigious schools world-wide. Both these organizations have growing membership. Given the vitality, profitability, and global appeal of business education and its credentials, and the absence of central US government or international control, there is a bubbling population of not-entirely reliable for-profit schools, sometimes dubbed "diploma mills," which provide an MBA credential whilst not being accredited as viable educational institutions.

The business school faculty are reasonably well paid, or at least those in the AACSB accredited schools are. A survey of almost 25,000 faculty in 485 such schools showed the average 2006 full-time salary rose four percent from 2005 to $96,000 (AACSB, 2006). These are "nine-month" salaries, suggesting faculty should be unburdened by teaching and administrative duties during the summer months, and so be free to research and write, preparing to deliver greater value as the academic year starts in the Fall. A US business school faculty member typically teaches during only two 13-week semesters per year. Their two 1½ hour class-per-week course loads may vary from two per year to four per semester, according to the quality and wealth of the school, and, perhaps, their Dean's discretion. Even so there are often informal arrangements which allow faculty to work a "four-day" week, leaving them free to do private consulting, for instance, one day per week during their teaching semesters.

Younger faculty may be supported with "two ninths" additional salary, to motivate them even more to do the work which yields the A-journal publications they need to gain tenure. These publications also score well in the AACSB's accreditation process and may do something to increase the school's visibility in the business and popular press. Finance professors are paid around $20,000 p.a. more than those of other disciplines while, curiously, the economists are paid less. The steady rise in professorial salaries over the last 20 years has created some odd situations, anomalies perhaps, in which new recruits may come in at salaries well above those of the majority of their elder, more experienced, and more published colleagues.

Most upper-tier schools – the "Doctoral/Research universities" – often run a four- or six-year "tenure clock" against which the new faculty must perform if they are to get tenure. They get a mid "clock" review which enables their colleagues to re-appraise them and, perhaps, encourage some career course correction. The review process, both mid-clock and final, may be done by an un-named group of faculty, and involves a detailed examination of the aspirant's research and publications. In most schools these publications are scored with a weighting system reflecting the perceived quality or reputation of the journal. The most prestigious journals, those on the A-list, vary according to the discipline. These lists are fairly stable, though new journals occasionally claw their way in after around ten years of hard editorial work and publisher support. New journals generally start because the established journals are unwilling to publish papers about new lines of research. Legitimating this new line often entails not only creating a wide community of scholars doing significant and compelling research, but also establishing a "home" journal. While many schools espouse the importance of teaching and service to the academic and institutional community, history indicates that well-received teaching and substantial community seldom count for much during the tenure review. Many schools allow the candidate to seek "outside letters of support" from professors at other schools who may well be more familiar with the candidate's research and publication than her/his colleagues can ever hope to be.

The consumption of management education

The 895 US schools recognized by the NCES graduated around 139,000 Master's students in the 2003–4 academic year. MBAs make up almost all this number, though some programs offer an MSc or various JD/ Masters combinations. Many of these US schools also offer undergraduate degrees, but an additional 800 or so NCES recognized schools offer only undergraduate (four-year) and associate level (two-year) degrees. In total, some 1,650 recognized US schools graduated over 300,000 Business Bachelor and over 90,000 Business Associate students. These 2003–4 numbers were usefully up from 127,000 Masters, 292,000 Bachelors, and 89,000 Associates in 2002–3.

Many US schools require applicants to provide GMAT (General Management Admission Test) scores. The GMAT is an effective monopoly and is administered around the world and on-line by GMAC. It follows that the volume of GMAT tests being taken is a useful measure of the health of the business education industry. Over 202,000 tests were taken in the year concluding October 2006, up about 1.9 percent on the 2005 figure. The breakdown is interesting, for there is a steady shift away from the US, with non-US tests rising 3.7 percent, and so faster than the number of US tests which rose only 0.9 percent. This statistic may not be entirely indicative of the numbers of prospective students, for approximately 21 percent of the GMAT tests are taken by applicants who have taken the test before. GMAC allows a person to take the GMAT up to 5 times within a given 12-month period, charging them $250 per test.

In a Podcast available on the GMAC website (www.gmac.com) David Wilson, GMAC's President and CEO reported 2006 BSchool recruitment was rising, more female and minority students were applying, and there was a substantial trend towards foreign students coming into the US, after some post 9/11 difficulties and, perhaps more interestingly, towards US students enrolling in non-US schools (up 62 percent in 2006). He argued that the MBA has global currency and is no longer a qualification of influence only in the US and among US firms. It is now considered the professional qualification for managers everywhere. Likewise John Fernandes, AACSB President and CEO, argued the MBA remains the world's popular, flexible, and successful degree (Fernandes, 2005).

Tuitions, donations, and endowments

The rising costs of business school education have long been a concern to business school administrators and parents. In many universities the costs of business education are not much different from those of other non-business programs. Science programs tend to be more expensive. In 2006 in the US average tuition and fees for undergraduate education is around $22,000 per annum for four-year private schools, $5,800 for public schools, and $2,200 for two-year public schools. The latter, being differently constituted and chartered, and typically supported by local as opposed to state taxes, are able to attract a substantial number of students who after getting their Associate degree, then go on to the four-year state school to complete their Bachelor degree. Business schools are also often able to set their own tuitions. Again these vary widely. Notre Dame's tuition charges are $17,160 per semester for their four-semester on-campus MBA program, while Stanford charges $43,380 in tuition alone with a suggested budget of around $70,000 per semester (www.stanford.edu/mba/financialaid/budget.html). Most of the upper-tier schools' students graduate with hefty, even six-figure, loans they have to spend several years repaying.

Many business schools are supported and extended by substantial gifts and giving programs. Much of this giving goes to help the needier students. In 2006 Philip Knight, Nike's founder, gave Stanford's Business School a record $105 million. Dozens of other schools receive lesser gifts, often in exchange for naming the school after the donor (http://aacsb.edu/members/communities/interestgrps/donors.asp). The AACSB reported that in 2003 some 14 percent of the top 387 US BSchools' operating funds came from gifts and endowment income. On average, each employs two full-time fundraising staff. For example, it costs $1.5 million to endow a chair, $500,000 a professorship, and $25,000 to fund a scholarship.

The rankings

The wide variation of tuitions underscores that not all MBAs are equal. While Wilson and Fernandes trumpet the universality of the MBA label there are clearly tremendous variations in the value of the credential and the educational experience to the students who do the paying. The experience of a purely on-line MBA, such as one might obtain from, say, the University of Phoenix's mega-program, or from Capella University, differs from that of spending two years at, say, NYU's Stern School, Emory's Goizueta School, or the Illinois Institute of Technology. The rankings provided by Business Week (http://www.businessweek.com/

bschools/06/full_time.htm) and US News & World Report (http://www. usnews.com/usnews/edu/grad/rankings/mba/brief/mbarank_brief.php) fill this gap, helping prospective students and recruiters make their choices. Unfortunately, program quality is a deeply contested idea, and an enormous and largely fruitless debate has ensued. It is worth noting that 17 of the top 25 programs have been so regarded since the rankings began (Policano, 2005). So there is not much opportunity for change. Indeed there may be something of a self-regenerating or self-organizing system at work, particularly as much of the data provided is carefully shaped and manufactured. The AACSB has attempted, unsuccessfully, to get to grips with these issues, seeking alternative and more authoritative measures, but these rankings and reputations may be not under the control of any of the business education's actors (AACSB, 2005). It was a clear step forward when Business Week and US World & News Report agreed to have the survey data provided by the schools professionally audited.

The business education industry's evident continued growth and vitality, both rising numbers and prices within the US and increased circulation and exchange with the world beyond, raises interesting questions about what, if anything, might lead to strategic change at a time when almost everything else in the economy is changing. The less-costly MBA programs, especially those offered on-line, have served more to increase the market than to attack the higher priced chalk-and-talk programs. This is in spite of the fact that the texts used are largely the same at all levels of the industry. The management text and journal business is very lucrative. The Harvard Business School, along with a handful of other publishers, has also made a highly successful business out of providing their own faculty, and the rest of the world, with carefully crafted case-studies, the apparent hall-mark of the MBA program's unique pedagogy. While the content of MBA programs seems largely commoditized, there are clearly dimensions around the classroom experience, class size, interaction with outstanding teachers, and the socialization processes of time shared on campus, that sustain the business's reputation differentials.

The future

The business education business is perpetually nervous, highly conscious of its critics within the academy and within business. In spite of Wilson's and Fernandes's brave talk, the industry remains awash with doubts. One cause for concern is to do with the pedagogy and technology adopted in both the in-class and on-line MBA programs, for there is no great difference in the material, the method of delivery, or the student's educational experience. This technology is extremely faculty-intensive and, as an AACSB 2002 report noted, the industry's expansion is making the obviously limited supply of teachers a strategic concern (AACSB, 2002). It may have led to the evident substantial inflow of faculty from overseas and a high acceptance of females, both probably highly beneficial effects. The report also tipped its hat towards the ongoing debate about the relevance of the MBA program's content to the work that the graduating students would be asked to do. But given these concerns have been part of the industry for many years, they seem to remain far from urgent (Spender, 2005).

Bibliography

AACSB. (2002). *Management Education At Risk*. St. Louis MO: AACSB International.

AACSB. (2005). *The Business School Rankings Dilemma*. Tampa FL: AACSB.

AACSB. (2006). *2005–2006 Salary Survey*. Tampa FL: AACSB.

Fernandes, J. (2004). "Adapting to Market Place Demands." *CEO Strategy*(October), 24–26.

Fernandes, J. (2005). "The World's Most Popluar Degree – the MBA – Is Alive and Well." *AACSB eNewsline*, 4(6), 1–2.

GMAC. (2006a). *Corporate Recruiters Survey*. McLean VA: GMAC.

GMAC. (2006b). *Corporate Recruiters Survey – General Data Report*. McLean VA: GMAC.

GMAC. (2006c). *MBA Alumni Perspectives Survey – Comprehensive Data Report*. McLean VA: GMAC.

Policano, A. J. (2005). "What Price Rankings?" *BizEd* (September/October), 26–32.

Spender, J.-C. (2005). "Speaking about Management Education: Some History of the Search for Legitimacy and the Ownership and Control of Management Knowledge." *Management Decision incorporating the Journal of Management History*, 43(10), 1282–1292.

17

Business Education in Latin America

Georges Blanc

A specific context

Although there are no homogeneous statistics describing the business education system in Latin America (L.A. in this text), each country developing its own data, there are common characteristics of the system, rooted in a homogeneous economical and social context:

- The economy is emerging : $ 3,000 revenue/capita on average ,versus $ 24,000 in advanced countries; 5 percent annual GDP growth versus 8 percent in South and Southeast Asia; a large informal sector composing 50 percent of the economically active population, and providing around 30 percent of GDP, whereas it represents on average 10 percent in developed economies;
- In spite of progressive market liberalization, the state-owned sector remains important, and it is common, even after privatization, to still have national monopolies and monopsonies; the same scenario of an imperfect market can be found in the financial area, and the stock exchanges are narrow and lack transparency;
- on the other side, small-size businesses (under 100 employees), mostly family-owned (99 percent according to some evaluations !), represents 90 percent of the jobs, instead of 70 percent of the jobs in Europe (where small business is defined under 500 employees); although some big private local companies have developed recently, most significant private firms are subsidiaries of US , European and Japanese multinationals;
- history and culture have developed a specifically "Latin" administrative paradigm, marked by the Spanish and Portuguese Catholic conquerors, far from the Anglo-Saxon culture, especifically when dealing with business institutions and spirit.

The historical perspective shows a good parallelism with the development of business education in Europe. After the first course, launched in 1958 by the Fondation Getulio Vargas of Sao Paulo ("Postgrade in Administration"), one year before the first MBA (Insead) in Europe, different MBA programs appeared chaotically in the 60s and the 70s, mostly with the help of US Business Schools such as Stanford and Harvard, and the creation process extended and accelerated during the 80s and 90s, but without a real rationalization. "The alien nature and structure of the MBA vis-à-vis the Latin American postgraduate educational systems, the lack of regulatory framework and/or external controls and audits, and most importantly, the luring image of the "three magic letters" has tempted many institutions to offer "MBAs' that are nothing but misnomers. For instance in Brazil, one of the largest and fastest growing markets of the region, it is possible to take a so-called MBA that lasts only 5 days or have less than 40 contact hours; in addition some of these courses do not require an adequate academic background, and/or appropriate business experience."(Carlos Ramos; in *Business leadership Review 2005)*

But the consolidation and normalization increased over these last years, both through the growing influence of the rankings (locally and at world level) and from the pressure coming from the accreditation mechanisms: 22 L.A. Business Schools were accredited at the end of 2005, half of them having already more than one accreditation (AASCB, EQUIS, AMBA, SACS).

Most Latin American universities and other high education institutes, except very isolated cases, have focused their efforts more on the teaching of foreign administrative theories than on the adaptation of these to their own reality, or even than creating their own theories:

- Latin American research and development, whatever the field considered, represents less than 2 percent of the world projects, versus 43 percent for the US, remembering that L.A. represents 6 percent of world GNP;
- most curricula, teaching texts and references, cases and knowledge material in general used in the business administration programs, come from North America, with only a minor adaptation in the most advanced institutions; An MBA is perceived more and more as a commodity;
- the perceived value of any local MBA relies heavily on the partnerships with US or European Business Schools, including foreign visiting professors and students going abroad for a period. The best institutions have been able to build a "double MBA titulation" with one or several renowned US or European institutions: Texas-Austin

for instance has this type of agreement with the Fondation Getulio Vargas (Bra), with the Università Cattolica del Sacro Cuore of Chile, with EGADE Monterrey (Mex); and HEC Paris with the same Latin American institutions plus Torcuato Di Tella (Arg).

To substitute the lack of homogeneous statistics at Latin American level, we show at the end of this chapter the widely recognised ranking of MBAs (here in the August 2006 edition), proposed by the review *America Economia*, published in Spanish and in Portuguese. Other data could be found only at country level, and very often concerns exclusively State and Federal universities, whereas there are some good business schools in the private sector.

A pervasive lack of innovation

First of all, there is very little innovation in the structure of the cursus and the teaching methods: most Business Schools try to stay as close as possible to the US MBA standards, with the best ones struggling to deliver a quality at the level of the world's 80th to 100th ranked (*Financial Times*). Traditional Universities maintain a Master's model ("Mestrado") or a post-graduation model, very often deeply character-ized by its original objective of training academics (a tradition in L.A. to supply the scarcity of Doctoral programs in the past) and not ori-ented towards practitioners. In Brazil for instance, some rare MBAs have been recognized as "Mestrado stricto sensu"; but most MBAs are only considered as "Post-graduation lato sensu," which means a low academic credibility.

As far as the teaching content is concerned, there is very little formal deviation from standard MBAs. Nevertheless, it is interesting to observe that, while most MBA programs in the world are criticized for their rela-tive lack of social sciences soft approach, the L.A. culture would tend to value this aspect more, insisting on psycho-sociological background, human relations, leadership, and this appears more clearly in the con-tent of Executive MBAs and in-company programs.

The main difficulty lies with the case method, which is not a natural approach in the Latin culture, being more prone to deliver structured messages through long lectures, where the case ended summarized and pre-digested as a strict illustration of the concepts. Local cases are not only very limited in number – most academics giving a large preference to Harvard cases - but they are rarely oriented towards decision-making; rather they are a bare description of a company, generally as a success story, few L.A. companies agreeing to open a debate on critical issues. Thus students are rarely placed in a decision-making-in-uncertainty type of situation, but they are in general taught the "right way" of managing, or doing business using the "right tool."

But innovation in knowledge is certainly the field where the economic and social developing context creates the most difficulties. Driven by the urgent need of educating their large population, L A universities have not perceived that the principal product of universities in the developed world is research, with education only a sub-product. Even the best institutions (such as EGADE Monterrey in Mexico, INCAE in Costa Rica, the Università Cattolica del Sacro Cuore of Chile, FIA-USP and Fondation Getulio Vargas in Brazil), with 40 to 70 PhDs each in their staffs, are publishing in A-level reviews supports 3 or 4 times less than the universities ranked between 50th and 100th in the US and Europe. Even worse, the small quantity of research produced relies essentially on the personal initiative, the will and the isolated efforts of some professors, very often without the support of any specific grant as is the rule in the US, and in spite of a much heavier burden of teaching hours (from two to four times more) than their First World colleagues.

The situation has been changing positively during the past five to eight years, with the help of associations such as BALAS and CLADEA, organizing conferences and facilitating publications. Good reviews in Spanish or Portuguese, with peers control, appear and develop in Mexico, Argentina, Chile and Brazil, offering a step toward potential publications in world standard-A reviews. But statistics for the 2001–03 period reveal that only 138 texts from professors teaching in L.A. business institutions have been published in reviews surveyed by the Institute for Scientific Information (ISI) . The break down by country of the list of papers "with international quality," according to Abarca & al. in *Bumeran,* a Chilean data bank, is:

Mexico	30%
Chile	27%
Brazil	15%
Argentina	14%
Costa Rica	9%

The move towards accreditation (quoted before) also strongly motivates the academics to engage in consistent research. In the same way, the ranking of *America Economia* in 2003 introduced the creation of knowledge as a fundamental criterion. As a consequence, the number of good publications from L.A. authors has increased sharply over these past three years.

Centers of excellence can now develop (see MBAs ranking in exhibit), mainly in the big cities of L.A., where there are greater intellectual reserves. The risk is that they might grow as islands, more linked to their US and European counterparts than to the local environment. Considering the necessities of the context, it is obvious that most national public education universities, particularly those localized in the poorer areas, should first devote their efforts towards the consolidation in their immediate environment of the basic systems of health, education, agriculture and public services, but also towards industrial and small business development. Some academics from the best L.A. institutions are tackling the challenge of developing A-level type of research based on the local economic and social needs, involving researchers from universities localized in poor areas, and with the intellectual and financial help of recognised US and European Institutions, giving birth to an interesting model (see Exhibit 17.1).

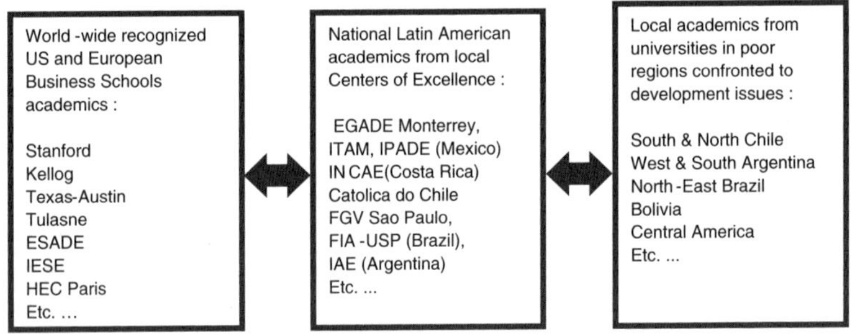

Exhibit 17.1   The Pivotal role of the leading Latin American business schools

Digging more into the local context

There is now a growing faculty entering more and more in L.A. institutions with PhDs obtained in the finest world universities; the challenge is to help them to become acquainted with the local business environment from different perspectives, so as to be able to adapt successfully the foreign models and practices to the local needs, and, as we suggested earlier, to create, whenever possible, new theories based on this local context.

Esteban Brenes, Dean of INCAE (Costa Rica), in *Business Leadership Review*, said:

> ...in my opinion, the local development of knowledge requires a rather different process from the one applied to the adaptation of business models and practices in other parts of the world. The schools should encourage and make sure that their faculty a) devote enough time for consultancy activities and b) are properly engaged in business activities in the region.

Leaving apart consultancy stricto-sensu, which is difficult to control from an education-oriented institution, action-research is a key option for L.A. academics, as it allows them to get in-depth knowledge of the business and managerial issues, generates a narrower link university-industry (reciprocal trust is a key for success), and opens the doors for writing cases and other applied materials. The difficulty is that most PhDs programs in the world, as well as most A-level reviews, leave little space for this specific approach of research, and thus any academic engaging in this way could find more difficulty in receiving the world peers recognition. This is a point that our international academic community should think about seriously, as it also applies to Eastern Europe, Asia, the Middle East and Africa, and even to any organization which is not totally immersed in the Anglo-Saxon model!

Besides the need for spreading business education among the 20 to 30 year-olds, who represent a much bigger proportion of the population than in First World countries, and who put a huge demand pressure on L.A. university systems, there is a strong need to better examine the modern business administration approaches, using a hybrid perspective (local/universal), among executives and decision-makers in general. Executive education should no longer be treated, particularly by L.A. State-controlled universities, as a marginal way to make some money (and finding alternative sources of money is absolutely vital for them!), but as a fully fledged mission, as important as training young people. The needs and the explicit demands are very high. But mainly it gives the opportunity of working much nearer from the field, as it gets to:

1. rethinking completely the MBA model when it comes to Executive MBA,
2. developing an effective system of diagnosis to build in-company programs,
3. focusing specifically on small business needs.

31 of the 40 first institutions ranked by *America Economia* (see exhibit) have developed some sort of executive MBA, but very few of them have clearly departed (except for the timing) from the basic MBA model. The best in the field are those who did not consider developing a basic full-time MBA, but rather focused on in-company programs first, considering their EMBA as one product among others. The case in point is Fondation Dom Cabral (Brazil) which struggles around the 15th rank in the *America Economia* MBA-EMBA classification, but which is the only L.A. institution ranked by the *Financial Times* among the best in world for in-company tailored executives programs, ahead of famous US and European business schools!

As a never ended conclusion

Centers of excellence in business administration are now developing in Latin America, with teaching and researching productions at world level (see Table 17.1); they already play an important role in the development of their countries, through the education of young students and, in many cases, the training of executives. Consultancy, action-research and in-company training programs should allow the new PhDs to dig more into their local context and come out with more suitable knowledge. But they should also look for, as a new mission, a contribution to the development of the other local institutions (mostly public universities), struggling within a poverty internal context and external environment, enhancing their capacity in teaching and researching, and thus leveraging the efforts for economic and social development.

Table 17.1 Business Schools in Latin America : Ranking 2006 (adapted from America Economia)

Ranking 2006	Business school	Country	Faculty				International faculty (US & EU)	International alliances	International accreditation
			Full time equivalent 2006	% MBA/MSC US & EU	% PhD US & EU	% Local PhD	Foreign with PhD from US & EU	Partnerships & joint degrees	
1	INCAE	Costa Rica Nicaragua	43	7.0	88.3		38	FIU, Case Western reserve, ESADE, HHL Leipzig, Thunderbird	AACSB, EQUIS, SACS
2	ITAM (Instituto Tecnológico autónomo de Mexico)	Mexico	84	8.3	84.5	4.8	71	Arizona State, ESADE, FIU	AACSB, AMBA
3	Fundação cetúlio Vargas – EAESP (Sâo Paulo)	Brazil	97	6.2	26.8	56.7	26	Texas-Austin, HEC Paris, U. Nova de Lisboa	AACSB, EQUIS, AMBA
4	Universidad Adolfo Ibañez	Chile	34	14.7	64.7		22	Thunderbird, Case Western reserve, ESADE, FIU	AACSB, AMBA
5	Pontificia Universidad Católica de Chile	Chile	25	44.0	52.0		13	Texas-Austin, HEC Paris	AACSB
6	EGADE (Tec de Monterrey, Campus Monterrey)	Mexico	61	2.0	77.0	20.0	47	Texas-Austin, S. Diego, ESADE, Pepperdine, Calgary, FIU, WHU, ILL. Tech, HEC Paris, Reuitinglen, Rouen, ESSEC, UNC Charlotte	AACSB, EQUIS, SACS
7	Universidad de Chile, Escuela de Postgrado Ec. Y negocios	Chile	36	11.1	83.3		30	Tulane	AMBA, AACSB

Continued

Table 17.1 Continued

Ranking 2006	Business school	Country	Faculty				International faculty (US & EU)	International alliances	International accreditation
			Full time equivalent 2006	% MBA/MSC US & EU	% PhD US & EU	% Local PhD	Foreign with PhD from US & EU	Partnerships & joint degrees	
8	IAE (Esc. De Dirección y negocios, Universidad austral	Argentina	33	6.1	69.7		23	IESE, FIU	AACSB, EQUIS, AMBA
9	Universidad de Chile – Ingeniería industrial	Chile	27	15.0	78.0		21	HHL Leipzig	
10	Coppead – UFRJ	Brazil	23	0	43.5	56.5	10	Florida Internacional University	EQUIS
11	IPADE	Mexico	59	2.0	14.0	0	8		AACSB
12	Fundação Instituto de Administracão (FIA), USP	Brazil	26	0	30.8	69.2	8	Université Pierre Mendès France	AMBA
13	Universidad de los Andes – Administración	Colombia	34	20.6	70.6		24	Tulane, FIU	EQUIS, AMBA
14	IESA	Venezuela	39	12.8	64.1		25	FIU	AACSB, AMBA
15	TEC de Monterrey, Campus ciudad de México EU de Texas EM Austin	Mexico	39	7.6	79.0	10.0	31	Universidad de Texas-Austin, HEC Paris, Pepperdine, San Diego, Les Heures	SACS, AACSB
16	FDC – Fundação DOM Cabral	Brazil	17	0	52.9	17.6	9		AMBA
17	IBMEC, Rio de Janeiro	Brazil	33	0	42.0	39.0	14	University of Arkansas, R. Schuman	
18	Universidad Torcuato di Tella	Argentina	14	21.4	50.0		7	HEC Paris	

19	ESAN, Universidad ESAN	Peru	32	18.8	25.0		8	Arizona State, ESADE, Texas-Austin, Leipzig	AMBA
20	Universidad Anahuac Sur	Mexico	22	50.0	18.2	27.3	4	Claremont, EAE, FCO de Vittoria, Ecole Supérieure de Gestion, ILI	
21	Universidad del desarrollo	Chile	20	30.0	40.0		8	George Mason, Cincinnati, Babson, Montpellier	AMBA
22	Fundação cetúlio Vargas – EBAPE (Rio de Janeiro)	Brazil	32	0	50.0	50.0	16	Instituto Superior de Ciencias del trabajo y la empresa (ISCTE)	
23	Universidad del Cema	Argentina	17	17.6	52.9		9		AMBA
24	Centrum, Pontificia Universidad católica de Perù	Peru	50	18.0	46.0		23	Laval, Maastricht School of Management, Tulane	AMBA
25	Universidad Alberto Hurtado	Chile	16	18.8	56.3		9		
26	Business School Sao Paulo	Brazil	12	16.7	16.7	25.0	2		
27	Universidad Anáhuac Norte	Mexico	23	39.1	30.4	8.7	6	Cantabria, FIU, EADA, Macquarie University, Texas Tech, Claremont	
28	Universidad del Pacifico	Peru	16	50.0	18.8		3	Pittsburg, IE	AMBA
29	Universidad Santa María	Chile	35	8.6	74.3		26	Boconi, Lleida, Pittsburg, Politécnica de Cataluña	
30	Universidad ORT	Uruguay	24	41.7	20.8		5	FIU, Royal Agricultural Collage	

Continued

Table 17.1 Continued

Ranking 2006	Business school	Country	Faculty				International faculty (US & EU)	International alliances	International accreditation
			Full time equivalent 2006	% MBA/MSC US & EU	% PhD US & EU	% Local PhD	Foreign with PhD from US & EU	Partnerships & joint degrees	
31	Universidad de las Américas, Puebla	Mexico	21	9.5	61.9	14.3	13	EBS Paris, Texas Christian, Montpellier, Reims, INSEEC	SACS
32	PAD, Escuela de Dirección de la Universidad de Piura	Peru	16	25.0	25.0		4		
33	Universidad de Belgrano	Argentina	17	11.8	5.9		1	Les Heures, Euromed Marseille Ecole de management	
34	Universidad San Ignacio de Loyola	Peru	90	55.6	22.2		2	Québec (UQAM), Montpellier	
35	Universidad de Santiago de Chile	Chile	12	40.0	33.0		4	Esc. Superior de comercio Montpellier, Reims	
36	Universidad de Talca	Chile	14	21.4	50.0		7	HHL Leipzig, Montpellier	
37	IDE – Escuela de Dirección de empresas	Ecuador	8	25.0	12.5		1		
38	Escuela de postgrado en Administración de empresas, ESPOL	Ecuador	60	16.6	33.3		2	UQAM	
39	EAFIT	Colombia	38	13.2	21.1		8	Leipzig GS, IECS Strasbourg, EAE	
40	Universidad Americana	Paraguay	14	7.1	7.1		1	CESMA, San Diego State	

18
Management Education in Asia

Christian Koenig and Pierre Tapie

Introduction: diversity and the challenge of growth

"Asia is back" or "Asian renaissance" are but a couple of the expressions that abound to describe the formidable dynamics of this part of the world, where a large number of countries enjoy a sustained high growth unprecedented in economic history.

This revival of Asia calls for an equally formidable development of higher education, in science, technology and management in particular. The challenge is daunting for several reasons. First of all, fast economic growth requires bridging a growing gap between the management needs of various types of companies and the capacity of academic institutions to train enough managers able to tackle the intricacies of the local context, as well as understand the global imperative of business. Management education has to cater for the needs of firms investing massively in Asia, and for those of Asian firms facing the growth of local as well as international markets.

Secondly, as distinct from Eastern Europe or Latin America, where countries share some historical, cultural or economic traits, Asia is marked by an extraordinary diversity of cultures, climates, levels of education and economic development, from rising economic power in a country like Vietnam to post-industrial society in Japan; from an immensely populated, fast-developing country like India to the "little red dot" of rich and modern Singapore striving to become a higher education hub for Asia. And whereas China has embraced foreign investment for a long time, attracting more than half of foreign direct investment (FDI) in Asia, India is a rather late comer in this respect, attracting today US $ 7 billion worth of FDI, compared to US $ 70 billion for China. Countries also differ in terms of the status of private vs. state-owned companies and in terms of the role of family-dominated conglomerates, as seen in India or the Philippines.

Obviously, this diversity is reflected in the way management education has been considered or has developed in different countries. This short chapter cannot adequately do justice to this diversity, but will focus, at the risk of making sweeping generalizations, on some major characteristics and challenges, and some original avenues for developing world-class management education.

Non-Asian influences in the development of management education

One of the few common traits among Asian management education institutions, although not always pervasive, is the role played by foreign institutions, particularly American, in their historical development. While in many cases this influence was limited to the setting up of business schools, it still plays a considerable role in countries like China, where foreign schools operate in one form or another to serve the needs of companies.

Harvard Business School is notable for having helped the establishment of many schools around the world or for training faculty to set up schools. One early example is AIM (Asian Institute of Management) in Manila, created in 1968. With a similar intellectual and pedagogical filiation, Keio Business School was created in Tokyo in 1978 as a separate entity from Keio University, a prestigious private university. But as early as 1961, MIT's Sloan School of Management was involved in the creation of the first Indian Institute of Management in 1961 in Calcutta.

This also reflected in the training of faculties in many Asian countries. For instance, Euh (2007) underlines that 90 percent of professors in top Korean business schools (e.g. Seoul National University, Korea University, KAIST, Yonsei) received their PhDs from American universities. Similar trends are to be observed, albeit to a smaller extent, in many other Asian countries, but much less so in India. Obviously, this helps develop locally competencies that students often tend to look for by going abroad to study - in the US, predominantly, or in Europe – more and more.

Another indicator is the rapid growth of programs led by American or European schools in China, either as stand-alone organizations like CEIBS (China European International Business School) in Shanghai or through multiple partnerships with top Chinese universities in Beijing, Shanghai and Hong Kong. Shared MBA programs or joint Executive

MBAs have flourished, many universities having partnerships of different forms with a number of different American or European schools.

India is something of an oddity in this respect. The original Indian Institutes of Management (IIMs) in Calcutta and Ahmedabad date back to 1961, and only four others have been added since then. The IIMs, like their equivalent Indian Institutes of Technology (IITs), are stand-alone state institutions but are not affiliated to universities and do not deliver university degrees: their flagship program is the PGP (Postgraduate Program), which does not bear the name of MBA. IIMs are also extremely selective: about 170,000 top holders of Bachelor's degrees apply each year to IIM Ahmedabad, the most selective of all, for only 280 seats.[1] Faculty and students are essentially Indian, even though graduates are much sought after by MNCs for enviable positions abroad. The IIMs are also the oldest business schools in Asia; these are probably now the institutions which have most blended the western origin of management knowledge with their own local cultures and traditions.

Yet another original development is the creation of ISB (Indian School of Business) in Hyderabad, in 1998, with the support of the Kellogg School (Northwestern University) and Wharton, involving in particular prominent Indian faculty from these universities, often educated firstly in the IIMs and then in a US university for their PhDs.

In a similar vein, privately-funded Cheung Kong Business School was established in Beijing to supplement public institutions, offering executive programs taught by Chinese *faculty* (not doctoral students) recruited from American universities.

All these efforts, based on extreme selectivity or on some sort of unique blend of local and international teaching competencies, aim to offer world-class programs to aspiring or well-established business leaders.

Finally, the unique case of Singapore should be mentioned because this small island with a population of 4.3 million has made major steps forward to become an Asian leader in the knowledge economy, by investing and attracting investment in research and higher education. Its standard of living, location, high-quality infrastructures and use of English all contribute to the success of the "global schoolhouse policy." Many European and American institutions have established permanent bases or campuses in Singapore. In management education, INSEAD, University of Chicago GSB and ESSEC have opened campuses, either duplicating programs offered on their main campus or offering teaching tracks dedicated to exposing their students to Asian issues. More recently, the University of New South Wales, part of the leading "Group of Eight" Australian universities, has started a comprehensive campus, offering in particular undergraduate programs in commerce.

In addition, in the late 1990s, the Singapore government decided to introduce diversity and emulation on the national higher education stage. The two universities, Nanyang Technology University (NTU) and National University of Singapore (NUS) both enjoyed enviable positions, including with their business faculties. But the State commissioned the Wharton School for the overall design and program architecture of a new university, with a different format of programs and degrees, directly inspired by the American system: Singapore Management University. In a matter of years, SMU has become a university of 5000 students with an international faculty teaching in six different schools.

All this is part of a deliberate policy of making Singapore a place of reference for higher education in Asia, thus making the knowledge economy contribute to sustained economic growth.

Diversity of degree status

The differences in histories, governance, and growth have led to a wide variety of management degrees in Asia.

In India, this is reflected by the fact that the six IIMs built their fame on their highly selective PGP (Postgraduate program), while the name "MBA" degree was reserved by rule for universities. The PGP mostly recruits students with little or no experience. For this reason, IIMs usually do not appear in the major rankings even though they are considered in Asia as top MBAs.

In response to the needs generated by the opening up of the Indian economy, IIMs and other institutions have slightly enlarged their enrollment and joined other institutions and universities in offering a wider range of programs, with a number of specialized PGPs. For instance, IIM Ahmedabad now offers a PGP in agri-business and one in public management and policy. IIM Bangalore, created in 1973, leverages on its business environment with a program on software industries, but also one on public management. The necessary empowerment of the Indian public sector certainly calls for such a high-quality program, which adds to the needs of the private sector. Several IIMs and other non-universities now offer the equivalent to the Executive MBA, namely, the "PGPX" or Exec PGP, for instance at XLRI (Xavier Labour Relations Institute) and, since this year, at IIM Ahmedabad.

Yet, also proliferating are programs offered by astute "academic entrepreneurs" who realize that churning out management certificates may serve the recruiting needs of some companies while being a profitable business in itself. Nobody knows exactly how many MBA programs there are in India, certainly more than 900. This entrepreneurial growth is reinforced by India's student demographics: between 2000 and 2015, the student population in India will have increased from 11 to 41 million! The growth potential for management studies, whether at Bachelor's level or at MBA/PGP level, is enormous.

The experience in China is radically different. The country has long embraced foreign investment, thereby underlining the need for training managers with both adequate technical skills but also an aptitude to deal, often in English, with a diversity of expatriate executives. The development of management programs in the top universities like Beida (Peking University), Tsinghua or Fudan is relatively recent, and draws on a multiplicity of partnerships. The Guanghua School of Management celebrated its 20th anniversary in 2005, but the first MBA program in China appeared only in 1991, while the top universities kept providing highly selective undergraduate programs, and started offering specialized Master's programs, e.g. in finance. A remarkable trait of management education in China, in addition to its rapid growth and the proliferation of partnerships, is the fact that many MBA students gained their experience in State-owned enterprises, in an environment not necessarily conducive to managerial talent the way it is understood or practiced in foreign companies investing in China.

A related trait is the immense number of needs in executive education, which has an impact on enrolment of Executive MBAs: these programs developed even more recently and tend to recruit much more senior participants in China than they would in western schools. Management education will thus continue to develop in China, just as higher education at large will develop at an unprecedented rate. The number of students has almost doubled in the last 4 years, but remains much smaller in proportion than the average European country or Japan. Whilst 25 percent of Europeans between the age of 25 and 65 hold a university degree and 34 percent in Japan, the proportion is closer to 5 percent in China. This formidable growth perspective obviously encourages foreign universities to be part of the expansion game.

However, due to the strict regulation of the population in China, a large part of this increase will take place between 2004 and 2008, with growth rates of 30 percent annually. In the period 2000–2015, China's student population will only double (up to 40 million), while India's will quadruple. This is one of the reasons why foreign universities are rushing to China: places have to be taken in the next few years.

In Japan, earlier endeavors in management education at the beginning of the twentieth century were the realm of schools or faculties of commerce, in private universities like Waseda University or prestigious institutions like Keio University; business schools in the modern sense appeared much later. As a matter of fact, the faculty of commerce at Keio and Keio Business School are managed separately and are located on separate campuses, while only recently has Waseda Business School been integrated into the school of commerce. It is interesting to note that professional experience is recommended but is not a criterion for admission to Waseda's MBA.

Yet, despite decades of stability, and in a country where business schools, as they are known in Europe or the USA, were rare, Japan is bound to undergo major changes since the law on university reform of April 2004. For the first time, graduate professional education appeared in Japan, first in law, with the creation of 73 law schools within two years, then in business. The tradition in Japan had been a combination of very strict selection in the top universities, and professional training by their employers once students had graduated. Therefore graduate studies were mostly of an academic type, aimed at training future professors. Yet, changes in habits, labor market practices, and the end of the life-long employment policy demand young graduates with more autonomy, more knowledge and know-how, in order to be more innovative and take up responsibility at a relatively younger age. This will lead to new developments in management education, but for reasons that are thus very different from those prevailing in China or India. Unlike China and India, Japanese demography plays a negative role in that development: between 1991 and 2010, the age cohort entering university will have decreased by 40 percent. However, the need for these new independent professionals, at a graduate level of education, is increasing.

Opportunities and challenges

The growth and diversity of management education in Asia raises a number of issues related to its sustainability, efficiency, potential regional partnerships, academic rigor and relevance.

An initial imperative will certainly be to develop Asian content and research (see Euh, 2007; Li *et al.*, 2005; Montgomery, 2006). There is general consensus that this is clearly lacking in programs that are generally inclined to mimic western schools or use imported teaching material. The varying extent of family or State ownership and regulation, the structure of primary and secondary education, rules of access to higher education, differences in ranges of stakeholders, political systems and democratic traditions are all part of the institutional context that affects the efficiency and relevance of importing western concepts of management. (For an example of the roles played by these institutional differences in post-war Europe, see Djelic, 2000). They affect not only how business is done but the gamut of managerial competencies required and career patterns. Efforts to develop Asian versions of textbooks are steps in the right directions, and institutions like AIM in the Philippines or Nanyang Business School in Singapore have developed structures to produce Asian cases.

Similarly, differences in, for instance, attitudes to brands, in risk-taking and investment behavior, in the notion of service quality, or in leadership styles are such that they command specific Asian research in these areas. This is related to another challenge on the status of research itself, in institutions which have done an excellent job in recruiting able students and at teaching, but do not necessarily have a research tradition (on the case of India, see Tirupati, 2006).

This has several impacts. First of all, this probably requires the creation of appropriate, high-quality publications to support this enhanced research effort. It may be a difficult move: because rankings have become an essential part of each school's marketing effort, all strive frantically to publish in the same, usually US-based, publications (see Montgomery, 2006) at the expense of relevance and efficiency. A related impact obviously has to do with faculty development. Excellence of a few institutions in each and every Asian country cannot hide the lack of resources and of research culture in many others. This is compounded with the current shortage of PhDs in Europe and the USA, meaning that only institutions with adequate funding can play this expensive game of attracting a rare resource. Finally, topics which have emerged as important in the curricula of most schools in Europe or the US, such as corporate social responsibility and ethics, receive only scant treatment in most Asian programs.

Several approaches can be used to take on these challenges, in a period where Asian institutions will need time to develop their own materials, cases or research. Considering the fast speed of change in Asia, especially within the two demographic giants, collaborative programs of research or education will probably be among the most relevant. Addressing how an identical issue is tackled in two or three regions of the world, and why they are so differently managed, enables exploration of how cultural or historical roots can be either an explanation for the state-of-the-art of the present, or a factual and objective constraint, more endogenous than exogenous, which will have to be seriously taken into account in order to avoid failure. Such sustainable partnerships can create new abilities within partner institutions, better suited to undertaking comparative studies, or to find new solutions which have never been tried in one of the contexts. From its collaborative ventures with IIM Ahmedabad, Seoul National University, or Beida, ESSEC has garnered experience of these situations where collaboration, if properly handled, can be efficient and save time and energy, even if transactions do take some time.

But one of the remaining challenges is the cross-cultural ability to share concepts, ideas and views between professors and students, or even between scholars, with a very different cultural background. The way of *thinking* is so different between Asia and the rest of the world, and between and within Asian countries!

In his well-known provocative book, "Can Asians think?" Kishore Mahbubani (2004) was exploring the difficulties, for a new generation of Asians, to think differently by themselves. He emphasized that the Asian traditions were the respect of ancestors' paradigms, while modernity was often a desire to mimic western ideas or products. This tension between replication and mimetism is strengthened by the taste of new Asian generations for newness for the sake of newness: any fashion, habit, innovative object, may be considered desirable and relevant, even though it may be disposed of after a short while. Youngsters in large urban areas like Tokyo or Shanghai are probably displaying the extreme of these behaviors, when everyone copies the last fashion.

A key challenge in Asia, especially in China and India, is the balance between economic growth and social development, the internal battle between the ultra-liberal move, of the Shanghai kind, and the long-term Chinese and Indian traditions to integrate social interest with economic thought and development. In this last respect, the European experience of development could be relevant for these giants: Asia and Europe share a history of dense population where environmental issues are huge, where the balance between short-term profits and long-term sustainable growth is a key concern, and where very old cultures are dealing with the most modern changes. European business schools are thus in an interesting position to work in partnership with their Asian counterparts to tackle the formidable task assigned to the latter: how to train creative and responsible leaders?

Bibliography

Djelic, Marie-Laure, *Exporting the American Model*, Oxford: Oxford University Press, 2000.

Euh, Yoon-Dae, Management education in Asia – Unlocking New Opportunities, presented at the Asian Business Conference, AIM, Manila, March 2007.

Farnsworth, Bradley, "Management Education and the Asian Century," *The Journal of the International Institute*, University of Michigan, vol. 2 (3), 2005.

Li Manfang, Wong Yim-Yu and Wang Qung, Management Education in the Greater China Economy: Challenges and Task, in Alon, Ilan and McIntyre, John, eds., *Business and Management Education in China: Transition, Pedagogy and Training*, World Scientific Publishing Company, 2005.

Mahbubani, Kishore, *Can Asians Think?*, 3rd edition, Singapore: Times Editios, 2004.

Montgomery, David B., Asian Management Education: Some Twenty-First Century Issues, *Journal of Public Policy and Marketing*, vol. 24 (1), Spring 2006, pp. 150–154.

Rao, Tripati, Management Education in India, *Asian Analysis*, Australian National University, February 2006.

19
Business Higher Education in the Arab Middle East and North Africa (MENA) Region

Lassaâd Mezghani

General context

The education systems of the MENA region have undergone several transformations over the last few decades. Prior to the colonial period, most countries of the region had a long-established history of Koranic-based education. After independence, the governments of these countries undertook the process of reforming their education systems to make them more coherent with their specific social and economic needs. One of the main points of this reform process was the nationalization of education, with emphasis placed on educating a number of national teachers able to replace a mainly foreign body of educators. In fact, during the colonial period, a limited number of positions were made available to the local population. Just before the Algerian war of liberation, for example, there were only 1,000 Algerian university graduates, and in Tunisia at independence just 700 students were enrolled. Therefore, efforts to nationalize instruction required an enormous development at all levels of education, coupled with measures aimed at significantly increasing and encouraging access. However, even today, there continues to be a strong foreign, mainly European and North American, influence over education including language, curricula design, degree structure and nomenclature, especially in higher education as developed below.

Higher education evolution/revolution

To accompany the development of these countries and to train professionals in the skills required to occupy positions formerly held by members of the departing colonials, a policy of open access was instituted at a majority of the higher education institutions in the region. Most of them required that students hold a secondary school degree for admission. However, some institutions, mainly in the arts and humanities, adopted more liberal admission rules by enrolling students without the *high school degree*, provided they could pass a competitive entrance test. This policy was justified by the fact that there was a relatively small number of secondary school graduates. With such a need for educated manpower, students were guaranteed employment upon graduation from university in the early years after independence.

Later on, after about two decades of open access policy, the goal of nationalizing education, administration and other government agencies had largely been achieved. Consequently, the new generation of university students is no longer guaranteed employment upon graduation, especially in the public sector. At the same time, the increasing number of students and overcrowded institutions led to the establishment of a new set of strict admission procedures. Generally, students holding a high school degree are still guaranteed access to higher education. However, those wishing to enter specific scientific and technical disciplines or high-demand programs are required to have a minimum grade point average and/or score minimum grades in major subjects such as mathematics and sciences. Some other institutions have even established their own entrance examination.

To have a more precise idea about the number of students in these countries, one can refer to the UNESCO Institute for Statistics (UIS) 2006 Global Education Digest. In the Arab States the number of students in higher education has increased by 7.9 percent per year between 1991 and 2004. This percentage is the second highest in the world after that of East Asia and the Pacific (8.1 percent) and followed by sub-Saharan Africa (7.2 percent). For the same period, this rate was 1.9 percent for North America and Western Europe.

Between 1991 and 2004, the number of students in higher education in this region increased from about two to seven million. In 2004, Egypt had the largest number of students in the region (33 percent). Along with Algeria (12 percent) and Saudi Arabia (10 percent), these three countries accounted for more than half of the total number of students in the region.

In 2004, the teaching staff in these countries was about 240,000. It follows almost the same proportions and distribution as for students.

According to the same statistics, there were about 177,000 internationally mobile students from the Arab States. This represents about 7 percent of the world total. Half of these students are from Algeria, Morocco, and Tunisia. Overall, this region has known the greatest rise in student mobility ratio, which increased from to 2.3 percent to 2.9 percent between 1999 and 2004. This rate is the third highest in the world after that of sub-Saharan Africa (5.9 percent) and Central Asia (3.9 percent). It should be noted that Mauritania, Morocco and Qatar have high outbound mobility ratios of 22 , 15 and 13 percent, respectively.

Two out of three internationally mobile students originating from Arab States pursue their higher education in Western Europe, and 12 percent in North America. The most popular destinations are: France (43 percent), USA (10 percent), and Germany (9 percent). Some 13 percent stay in the region with Jordan being the main destination for about 13,500 students coming from different Arab States.

Along with this important increase in enrollments, higher education in this region has known different revisions of curricula, including several reforms.

Nowadays, some countries have already established higher educational systems largely influenced since the beginning by the Northern American system. Some other countries, such as those of North Africa, are reforming their higher education systems in an effort to make them more internationally compatible, while making them more efficient and responsive to the needs of the local public and private sectors. Following the education reforms in Europe based on the Bologna model, the three-year bachelor's, two-year master's and three-year doctoral degrees are being considered and gradually implemented. In Tunisia, for example, a pilot group of institutions introduced, in 2006, three-year *license* degrees in different fields. The others should follow no later than in 2009.

As reported by the World Education Services (WES) (2006), this reform has become a regional reform since "Institutions and government departments involved in drafting and implementing the 'LMD' reforms (*License, Master, Doctorate*) have been working in a spirit of international cooperation. Not only have the three countries of the Maghreb consulted closely, but there has also been a high degree of cross-Mediterranean consultation and discussion, much of which has been undertaken with an eye to extending the European Higher Education Area beyond the physical boundaries of Europe to incorporate the three countries of the Maghreb in what would become the Euro-Mediterranean higher education and research area."

How about business education?

According to the UNESCO Institute for Statistics (UIS) 2006 Global Education Digest, where statistics are available, the ratio of graduates in the fields of social science, business and law is the highest, with an average of 31 percent for most of the countries of the region. Otherwise, they represent the second most popular fields of graduation for some of the countries. In fact, if the ratio in the fields of social sciences, business and law is low, that is because the educational science field is leading, which is the case for Oman - (education: 68 percent; social science, business and law: 13 percent) and Saudi Arabia - (education: 41 percent; social science, business and law: 15 percent).

It is important to note that there are no standardized statistics specific to business education in the MENA region. However, some reports (World Bank, UNESCO, WES...), in addition to some academic publications, are available to permit some analysis of the situation.

Nowadays, business managers in the MENA region face an economic environment that has been rapidly and radically changing. It seems that these changes did not result in a real economic prosperity in the region. In his speech in a conference on *Higher Education in the Middle East and North Africa,* Nabli (2002) states that "what remains troubling in my mind is that the MENA region has been unable to realize the gains from its substantial investments in education. This applies not only to higher education but to lower levels of education as well. Despite extraordinary progress over the last decades in increasing the level of education throughout the region, the payoffs have been very disappointing from an international context." Such a conclusion was reported by Gillespie and Riddle (2004) stating that trade liberalization in this region did not generate significant increased employment opportunities (Dasgupta, Nabli, Pissarides, and Varoudakis, 2003), and labor productivity has gradually declined since the 1990s (Gardner, 2003).

It is also argued that Middle East business leaders complain that the MENA workforce is ill-prepared for today's business environment (Rugh, 2002). The author states that these business leaders have called for educational reform in order to review the learning processes mainly based on rote learning and memorization pedagogy at all levels of the educational system in the region (Rugh, 2002). It is to be noted that these educational reforms have been moving slowly in MENA countries (UNESCO, 2002). As reported by Gillespie and Riddle (2004), Rugh notes that at a 2002 international conference on Arab higher education "a leading Arab businessman stated that the Middle East would not achieve its full economic potential 'unless we revolutionize our educational system and adopt a total change in our mindset'" (2002, 406–407). In addition, a World Bank report on Arab education argues that this educational revolution must "impart skills enabling workers to be flexible, to analyze problems, and to synthesize information gained in different contexts" (World Bank, 1998, 18). This sentiment has also been shared by educational academics (Cassidy, 2003).

Its seems that most MENA universities and higher education institutions teach foreign, mainly North American and European, business theories using "imported" text books, if any. There was no significant effort to adapt these theories to the local context or to develop their own ones. Most teaching materials and references as well as curricula in business programs come from either North America or Europe. In some countries, like those of North Africa, some minor adaptations are introduced to cope with local environments but, at the same time, some master's degrees are "imported" including faculty.

What could be done for business education?

As stated above, if the MENA workforce is ill-prepared for today's business environment mainly because of the learning processes, which are based on rote learning and memorization, it is probably time to consider the recommendations of Gillespie and Riddle (2004). The authors argue that the case method can provide an opportunity to exercise problem-solving and decision-making skills by placing students in the position of the managerial decision-maker. In fact, case-based learning experiences can help prepare MENA students for the changing and challenging business environment that MENA managers face in a global economy, enabling them to better navigate uncertainty by employing analytic and problem-solving skills to seek solutions to complicated business problems. Hence, can we talk about the need for case-based business education in the MENA region?

In 1940, a major work on the case method entitled "Because Wisdom Can't be Told" was written by Charles Gragg and published by Harvard Alumni Bulletin. The author argues that the case method opens "the way for students to make positive contributions to thought … and to prepare themselves for action." The case method is used to develop and sharpen students' analytical skills in business. Generally, a business case is a description of a real or a hypothetical business situation where the decision-maker, commonly the manager, faces a particular set of problems to solve. The students are asked to analyze the situation and suggest a plan of action in order to solve a particular problem. This allows the student to practice analytical skills on semi-structured situations using a common core of generally validated concepts in order to construct individual interpretations of the case and to comprehend managerial lessons. This methodology also allows the student to realize the lack of the one "right" answer to case studies. In addition, Gragg (1940, 5) argues that the case method stimulates "democracy in the classroom" since "no longer is the situation that of teacher on the one hand and a body of students on the other."

Gillespie and Riddle (2004) conclude that "As institutions, educational entities are embedded in the local cultural context. They are both affected by and affect change within local culture. To be effective, pedagogy must have a connection with local cultural values and norms. How suitable, then, is case-based teaching for the MENA classroom?"

Educators willing to use the case method in MENA educational institutions should be aware of how differences in culture and classroom norms might impact case-based learning in this region. In particular, it is important to keep in mind that the cultural background gives rise to a learning environment that is divergent from the Western one, where the case method was born and developed. Gillespie and Riddle (2004) argue that "Case method socialization and classroom-composition or process adaptations may be necessary to better fit the case method to local cultural values and norms." In fact, there is an opportunity but also a lot of work to be done to contribute to a greater understanding of MENA management challenges. Business case-writers face several challenges due to the difficulties in the local data-collection process and to cultural adaptations needs. But these obstacles can be overcome by sufficient and careful case-writer preparation.

How about business research?

Most of the MENA universities concentrate their efforts on the educational aspect considering that it constitutes the institutions main product. However, recently, some universities realized that education constitutes a sub-product while the main product is research and innovation.

As far as we know, there are no specific statistics on business academic research output in the region but it could be estimated to be among the world's lower average if not lowest. The question is: What could be done in this domain?

Research on business issues should not be independent from the local environment. In fact, one of the up to date subjects in Tunisia, for example, is: how to conduct research that would be beneficial for local firms? There is probably no one right answer to this question. However, action-research seems to be the most appropriate solution. This research methodology allows researchers and business managers to establish the missing link between the university and industry and why not other public institutions? This collaboration should allow university faculty to become familiar with business and managerial issues and concerns and, hence, use this knowledge to better design courses through adapting the content, writing case studies, and developing other teaching materials. The research policy in this region should also encourage their faculty to be involved in different local business activities (e.g. Chambers of Commerce) and to have some consultancy activities. Business educators cannot be separated from their natural environment (the business itself) if they are to play a real role in the environment adapted education.

Conclusion

LeClair (2004), Director of Knowledge Services, A.A.C.S.B.[1] International, states that business education is crucial in emerging economies because competitive industries demand leadership from skilled, knowledgeable managers. He recommends some insight to understand specific challenges in emerging economies by offering five observations to keep in mind when considering business education:

- Business **curricula** should be relevant locally: in any country or region, business education is linked to the historical, political, demographic, technological, and social realities.
- Educational achievement depends on **process** as much as content: if we want students to acquire management skills, educators should apply interactive, experiential learning models and integrate learning with business practice.
- **Student** and **faculty qualifications** must be appropriately matched to business programs: Business programs should be consistent with the educational backgrounds and experience of targeted students, and business school leaders ought to find innovative solutions to develop and maintain qualified faculties.
- Adequate **educational resources** and physical infrastructure are necessary to provide high-quality business education: business schools in emerging markets should offer sufficient educational resources (textbooks, cases, networked computers, databases, etc.) and have well-designed facilities that can support interactive and/or technology-based instruction.
- Business education **goes beyond** producing qualified graduates: business educators should share their management knowledge with

businesses and governmental agencies in their regions, and they should assist in building an entrepreneurial culture to contribute to their economic growth.

As a never ending conclusion, Nabli (2002) argues that "Improving the access to and content of higher education in MENA is of critical importance in the region's economic and social development. But greater investment in higher education is not a magic bullet. While expansion in higher education is important in the context of economic growth, the economic context in which these services are provided is equally important."

Bibliography

Cassidy, T.J., (2003), "Education in the Arab States: preparing to compete in the global economy," in Schwab, K. & Cornelius, P. (eds.), *The Arab World competitiveness report*, pp. 218–234. World Economic Forum: Geneva.

LeClair, D., (2004), "Business Education in Emerging Economies," in McIntyre, J.R. & Alon, I. (eds.), *Business education and emerging market economies: perspectives and best practices*, Kluwer Academic Publishers, Boston.

Dasgupta, D., Nabli, M.K., Pissarides, C., & Varoudakis, A., (2003), *Making trade work for jobs: international evidence and lessons for MENA*, The World Bank: Washington DC.

Gardner, E., (2003), *Creating employment in the Middle East and North Africa*, The International Monetary Fund: Washington DC.

Gillespie, K. & Riddle, L., (2004), "Case-Based Teaching in Business Education in the Arab Middle East and North Africa," in McIntyre, J.R. & Alon, I. (eds.), *Business education and emerging market economies: perspectives and best practices*, Kluwer Academic Publishers, Boston.

Gragg, C.I., (1940), "Because wisdom can't be told," *Harvard Alumni Bulletin*, October 19.

Nabli, M., (2002), "Challenges and Opportunities for the 21st Century," *Conference on Higher Education in the Middle East and North Africa*, May 23rd, Institut du Monde Arabe – Paris.

Rugh, W.A., 2002, "Arab education: tradition, growth, and reform," *The Middle East Journal*, 56(3), pp. 396–414.

UNESCO, (2006), *Recueil de données mondiales sur l'éducation 2006 : Statistiques comparées sur l'éducation dans le monde*, Institut de statistique de l'UNESCO (ISU), Montréal.

UNESCO, (2002), *Arab States: regional report*, UNESCO Institute for Statistics (UIS), Montreal.

World Bank, (1998), *Education in the Middle East and North Africa: a strategy towards learning for development*, The World Bank: Washington DC.

World Education Services (2006), "Education in the Maghreb: Algeria, Morocco & Tunisia," *World Education News and Reviews*, April. www.wes.org/ewenr/PF/06apr/pfpractical.htm

Notes

The US Baseline

1. Cruikshank, J. L. (1987). *Delicate Experiment: The Harvard Business School 1908–1945* Boston MA: Harvard Business School Press
   Gay, E. F. (1927). The Founding of the Harvard Business School. *Harvard Business Review, 4*, 397–400.
   Heaton, H. (1968). *A Scholar in Action: Edwin F. Gay.* New York: Greenwood Press.
2. Engwall, L., & Zamagni, V. (Eds.). (1998). *Management Education in Historical Perspective.* Manchester: Manchester University Press.
   Van Fleet, D. D., & Wren, D. A. (2005). Teaching History in Business Schools: 1982–2003. *Academy of Management Learning & Education, 4*(1), 44–56.
3. Spender, J.-C. (2005). Speaking about Management Education: Some History of the Search for Legitimacy and the Ownership and Control of Management Knowledge. *Management Decision incorporating the Journal of Management History, 43*(10), 1282–1292.
4. Sass, S. A. (1982). *The Pragmatic Imagination: A History of the Wharton School 1881–1981.* Philadelphia PA: University of Pennsylvania Press.
5. Contardo, I., & Wensley, R. (2004). The Harvard Business School Story: Avoiding Knowledge by Being Relevant. *Organization, 11*(2), 211–231.
6. Daniel, C. (1998). *The MBA: The First Century.* London: Routledge.
7. Bok, D. C. (1978). *The President's Report 1977–1978.* Cambridge MA: Harvard University.
8. Garten, J. (2005, April 17). The Need for Wider Horizons. *Financial Times.*
9. Emiliani, M. L. (2005). Is Management Education Beneficial to Society? *Journal of Management Decision, 42*(3/4), 481–498.
10. Livingston, J. S. (1971). Myth of the Well-educated Manager. *Harvard Business Review*(Jan-Feb), 79–89.
11. Hayes, R. H., & Abernathy, W. J. (1980). Managing Our Way to Economic Decline. *Harvard Business Review, July – Sept*, 67–77.
12. Linder, J. C., & Smith, H. J. (1992). The Complex Case of Management Education. *Harvard Business Review, 70*(5), 16–33.
    Smith, H. J., & Linder, J. C. (1992). H. Jeff Smith and Jane C. Linder Respond. *Harvard Business Review, 70*(6), 130.
13. Lataif, L. E. (1992). MBA: Is the Traditional Model Doomed? *Harvard Business Review, 70*(6), 128.
14. Bennis, W., & O'Toole, J. (2005). How Business Schools Lost Their Way. *Harvard Business Review, 83*(5), 96–104.
15. Mintzberg, H. (2004). Managers not MBAs: A Hard Look at the Soft Practice of Managing and Management Development. San Francisco CA: Berrett-Koehler Publishers.
16. Cheit, E. F. (1985). Business Schools and Their Critics, *California Management Review* (Vol. 27, pp. 43): California Management Review.

Pfeffer, J., & Fong, C. T. (2002). The End of Business Schools? Less Success Than Meets the Eye. *Academy of Management Executive, 1*(1), 78–95.

Pfeffer, J., & Fong, C. T. (2004). The Business School "Business": Some Lessons from the US Experience, *Journal of Management Studies* (Vol. 41, pp. 1501–1520): Blackwell Publishing Limited.

Porter, L. W., & McKibbin, L. (1988). *Management Education and Development.* New York: McGraw-Hill.

17. Hambrick, D. C. (1994). 1993 Presidential Address – What if the Academy Actually Mattered. *Aacademy of Management Review, 19*(1), 11–16.

Huff, A. S. (2000). 1999 Presidential Address – Changes in Organizational Knowledge Production. *Academy of Management Review, 25*(2), 288–293.

Mowday, R. T. (1997b). Reaffirming Our Scholarly Values. *Academy of Management Review, 22*(2), 335–345.

Pearce, J. L. (2004). What Do We Know And How Do We Really Know It? *Academy of Management Review, 29*(2), 175–179.

18. Hodgkinson, G. P., Herriot, P., & Anderson, N. (2001). Re-aligning the Stakeholders in Management Research: Lessons from Industrial, Work and Organizational Psychology. *British Journal of Management, 12* (Special Issue), S41–S48.

Starkey, K., Hatchuel, A., & Tempest, S. (2004). Rethinking the Business School, *Journal of Management Studies* (Vol. 41, pp. 1521): Blackwell Publishing Limited.

Starkey, K., & Madan, P. (2001). Bridging the Relevance Gap: Aligning Stakeholders in the Future of Management Research *British Journal of Management, 12*(Supplement 1), S3–S26.

19. Spender, J.-C. (2005). Speaking about Management Education: Some History of the Search for Legitimacy and the Ownership and Control of Management Knowledge. *Management Decision incorporating the Journal of Management History, 43*(10), 1282–1292.

20. Ghoshal, S. (2005). Bad Management Theories are Destroying Good Management Practices. *Academy of Management Learning & Education, 4*(1), 75–91.

Hayes, R. H., & Abernathy, W. J. (1980). Managing Our Way to Economic Decline. *Harvard Business Review, July – Sept*, 67–77.

21. Hambrick, D. C. (2005). Just How Bad Are Our Theories? A Response to Ghoshal. *Academy of Management Learning & Education, 4*(1), 104–107.

Pfeffer, J. (2005). Why Do Bad Management Theories Persist? A Comment on Ghoshal. *Academy of Management Learning & Education, 4*(1), 96–100.

22. http://www.aacsb.edu/publications/

23. Connolly, M. (2003). The End of the MBA as We Know It? *Academy of Management Learning and Education, 2*(4), 365–367.

24. Miles, R. E. (1985). The Future of Business Education, *California Management Review* (Vol. 27, pp. 63): California Management Review.

25. Morgeson, F. P., & Nahrgang, J. D. (2006). *Same as It Ever Was: Recognizing Stability in the Business Week Rankings.* Paper presented at the Academy of Management Annual Meeting.

26. Mowday, R. T. (1997a). Celebrating 40 Years of the Academy of Management Journal. *Academy of Management Journal, 40*(5), 1400–1413.

27. Fernandes, J. (2005). The World's Most Popular Degree – the MBA – Is Alive and Well. *AACSB eNewsline, 4*(6), 1–2.

28. Doria, J., Rozanski, H., & Cohen, E. (2003). What Business Needs from Business Schools. *Strategy + Business*(32), 39–45.

29. Ferraro, F., Pfeffer, J., & Sutton, R. I. (2005a). Economics Language and Assumptions: How Theories Can Become Self-Fulfilling. *Academy of Management Review, 30*(1), 8–24.
Ferraro, F., Pfeffer, J., & Sutton, R. I. (2005b). Reply: Prescriptions Are Not Enough. *Academy of Management Review, 30*(1), 32–35.

30. McCormack, M. H. (1984). *What They Don't Teach You at Harvard Business School*. London: Fontana/Collins.

31. Bolton, M. J., & Stolcis, G. B. (2003). Ties That Do Not Bind: Musings on the Specious Relevance of Academic Research. *Public Administration Review, 63*(5), 626.

32. Gordon, R. (1976). Rigour and Relevance in a Changing Institutional Setting. *American Economic Review, 66*(1), 1–10.
McCloskey, D. N. (2002). *The Secret Sins of Economics*. Chicago IL: Prickly Paradigm Press.

33. Johnson, H. T., & Kaplan, R. S. (1987). *Relevance Lost: The Rise and Fall of Managerial Accounting*. Boston MA: Harvard Business School Press.

34. Nguyen, D. Q. (1998). The Essential Skills and Attributes of an Engineer: A Comparative Study of Academics, Industry Personnel and Engineering Students. *Global Journal of Engineering Education, 2*(1), 65–74.

35. Benbasat, I., & Zmud, R. W. (2003). The Identity Crisis within the IS Discipline: Defining and Communicating the Discipline's Core Properties. *MIS Quarterly, 27*(2), 183–194.
King, J. L., & Lyytinen, K. (2004). Reach and Grasp. *MIS Quarterly, 28*(4), 539–551.

36. Metcalf, H. C. (1927). *Business Management as a Profession*. Chicago IL: A. W. Shaw Company.
Spender, J.-C. (2005). Speaking about Management Education: Some History of the Search for Legitimacy and the Ownership and Control of Management Knowledge. *Management Decision incorporating the Journal of Management History, 43*(10), 1282–1292.

37. Abbott, A. (1988). The System of Professions: An Essay on the Division of Expert Labor. Chicago IL: University of Chicago Press.

38. Trank, C. Q., & Rynes, S. L. (2003). Who Moved Our Cheese? Reclaiming Professionalism in Business Education. *Academy of Management Learning & Education, 2*(2), 189–205.

39. Trieschmann, J. S., Dennis, A. R., Northcraft, G. B., & Nieme Jr, A. W. (2000). Serving Constituencies in Business Schools: MBA Program versus Research Performance. *Academy of Management Journal, 43*(6), 1130–1141.

40. Pfeffer, J. (1993). Barriers to the Advancement of Organization Science: Paradigm Development as a Dependent Variable. *Academy of Management Review, 18*, 599–620.

41. Policano, A. J. (2001). Ten Easy Steps to a Top-25 MBA Program. *Selections, 1*(2), 39–40.
Policano, A. J. (2005). What Price Rankings? *BizEd*(September/October), 26–32.
Trank, C. Q., & Rynes, S. L. (2003). Who Moved Our Cheese? Reclaiming Professionalism in Business Education. *Academy of Management Learning & Education, 2*(2), 189–205.

42. Bok, D. C. (2003). Universities in the Marketplace: The Commercialization of Higher Education. Princeton NJ: Princeton University Press.

43. Baden-Fuller, C., Ravazzolo, F., & Schweizer, T. (2000). Making and Measuring Reputations – The Research Ranking of European Business Schools *Long Range Planning, 33*(October), 621–650.
Dichev, I. D. (1999). How Good Are Business School Rankings? *Journal of Business, 72*(2), 201–213.
Gioia, D. A., & Corley, K. G. (2000). The Rankings Game: Managing Business School Reputation *Corporate Reputation Review, 3*(4), 319–333.

44. Morgeson, F. P., & Nahrgang, J. D. (2006). *Same as It Ever Was: Recognizing Stability in the Business Week Rankings*. Paper presented at the Academy of Management Annual Meeting.

45. http://www.aacsb.edu/publications/Rankings/MediaRankingsTF.asp

46. Trieschmann, J. S., Dennis, A. R., Northcraft, G. B., & Nieme Jr, A. W. (2000). Serving Constituencies in Business Schools: MBA Program versus Research Performance. *Academy of Management Journal, 43*(6), 1130–1141.

47. Wensley, R. (forthcoming). Beyond Rigour and Relevance: The Underlying Nature of both Business Schools and Management Research. *British Journal of Management.*

48. Gordon, R., & Howell, J. (1959). *Higher Education for Business*. New York: Columbia University Press.
Pierson, F. C., & Others. (1959). The Education of American Businessmen: A Study of University-College Programs in Business Education. New York: McGraw-Hill.

49. Clegg, S. R., & Ross-Smith, A. (2003). Revising the Boundaries: Management Education and Learning in a Postpositivist World. *Academy of Management Learning & Education, 2*(1), 85–98.

50. Collins, D. (2000). Management Fads and Buzzwords: Critical-Practical Perspectives. London: Routledge.
Kieser, A. (1997). Rhetoric and Myth in Management Fashion. Organization, 4(1), 49–74.

51. North, D. C. (2005). *Understanding the Process of Economic Change*. Princeton NJ: Princeton University Press.

52. Foss, N. J., & Klein, P. G. (2005). *The Theory of the Firm and Its Critics: A Stocktaking and Assessment, Working Paper 2/2005* (No. CKG WP 2/2005). Copenhagen: Center for Knowledge Governance, Copenhagen School of Business.

53. Cohen, K. J., & Cyert, R. M. (1965). *Theory of the Firm: Resource Allocation in a Market Economy*. Englewood Cliffs NJ: Prentice-Hall.
Cyert, R. M., & March, J. G. (1963). *A Behavioral Theory of the Firm*. Englewood Cliffs NJ: Prentice-Hall.
Cyert, R. M., & Welsch, L. A. (Eds.). (1970). *Management Decision Making: Selected readings*. Harmondsworth Middx: Penguin Books.
Locke, R. R. (1996). *The Collapse of the American Management Mystique*. New York: Oxford University Press.

54. Baron, R., & Shane, S. (2005). *Entrepreneurship: A Process Perspective*. Mason OH: Southwestern Publishing Company.
Casson, M. (1982). *The Entrepreneur: An Economic Theory*. Oxford: Martin Robertson.

Kirzner, I. M. (1997). Entrepreneurial Discovery and the Competitive Market Process: An Austrian Approach, *Journal of Economic Literature* (Vol. 35, pp. 60): American Economic Association.

55. Foss, N. J. (1994). The Theory of the Firm: The Austrians as Precursors and Critics of Contemporary Theory. *Review of Austrian Economics, 7*(1), 31–65.
   Shackle, G. L. S. (1972). *Epistemics & Economics: A Critique of Economic Doctrines*. New Brunswick NJ: Transaction Publishers.
56. Shane, S. (2005). Where is Entrepreneurship Research Heading? Max Planck Institute.
   Shane, S., & Venkatraman, N. (2000). The Promise of Entrepeneurship as a Field of Research. *Academy of Management Review, 25*(1), 217–226.
57. Sawyer, R. K., & Others. (2003). *Creativity and Development*. Oxford: Oxford University Press.
58. Spender, J.-C. (2005). Speaking about Management Education: Some History of the Search for Legitimacy and the Ownership and Control of Management Knowledge. *Management Decision incorporating the Journal of Management History, 43*(10), 1282–1292.
59. Business Week On-Line. (5/25/2005). Bringing Shakespeare to B-School: Two Professors Sound Off on What's Missing from Most MBA Programs – from Real-World Relevance to the Bard's Wisdom [Electronic Version]. Retrieved August 19, 2006.
60. Archer, M. S. (2003). *Structure, Agency, and the Internal Conversation*. Cambridge: Cambridge University Press.
   von Glasersfeld, E. (2002). *Radical Constructivism*. London: Routledge / Falmer.
61. Pratt, J. W., & Zeckhauser, R. J. (Eds.). (1991). *Principals and Agents: The Structure of Business*. Cambridge MA: Harvard Business School Press.

1   Management Education as a System: A Case Study on Europe

1. If not indicated, figures come from chapters detailing management education in each European country (see part II).
2. http://ec.europa.eu/education/programmes/socrates/shorten.pdf
3. Le Monde, 6th December 2006, L'université de Cambridge va investir dans les hedge funds.
4. Wall Street Journal – *Europe's flat learning curve*, November 2006.

3   Exogenous Pressures Exerted on the System

1. Very early on, it has been clear that this target could not be reached. Yet, the repeated reference to an explicit and ambitious target had a positive effect on raising awareness throughout the EU on this important matter.

5   Strategic Implications for the Main Regions of the World

1. In addition, the best talents from developing countries have had a tendency to turn to hard science and Engineering, not so much to business studies. As

a result, PhD programs in Science and Engineering in the US and Europe are filled with non OECD doctoral students.

6 Strengthening a Management Education System: Back to the EU Case

1. The Bologna agreement organized mobility for Students across Europe. It took the form of the so-called 3–5-8 or L-M-D scheme (3 years for the Licence, 5 years for the Master, 8 years for the Doctorate). The Bologna agreement also created the ECTS (European Credit Transfer System) which, together with the organization of curricula in semesters, makes student mobility possible. This decision was made in 1999 and implemented in most EU member states by 2005 or so, with the exception of Germany where the change will be operational as of 2010. This clearly helped promote internal consistency within the EU university system and external visibility for non EU prospective students.

7 U.K. Business Schools

1. Exceptions to this include the University of Buckingham and privately-funded business schools such as Henley and Ashridge.

8 Management Education and Research in Germany

* **Acknowledgements:** We thank Stephanie Dameron, Thomas Durand, Georg Schreyögg and Ralf Reichwald for valuable feedback, suggestions and comments. All remaining weaknesses are solely the responsibility of the authors.

** This book is about future scenarios for business schools. "Business School," however, is not a common term in German management education and research. Therefore we first provide a brief look at the historic roots of the management field, its educational institutions, research journals and scholarly associations in German-speaking countries. The following sections overview higher education institutions and programs, with a special emphasis on preparation for academic careers.

1. "Handelshochschule" can be directly translated as "commercial high-school," but stands for a university-level educational institution, not a secondary school. For a more comprehensive historical overview of Betriebswirtschaftslehre in the German-speaking countries see: Albach 1990.
2. HHL-Leipzig Graduate School of Management, founded in 1898 as the Handelshochschule Leipzig, was the first German business school to be granted university status and is the only one which still runs under its historic label.
3. In 1906 Eugen Schmalenbach founded the "Zeitschrift für handelswissenschaftliche Forschung (ZfhF)," now called "Zeitschrift für betriebswirtschaftliche Forschung (ZfbF)" and recently complemented by the "Schmalenbach Business Review (sbr)" for the English-speaking audience. In 1908 Heinrich Nicklisch founded the "Zeitschrift für Handelswissenschaft und Handelspraxis (ZHH)," which has changed its name to "Die Betriebswirtschaft (DBW)." In 1924 Fritz Schmidt started the "Zeitschrift fürBetriebswirtschaft (ZfB)" which retains its original name.

4. See www.schmalenbach.org.
5. FSOG 2006; Rühli 2002, p. 115; Schneider 2001, p. 237.
6. BMBF 2003.
7. http://www.mba.uni-mannheim.de/
8. Wissenschaftliche Hochschulen in privater Trägerschaft.
9. Departments at Wissenschaftliche Hochschulen in staatlicher Trägerschaft.
10. C.f. Muller-Camen/Salzgeber 2005: In the following we will summarize key aspects of their analysis.
11. Oechsler 1999, p. 2 (As university professors in the German-speaking countries – Germany, Austria, Switzerland – feel and are organized as one academic community, e.g. in the Association of University Professors of Management (AUPM), we extend our view to all three countries whenever it makes sense.).
12. Clark 1983, p. 111ff.; Dorf 1999; Engwall 1999; Muller-Camen/Salzgeber 2005, p. 276.
13. Muller-Camen/Salzgeber 2005, p. 277.
14. BMBF 2003, p. 6.
15. BMBF 2003, p. 17.
16. FSOG 2006, see also Figure 8.1.
17. see: www.hrk.de (university rectors conference).
18. The Bertelsmann Stiftung was established by Reinhard Mohn as a charitable foundation in 1977. It is a majority shareholder of the German media corporation Bertelsmann AG.
19. dapm/CHE 2006.
20. Huff/Huff 2001; Starkey/Madan 2001; Bradley *et al.* 2004.
21. Hartung 2006; CHE 2004.
22. In addition there were traditionally a relatively large number of temporary and permanent C2 professors. We do not include details about this job category since it is no longer an available category in most settings and thus not an interesting career aspiration for academics reading this chapter.
23. FSOG 2006; Rühli 2002, p. 115; Schneider 2001, p. 237.
24. ZVS 2005, p. 2.
25. FSOG 2006.
26. Berghoff *et al.* 2005.
27. Berghoff *et al.* 2005.
28. Berghoff *et al.* 2005.
29. Solis (IZ Bonn), HWWA (Institut für Wirtschaftsforschung Hamburg), ECONIS (Institut für Weltwirtschaft Kiel) and BLISS (GBI Munich).
30. There are controversial views about this method of measuring weighted publication points as it only focuses on quantity, not quality of the research output.
31. Berghoff *et al.* 2005.
32. Macharzina/Wolf/Rohn 2004.
33. Macharzina/Wolf/Rohn 2004, p. 335.
34. Berghoff *et al.* 2005.
35. See f.i. Möslein 2005; Ivory *et al.* 2006.
36. Spender 2000.
37. http://www.dfg.de/en/research_funding/coordinated_programs/excellence_ initiative/general_information.html
38. Decision as of 13th October 2006.
39. For details see Reichwald 2006; Witte 2003.

10 Higher Education in Business:
The Case of Spain

1. The only exception to this general rule was the Faculty of Economics and Business of Seville which offered the first licentiate degree in Business in 1971 without a previous degree in Economics.
2. There was a slightly similar process in the private system, but for different reasons. The Law of 1991 allowed the creation of private universities and led many "ascribed" schools to become private universities (see section on private universities).
3. The only exception is the U. Carlos III MBA, currently the only public university master program with an international accreditation (Association of MBAs).
4. Thus "Finance and Accounting" includes Financial Management, Financial Ec onomics, Actuarial Sciences, Financial Mathematics, Managerial Accounting, Financial Accounting, and Auditing. "Management" includes General Management, Operations Management, Human Resource Management, and Managerial Economics.
5. With the new reform of the Law of Universities that is currently being discussed in the Spanish Parliament the CEU and TEU positions are going to disappear.

11 Management Education in Italy*

* The author would like to thank Prof Gianluca Colombo and the editors of the book for their suggestions and comments.
1. Source: SIDREA, 11th November 2005.
2. The competition among Universities results in a sort of market segmentation; in fact students can attend many bachelors that are supposed to offer an access to job (so-called profession- oriented bachelors) and few bachelors that are considered as a basis for the two year courses. This segmentation is probably due to the fact that in Italy there is no kind of vocational training at university level (like the German, Austrian and Swiss Fackulschule).
3. Source: G.tr., "Lo studente paga 803 € l'anno," Il Sole 24 Ore, lunedi 26 giugno 2006.
4. Source: G.TR, "Lo studente paga 803 € l'anno," Il Sole 24 Ore, 26 giugno, 2006.
5. Source: SIDREA – data from MIUR, November 2005.

12 Higher Management Education in the Netherlands

1. See the Ministry of Education, Culture and Sciences website : http://www.minocw.nl/persberichten/11382.
2. See the NVAO website: http://nvao.net/content.php?a=s&id=211.
3. The source is the Ministry of Education, Culture and Sciences website: http://www.minocw.nl/factsheets/339. VMBO (Voorbereidend Middelbaar Beroepsonderwijs) = preparatory secondary vocational education; MBO (Middelbaar Beroepsonderwijs) = secondary vocational education. The other terms have already been explained in the main text.

4. See the IB-Group website: http://www.ib-groep.nl/particulier/Informatie/ Studiefinanciering/Hoger_onderwijs/Prestatiebeurs.asp.
5. See NRC Handelsblad (a national Dutch newspaper), January 26, 2006.
6. See the KNAW website http://www.knaw.nl/, the NWO website http://www. nwo.nl, and the Bsik website http://www.senternovem.nl/bsik/index.asp.
7. See the Fontys Hogescholen website: http://www.fontys.nl/promotie/.
8. See the magazine Intermediair, June 6, 2005.
9. See the magazine Elsevier, December 13, 2004.
10. More information on which institutions offer what kind of business programs can be found at the Informatie Beheer Groep website: http://www.ib-groep. nl/zakelijk/HO/CROHO/Raadplegen_of_downloaden_CROHO.asp.
11. Most of the figures we use for this section were derived from the statistics on education published annually by the Dutch Central Bureau for Statistics ("Jaarboek Onderwijs in Cijfers 2006", Centraal Bureau voor de Statistiek, Voorburg/Heerlen, 2005), unless indicated otherwise.
12. The total is more than 100 percent, since several executives had studied in more than one discipline. We created rather broad categories. Since an explicit distinction between economics and business economics did not exist before the beginning of the nineteen eighties, we had to add economics to our business category. "Technical background" also includes the few individuals who studied mathematics, biology, and agricultural and pharmaceutical sciences. The category "different" contains the "softer" disciplines, in particular political sciences, sociology, psychology, communication, and human resource management, but also public administration and the combination of law and economics. We would like to express our gratitude to Loes Boumans for going through the elaborate process of gathering the raw data.
13. In 2003, total revenues for universities of 4,776 were divided over state funding 3,210 (67.2%), tuition 273 (5.7%), third party education 108 (2.3%), third party contract research 567 (11.9%), third party other 148 (3.1%), transitory posts 28 (0.6%), and other 443 (9.3%). For universities of professional education, total revenues were 2,448, divided over state funding 1,634 (66.8%), tuition 434 (17.7%), third party education 116 (4.7%), third party contract research 9 (0.4%), third party other 47 (1.9%), transitory posts 2 (0.1%), and other 205 (8.4%). All amounts of money are in millions of euros.
14. See the Ministry of Education, Culture and Sciences website: http://www. minocw.nl/factsheets/359#A773.
15. See the Ministry of Education, Culture and Sciences website: http://www. minocw.nl/organogram.
16. See the NVAO website, which contains a complete list and links to the separate approved VBIs: http://nvao.net/content.php?action=show&id=213.
17. See the Inspectorate of Education website: http://www.owinsp.nl/ and http://www.onderwijsinspectie.nl/watdoenwij/soortenonderwijs/ hogeronderwijs/.
18. See Noorderhaven, N. G. (2002), De grenzen van de Nederlandse bedrijfscultuur [the boundaries of Dutch business culture]. In R. Batenburg, T. van der Lippe and N. van den Heuvel, eds., *Met het Oog op de Toekomst van de Arbeid*, Den Haag: Elsevier Bedrijfsinformatie, 77–89.

13 Management Education and Research in Sweden

1. Professor of Organization Theory at the Stockholm School of Economics. E-mail: bengt.stymne@hhs.se
2. "Management" is not given as a program in the Swedish university system. The area that comes closest is "Företags-ekonomi" that translates to "Business economics." In the report we use the term "Business studies" to refer to this area.
3. The article will use the expression "Academic System" rather than "University System" to denote all the institutions of higher education and scientific research in Sweden. In addition to universities, other types of education providers are included.
4. The conversion rate used in this article is 1€=SEK 9.3
5. The source statistics from SACO reports figures separate for women and men. The male figure has been chosen because it represents the largest group. It should be pointed out that the figures for the two sexes follow each other very closely for the university staff.
6. The income tax in 2005 on a monthly salary of 2.000 € was 29 percent and on 6.000 43 percent.

14 Higher Management Education in Portugal

1. To contact the author:
   ISEG – School of Economics and Management
   Rua Miguel Lupi, 20
   1249–078 Lisboa, Portugal
   Tel: + 351–213925926
   jcneves@iseg.utl.pt

18 Management Education in Asia

1. In a way, despite differences in sheer numbers, this system resembles the French system of Grandes Ecoles, as independent, highly selective institutions.

19 Business Higher Education in the Arab Middle East and North Africa (MENA) Region

1. Association to Advance Collegiate Schools of Business – a network of close to 900 business schools dedicated to advancing business and management education worldwide.

Index